Cost-Benefit Analysis and the Environment

RECENT DEVELOPMENTS

OECD

ORGANISATION FOR ECONOMIC CO-OPERATION AND DEVELOPMENT

ORGANISATION FOR ECONOMIC CO-OPERATION AND DEVELOPMENT

The OECD is a unique forum where the governments of 30 democracies work together to address the economic, social and environmental challenges of globalisation. The OECD is also at the forefront of efforts to understand and to help governments respond to new developments and concerns, such as corporate governance, the information economy and the challenges of an ageing population. The Organisation provides a setting where governments can compare policy experiences, seek answers to common problems, identify good practice and work to co-ordinate domestic and international policies.

The OECD member countries are: Australia, Austria, Belgium, Canada, the Czech Republic, Denmark, Finland, France, Germany, Greece, Hungary, Iceland, Ireland, Italy, Japan, Korea, Luxembourg, Mexico, the Netherlands, New Zealand, Norway, Poland, Portugal, the Slovak Republic, Spain, Sweden, Switzerland, Turkey, the United Kingdom and the United States. The Commission of the European Communities takes part in the work of the OECD.

OECD Publishing disseminates widely the results of the Organisation's statistics gathering and research on economic, social and environmental issues, as well as the conventions, guidelines and standards agreed by its members.

This work is published on the responsibility of the Secretary-General of the OECD. The opinions expressed and arguments employed herein do not necessarily reflect the official views of the Organisation or of the governments of its member countries.

Publié en français sous le titre :
Analyse coûts-avantages et environnement
DÉVELOPPEMENTS RÉCENTS

Foreword

*I*n the early 1970s, when the OECD Environment Directorate was established, the question of how to evaluate in monetary terms the environmental damages – or the benefits of damage reductions – was identified as a key issue. Several publications were produced, designed to help analysts and policy makers. These included technical handbooks and manuals designed to "communicate" the main tenets of environmental cost-benefit analysis to policy analysts and decision makers. They also included analysis of the "political economy" of cost-benefit analysis (e.g. political and social obstacles to its use), and applications in specific areas, such as biodiversity valuation.

Cost-benefit analysis is now recognised as an indispensable tool for policy design and decision making. As environmental policies are becoming more complex and challenging (e.g. global warming, biodiversity loss, and health impacts of local air and water pollution), a number of countries and the European Commission have introduced legal provisions requiring impact and cost-benefit assessments of major policies and regulations. Over the last 5-10 years, considerable progress has been made in the conceptual framework and techniques of environmental cost-benefit analysis. This report takes stock of these recent developments, and as such provides a timely and indispensable contribution to those in charge of policy and regulatory cost-benefit assessments. Handbooks need to be technically rigorous, but their purpose and main content also need to be understandable to policy-makers. It is my hope that this report strikes that balance.

This report was drafted by David W. Pearce, Susana Mourato and Giles Atkinson, under the supervision of the OECD Working Party on National Policies. Financial support was provided by the United Kingdom Department of the Environment, Food and Rural Affairs and the Norwegian Ministry of Environment. The Italian Ministry of Environment and Territory hosted a workshop in Rome in October 2004 for a detailed discussion of a first draft. The work was co-ordinated by Jean-Philippe Barde, Head of the National Policies Division of the OECD Environment Directorate.

Lorents G. Lorentsen

Director

OECD Environment Directorate

Authors' Acknowledgements. This volume arose as the product of a discussion between one of the authors (David W. Pearce) and the OECD Secretariat. OECD has a distinguished history of pioneering economic analysis of environmental issues, including cost-benefit analysis and the monetary valuation of environmental impacts. But there was no publication that brought together some of the recent developments in cost-benefit analysis, and, given its record, OECD seems the right place to locate such a study. We hope the volume will be useful both to academics and, more importantly, practitioners, since cost-benefit analysis is now widely practised and used. To this end, each chapter concludes with a "decision-maker's guide" to the central points raised in the chapters. For busy people with little time to devote to sustained study of the literature, some of the theoretical developments are not easy to understand. We have done our best to explain what we understand the contributions to be, but we recognise that many readers will not have the time to work through each chapter. The decision-maker's guide at the end of each chapter is therefore designed to offer some intuition as to the nature of the insights so that, at the very least, someone receiving or commissioning work in cost-benefit analysis has some idea of what they should expect from up-to-date analysis. Unfortunately, the very nature of the theory is such that it will not be instantly understood by everyone, not even by economists. Hence we urge those who do have time to work their way through the chapters that are of interest to them.

The work would never have been completed without the advice and understanding of Jean-Philippe Barde of the OECD Environment Directorate. We wish to thank him for all his patience and helpful comments. Parts of the document were discussed at an OECD Working Party in Paris on National Environmental Policy in May 2004: we are indebted to the delegates there for very useful comments which helped us redirect the work effort. Most of the contents were further discussed at a special Workshop on Recent Developments in Environmental Cost-benefit Analysis hosted by the Italian Ministry of Environment and Territory in Rome in October 2004. We are indebted to the various experts there for helpful suggestions on corrections and on new material that now appears in this final version of the volume. Section 14.10 has been prepared by Pascale Scapecchi of the OECD Environment Directorate – we truly appreciate her contribution.

Finally, we are indebted to our colleagues at University College London who have helped shape our understanding of the issues in question. Above all, we thank Joe Swierzbinski who has commented on selected chapters and whose graduate teaching notes reach standards of expositional elegance that are unequalled in the literature. We have all learned a great deal from him.

David W. Pearce

In Memoriam

This project and this book were initiated in 2003, under the initiative of David Pearce who took a leading role in carrying it through to its completion. Prior to publication, David suddenly passed away on the 8th September 2005. David contributed to the work of the OECD for 34 years, in the course of which he made significant contributions to environmental economics and sustainable development. David Pearce's "opus" and influence are immense, and his capacity to link sound conceptual analysis with the political economy of environmental policy has helped to shape environmental policies in OECD countries. He was a mentor and a friend, and will be sorely missed. It has been our great privilege to work with him.

Jean-Philippe Barde

Table of Contents

11

List of figures

ISBN 92-64-01004-1
Cost-Benefit Analysis and the Environment
Recent Developments
© OECD 2006

Executive Summary

Introduction

The OECD has long championed efficient decision-making using economic analysis. It was, for example, one of the main sponsors of the early manuals in the late 1960s on project evaluation authored by Ian Little and James Mirrlees.* Since then, cost-benefit analysis has been widely practised, notably in the fields of environmental policy, transport planning, and healthcare. In the last decade or so, cost-benefit analysis has been substantially developed both in terms of the underlying theory and in terms of sophisticated applications. Many of those developments have been generated by the special challenges that environmental problems and environmental policy pose for cost-benefit analysis. The OECD has therefore returned to the subject in this new and comprehensive volume that brings analysts and decision-makers up to date on the main developments.

History and uses of CBA

The history of cost-benefit analysis (CBA) shows how its theoretical origins date back to issues in infrastructure appraisal in France in the 19th century. The theory of welfare economics developed along with the "marginalist" revolution in microeconomic theory in the later 19th century, culminating in Pigou's *Economics of Welfare* in 1920 which further formalised the notion of the divergence of private and social cost, and the "new welfare economics" of the 1930s which reconstructed welfare economics on the basis of ordinal utility only. Theory and practice remained divergent, however, until the formal requirement that costs and benefits be compared entered into water-related investments in the USA in the late 1930s. After World War II, there was pressure for "efficiency in government" and the search was on for ways to ensure that public funds were efficiently utilised in major public investments. This resulted in the beginnings of the fusion of the new welfare economics, which was essentially cost-benefit analysis, and practical decision-making. Since the 1960s CBA has enjoyed fluctuating fortunes, but is now recognised as the major appraisal technique for public investments and public policy.

Theoretical foundations

The essential theoretical foundations of CBA are: benefits are defined as increases in human wellbeing (utility) and costs are defined as reductions in human wellbeing. For a project or policy to qualify on cost-benefit grounds, its social benefits must exceed its social costs. "Society" is simply the sum of individuals. The geographical boundary for CBA is usually the nation but can readily be extended to wider limits. There are two basic

* Little, I and J. Mirrlees (1974), *Project Appraisal and Planning for Developing Countries*, Oxford, Oxford University Press (The "OECD Manual").

aggregation rules. First, aggregating benefits across different social groups or nations involves summing willingness to pay for benefits, or willingness to accept compensation for losses (WTP, WTA respectively), regardless of the circumstances of the beneficiaries or losers. A second aggregation rule requires that higher weights be given to benefits and costs accruing to disadvantaged or low income groups. One rationale for this second rule is that marginal utilities of income will vary, being higher for the low income group. Aggregating over time involves discounting. Discounted future benefits and costs are known as present values. Inflation can result in future benefits and costs appearing to be higher than is really the case. Inflation should be netted out to secure constant price estimates. The notions of WTP and WTA are firmly grounded in the theory of welfare economics and correspond to notions of compensating and equivalent variations. WTP and WTA should not, according to past theory, diverge very much. In practice they appear to diverge, often substantially, and with WTA > WTP. Hence the choice of WTP or WTA may be of importance when conducting CBA.

There are numerous critiques of CBA. Perhaps some of the more important ones are: *a)* the extent to which CBA rests on robust theoretical foundations as portrayed by the Kaldor-Hicks compensation test in welfare economics; *b)* the fact that the underlying "social welfare function" in CBA is one of an arbitrarily large number of such functions on which consensus is unlikely to be achieved; *c)* the extent to which one can make an ethical case for letting individuals' preferences be the (main) determining factor in guiding social decision rules; and *d)* the whole history of neoclassical welfare economics has focused on the extent to which the notion of economic efficiency underlying the Kaldor-Hicks compensation test can or should be separated out from the issue of who gains and loses – the distributional incidence of costs and benefits. CBA has developed procedures for dealing with the last criticism, *e.g.* the use of distributional weights and the presentation of "stakeholder" accounts. Criticisms *a)* and *b)* continue to be debated. Criticism *c)* reflects the "democratic presumption" in CBA, *i.e.* individuals' preference should count.

The stages of CBA

Conducting a well-executed CBA requires the analyst to follow a logical sequence of steps. The first stage involves asking the relevant questions: what policy or project is being evaluated? What alternatives are there? For an initial screening of the contribution that the project or policy makes to social wellbeing to be acceptable, the present value of benefits must exceed the present value of costs.

Determining "standing" – *i.e.* whose costs and benefits are to count – is a further preliminary stage of CBA, as is the time horizon over which costs and benefits are counted. Since individuals have preferences for when they receive benefits or suffer costs, these "time-preferences" also have to be accounted for through the process of discounting. Similarly, preferences for or against an impact may change through time and this "relative price" effect also has to be accounted for. Costs and benefits are rarely known with certainty so that risk (probabilistic outcomes) and uncertainty (when no probabilities are known) also have to be taken into account. Finally, identifying the distributional incidence of costs and benefits is also important.

Decision rules

Various decision rules may be used for comparing costs and benefits. The correct criterion for reducing benefits and costs to a unique value is the net present value (NPV) or "net benefits" criterion. The correct rule is to adopt any project with a positive NPV and to rank projects by their NPVs. When budget constraints exist, however, the criteria become more complex. Single-period constraints – such as capital shortages – can be dealt with by a benefit-cost ratio (B/C) ranking procedure. There is general agreement that the internal rate of return (IRR) should not be used to rank and select mutually exclusive projects. Where a project is the only alternative proposal to the status quo, the issue is whether the IRR provides worthwhile additional information. Views differ in this respect. Some argue that there is little merit in calculating a statistic that is either misleading or subservient to the NPV. Others see a role for the IRR in providing a clear signal as regards the sensitivity of a project's net benefits to the discount rate. Yet, whichever perspective is taken, this does not alter the broad conclusion about the general primacy of the NPV rule.

Dealing with costs

The cost component is the other part of the basic CBA equation. As far as projects are concerned, it is unwise to assume that because costs may take the form of equipment and capital infrastructure their estimation is more certain than benefits. The experience is that the costs of major projects can be seriously understated. The tendency for policies is for their compliance costs to be overstated. In other words there may be cost pessimism or cost optimism. In light of this it is important to conduct sensitivity analysis, *i.e.* to show how the final net benefit figure changes if costs are increased or decreased by some percentage. Ideally, compliance costs would be estimated using general equilibrium analysis.

Politicians are very sensitive about the effects of regulation on competitiveness. This is why most Regulatory Impact Assessment procedures call for some kind of analysis of these effects. A distinction needs to be made between the competitiveness of nations as whole, and the competitiveness of industries. In the former case it is hard to assign much credibility to the notion of competitiveness impacts. In the latter case two kinds of effects may occur. The first is any impact on the competitive nature of the industry within the country in question – *e.g.* does the policy add to any tendencies for monopoly power? If it does then, technically, there will be welfare losses associated with the change in that monopoly power and these losses should be added to the cost side of the CBA, if they can be estimated. The second impact is on the costs of the industry relative to the costs of competing industries in other countries. Unless the industry is very large, it cannot be assumed that exchange rate movements will cancel out the losses arising from the cost increases. In that case there may be dynamic effects resulting in output losses.

Policies to address one overall goal may have associated effects in other policy areas. Climate change and conventional air pollutants is a case in point. Reductions in climate gases may be associated with reductions in jointly produced air pollutants. Should the two be added and regarded as a benefit of climate change policy? On the face of it they should, but care needs to be taken that the procedure does not result in double counting. To address this it is important to consider the counterfactual, *i.e.* what policies would be in place without the policy of immediate interest. While it is common practice to add the benefits together, some experts have cast doubt on the validity of the procedure.

Finally, employment effects are usually also of interest to politicians and policy-makers. But the extent to which they matter for the CBA depends on the nature of the economy. If there is significant unemployment, the labour should be shadow priced on the basis of its opportunity cost. In turn this may be very low, *i.e.* if not used for the policy or project in question, the labour might otherwise be unemployed. In a fully employed economy, however, this opportunity cost may be such as to leave the full cost of labour being recorded as the correct value.

Total economic value

The notion of total economic value (TEV) provides an all-encompassing measure of the *economic value* of any environmental asset. It decomposes into use and non-use (or passive use) values, and further sub-classifications can be provided if needed. TEV does not encompass other kinds of values, such as intrinsic values which are usually defined as values residing "in" the asset and unrelated to human preferences or even human observation. However, apart from the problems of making the notion of intrinsic value operational, it can be argued that some people's willingness to pay for the conservation of an asset, independently of any use they make of it, is influenced by their own judgements about intrinsic value. This may show up especially in notions of "rights to existence" but also as a form of altruism. Any project or policy that destroys or depreciates an environmental asset needs to include in its costs the TEV of the lost asset. Similarly, in any project or policy that enhances an environmental asset, the change in the TEV of the asset needs to be counted as a benefit. For instance, ecosystems produce many services and hence the TEV of any ecosystem tends to be equal to the discounted value of those services.

Revealed preference valuation

Economists have developed a range of approaches to estimate the economic value of non-market or intangible impacts. There are several procedures that share the common feature of using market information and behaviour to infer the economic value of an associated non-market impact.

These approaches have different conceptual bases. Methods based on hedonic pricing utilise the fact that some market goods are in fact bundles of characteristics, some of which are intangible goods (or bads). By trading these market goods, consumers are thereby able to express their values for the intangible goods, and these values can be uncovered through the use of statistical techniques. This process can be hindered, however, by the fact that a market good can have several intangible characteristics, and that these can be collinear. It can also be difficult to measure the intangible characteristics in a meaningful way.

Travel cost methods utilise the fact that market and intangible goods can be complements, to the extent that purchase of market goods and services is required to access an intangible good. Specifically, people have to spend time and money travelling to recreational sites, and these costs reveal something of the value of the recreational experience to those people incurring them. The situation is complicated, however, by the fact that travel itself can have value, that the same costs might be incurred to access more than one site, and that some of the costs are themselves intangible (*e.g.* the opportunity costs of time).

Averting behaviour and defensive expenditure approaches are similar to the previous two, but differ to the extent that they refer to individual behaviour to avoid negative intangible impacts. Therefore, people might buy goods such as safety helmets to reduce accident risk, and double-glazing to reduce traffic noise, thereby revealing their valuation of these bads. However, again the situation is complicated by the fact that these market goods might have more benefits than simply that of reducing an intangible bad.

Finally, methods based on cost of illness and lost output calculations are based on the observation that intangible impacts can, through an often complex pathway of successive physical relationships, ultimately have measurable economic impacts on market quantities. Examples include air pollution, which can lead to an increase in medical costs incurred in treating associated health impacts, as well as a loss in wages and profit. The difficulty with these approaches is often the absence of reliable evidence, not on the economic impacts, but on the preceding physical relationships.

Stated preference valuation: contingent valuation

Stated preference techniques of valuation utilise questionnaires which either directly ask respondents for their willingness to pay (accept), or offer them choices between "bundles" of attributes and from which choices the analysts can infer WTP (WTA).

Stated preference methods more generally offer a direct survey approach to estimating individual or household preferences and more specifically WTP amounts for changes in provision of (non-market) goods, which are related to respondents' underlying preferences in a consistent manner. Hence, this technique is of particular worth when assessing impacts on non-market goods, the value of which cannot be uncovered using revealed preference methods.

This growing interest in stated preference approaches has resulted in a substantial evolution of techniques over the past 10 to 15 years. For example, the favoured choice of elicitation formats for WTP questions in contingent valuation surveys has already passed through a number of distinct stages. This does not mean that uniformity in the design of stated preference surveys can be expected any time soon. Nor is this particularly desirable. Some studies show how, for example, legitimate priorities to minimise respondent strategic bias by always opting for incentive compatible payment mechanisms must be balanced against equally justifiable concerns about the credibility of a payment vehicle. The point is the answer to this problem is likely to vary across different types of project and policy problems.

There remain concerns about the validity and reliability of the findings of contingent valuation studies. Indeed, much of the research in this field has sought to construct rigorous tests of the robustness of the methodology across a variety of policy contexts and non-market goods and services. By and large, one can strike an optimistic note about the use of the contingent valuation to estimate the value of non-market goods. In this interpretation of recent developments, there is a virtuous circle between translating the lessons from tests of validity and reliability into practical guidance for future survey design. Indeed, many of the criticisms of the technique can be said to be imputable to problems at the survey design and implementation stage rather than to some intrinsic methodological flaw. Taken as a whole, the empirical findings largely support the validity and reliability of contingent valuation estimates.

Stated preference valuation: choice modelling

Many types of environmental impact are multidimensional in character. Hence an environmental asset that is affected by a proposed project or policy often will give rise to changes in component attributes each of which command distinct valuations. The application of choice modelling (CM) approaches to valuing multidimensional environmental problems has been growing steadily in recent years. CM is now routinely discussed alongside the arguably better-known contingent valuation method in state-of-the-art manuals regarding the design, analysis and use of stated preference studies. While there are a number of different approaches under the CM umbrella, it is arguably the *choice experiment* variant (and to some extent, *contingent ranking*) that has become the dominant CM approach with regard to applications to environmental goods. In a choice experiment, respondents are asked to choose their most preferred option from a choice set of at least two options, one of which is the status quo or current situation. It is this CM approach that can be interpreted in standard welfare economic terms, an obvious strength where consistency with the theory of cost-benefit analysis is a desirable criterion.

Much of the discussion about, for example, validity and reliability issues in the context of contingent valuation (CV) studies applies in the context of the CM. While it is likely that on some criteria, CM is likely to perform better than CV – and *vice versa* – the evidence for such assertions is largely lacking at present. While those few studies that have sought to compare the findings of CM and CV appear to find that the total value of changes in the provision of the same environmental good in the former exceeds that of the latter, the reasons for this are not altogether clear. However, whether the two methods should be seen as always competing against one another – in the sense of say CM being a more general and thereby superior method – is debatable. Both approaches are likely to have their role in cost-benefit appraisals and a useful contribution of any future research would also be to aid understanding of when one approach should be used rather than the other.

Option value

The notion of *quasi option value* was introduced in the environmental economics literature some three decades ago. In parallel, financial economists developed the notion of "*option value*". QOV is not a separate category of economic value. Rather it is the difference between the net benefits of making an optimal decision and one that is not optimal because it ignores the gains that may be made by delaying a decision and learning during the period of delay. Usually, QOV arises in the context of irreversibility. But it can only emerge if there is uncertainty which can be resolved by learning. If the potential to learn is not there, QOV cannot arise.

Can QOV make a significant difference to decision-making? Potentially, yes. It is there to remind us that decisions should be made on the basis of maximum feasible information about the costs and benefits involved, and that includes "knowing that we do not know". If this ignorance cannot be resolved then nothing is to be gained by delay. But if information can resolve it, then delay can improve the quality of the decision. How large the gain is from this process is essentially an empirical question since QOV is the difference in the net benefits of an optimal decision and a less than optimal one.

WTP versus WTA?

Traditionally, economists have been fairly indifferent about the welfare measure to be used for economic valuation: willingness to pay (WTP) and willingness to accept compensation (WTA) have both been acceptable. By and large, the literature has focused on WTP. However, the development of stated preference studies has, fairly repeatedly, discovered divergences, sometimes substantial ones, between WTA and WTP. These differences still would not matter if the nature of property rights regimes were always clear. WTP in the context of a potential improvement is clearly linked to rights to the status quo. Similarly, if the context is one of losing the status quo, then WTA for that loss is the relevant measure. By and large, environmental policy tends to deal with improvements rather than deliberate degradation of the environment, so there is a presumption that WTP is the right measure. The problems arise when individuals can be thought of as having some right to a future state of the environment. If that right exists, their WTP to secure that right seems inappropriate as a measure of welfare change, whereas their WTA to forego that improvement seems more relevant. In practice, the policy context may well be one of a mixture of rights, *e.g.* a right to an improvement attenuated by the rights of others not to pay "too much" for that improvement.

Finding out why, empirically, WTA and WTP differ also matters. If there are legitimate reasons to explain the difference then the preceding arguments apply and one would have to recommend that CBA should always try to find both values. The CBA result would then be shown under both assumptions. But if the observed differences between WTA and WTP are artefacts of questionnaire design, there is far less reason to be concerned at the difference between them. The fallback position of their approximate equality could be assumed. Unfortunately, the literature is undecided as to why the values differ. This again suggests showing the CBA results under both assumptions about the right concept of value.

Valuing ecosystem services

Research is now being conducted on the value of ecosystem services. The aim is to estimate the total economic value (TEV) of ecosystem change. The problems with valuing changes in ecosystem services arise from the interaction of ecosystem products and services, and from the often extensive uncertainty about how ecosystems function internally, and what they do in terms of life support functions. Considerable efforts have been made to value specific services, such as the provision of genetic information for pharmaceutical purposes. The debate on that issue usually shows how complex valuing ecosystem services can be. But even that literature is still developing, and it does not address the interactive nature of ecosystem products and services.

Once it is acknowledged that ecosystem functioning may be characterised by extensive uncertainty, by irreversibility and by non-linearities that generate potentially large negative effects from ecosystem loss or degradation, the focus shifts to how to behave in the face of this combination of features. The short answer is that decision-making favours precaution. But just what precaution means is itself a further debate.

Discounting

Some advances have been prompted by the alleged "tyranny of discounting" – the fact that discounting has a theoretical rationale in the underlying welfare economics of CBA, but with consequences that many seem to find morally unacceptable. This unacceptability arises from the fact that distant future costs and benefits may appear as insignificant present values when discounting is practised. In turn, this appears to be inconsistent with notions of intergenerational fairness. Current activities imposing large costs on future generations may appear insignificant in a cost-benefit analysis. Similarly, actions now that will benefit future generations may not be undertaken in light of a cost-benefit analysis.

The weakness of the conventional approach, which assumes that one positive discount rate is applied for all time, is that it neither incorporates uncertainty about the future nor attempts to resolve the tyranny problem. Additionally, the assumption of a constant discount rate is exactly that – an assumption. The "escapes" from the tyranny problems centre on several approaches.

First, many studies find that very often (but not always), people actually discount "hyperbolically", i.e. people actually do use time-declining discount rates. If what people do reflects their preferences, and if preferences are paramount, there is a justification for adopting time-declining discount rates.

Second, there is also uncertainty about future interest rates: here it can be shown that uncertainty about the temporal weights – i.e. the *discount factor* – is consistent with a time-declining certainty equivalent *discount rate*. Introducing uncertainty about the state of the economy more generally can be shown also to generate time-declining rates, if certain conditions are met.

Third, by positing the "tyranny" problem as a social choice problem in which neither the present nor the future dictates outcomes, and adopting reasonable ethical axioms can be shown to produce time-declining rates.

In terms of the uncertainty and social choice approaches, the time-path of discount rates could be very similar with long term rates declining to the "lowest possible" rates of, say, 1%.

But time-consistency problems remain and some experts would regard any time-declining discount rate as being unacceptable because of such problems. Others would argue that the idea of a long-run optimising government that never revises its "optimal" plan is itself an unrealistic requirement for the derivation of an optimal discount rate.

Valuing health and life

Considerable strides have been made in recent years in terms of clarifying both the meaning and size of the "value of a statistical life" (VOSL). One of the main issues has been how to "transfer" VOSLs taken from non-environmental contexts to environmental contexts. Non-environmental contexts tend to be associated with immediate risks such as accidents. In contrast, environmental contexts are associated with both immediate and future risks. The futurity of risk may arise because the individual in question is not at immediate risk from *e.g.* current levels of pollution but is at risk in the future when there is greater vulnerability to risk. Or futurity may arise because the risk is latent as with diseases such as asbestosis or arsenicosis. All this suggests *a)* that valuations of immediate risk might be transferred to environmental immediate risk contexts (provided that the perception of the risk is the same) but *b)* future risks need to be valued separately.

In terms of practical guidelines, the age of the respondent who is valuing the risk matters. Age may or may not be relevant in valuing immediate risks – the literature is ambiguous. The general rule, then, is to ensure that age is controlled for in any primary valuation study. For "benefits transfer" the rule might be one of adopting a default position in which immediate risks are valued the same regardless of age (*i.e.* the VOSL does not vary with age), with sensitivity analysis being used to test the effects of lower VOSLs being relevant for older age groups. Age is very relevant for valuing future risks. Thus a policy which lowers the general level of exposure to pollution should be evaluated in terms of the (lower than immediate VOSL) valuations associated with younger people's valuations of future risks, plus older persons' valuation of that risk as an immediate risk.

Some environmental risks fall disproportionately on the very young and the very old. A complex issue arises with valuing risks to children. The calculus of willingness to pay now seems to break down since children may have no income to allocate between goods, including risk reduction, may be ill-informed about or be unaware of risks, and may be too young to articulate preferences anyway. The result is that adults' valuations of the risks *on behalf of* children need to be estimated. The literature on which to base such judgements is only now coming into existence. Preliminary findings suggest that the resulting values of WTP may be higher for adults valuing on behalf of children than they are for adults speaking on behalf of themselves. The safest conclusion at this stage is that bringing the effects on children into the domain of CBA is potentially important, with a default position being to use the adult valuations of "own" life risks for the risks faced by children.

Equity

One important issue is equity or the distributional incidence of costs and benefits. Incorporating distributional concerns implies initially identifying and then possibly weighting the costs and benefits of individuals and groups on the basis of differences in some characteristic of interest (such as income or wealth). First, there is the relatively straightforward but possibly arduous task of assembling and organising raw (*i.e.* unadjusted) data on the distribution of project costs and benefits. Second, these data could then be used to ask what weight or distributional adjustment would need to placed on the net benefits (net costs) of a societal group of interest for a given project proposal to pass (fail) a distributional cost-benefit test. Third, explicit weights reflecting judgement about society's preferences towards distributional concerns can be assigned and net benefits re-estimated on this basis.

A crucial question then is where should cost-benefit analysts locate themselves upon this hierarchy? Given that cost-benefit appraisals are sometimes criticised for ignoring distributional consequences altogether then the apparently simplest option of cataloguing how costs and benefits are distributed could offer valuable and additional insights. This suggests that, at a minimum, cost-benefit appraisals arguably should routinely provide these data. Whether more ambitious proposals should be adopted is a matter of deliberating about whether: first, the gains in terms of being able to scrutinise the (weighted) net benefits of projects in the light of societal concerns about both efficiency and equity outweighs; second, the losses arising from the need for informed guesswork in interpreting the empirical evidence with regards to the treatment of the latter.

On the one hand, empirical evidence about the "correct" magnitudes of distributional weights can be usefully employed in distributional CBA as its application to the case of climate change illustrates. On the other hand, even apparently small changes in assumptions about the size of distributional weights – indicated by the range of values in available empirical studies – can have significant implications for recommendations about a project's social worth. This finding should not be a surprise for it primarily reflects the complexity involved in trying to disentangle society's distributional preferences. As a practical matter, the danger is whether the most ambitious proposals for distributional CBA generate more heat than light. While it would worthwhile for research to seek further understanding of these preferences – perhaps making greater use of stated preference methods – in the interim, estimating implicit weights might be the most useful step beyond the necessary task of cataloguing the distribution of project cost and benefits.

Sustainability and CBA

While there remains a debate about what it means for development to be sustainable, there is now a coherent body of academic work that has sought to understand what a sustainable development path might look like, how this path can be achieved and how progress towards it might be measured. Much of this work considers the pursuit of sustainable development to be an aggregate or macroeconomic goal. Comparatively little attention has been paid to the implications of notions of sustainability for CBA. However, a handful of recommendations do exist with regards to how cost-benefit appraisals can be extended to take account of recent concerns about sustainable development.

According to one perspective there is an obvious role for appraising projects in the light of these concerns. This notion of strong sustainability starts from the assertion that certain natural assets are so important or critical (for future, and perhaps current, generations) so as to warrant protection at current or above some other target level. If individual preferences cannot be counted on to fully reflect this importance, there is a paternal role for decision-makers in providing this protection. With regards to the relevance of this approach to cost-benefit appraisals, a handful of contributions have suggested that sustainability is applicable to the management of a *portfolio* of projects. This has resulted in the idea of a shadow or compensating project. For example, this could be interpreted as meaning that projects that cause environmental damage are "covered off" by projects that result in environmental improvements. The overall consequence is that projects in the portfolio, on balance, maintain the environmental status quo.

There are further ways of viewing the problem of sustainable development. Whether these alternatives – usually characterised under the heading "weak sustainability" – are complementary or rivals has been a subject of debate. This debate would largely dissolve if it could be determined which assets were critical. As this latter issue is itself a considerable source of uncertainty, the debate continues. However, the so-called "weak" approach to sustainable development is useful for a number of reasons. While it has primarily be viewed as a guide to constructing green national accounts (*i.e.* better measures of income, saving and wealth), the focus on assets and asset management has a counterpart in thinking about project appraisal. For example, this might emphasise the need for an "asset check". That is, what the stocks of assets are before the project intervention and what they are likely to be after the intervention? It might also add another reason for the tradition in cost-benefit analysis of giving greater weight to projects which generate economic resources for saving and investment in economies where it is reckoned that too little net wealth (per capita) is being passed on to future generations.

Benefits transfer

Benefits or value transfer involves taking economic values from one context and applying them to another. Transfer studies are the bedrock of practical policy analysis in that only infrequently are policy analysts afforded the luxury of designing and implementing original studies. In general then, analysts must fall back on the information that can be gleaned from past studies. This is likely to be no less true in the case of borrowing or transferring WTP values to policy questions involving environmental or related impacts. Almost inevitably, benefits transfer introduces subjectivity and greater uncertainty into appraisals in that analysts must make a number of *additional* assumptions and judgements to those contained in original studies. The key question is whether the added subjectivity and uncertainty surrounding the transfer is acceptable and whether the transfer is still, on balance, informative.

Surprisingly given its potentially central role in environmental decision-making, there are no generally accepted practical transfer protocols to guide analysts. However, a number of elements of what might constitute best practice in benefits transfer might include the following. First, the studies included in the analysis must themselves be sound. Initial but crucial steps of any transfer are very much a matter of carefully scrutinising the accuracy and quality of the original studies. Second, in conducting a benefits transfer, the study and policy sites must be similar in terms of population and population characteristics. If not then differences in population, and their implications for WTP values, need to be taken into account. Just as importantly, the change in the provision of the good being valued at the two sites also should be similar.

The holy grail of benefits transfer is the consolidation of data on non-market values in emerging transfer databases. Yet, while databases are to be welcomed and encouraged, these developments still need to be treated with some caution. Thus, there is a widely acknowledged need for more research to secure a better understanding of when transfers work and when they do not as well as developing methods that might lead to transfer accuracy being improved.

However, a competent application of transfer methods demands informed judgement and expertise and sometimes, according to more demanding critics, as advanced technical skills as those required for original research. At the very least, it suggests that practitioners should be explicit in their analysis about important caveats regarding a proposed transfer exercise as well as take account of the sensitivity of their recommendations to changes in assumptions about economic values based on these transfers.

CBA and other decision-making guidance

A significant array of decision-guiding procedures are available and include cost-effectiveness analysis (CEA) and multi-criteria analysis (MCA). These procedures vary in their degree of comprehensiveness, where this is defined as the extent to which all costs and benefits are incorporated. In general, only MCA is as comprehensive as CBA and may be more comprehensive once goals beyond efficiency and distributional incidence are considered. All the remaining procedures either deliberately narrow the focus on benefits, *e.g.* to health or environment, or ignore cost. Procedures also vary in the way they treat time. Environmental Impact Assessment and Life Cycle Analysis are essential inputs into a CBA, although the way these impacts are dealt with in "physical terms" may not be the same in a CBA. They are not decision-making procedures in their own right. Risk assessments tend to be focused on human health only but ecological risk assessments are also fairly common. Once again, neither enables a comprehensive decision to be made.

Some political economy

Political economy, or "political economics", seeks to explain why the economics of the textbook is rarely embodied in actual decision-making. CBA is very much a set of procedures derived from an analytical framework that is as theoretically "correct" as possible. Unsurprisingly, actual decisions may be made on very different bases to this analytical approach. The reasons lie in the role played by "political" welfare functions rather than the social welfare functions of economics, distrust about or disbelief in monetisation, the capture of political processes by those not trained in economics, beliefs that economics is actually "common sense" and easily understood, and, of course, genuine mistrust of CBA and its theoretical foundations based on the debates that continue within the CBA community and outside it. But explaining the gap between actual and theoretical design is not to justify the gap. Theoretical economists need a far better understanding of the pressures that affect actual decisions, but those who make actual decisions perhaps also need a far better understanding of economics.

ISBN 92-64-01004-1
Cost-Benefit Analysis and the Environment
Recent Developments
© OECD 2006

Chapter 1

Introduction

The OECD has a long history of giving guidance on the social evaluation of projects (investments) and policies. In the late 1960s and in the 1970s it was instrumental in developing social cost-benefit analysis. Since that time, cost-benefit analysis has enjoyed widespread application and the theory has developed further. In the last few years, some major advances have taken place in the underlying theory, and this is the justification for the current volume. This chapter outlines the history of cost-benefit analysis (CBA), explains why it remains a powerful aid to decision-making, and gives a brief overview of the extent to which CBA is currently in use in OECD countries.

1.1. Purpose of this volume

The OECD has a long and distinguished history in terms of developing cost-benefit analysis (henceforth, CBA[1]) and producing manuals and guidance for its dissemination. In 1968 the OECD Development Centre published Ian Little and James Mirrlees' *Manual of Industrial Project Analysis* (Little and Mirrlees, 1968) which later became one of the classics of cost-benefit analysis (Little and Mirrlees, 1974). The other two major manuals of the time had been prepared for UNIDO (Dasgupta *et al.* 1972. See also UNIDO, 1980) and for the World Bank (Squire and van der Tak, 1975). The focus of these volumes was very much on the application of CBA to the developing world where market distortions could be expected to be more pervasive than in developed countries. The need to appraise projects and policies using the prices that would prevail in competitive markets ("shadow prices" or "accounting prices") was therefore more urgent. Nonetheless, CBA was beginning to be applied in developed countries at about the same time. The principles were the same but there was perhaps more emphasis in developed country applications on shadow prices in contexts where markets did not exist at all (accident risks and time savings being notable early examples).

Since the 1970s, OECD has returned to the subject of CBA on an occasional basis, producing documents aimed more precisely at: environmental policies and projects (Pearce and Markandya, 1989; Pearce *et al.* 1994; Winpenny, 1995); biodiversity (Biller 2001; Pearce *et al.* 2002); air pollution (OECD, 1981); environmental and health risks of products (OECD, 1983; Postle *et al.* 2002), and transport (ECMT, 1998).

Outside of the OECD, numerous texts and manuals have appeared, many covering the general field of CBA (*e.g.* Sugden and Williams, 1978; Pearce and Nash, 1981; Pearce, 1986; Schmid, 1989; Walshe and Daffern, 1990; Brent, 1996; Boardman *et al.* 2001). Other have covered the detailed procedures for estimating shadow prices, especially in developing countries (*e.g.* Ray, 1984; Dinwiddy and Teal, 1996; Londero, 1996, 2003), while yet others have specialised in the environmental context (*e.g.* Johansson, 1993; Hanley and Spash, 1993) or agriculture (*e.g.* Gittinger, 1984). As a further instance of the revival of CBA, a classic text from 1982 (Just, Hueth and Schmitz, 1982) was revised and reissued in 2004 to some considerable acclaim (Just, Hueth and Schmitz, 2004). At the level of official guidance, Canada issued CBA guidance for regulatory programmes (Government of Canada, 1995) and the USA issued a detailed manual on regulatory impact analysis in the environmental context (US EPA, 2000).

Given this wealth of exploration of the principles of CBA and practical guidance on how to use it, what justification can there be for yet another publication? The answer is that in recent years, there have been a number of generally uncorrelated developments in the theory of CBA that, taken together, alter the way in which many economists would argue CBA should be carried out. Interestingly, quite a few of those developments have come from concerns associated with the use of CBA in the context of policies and projects with significant environmental impacts. Those concerns have tended to centre on:

- the fact that most environmental goods and services have *no obvious markets*, so that environmental impacts can quickly become ignored or downplayed in a CBA because the implicit "price" of the environment appears to be zero;

- the role that *discounting* plays in CBA, making what seem intuitively to be large problems faced by future generations disappear through the practice of placing lower weight on future damages; and

- the fact that CBA tends to work with measures of benefit and cost based on *willingness to pay* which, in turn, is heavily influenced by ability to pay (income, wealth). The result is a cost-benefit rule for sanctioning or rejecting projects or policies that is biased in favour of those with higher incomes, raising issues of distributional fairness.[2] These distributional concerns have been emphasised in a separate political movement relating to "environmental justice", the presumption that environmental quality is unfairly distributed, with the poor or ethnic minorities suffering the worst environments (Pearce, 2003).

Other developments include the way *uncertainty* and potential *irreversibility* are treated in CBA, the sensitive issue of the valuation of *health risks*, especially to poor people and to children, and the extent to which *multi-functional ecosystems* can be valued in money terms.

These concerns have spilled over into OECD's past work. For example, the issue of non-market valuation was addressed, albeit briefly, in Pearce and Markandya (1989). A special OECD symposium on valuing child health was held in 2003 (OECD, 2005). The distributional issue has been the subject of a significant OECD symposium in 2003 (Serret and Johnstone, 2005). So far, OECD has not tackled the complex issue of discounting.

What is missing, however, is a document in which all these issues are addressed and in which the implications for the practice of CBA are spelled out. This is the purpose of the current volume. It is essential to be clear what the volume is not. *It is not a comprehensive manual of CBA.* It does not tell readers how to conduct a CBA. It focuses solely on recent developments, although the early chapters set out a very brief résumé of the basic principles in order to remind readers of the background. It does try to explain the recent changes and to show what they might mean for the practice of CBA. As such, it should be of value not only to those who practise CBA on a regular basis, but also to those who are too busy to consult what are sometimes quite complex articles and books. Some of the theoretical developments are controversial and it should not be assumed that there is a complete consensus on each and every issue. Where there is a debate we have tried to indicate what the nature of that debate is.

1.2. A very brief history of cost-benefit analysis

Central to CBA as it applies to environmental issues is the idea of an externality – a third party detrimental (or beneficial) effect for which no price is exacted. Pollution would be the most obvious example. In an unregulated market, polluters would have no incentive to account for the suffering and damage borne by third parties. A CBA approach, on the other hand, would weigh up the profits of the polluter against the damage done, each measured in money terms. Only if profits exceed damage would the polluter's activities be efficient. The notion of an externality was already familiar from the work of Sidgwick (1883) and Marshall (1890), but it was Pigou (1920) who developed the notion of the divergence between private and social cost, the divergence being the value of the externality. The underlying valuation procedure is the same for profits as for pollution damage. In each case, the money value of these benefits and costs reflects human preferences as expressed through willingness to pay. In short, the basic value judgement of CBA is that individuals' preferences should count and that preferences are revealed through choices in the market place.

That policies could be evaluated in terms of their costs and benefits defined in terms of human preferences and willingness to pay, was established by Dupuit (1844, 1853) much earlier in 19th century. Dupuit's concern was with the economic justification for constructing roads and bridges, and he showed that the net benefits of construction were measured by the sum of the consumers' surplus. The body of modern-day welfare economics which underlies CBA was established by Hicks (1939, 1943), Kaldor (1939) and others in the 1930s and 1940s. Pareto (1848-1923) had argued in his *Cours d'Économie Politique* in 1896 that the only objective test of whether or not social improvement had been brought about by a change in the existing state was if some people were made better off and no-one was made worse off, a highly restrictive condition known as the "Pareto condition". The strict Pareto principle – whereby a policy is "good" if at least some people *actually* gain and no-one *actually* loses – was clearly stultifying. Virtually all real-life contexts involve gainers and losers. The Kaldor-Hicks "compensation principle" established the idea of hypothetical compensation as a practical rule for deciding on policies and projects in these real-life contexts. All that is required is that gainers *can* compensate losers to achieve a "potential" Pareto improvement.[3] The compensation principle thus establishes the *prima facie* rule that benefits (gains in human well-being) should exceed costs (losses in human well-being) for policies and projects to be sanctioned.

These theoretical developments were not without their critics. Samuelson (1942) had argued that consumer's surplus had no practical validity because one could not assume that the marginal utility of income was constant. Scitovsky (1941) had shown that there was a potential contradiction in the hypothetical compensation principle. Since a change making some better off and some worse off would change the distribution of income it was possible for those who lost to (hypothetically) compensate those who gained to return to the original situation. All-round attacks on welfare economics came from Ian Little in his *Critique of Welfare Economics* (Little, 1950, 2002) and from Jan de Graaff in his *Theoretical Welfare Economics* (de Graaff, 1957). Lipsey and Lancaster (1956-7) had also produced the general theory of the "second best" which showed that if a distortion (a deviation from marginal cost pricing say) existed in one market, correcting that deviation could not be assumed to improve social welfare if there was also a deviation in another market. Since CBA tends to adopt a partial equilibrium approach, this means that a project or policy might pass a cost-benefit test without necessarily improving overall social welfare. Finally, Arrow (1951) had established in his *Social Choice and Individual Values* that there exists no way to decide whether something is a social improvement or not, if we insist that social rankings are based on individual preferences and on certain "reasonable" criteria. But CBA is a procedure for aggregating individuals' preferences, so that CBA must fail the Arrow "impossibility" theorem as well. There is no "reasonable" way of going from individuals' preferences to a social ordering of different states. Arrow's theorem related to individuals' preferences being expressed in an *ordinal* fashion, *i.e.* preferences are capable of being ordered but the "distance" between them could not be measured, since this was the welfare economics climate of the time. For example, an ordinal ranking of states x, y, z could be $U(x) > U(y) > U(z)$, where "U" simply means "utility" or "well-being". With ordinal ranking no meaning can be attached to the "distance" U(x) – U(y), say. The *intensity of preference* cannot be measured. In contrast, *cardinal* orderings would enable values to be attached to the distances for purposes of comparison, *e.g.* if U(x) – U(y) = 9 and U(y) – U(z) = 3, the former can be said to be three times the latter. A scale might be strictly cardinal if the scale has a "real" origin, rather like measures of height and weight and geographical distance. If it is necessary to avoid another widely discussed problem, that of (the impossibility of) *interpersonal comparisons of utility*, then the various intervals between U(x), U(y), etc., should mean the same thing for all individuals. For example, it would imply that $U^1(x) - U^1(y) > U^2(x) - U^2(y)$, where 1 and 2 are different people. Otherwise preferences cannot be aggregated. But if cardinal utility and interpersonal comparisons both apply, then CBA would appear to be valid since preference s can be aggregated. The whole spirit of the Arrow theorem was to show that *ordinal* preferences could not be aggregated in a context where there is no interpersonal comparison of utility. The view that interpersonal comparisons were themselves impossible had become widely accepted with the publication of Lionel Robbins' famous essay in 1938 (Robbins, 1938). Interpersonal comparisons become essential with the hypothetical compensation test. If compensation is *actually* paid no problem arises. But if it is not actually paid then it is necessary to know if the gainers really could compensate the losers, *i.e.* the relative size of the gains and losses must be known, which means comparing utilities across different people. The essential point about aggregating preferences is that if interpersonal comparisons of utility cannot be made, then the Arrow theorem applies and *all* non-dictatorial mechanisms for aggregating individual preferences are imperfect in the sense of permitting inconsistent social orderings. If interpersonal comparisons can be made, CBA is "saved" and the Arrow theorem does not apply.

This digression on the theoretical developments is necessary in order to show that the development of CBA borrowed heavily from the theoretical literature but that, perhaps more interestingly, it took place *despite* many problems. It seems clear that the architects of CBA knew fully what the various criticisms were. One reason CBA proceeded despite these problems is almost certainly the recognition that many of the criticisms were equally applicable to any competing rule for aggregating preferences: Arrow's theorem for example was not specific to the welfare economics developed by Hicks and others, although it focused on that welfare economics because what Hicks had attempted to do was to reconstruct welfare economics based on ordinal preferences only. In this respect, CBA may well have been "the best game in town". Everything else was worse. Other criticisms seemed also to be less important in the real world of policy: partial equilibrium analysis, for example, seems appropriate so long as there are no major repercussions elsewhere in the economy from a given project or policy, as is often (but not always) the case.

Practical guidelines for using welfare economics in the guise of cost-benefit analysis were drawn up first for the water sector in the USA. The US Flood Control Act of 1936 declared that the control of flood waters was "in the interests of the general welfare" and the role of the Federal Government was to "improve or participate in the improvement of navigable waters … for flood control purposes if the benefits to whomsoever they accrue are in excess of the estimated costs". While this appears to be a clear invocation of the benefit-cost rule, the notion of cost was actually restricted to construction costs and did not embrace wider social losses – *e.g.* displacement of people because of dam construction. Similarly, the notion of a benefit was not clearly defined in the Act, and there are considerable doubts as to whether many of the projects undertaken because of the Act would have passed a modern-day CBA test.

In the early 1950s attempts were made to codify the benefit-cost rules, notably in the Federal Inter-Agency River Basin Committee's *Green Book* of 1950 and the Bureau of Budget's *Budget Circular A-47* of 1952. Considerable attention was also being devoted to the wider issue of "efficiency in government", especially military spending, by bodies such as the Rand Corporation. In 1958 three seminal works appeared: Eckstein's *Water Resource Development* (Eckstein, 1958); Krutilla and Eckstein's *Multipurpose River Development* (Krutilla and Eckstein, 1958); and McKean's *Efficiency in Government Through Systems Analysis* (McKean, 1958). The feature of these works was the synthesis of practical concerns with the theoretical welfare economics literature of the 1930s and 1940s. What these volumes showed was that benefits and costs had precise meanings and that they were potentially measurable. Importantly, they established that gains and losses reflected preferences or "utility", and that cost had always to be interpreted as opportunity cost, the value of the project or policy that is foregone by choosing a specific action. The 1958 volumes were followed by another major work of guidance for water investments – Maass (1962).

By the early 1960s, then, the basic principles of CBA had been set out, although many of the later concerns were either not discussed or were subjected to very rudimentary treatments. Costs and benefits had rigorous definitions and the benefit-cost rule, an efficiency rule, for sanctioning investments and policies was firmly established. Some of the theoretical literature had attempted to address distributional concerns, *i.e.* to worry about who gains and loses, and these concerns ultimately led to distributional weighting schemes of the kind set out in the 1970s manuals. The issue of the discount rate at which to discount future costs and benefits had long been discussed, but without any real consensus. Lind (1982) reports on a 1977 conference at Resources for the Future in Washington DC aimed at agreeing a rate for use in water resource projects. The end result was an unhelpful range of numbers from 2% to 20%! While the range that is likely to be quoted today would probably not be so large, it seems fair to say that the choice of "the" discount rate remains as controversial now as it was 40 years ago, despite major symposia on the subject (Lind *et al.* 1982; Portney and Weyant, 1999).

1.3. Why use CBA?

This volume is not a defence of CBA, nor a critique of other procedures sometimes used to give guidance on how to choose policies and projects, although we look briefly at other procedures in Chapter 18. Our aim is to describe recent developments in CBA and illustrate their applications. Arguments for and against CBA have been well rehearsed elsewhere (for critiques see, for example, Sagoff 1988 and 2004; Heinzerling and Ackerman, 2004. See also Pearce, 2001 for the sources of controversy). Nonetheless, it is in order to outline some of the reasons why economists tend to favour CBA (not unanimously, however).

The first rationale for using CBA is that it provides a model of rationality. In the world of politics decisions are not always made on the basis of thinking rationally about gains and losses. Independently of its use of money measures of gain and loss, CBA forces the decision-maker to look at who the beneficiaries and losers are in both the spatial and temporal dimensions. It avoids what might be called "lexical" thinking whereby decisions are made on the basis of the impacts on a single goal or single group of people. For example, policies might be decided on the basis of human health alone, rather than on the basis of health and ecosystem effects together. CBA's insistence on all gains and losses of "utility" or "well-being" being counted means that it forces the wider view on decision-makers. In this respect, CBA belongs to a group of approaches to policy analysis which do the same thing. For example, cost-effectiveness analysis (CEA) and multi-criteria analysis (MCA) impose a discipline in terms of defining goals (working out what it is that the policy should achieve) and differentiating costs from indicators of achievement of the goals (see Chapter 18).

Secondly, CBA is clear in its requirement that any policy or project should be seen as one of a series of options. Hence setting out the alternatives for achieving the chosen goal is a fundamental prerequisite of CBA. Again, this feature is shared by some other policy analysis procedures, such as CEA and MCA.

Third, CBA should make the decision-maker include in the list of alternative options variations in the *scale* of a policy or project. Unlike CEA and MCA, CBA has the capacity to determine the *optimal scale* of the policy. This would be where net benefits are maximised. Any guidance procedure that expresses benefits and costs in different units, which is the case with MCA and CEA, cannot define this optimum (see Chapter 18). In the same vein, CBA offers a rule for deciding if anything at all should be chosen. CEA and MCA can decide only between alternatives to do something. They cannot address the issue of whether any option should be chosen. Again, this arises because numerator and denominator in CBA are in the same units, whereas they are not in CEA and MCA.

Fourth, while it is often ignored in practice, properly executed CBA should show the costs and benefits accruing to different social groups of beneficiaries and losers. As will be seen in Chapter 14, social concerns about differential impacts can be accounted for by the use of distributional weights. Thus, CBA has the capacity to express costs and benefits either in units of money reflecting willingness to pay, or in units of "utils" – willingness to pay weighted by some index of the social importance attached to the beneficiary or loser group.

Fifth, CBA is explicit that time needs to be accounted for in a rigorous way. This is done through the process of discounting which, we have seen, is nonetheless controversial. It is impossible not to discount. Failing to discount means using a discount rate of 0% which means that USD 1 of gain 100 years from now is treated as being of equal value to USD 1 of gain now. Zero is a real number. But it is true that what the "correct" real number is, continues to be debated. Chapter 13 looks at recent developments in discounting. Note that the treatment of time in other decision-making guidance is far from clear.

Sixth, CBA is explicit that it is individuals' preferences that count. To this extent, CBA is "democratic", but some see this as a weakness rather than a strength since it implies that preferences should count, however badly informed the holders of those preferences might be. They also argue that there are two kinds of preference, those made out of an individual's self-interest and those made when the individual expresses a preference as a citizen. There are clearly pros and cons to the underlying value judgement in CBA, namely that preferences count.

Finally, CBA seeks explicit preferences rather than implicit ones. To this extent, CBA looks directly for what people want, either in the market place or in "constructed" markets – see Chapters 8-9 –, or indirectly by seeing how preferences affect a complementary market – see Chapter 7. All decisions, however they are made, imply preferences and all decisions imply money values. If a decision to choose Policy X over Policy Y is made, and X costs USD 150 million and Y costs USD 100 million, then it follows that the benefits of X must exceed the benefits of Y by at least USD 50 million. The unavoidability of money values was pointed out by Thomas (1963). It may be that leaving decisions to reveal implicit values is better than seeking those values explicitly. But CBA is clear in favouring the latter.

Readers may find one or more of these features of CBA attractive enough to justify the use of CBA. Or they may disagree. It is not the purpose of this volume to persuade anyone, one way or the other.

1.4. Guidance on environmental CBA in OECD countries: some examples

As noted earlier, there is an extensive academic literature on CBA, some of which may not use the term "cost-benefit analysis" but instead refers to "policy evaluation" or "project appraisal". Detailed official guidance on how to carry out CBA is much rarer and tends to be confined to those countries where CBA is part of the process of "regulatory impact analysis" (RIA), (or, sometimes, "appraisal" or "assessment"). OECD has issued its own guidelines on RIA (OECD, 1997) and also maintains an *Inventory of RIA Procedures* (OECD, 2004). OECD (2004) states that CBA is the "most desirable" form of RIA but notes that it is not used in many countries because of the difficulties of placing money values on a comprehensive range of costs and benefits. In other words, the existence of RIA procedures cannot be taken as an indication that CBA is used. It is more likely it will not be used than that it will be. The following case examples illustrate the availability of central guidance and the extent to which CBA is used in selected countries.

1.4.1. *The USA*

In the environmental policy context in the USA, which is the main concern here, CBA is widely used. The major piece of legislation in this respect was Executive Order 12291 (1981) which required a benefit-cost assessment of new regulations for rules which impose significant costs or economic impacts. EO 12991 required that, for any new regulation, "the potential benefits outweigh the costs" and that of all the alternative approaches to the given regulatory objective, the proposed action will maximise net benefits to society. EO 12291 helped to engrain cost-benefit thinking in federal agencies, although actual cost-benefit studies were applied in a non-uniform manner across agencies. Several court cases in the USA have established that CBA cannot be used by agencies unless explicitly authorised by statute. However, even where analysis of costs and benefits was not explicitly required, the US EPA tended to adopt regulations on the basis of CBA studies. Thus, compared to Europe, CBA is far more influential in the USA than a simple comparison of formal requirements would suggest.

Whether CBA is actually used more than the statutes require, it remains the case that US legislators quite clearly regard CBA as not being relevant in a number of regulatory contexts. It is tempting to think that this has something to do with doubts about the credibility of *benefit* estimates, but it is significant that, while the *costs* of regulation are given more consideration than the benefits, several statutes and corresponding court cases specifically exclude even the costs from consideration in standard setting.

EO 12991 was superseded by EO 12866 in 1993. This replaced the "benefits outweigh costs" provision with "benefits justify costs". Benefits include "economic, environmental, public health and safety, other advantages, distributive impacts and equity" and may not all be quantified. In effect there was no formal requirement that benefits actually exceed costs in a quantitative sense. Some commentators have suggested that EO 12866 endorses CBA as an "accounting framework" rather than an "optimising tool". In a review of US regulations 1981-1996, Hahn (2000) found that benefits or cost savings were assessed in 87% of cases, but that benefits were given monetary values in only 26% of cases. For environmental statutes, the relevant proportions were 83% and 23% respectively.

In some cases balancing of costs and benefits has been explicitly rejected by US court rulings. Notions of "public trust" doctrine have often been used to justify this neglect of a cost-benefit approach. Public trust is best defined in the context of damage liability where an agent damages the environment and is held liable for those damages. But similar notions, not always expressed in terms of the language of the public trust doctrine, have been used to reject cost-benefit comparisons. Under public trust, a nation's natural resources are held in trust for all citizens, now and in the future. Combined with *parens patriae* – the role of the state as guardian of persons under legal disability – public trust gives the state a right to protect the environment on behalf of its citizens. This right exists independently of ownership of the resource and derives from the state's duty to protect its citizens. Moreover, whereas CBA works with the public's preferences, public trust works with the restoration of the environmental asset itself. As Kopp and Smith (1993) put it:

> "Damage awards for injuries to natural resources are intended to maintain a portfolio of natural assets that have been identified as being held in public trust... Because this compensation is to the public as a whole, the payment is made to a designated trustee and the compensation takes the form of in-kind services..." (Kopp and Smith, 1993, p. 2).

Outside of the liability context, it has been argued that public-trust style doctrine has influenced the courts in ruling that US EPA is authorised to regulate without reference to costs and benefits. More generally, there is a debate in the USA as to how far CBA should be used for environmental regulations and how far practice follows Office of Management and Budget (OMB) guidance (Lutter, 2001). However, the US Environmental Protection Agency does have extensive guidelines for preparing economic analyses of regulations (US EPA 2000). These are intended to comply with the OMB requirements for using some form of CBA for major regulations (mainly those with costs over USD 100 million and/or with potentially significant effects on employment and competitiveness). The guidance covers most of the issues that anyone practising CBA would have to address, along with other issues such as impacts of regulations on innovation, business, and competitiveness. Despite its length (over 200 pages) the guidelines remain very much an extensive checklist, with, for example, around 15 pages being devoted to valuation techniques. This perhaps underlines why comprehensive guidance of the "manual" kind does not generally exist: the practise of CBA requires considerable practical experience as well as theoretical understanding. No one "manual" could possibly encompass all that is required to carry out a CBA, as the US EPA guidelines show. However, the US EPA guidance remains the most elaborate set of guidelines in any OECD country.

1.4.2. *Canada*

The Canadian Government (1995) has issued general guidelines for CBA as applied to any regulation, *i.e.* the guidance is not specific to environmental policy. Prepared by external consultants, the guidance is non-technical and is not aimed at professional economists. As such it is far less comprehensive than the US EPA guidelines and provides only a beginning for anyone seeking to carry out a CBA. Nonetheless, it is effective in introducing the reader to "cost-benefit thinking".

1.4.3. *The United Kingdom*

The UK has RIA procedures which are brought into operation when regulations are thought to have significant impacts on business or the voluntary sector. RIA was made mandatory for regulations in 1998. Each government department has a Regulatory Impact Unit (RIU) and a centralised RIU exists in the Cabinet Office. The most recent guidance is given in UK Cabinet Office (2003), although additions have been made to this document via the Cabinet-Office website (*www.cabinet-office.gov.uk/regulation'ria-guidance/asp*). The guidance tells practitioners how to conduct an RIA in the sense of giving guidance on structure and issues to look out for. Each RIA must consider costs and benefits and their distribution. The guidance does not, however, indicate how to value costs and benefits in monetary terms. Outline guidance for this is given by the UK Treasury (2002) in its "Green Book".

1.4.4. *The European Union*

The European Commission is committed to applying some form of cost-benefit test to its Directives. In the context of environmental legislation, Article 130r of the Treaty on European Union (1992) requires that:

> "in preparing its policy on the environment, the Community shall take account of – available scientific and technical data, environmental conditions in the various regions of the Community, *the potential benefits and costs of action or lack of action*, and the economic and social development of the Community as a whole and the balanced development of its regions" (italics added).

There is no implication in Article 130r that Directives need to pass a cost-benefit test for each and every Member State affected by the Directive, nor that the comparison of costs and benefits takes the form that economists would regard as conforming to CBA.

In 2003 general impact appraisal procedures were introduced for all Commission proposals deemed to have significant impacts of an economic, social or environmental kind. Preliminary impact statements are used to narrow the choice of options and formally adopted options must be subject to an Extended Impact Assessment. However, these Assessments are not required to adopt cost-benefit analysis as the methodology for appraisal, and no formal requirements, beyond comparing costs and benefits in some form, are required. As far as Regional schemes are concerned ("structural and cohesion funds") a guidance document on CBA does exist. This focuses mainly on conventional project appraisal issues but does have a brief section on valuing environmental impacts in money terms (Florio 2004).

Pearce (1998a) surveyed the extent to which early environmental Directives were subject to formal appraisal – whether CBA, cost-effectiveness, multi-criteria or some form of environmental impact assessment. The general finding was that up to around 1990 very few formal appraisals were conducted. In the 1990s formal appraisal increases primarily in the sphere of water pollution and air pollution, but they varied significantly in quality and in the extent to which they provide a clear comparison of costs and benefits. More recently, the Commission has either commissioned CBA studies, or carried them out "in house", or have cited CBA studies carried out in some Member States. In a review of recent Directives, Pearce (2004b) noted that CBA studies existed in a number of cases but that it was unclear if a CBA "test" for those policies had been met. However, as with most policy making, CBA is not the sole criterion for accepting or rejecting policies. In the case of the European Union there are additional complexities. The requirement to avoid competitive distortions within the Community (the "Single Market") means that standards for environmental quality are not permitted to vary between Member States (although there may be derogations and staged timings). But harmonised standards may well be inimical to economic efficiency if preferences for environmental quality and/or costs of compliance vary geographically, as seems likely. Hence a CBA test may well not be passed.

Notes

1. In North America cost-benefit analysis is more often term "benefit-cost analysis" (BCA). The terms are interchangeable.

2. This last concern was actually integral to the early manuals dealing with developing country issues, i.e. social weights were applied to correct for the distributional incidence of costs and benefits. To this extent, CBA has come full circle with the 1970s procedures being reintroduced in a number of applications of CBA.

3. Pigou regarded actual payment as being necessary and the task of the economist was to work out how such payments could be made. As noted, however, CBA has proceeded on the basis of saying that if the polluter *could* compensate the losers and still have a net profit, then the polluting activity passes a cost-benefit test.

ISBN 92-64-01004-1
Cost-Benefit Analysis and the Environment
Recent Developments
© OECD 2006

Chapter 2

The Foundations of Cost-benefit Analysis

The underlying theory of CBA has been developed most over the past 50 years. It is based on the notion of a human preference. Preferences are linked to "utility" or "wellbeing" by rigorous rules and axioms. In turn, CBA provides rules for aggregating preferences so that it is possible to speak of a "social" preference for or against something. Preferences are revealed in market places through decisions to spend, or not spend, money. Hence "willingness to pay" becomes the primary means of measuring preferences and money becomes the measuring rod that permits aggregation of preferences. For potential losses, "willingness to accept compensation" might also be used. CBA remains controversial in the eyes of some and this chapter provides a brief overview of the main debates.

2.1. Utility, well-being and aggregation

The theoretical foundations for CBA can be briefly summarised as:

a) the preferences of individuals are to be taken as the source of value. To say that an individuals' well-being, welfare or utility is higher in state A than in state B is to say that he/she prefers A to B.

b) preferences are measured by a willingness to pay (WTP) for a benefit and a willingness to accept compensation (WTA compensation) for a cost.*

c) it is assumed that individuals' preferences can be aggregated so that social benefit is simply the sum of all individuals' benefits and social cost is the sum of all individuals' costs. Effectively some degree of cardinalisation of utility is assumed.

d) if beneficiaries from a change can *hypothetically* compensate the losers from a change, and have some net gains left over, then the basic test that benefits exceed costs is met. This is the Kaldor-Hicks compensation test discussed in Chapter 1.

Costs and benefits will accrue over time and the general rule will be that future costs and benefits are weighted in such a way that a unit of benefit or cost in the future has a lower weight than the same unit or benefit cost occurring now. This temporal weight is known as the *discount factor* and this is written:

$$DF_t = \frac{1}{(1+s)^t} \qquad\qquad [2.1]$$

where DF_t means the discount factor, or weight, in period t, and s is the *discount rate*. As long as projects and policies are being evaluated from society's point of view, s is a *social* discount rate. The rationales for discounting are given in Chapter 13.

2.2. The decision rule

The basic decision rule for accepting a project or policy is:

$$\left\{ \sum_{i,t} WTP^G_{i,t}.(1+s)^{-t} - \sum_{i,t} WTP^L_{i,t}.(1+s)^{-t} \right\} > 0 \qquad\qquad [2.2]$$

where i is the ith individual and t is time. In this formulation, benefits are measured by WTP to secure the benefit (G refers to gainers), and costs are measured by WTP to avoid the cost (L refers to losers). If the "losers" from the project or policy have legitimate property rights to what they lose, then WTP should be replaced by WTA, and the equation would read:

$$\left\{ \sum_{i,t} WTP^G_{i,t}.(1+s)^{-t} - \sum_{i,t} WTA^L_{i,t}.(1+s)^{-t} \right\} > 0 \qquad\qquad [2.3]$$

---

* The notions of WTP and WTA can be extended to include WTP to avoid a cost and WTA compensation to forego a benefit.

The difference, then, is that losses in [2.3] are measured by WTA and not by WTP. We observe later that WTA can differ significantly from WTP – see Chapter 11.

In [2.2] and [2.3], WTP and WTA are discounted so that when summed over time the resulting magnitude is known as a *present value* (PV). A present value is simply the sum of all the *discounted* future values. [2.3] might therefore be written very conveniently as:

$$PV\ (WTP) - PV(WTA) > 0 \tag{2.4}$$

2.3. Aggregation rules

In [2.2] and [2.3] WTP and WTA are summed across individuals in accordance with the aggregation rule which defines "society" as the sum of all individuals. There are no hard and fast rules for defining the geographical boundaries of the sum of individuals. Typically, CBA studies work with national boundaries so that "society" is equated with the sum of all individuals in a nation state. But there will be cases where the boundaries need to be set more widely. Some examples illustrate.

In the context of acid rain, those who suffer damage caused by emissions from one country may be in an entirely different country. This is because acid rain (sulphur and nitrogen oxides – SO_X, NO_X – and some other pollutants) are transboundary pollutants, travelling across national boundaries. There are two main reasons why the damage to another country would be relevant to a CBA in the emitting country: *a)* a moral judgement that others' suffering should count, *b)* legal obligations arising from transboundary pollution agreements. Hence a CBA might appear in a two-part form. The first part would show the costs of acid rain abatement in the country in question, and the benefits *to that country* of the abatement. The second part would show the same costs but the benefits would be shown as those accruing both to the country in question and all other countries that benefit from the pollution abatement.

In some cases, the boundary may be the world as a whole. Emissions of greenhouse gases, for example, cause damage worldwide. The same principles, moral and legal, can be used to justify including these world-wide damages in a CBA conducted for one emitting country.

The issue of "who counts" in a CBA is known as the issue of "standing". But even when standing has been agreed, other ethical principles might be invoked to determine the aggregation rule applicable to geographical boundaries. Again, there are no hard and fast rules. If the well-being of people in country B matters as much to country A as the well-being of A's own people, as measured by money, then the aggregation rule would be one of adding up benefits and costs regardless of to whom they accrue. In this case, USD 1 of gain/loss to B matters as much as USD 1 of gain/loss to A. A more "utilitarian" rule would take account of income or wealth differences. For example, if the inhabitants of B are poor and the inhabitants of A are rich, allowance might be made for the likelihood that USD 1 of gain/loss to a poor person will have a higher utility than USD 1 of gain/loss to a rich person. This allowance for variations in the marginal utility of income is one fairly popular form of "equity weighting". Equity weighting is discussed further in Chapter 15.

Equations [2.2] and [2.3] also aggregate across time. However, what is aggregated is the discounted value of WTP (WTA), not the absolute values. A simple example makes this clear. Suppose benefits and costs are distributed across time as follows:

	Year 1	Year 2	Year 3	Year 4
Benefit	0	80	60	40
Cost	−100	20	20	20
Net benefit	−100	60	40	20
Discount factor*	0.952	0.907	0.864	0.823
Discounted net benefits	−95.2	54.4	34.6	16.5

* Assumes a discount rate of 5%.

The minus sign indicates a cost. The discount factor is computed from equation [1], with an assumed discount rate of 5%. The final row shows the discounted net benefits. When these are summed, it will be found that there are positive net benefits of 105.5 which can be compared to the costs of 95.2, i.e. there is a positive net present value (NPV). The example also illustrates the notion of a "base year", i.e. the year to which future costs and benefits are discounted. In this case there is a year 0 so that costs in year 1 are discounted back to year 0 to obtain the present value of year 1 costs (the first column of numbers). A more usual practice is to set the base year as the one in which the initial costs – usually a capital outlay – occurs. Again, there are no hard and fast rules. Any base year can be chosen, so long as the resulting procedures are consistent.

2.4. Inflation

The values of WTP and WTA in the above equations are in real money terms. What this means is that any effects of inflation are netted out. This does not mean that benefits and costs will not rise (or fall) over time. They may do this for any number of reasons. But inflation – a rise in the general level of prices – is not relevant. This again means that a base year issue arises. The choice of the year in which prices are expressed can vary. The usual procedure is to value all costs and benefits at the prices ruling in the year of the appraisal, but it is perfectly possible to change the year prices to conform with some other rule, e.g. in order to compare the results of one study with another study.

To illustrate the procedure for netting out inflation, consider the same example above but with WTP and WTA expressed in current prices, i.e. the prices ruling in the year they occur. The table assumes an inflation rate of 3% per year. Then the benefits and costs appear as in the first row of the table. Netting out inflation means adopting a base year, in this case year 0 again, and computing benefits and costs at constant prices. The distinction between inflation and discounting should ten be clear: the first step is always to ensure that benefits and costs are expressed in constant prices, and it is these magnitudes that are then discounted.

	Year 1	Year 2	Year 3	Year 4
Net benefit in current prices	−103	63.6	43.7	22.5
Netting out inflation at 3% p.a. = net benefit in constant year 0 prices	−100	60.0	40.0	20.0
Discount factor*	0.952	0.907	0.864	0.823
Discounted net benefits	−95.2	54.4	34.6	16.5

2.5. Benefits, costs, WTP and WTA

The more familiar form of [2.2] and [2.3] simply speaks of benefits and costs, *i.e.*:

$$\{\sum_{i,t} B_{i,t}.(1+s)^{-t} - \sum_{i,t} C_{i,t}.(1+s)^{-t}\} > 0$$

or

$$\sum_{i,t} (B_{i,t} - C_{i,t}).(1+s)^{-t} > 0 \qquad [2.5]$$

The notions of WTP and WTA need a little more exploration. A gain in an individual's well-being, utility, welfare or well-being can be measured by the maximum amount of goods or services – or money income (or wealth) – that he or she would be willing to give up or forego in order to obtain the change. Alternatively, if the change reduces well-being, it would be measured by the amount of money that the individual would require in compensation in order to accept the change. Consider an individual in an initial state of well-being U_0 that he/she achieves with a money income Y_0 and an environmental quality level of E_0:

$$U_0 (Y_0, E_0) \qquad [2.6]$$

Suppose that there is a proposal to improve environmental quality from E_0 to E_1. This improvement would increase the individual's well-being to U_1:

$$U_1 (Y_0, E_1) \qquad [2.7]$$

We need to know by how much the well-being of this individual is increased by this improvement in environmental quality, *i.e.* $U_1 - U_0$. Since utility cannot be directly measured, we seek an indirect measure, namely the maximum amount of income the individual would be willing to pay (WTP) for the change. The individual is hypothesised to be considering two combinations of income and environmental quality that both yield the same level of well-being (U_0): one in which his income is reduced and environmental quality is increased, and a second in which his income is not reduced and environmental quality is not increased, *i.e.*:

$$U_0 (Y_0 - WTP, E_1) = U_0 (Y_0, E_0) \qquad [2.8]$$

The individual adjusts WTP to the point at which these two combinations of income and environmental quality yield equal well-being. At that point WTP is defined as the monetary value of the change in well-being, $U_1 - U_0$, resulting from the increase in environmental quality from E_0 to E_1. This WTP is termed the individual's *compensating variation*, and it is measured relative to the initial level of well-being, U_0.

An alternative is to ask how much an individual would be willing to accept (WTA) in terms of additional income to forego the improvement in environmental quality and still have the same level of well-being as if environmental quality had been increased. The individual is then considering the combinations of income and environmental quality that yield an equal level of well-being (U_1):

$$U_1 (Y_0 + WTA, E_0) = U_1 (Y_0, E_1) \qquad [2.9]$$

where WTA is a monetary measure of the value to the individual of the change in well-being ($U_1 - U_0$) resulting from the improvement in environmental quality. This is termed the *equivalent variation*. It is measured relative to the level of well-being after the change, W_1. Here the monetary measure of the value of the change in well-being could be infinite

45

if no amount of money could compensate the individual for not experiencing the environmental improvement.

Analogous measures for policy changes that result in losses in well-being can be derived. In this case the compensating variation is measured by WTA, and the equivalent variation is measured by WTP. Suppose the move from E_0 to E_1 results in a reduction in the individual's well-being. Then, the compensating variation is the amount of money the individual would be willing to accept as compensation to let the change occur and still leave him or her as well off as before the change:

$$U_0 (Y_0 + WTA, E_1) = U_0 (Y_0, E_0) \qquad [2.10]$$

The required compensation could again, in principle, be infinite if there was no way that money could fully substitute for the loss in environmental quality.

The equivalent variation is the amount of money the individual would be willing to pay to avoid the change:

$$U_1 (Y_0 - WTP, E_0) = U_1 (Y_0, E_1) \qquad [2.11]$$

In this case the equivalent variation measure of the value to the individual of the change in well-being resulting from a deterioration in environmental quality from E_0 to E_1 is finite and limited by the individual's income.

Table 2.1 summarises the various measures of welfare gains and losses.

Table 2.1. **Compensating and equivalent variation measures**

	Compensating variation = Amount of Y that can be taken from an individual *after* a change such that he/she is as well off as they were *before* the change	Equivalent variation = If a change does *not* occur, the amount of Y that would have to be given to the individual to make him/her as well off as if the change did take place
Increase in human welfare	$U_0 (Y_0 - WTP, E_1) = U_0 (Y_0, E_0)$	$U_1 (Y_0 + WTA, E_0) = U_1 (Y_0, E_1)$
Decrease in human welfare	$U_0 (Y_0 + WTA, E_1) = U_0 (Y_0, E_0)$	$U_1 (Y_0 - WTP, E_0) = U_1 (Y_0, E_1)$

2.6. WTP "versus" WTA

Until a few decades ago, most economists assumed that the difference between compensating and equivalent variation measures of change in well-being would be very small and of no practical policy relevance. That is, for CBA purposes, it mattered little if WTP or WTA was used in either of the relevant contexts (a gain, and a loss). There are theoretical reasons for supposing that WTP and WTA should be very similar. But empirical estimation of these magnitudes has tended to show that they do vary, sometimes significantly, and with WTA > WTP. Depending on one's view of the evidence that WTA and WTP differ in practice, the choice of WTA or WTP could matter substantially for CBA. Accordingly, this issue is deferred for a fuller discussion in Chapter 11.

2.7. Critiques of CBA

The purpose of this volume is to guide experts and policy-makers to recent developments in the theory and practice of CBA. As such, we have not accounted for the various critiques that have been made of CBA or its underlying welfare economics foundations. This section guides the reader to some of the critiques, but does not develop them in any way.

First, welfare economics or, more strictly, "neoclassical welfare economics" which culminates in the Kaldor-Hicks compensation principle, has always been the subject of debate. It has to be recognised that the compensation principle was an attempt to overcome the seeming sterility of the "Pareto principle" for deciding whether or not policies or projects were welfare-improving, all in a context where it was alleged that individuals' utilities could not be compared on a consistent basis (the "impossibility" of interpersonal comparisons of utility). The Pareto rule was sterile because it said that a policy was a good policy if and only if no-one suffered a welfare loss and at least one person experienced a gain. Today such situations tend to be termed "win-win" measures. Unsurprisingly, it is quite hard to find examples of win-win solutions: someone always loses in one way or another. The Kaldor-Hicks rule, or "potential Pareto improvement" rule, says that so long as gainers can compensate losers and still have some net gains left over, the policy is a good policy. In a sense, what is happening is that the Pareto rule is being "mimicked" but with two important provisions: *a)* compensation need not actually be paid, and *b)* interpersonal comparisons of welfare are not being made because one can think of the compensation as some form of bargain in which the loser decides how much he/she needs for their original level of well-being to be unchanged. While such a solution to the Pareto sterility issue is in many ways ingenious, it produces a number of potential inconsistencies which have been noted over the years. Details of these theoretical criticisms are not provided here. Most relate to issues of what happens to income distribution as the policy or project is implemented. In theory it could change in such a way that the policy originally sanctioned by the potential compensation principle could also be negated by the same principle – i.e. benefits exceed costs for the policy, but the move back to the original pre-policy state could also be sanctioned by CBA. This is the "Scitovsky paradox" (Scitovsky, 1941). Another problem arising from the fact that policies may change income distributions (and hence relative prices) is the "Boadway paradox" (Boadway, 1974). A possibility is that the policy showing the highest net benefits may not, in fact, be the best one to undertake. Bergson (1938) showed that one of the "escapes" from these problems could be to assume a "social welfare function" – a rule that declared how aggregate welfare would vary with the set of all individuals' welfare. The problem is one of finding a social welfare function that might be regarded as a socially "consensus" function – there are many possible functions and no practical prospect of deciding which one to use. Most notably, Arrow (1951) showed that one cannot construct such a function without traversing one or more of a set of "axiomatic" rules that would seem sensible. This is the "Arrow impossibility theorem". An enormous literature has been devoted to various "escapes" from the Arrow impossibility theorem, *e.g.* by relaxing one or more of the underlying axioms, or by imposing moral rules about the "just" distribution of welfare within society. But just as there are many ways of aggregating individuals' welfare to get different social welfare functions, so there are many different concepts of what constitutes a just division of welfare in society.

Critics of CBA, which rests on an underlying social welfare function in which it is possible to add up individuals' welfare, cite this historical sequence of objections and counter-objections to welfare economics as a dominant reason why CBA is not credible. An excellent summary (which oddly excludes the Arrow social welfare function issue) is given by Gowdy (2004). One problem, however, is that social decision-making necessarily is about weighing up gains and losses and deciding on the relative importance of different individuals' gains and losses. In short, it is very hard to see how the problems that afflict CBA can be avoided by alternative approaches.

A second line of criticism has focused on CBA's underlying value judgement that individuals' preferences should count in any social decision-making rule. Few advocates of CBA argue that this is an exclusive and comprehensive rule, *i.e.* it is not the only value judgement that is relevant. But once this is admitted, it opens up a debate on when individuals' preferences count and when they do not. There appear to be no hard and fast rules and this means that the use of CBA in certain contexts is always going to be controversial. Examples are its use in determining optimal levels of crime control, but the environment is probably the most controversial area. In some cases this is because critics believe other species have "intrinsic rights" which are not amenable to analysis using human preferences (unless humans can be judged to take those rights into account when expressing their own preferences). Hence those who believe in a "rights-based" approach will find CBA unacceptable. Others believe that individuals are poorly informed about the environment and its importance as a life-support asset. In that case guiding policy with measures of human preference could risk other social goals, even human survival itself. Belief in "rights" is perhaps an example of what has been called "endogenous preferences", preferences that are formed by the social context of decision-making, by how others behave, by institutions and social conditioning (Gowdy, 2004). A CBA advocate might respond by accepting such endogeneity and then asking what difference it makes to CBA rules which, after all, take the preferences as given, however they are formed. Nonetheless there is a growing interest in why people hold the preferences they do – their motivation – and perhaps in judging some motivations to be acceptable while others are not. Once again, moral notions enter the analysis. Equally, those who advocate a "moral" cost-benefit analysis may not always recognise that CBA adopts the wants-based approach because of observation that this is what often determines human behaviour. Moral notions may also determine human behaviour and it is not clear that such motivations cannot be encompassed in the CBA framework. Perhaps the single most debated issue is the extent to which wants-based approaches should be criticised because they are based on "self-interest". Arguably, self interest has become confused with "greed" and a failure to be sensitive to the wants and needs of others. There is nothing in the notion of an individual preference that dictates this conclusion, but it is a widespread perception of the critics of CBA.

As it happens, some of the critiques of CBA raise issues that are explicitly addressed in this volume. That is, some of the "recent developments" in CBA quite explicitly try to address the criticisms, for example on willingness to pay as a measure of preferences (Chapter 11), discounting (Chapter 13), distribution and equity (Chapter 15) and sustainability (Chapter 16). How successful they are is for the reader to judge.

2.8. Summary and guidance for decision-makers

The theoretical foundations of CBA can be summarised as follows:

- Benefits are defined as increases in human well-being (utility).
- Costs are defined as reductions in human well-being.
- A project or policy to qualify on cost-benefit grounds, its social benefits must exceed its social costs.
- "Society" is simply the sum of individuals.

- The geographical boundary for CBA is usually the nation but can readily be extended to wider limits.

- Aggregating benefits across different social groups or nations can involve summing willingness to pay/accept (WTP, WTA) regardless of the circumstances of the beneficiaries or losers, or it can involve giving higher weights to disadvantaged or low income groups. One rationale for this is that marginal utilities of income will vary, being higher for the low income group.

- Aggregating over time involves discounting. The rationale for discounting is given later. Discounted future benefits and costs are known as present values.

- Inflation can result in future benefits and costs appearing to be higher than is really the case. Inflation should be netted out to secure constant price estimates.

- The notions of WTP and WTA are firmly grounded in the theory of welfare economics and correspond to notions of compensating and equivalent variations.

- WTP and WTA should not, according to past theory, diverge very much. In practice they appear to diverge, often substantially, and with WTA > WTP. Hence the choice of WTP or WTA may be of importance when conducting CBA.

There are numerous critiques of CBA. Perhaps some of the more important one are:

- The extent to which CBA rests of robust theoretical foundations as portrayed by the Kaldor-Hicks compensation test.

- The fact that the underlying "social welfare function" in CBA is one of an arbitrarily large number of such functions on which consensus is unlikely to be achieved.

- The extent to which one can make an ethical case for letting individuals' preferences be the (main) determining factor in guiding social decision rules.

Finally, and issue to which we return in Chapter 15 (on equity), the whole history of neoclassical welfare economics has focused on the extent to which the notion of economic efficiency underlying the Kaldor-Hicks compensation test can or should be separated out from the issue of who gains and loses – the distributional incidence of costs and benefits. Various "schools of thought" have emerged. Some argue that distributional incidence has nothing to do with CBA: CBA should be confined to "maximising the cake" so there is more to share round according to some morally or politically determined rule of distributional allocation. Others argue that notions of equity and fairness are more engrained in the human psyche than notions of efficiency, so that distribution should be considered as a prior moral principle, with efficiency taking second place. Yet others would agree with the second school but would argue that precisely because efficiency is "downgraded" in social discourse that is all the more reason to elevate it to a higher level of importance in CBA. Put another way, one can always rely on the political process raising the equity issue, but not the efficiency issue. As we see in Chapter 3, certain minimum requirements for practice emerge. At the very least, a "proper" CBA should record not just the aggregate net gains from a policy, but the gains and losses of different groups of individuals.

2.9. Further reading

While there are many textbooks on CBA, a comprehensive text that assesses some of the recent developments and which provides a thorough grounding in technique is A. Boardman, D. Greenberg, A. Vining, and D. Weimer (2001), *Cost-benefit Analysis: Concepts and Practice*, 2nd edition, Upper Saddle River NJ, Prentice Hall. An excellent and comprehensive text on welfare economics is Just, R., Hueth, D. and Schmitz, A. (2004), *The Welfare Economics of Public Policy: a Practical Guide to Project and Policy Evaluation*, Cheltenham, Edward Elgar.

A provocative and clear critique of CBA (or, rather, neoclassical welfare economics) is given in John Gowdy's "The revolution in welfare economics and its implications for environmental valuation and policy", *Land Economics*, 2004, 80 (2): 239-257.

ISBN 92-64-01004-1
Cost-Benefit Analysis and the Environment
Recent Developments
© OECD 2006

Chapter 3

The Stages of a Practical Cost-benefit Analysis

Conducting a well executed CBA requires the analyst to follow a logical sequence of steps. This chapter provides an overview of those steps, beginning with the nature of the problem being addressed and the alternative options for dealing with it. Determining "standing" – i.e. whose costs and benefits are to count – is a further preliminary stage of CBA, as is the time horizon over which costs and benefits are counted. Since individuals have preferences for when they receive benefits or suffer costs, these "time-preferences" also have to be accounted for through the process of discounting. Similarly, preferences for or against an impact may change through time and this "relative price" effect also has to be accounted for. Rarely are costs and benefits known with certainty so that risk (probabilistic outcomes) and uncertainty (when no probabilities are known) also have to be taken into account. Finally, identifying the distributional incidence of costs and benefits will be important.

3.1. The questions to be addressed

While it may seem obvious, the first and fundamentally most important issue to be addressed in practical CBA is what question is being asked. CBA is applicable to *policies* and to *projects* (investments). The context may be either *ex ante* – determining whether something that has not yet been done should be done – or *ex post* – finding out whether something that has been done should have been done. The reason for doing *ex ante* CBA is to find out whether what are often significant sums of money should be spent in the public interest. The rationale for *ex post* CBA is that, while it cannot reverse expenditure already made, it can *a)* cast light on the accuracy of the *ex ante* CBA, or *b)* cast light on whatever decision rule was used to justify the policy/project. In both cases, *ex post* CBA is designed to assist the process of *learning* about what does and what does not contribute to overall social well-being.

Any analysis begins with the set of *options* that are available. Usually there is some reasonably defined goal, *e.g.* improving air or water quality. Consider air quality goals. There may be different options with respect to the extent of control, *i.e.* the issue is what environmental quality target to set, or there may be different ways of reaching any given target. Options tend to be sifted into feasible and non-feasible ones, and other issues such as the political factors driving the policy will also tend to limit the options. An option that is often ignored is *when* to commence the policy (or project). This option should be considered whatever the policy or project in question, but Chapter 10 shows that issues of timing can be very important when there is uncertainty and irreversibility, *i.e.* the future is not known with certainty and the policy decision commits government to an action that cannot be changed subsequently. Chapter 4 discusses the formal ways in which choices between options are determined.

So, the first question is:

● What are the options under consideration?

The next question that is likely to arise is:

● Should project X or policy X be undertaken at all?

The answer to this question will be "yes" if the present value of expected (*ex ante*) benefits exceed expected costs, and "no" if expected costs exceed benefits. Note that all this assumes that CBA is either *the* relevant decision-guiding criterion or is *one* of the relevant criteria. In what follows, we assume CBA is always relevant. In making this assumption, the relevance of other factors – political, ethical etc. – is ignored. In reality, of course, these factors will often influence decisions. But CBA is there as a check on those decisions, so it is always sensible to carry out a CBA wherever practicable. The answer to the above question is then:

● Proceed if E(B) > E(C). Do not proceed if E(B) < E(C).

where B is the present value of benefits and C is the present value of costs, and the "E" reminds us that in the *ex ante* context, benefits and costs are anticipated or estimated.

In the *ex post* context, the question will be:

● Should project X or policy X have been undertaken?

If *ex post* benefits exceed costs then the policy decision is confirmed. If costs exceed benefits then the analysis indicates that *ex ante* appraisal procedures need to be revisited to find out what went wrong. Perhaps there was "appraisal optimism" which is quite common in decision-making – see Chapter 5. There is a temptation to exaggerate benefits and under-estimate cost escalations. Perhaps wrong assumptions were made. Perhaps the *ex ante* CBA was not carried out in a rigorous fashion. *Ex post* assessments can also cast light on decision-making procedures. Many, if not most, decisions are not actually made with the aid of a CBA. Conducting *ex post* CBA can cast light on the extent to which actual decision-making procedures are imposing an efficiency cost on society (*i.e.* net social costs). The answer to the second question, then, is:

● Yes, if B > C. No if C > B

Note that the "E" no longer applies because the costs and benefits in question are actual – they have been realised.

The next question that can and should be asked is:

● What is the optimal scale of the policy or project?

If the project consists of building a road, say, CBA can say something about whether the road should be two lanes or three. If there is a policy of improving environmental quality, CBA can inform decision-makers about the optimal or desirable level of air quality. The basic rule for determining optimal scale is very simple: optimal scale is where the marginal social benefits of the project/policy are just equal to the marginal costs of the project policy. "Marginal" here simply means "small change in". So the marginal benefit of a policy is the extra benefit that accrues to society from one small change in the "quantity" of the policy, *e.g.* a small amount of air quality improvement. Annex 3.A1 shows this formally.

CBA can be used to decide which of a set of competing projects/policies should be undertaken. In the previous examples, only one policy/project was under consideration (henceforth we shall use "policy" to refer to policies or projects). It is important to determine at the outset whether there are alternatives to the single policy. Very often, only one option is presented. Even if this option passes a cost-benefit test (benefits exceed costs), it does not mean it is the best thing to do. There may be alternatives that yield higher net benefits for the same cost outlay. A basic rule, then, is for the adviser or analyst to raise the issue of the alternatives even if none is presented. One reason often advanced for considering only one policy is that it is a statutory duty, *i.e.* some law exists which mandates that this policy be adopted. In such circumstances different views arise. First, if something is a statutory duty, then it could be argued that it makes little sense to undertaken a CBA. It will be done whether benefits exceed costs or not. If this view is adopted, it remains very important to ensure that the costs of meeting the statutory goal are minimised. A second view, however, utilises the rationale for *ex post* CBA. Whether something is currently a statutory duty does not mean that similar policies should be statutory in the future. If statutory duties can be shown systematically to impose net costs on society, it is important to factor this into any future review of those obligations.

The answer to the question about scale is therefore:

● Design the policy to achieve the point where marginal benefits just equal marginal costs.

The rules for choosing between alternatives are not transparently obvious. Chapter 4 looks at these in more detail. The most common context in which alternatives exist is that of mutual exclusion. Given three alternatives, A, B and C, each is mutually exclusive – we can only have one of them. Other contexts arise in which mixtures of alternatives may be obtained. Effectively, A, B and C are extended to include yet more options such as AB (mostly A but some of B), BA (mostly B, but some of A) etc. To make the analysis simple, assume that full mutual exclusivity obtains. Then, A, B and C are evaluated with respect to a benchmark (baseline, counterfactual) which is usually the status quo. The decision-maker wants to know if A, B and C improve social well-being relative to the status quo (doing nothing new), and, if so, which one gives the best social return. The basic rule for making this choice is:

● *Provided each option costs the same*, choose the option with the highest net benefits.

The chances that A, B and C will each cost the same is, of course, fairly remote. When costs differ, the decision rule is more complex and is discussed in Chapter 4. The basic reason for the complexity is that the inclusion in the options of the highest cost alternative implies that expenditure up to this level would at least be contemplated. But suppose the most expensive option cost 50% more than the next most expensive option. Choosing the cheaper option might secure less net benefits but it would also release the saved costs. These funds could be invested in yet another policy which could secure some further net benefits. Essentially, the idea is to try and compare like with like. If the most expensive policy (C) costs 100 units, the next most expensive (B) 67 units, and the cheapest one (A) 50 units, then the proper comparison is between:

A + the additional benefits of spending 100-50 = return on 50 "saved";

B + the additional benefits of spending 100-67 = return on 33 "saved";

C.

Another form of mutual exclusivity involves *timing*. Policies are usually presented with some desired starting date. But starting dates should actually be chosen so as to maximise net benefits. The question is then:

● When should the policy commence?

A desirable procedure is to ask what would happen if the policy was postponed for one year. Chapter 4 looks at this issue and shows the basic rules that need to be followed. Chapter 10 looks at a special situation in which postponing a decision can be shown to be beneficial. This situation arises when decisions are irreversible and when postponement facilitates learning more about the likely costs and benefits: so-called *option value* or *quasi option value*. The overriding answer to the timing question is therefore:

● Time the policy so as to maximise net social benefits

The final context is one in which policies are not mutually exclusive and several or even many can be implemented. However, all decision-making takes place in a context of a budget constraint or "capital rationing". This simply means that one cannot do everything because costs would exceed the available budget. The question then is:

● Which policies should be undertaken first, or, how should policies be ranked in order of importance?

Chapter 4 looks at this issue and shows that, contrary to intuition, policies should not be ranked by their net benefits but by their *benefit–cost ratios*.

The clarification of questions can be summarised follows:

- Establish the context. Where possible, avoid contexts in which there is a single option because there may be alternatives with higher net benefits.

- Consider the issue of scale. The same policy but on a different scale amounts to providing an alternative to the initial proposal.

- Establish what the alternatives are, and the degree to which they are mutually exclusive.

- Where costs are the same across mutually exclusive alternatives, choose the one with the highest net benefits.

- Where costs differ across the alternatives, "normalise" the policies by comparing each policy with the highest cost policy, allowing for the beneficial use of money "saved" by adopting lower cost policies.

- Do not accept that a policy has to be implemented on a single date. Consider the start date to be another alternative and seek to maximise net social benefits. Put another way, consider the costs and benefits of delay.

- Where there is a budget and range of policies all of which could be implemented, rank the policies by the ratio of their benefits to costs. Work down the ranking list until the budget is exhausted.

3.2. The issue of standing

"Standing" refers to the issue of whose benefits and costs counts. This was discussed in Chapter 2. The basic rule is that benefits and costs to all nationals should be included, whilst benefits and costs to non-nationals should be included if *a)* the policy relates to an international context in which there is a treaty of some kind (acid rain, global warming), or *b)* there is some accepted ethical reason for counting benefits and costs to non-nationals.* Note that any number of rules about the relative weights to be given to nationals and non-nationals could be devised – see Chapter 15.

3.3. Assessing the impacts

CBA works on the basis that any gain or loss to anyone who has standing must be included in the CBA. Chapters 1 and 2 showed that gains and losses (benefits and costs) are defined according to individuals' preferences. While it would be perfectly possible to substitute other preferences for those of society's individuals (*e.g.* using experts' or politicians' preferences) there is a strong presumption in CBA that individuals' preferences should be the basis for evaluation. This is because *a)* experts and politicians have other opportunities to influence the decision in question, and *b)* CBA is designed as a check on decisions made within the political process. It is, in effect, a means of ensuring accountability to public preferences.

---

* The issue of standing is especially relevant in the economics of crime, which has some links to environmental contexts. If criminals' utility has equal standing to that of victims, one can end up with the morally perverse result that theft is simply a transfer of goods from one agent to another and hence has no economic effect. In practice, the fact that the transfer is coercive means that criminals' utility does not have equal standing to that of the victim. In the act of crime, criminals' utility should not count.

55

Any impact of the policy that affects individuals' well-being is therefore a proper impact for inclusion in the CBA. Impacts may have quite complex pathways. For example, the policy may be aimed at improving air quality. One could directly ask individuals how they value that change, or the procedure could be indirect. An indirect route would be to elicit from individuals their preferences for improvements in a health end-state such as difficulties in breathing due to respiratory disease. The link between air pollution and respiratory disease would then be the subject of an expert assessment.

Tracing and measuring impacts is the necessary precursor to valuing those impacts by measuring preferences for or against the impacts. As far as environmental impacts are concerned, the procedure for doing this is a combination of *environmental (impact) analysis* (EA or EIA) and *life cycle analysis* (LCA). EIA measures the various environmental changes arising from the policy, leaving the impacts measured in physical units which will vary from one impact to another. LCA really amounts to EIA but with the provision that the impacts are measured across the entire life cycle in question. A policy to recycle more waste materials, for example, would need to take account of the upstream savings in virgin materials. Using less virgin material – timber, say – would mean that various environmental impacts from forestry could be reduced. Those reduced environmental impacts are a benefit that can legitimately be credited to the recycling policy.

In practice, the "marriage" between CBA, EIA and LCA is not so straightforward. This is because EIA and LCA often adopt conventions of measurement that would not be accepted in CBA. An example would be the common assumption in EIA and LCA that any reduced consumption of primary resources such as oil or bauxite should be counted as a beneficial impact. In CBA, however, the analyst would need to establish if this is an economic benefit or not. Since natural resources appear to be scarce, it seems intuitively acceptable to count saved natural resources as a benefit. But the economic analyst might argue that this scarcity is already reflected in the price of natural resources. If so, there are no additional benefits to be added in – they are already included in the observed prices of natural resources. The contrasts between CBA and current conventions in LCA are discussed in Pearce *et al.* (1998).

The simplest way to think of the basic rule in CBA that tries to capture the essence of EIA and LCA is to adopt the "with/without" principle:

- Any gain that arises because of a policy, regardless of to whom it accrues, when it accrues, or at what stage of the life cycle it occurs, is a benefit that needs to be counted in the CBA. Similarly for costs.

3.4. Impacts and time horizons

Each and every impact identifying in the EIA/LCA process must also be determined for each year. The issue arises of how far into the future these impacts should be estimated. There are no hard and fast rules. In the early years, when CBA was confined to assessing the worth of investment projects, the rule was that the time horizon – the point beyond which costs and benefits are not estimated – was set by the physical or economic life of the investment. For infrastructure such as roads, ports, water etc. this was usually set at a minimum of 30 years and a maximum of 50 years. Such rules applied even to longer lived assets, *e.g.* housing developments which might last over 100 years. The transition to the CBA of policies has made this rule less compelling because it is unclear how long the effects of policies last. Moreover, some environmental policies have quite explicit long-term goals, *e.g.* biodiversity conservation and global warming control. Others have argued that the rule about time horizons should be set according to either the uncertainty of future estimates or the extent to which discounting makes future gains and losses insignificant. In the former case, the argument is that we cannot honestly say what will happen after 30 or 40 years, so pretending that estimates are accurate after that is dishonest. The uncertainty of the estimates is simply too wide. The latter case arises because any positive discounting of long distant future events quickly reduces the present value of those events to very small numbers. For example, USD 1 billion of damage in 100 years time at a discount rate of 5% would appear in the CBA as a damage of:

$$\text{USD 1 billion}/(1.05)^{100} = \text{USD 7.6 million}$$

Chapter 13 reconsiders the standard discounting formula and raises the prospect of a time-declining discount rate. If this is accepted, then the argument that time horizons should be set according to when the present value of the future impact is insignificant, itself becomes suspect.

3.5. Finding money values

Once physical impacts have been identified and measured they must be expressed relative to some baseline, usually the "do nothing" situation. Thus, air pollution changes from a policy might consist of reductions of X micrograms per cubic metre of particulate matter (PM), Y of sulphur oxides (SO_X) and Z of nitrogen oxides (NO_X). The changes in PM will have beneficial health effects which in turn can be expressed in terms of various health "end states". These are likely to consist of reductions in premature mortality, reduced respiratory hospital admissions, reduced "restricted activity days" (days when activity is less than would be the case for normal health), and so on. The SO_X and NO_X reductions will also give rise to some health benefits but will additionally generate improvements in ecosystems since these two pollutants (with others) result in acidification and eutrophication. Again, therefore, these ecosystem effects need to be described with some convenient indicator. Finally, the changes in health end states and in ecosystems need to be valued in money terms. The procedures for doing this are described in Chapters 6-9 and 17. What is essential is that the values derived be applicable to the health and ecosystem end states. For example, if water quality improves from "good" to "very good", individuals' preferences must be definable over this change. One common problem in CBA – the "correspondence problem", and a major reason why it can be limited in practical use, is that scientific information on ecosystem change does not correspond to indicators that individuals recognise. The correspondence problem is less important in the context of health so long as health end states can be defined in recognisable units such as days away from work, or extra days with eye irritation, etc.

Box 3.1 illustrates a case study in which this sequence of "impact pathways" was adopted.

3.6. Selecting a discount rate

The choice of the discount rate, s, is one of the most debated issues in CBA. Because of this, a detailed analysis is deferred until Chapter 13. For the moment, the analysis proceeds as if there is one, constant discount rate, *i.e.* s is the same regardless of which year in the project or policy life cycle is looked at. Chapter 13 entertains the possibility that s actually varies with time.

57

Box 3.1. **Achieving air quality targets in Europe**

The European Union has set air quality targets for the year 2010 with respect to various pollutants. The ones selected here are NO_2, SO_2 and PM. The ambient concentration levels of these pollutants associated with the future standards are compared to the projected concentrations in a "reference scenario", *i.e.* the ambient air quality that would prevail if the standards were not mandated. The standards are consistent with a 10% reduction in emissions of sulphur oxides, 8% for nitrogen oxides and 50% for particulate matter, all relative to the reference scenario. Using epidemiological information about dose-response relationships, the change in ambient concentration of each pollutants can be linked to various health end-states. Those chosen are short-term (or "acute") effects: reduced mortality, reduced hospital admissions, reduced respiratory symptoms in children (PM only), and restricted activity days for adults. Long term ("chronic") effects include reduced mortality and reduced respiratory illness. Values for these impacts were taken from the literature showing how individuals are willing to pay for reductions in these health end states including "values of statistical life" taken from studies looking at willingness to pay to reduce life risks.

A second category of effects is related to material damage, *e.g.* acidic corrosion of buildings. It is easy to see that reduced corrosion avoids cleaning and repair costs. The study in question did assess these benefits in money terms for sulphur oxides only. Other impacts, notably, ecosystem effects (forests, wetlands, soil etc.), reduced damage to crops, and changes in visibility were not quantified or valued. Hence total benefits will be understated to the extent that these effects are excluded. Significant uncertainties surround some of the dose-response functions and more uncertainty attaches to the valuation estimates, especially those relating to life risk reduction.

The resulting benefits and costs are shown below. They all relate to cities since rural areas were found to comply with the standards without specific action.

Costs per annum		Benefits per annum	
SO_2	EUR 4 to 48 million	Short-term mortality	EUR 0 to 8 153 million
NO_X	EUR 5 to 285 million	Hospital admissions	EUR 2 to 6 million
PM	EUR 50 to 300 million	Long-term mortality	EUR 5 438 to 58 149 million
		Other morbidity	EUR 2 million
		Materials	EUR 58 million
Total	**EUR 59 to 633 million**	**Total**	**EUR 5 500 to 66 368 million**

Several observations can be made. First, morbidity and material damage reduction are unimportant. Second, acute health effects are significantly less important than chronic health effects, and acute effects may in fact have a negligible value due to the very brief periods of life that are "saved" by reduced episodes of acute pollution. Third, the range of cost values is very wide, by an order of magnitude. The range for benefits is similarly very large, again by an order of magnitude. The explanation for this wide range lies in the dominant effect of mortality reductions on the estimates, and the fact that a wide range of values of reduced mortality riskare used (EURO 0.36 to 10 million per "statistical life"). Fourth, but not shown here, some 90% of the benefit arises from PM reduction. This is explained by the fact that the standards require the biggest reduction in PM (50%) and the fact that PM is implicated in the biggest amount of health damage. Fifth, the results are shown in a somewhat unusual fashion, *i.e.* comparing annual benefits and annual costs rather than present values. The study omits any mention of a discount rate, but it is extremely unlikely that undiscounted benefits and costs are the same for each year. It is

Box 3.1. **Achieving air quality targets in Europe** (*cont.*)

possible that the authors believed they could avoid dealing with the choice of a discount rate, an often controversial feature of CBA. But discounting is still relevant – see Annex 3.A1. This is an unsatisfactory feature of the study. Finally, benefits appear to exceed costs again by an order of magnitude, whether low or high estimates are taken.

Since this study there has been a substantial debate about the validity of applying risk values to chronic mortality in the manner shown, and it seems likely that the consensus now would be that the health benefits in this study are significantly lower. Recall, however, that the study omits several other kinds of benefit.

Source: Olsthoorn *et al.* 1999.

3.7. Accounting for rising relative valuations

It is not unusual to find discounting, inflation and relative price changes being confused in a CBA. They are three very different things. Discounting arises because of the underlying value judgement in CBA, and taken from welfare economics, that individuals' preferences count. As long as individuals prefer now to later, this value judgement must be applied to time. The discounting of future benefits and costs is thus determined by the rate at which individuals express this "time preference. Inflation, as was noted, is simply a rise in the *general* price level. While it does not matter strictly which year's prices are used in a CBA, it is important to select just one year and to net out all future inflation. Typically, the "base year" is chosen and all costs and benefits are valued at the prices ruling in that year. Suppose this year is Year 1 and that the price level has an index of 100 in that year. Inflation might run at, say, 3% per annum, so that a benefit in year 10 might appear to be $(1.03)^{10}$ = 1.34 times higher than the same benefit in year 1. CBA proceeds by dividing the benefit in year 10, valued at year 10 prices, by 1.34 to express it in year 1 prices. The basic rule is simple: net out all general price changes.

A relative price change is different again. What this says is that some benefits and costs attract a higher valuation over time *relative to the general level of prices*. This might be because the benefit or cost in question has a positive income elasticity of willingness to pay, perhaps because it is simply valued more at higher incomes. It can be important to include this rising (or falling) relative valuation in a CBA, and it is especially important for environmental impacts. For example, it may be surmised that, as the overall stock of environmental assets diminishes over time, each unit of the environment will attract a higher "price". This reflects a positive *income elasticity of willingness to pay for the environment*. Annex 3.A1 shows in more detail how this is accounted for.

Pearce (2003a) surveys the evidence on the income elasticity of WTP for environmental improvements. The empirical estimates suggest that the income elasticity of WTP for environmental change is less than unity, and numbers like 0.3-0.7 seem about right.

3.8. Dealing with risk and uncertainty

While conventions vary, it seems fair to distinguish risk from uncertainty. A risk context is one where benefits and/or costs are not known with certainty, but a probability distribution is known. Sometimes these probability distributions can be very crude. On some occasions they can be sophisticated. A context of uncertainty is different. There is no known probability distribution. Usually, end points are known, *i.e.* it is known or expected that the value cannot be less than a number, and that it cannot be more than another number. In other cases, there may be pure uncertainty in the sense that "anything may happen". By and large, approaches to the integration of risk and uncertainty into CBA have not changed much in recent years, although the presence of uncertainty with other features of a decision, *e.g.* irreversibility, do give rise to interesting developments which are discussed in Chapter 10. These developments are important because there is a sense in which some form of irreversibility is present in all decisions, even if it is simply the fact that, once funds are committed to a policy it is difficult to "un-commit" them.

For the moment, the rules for handling risk and uncertainty outside this irreversibility context are as follows:

● If the context is one where probabilities are known (risk rather than uncertainty) and the decision-maker is *risk-neutral*, then the appropriate rule is to take the *expected value* of benefits and costs. Thus if benefit of B_1 is thought to occur with probability p_1, benefit of B_2 occurs with probability of p_2, and so on, the expected value of benefits is simply:

$$\sum_i p_i . B_i$$

Risk-neutrality means that the decision-maker is indifferent between any two probability distributions each with the same mean. Yet two distributions could have very different measures of dispersion and still have the same mean. Risk-neutrality implies that the decision-maker does not care about what may be probabilities that very small returns, or even negative returns, might be made from the policy or project. Reasons for supposing risk-neutrality is not an unreasonable assumption relate to the fact that CBA tends to be confined to government decisions. Governments can "pool" the risks of decisions in at least two ways: first by having many policies each with different risk profile, and second by having the cost spread out across millions of people, taxpayers. In short, risk-neutrality may be a reasonable assumption is we can assume risk-pooling.

● Where the context is one of risk (probabilities known) but the decision-maker is *risk-averse*, i.e. he or she attaches a higher weight to, say, negative benefits rather than positive benefits, the expected value rule gives way to an *expected utility* rule. The same process as before takes place but this time the relevant calculation is:

$$\sum_i p_i . U(B_i)$$

The expression above shows expected utility and this is most easily thought of as reflecting a set of weights that the decision-maker attaches to the outcomes. More formally, these weights are embedded in an *benefit utility function*. Provided some specific form can be given to this function, it is possible to compute what is called the *certainty equivalent* level of benefit that corresponds to the probabilistic level of benefits. It is this certainty equivalent level that would be entered into the CBA formula – see Annex 3.A1.

● If the context is one of *uncertainty*, i.e. the distribution of benefits (costs) is not known, then, at the very least, CBA requires that a *sensitivity analysis* is performed. Sensitivity analysis requires that the CBA is computed using different values of the parameters about which there is uncertainty. Such procedures require some assumption about likely minima and maxima, but do not make assumptions about the distribution of values between these limits. For example, if a discount rate of 4% is chosen as the central case, then, say, 2 and 6% could also be chosen for a sensitivity analysis. One possible outcome is that the sign of the net benefits will be unaffected by these alternatives. In which case the analysis is said to be "robust" with respect to these assumptions. In other cases, changing assumptions may alter the CBA result. If so, then some judgement has to be made about the reasonableness of the chosen values.

● Still in the context of uncertainty, various decision rules have been proposed. These essentially reduce to setting out *payoff matrices* which show the effect on a chosen parameter value of certain "states of nature". If state of nature 1 occurs, then benefits may be B1; if condition 2 occurs, benefits would be B2, and so on. Since the context is uncertainty, we cannot say what the probabilities of these states of nature are. In turn, benefits might vary according to some variation in the policy option. So, for N states of nature and S policy options (strategies) there will be NxS payoffs. Various decision rules then select the strategy. By and large, the rules vary according to the decision-maker's degree of optimism or pessimism. A very optimistic person might go immediately for the strategy giving the maximum payoff, regardless of the fact that alternate states of nature might produce very low payoffs for that strategy. A very pessimistic person might focus solely on the worst outcomes and choose a strategy that "assumes the worst", and so on. There are no basic rules for choosing one decision rule over another: the choice depends on the decision-maker's attitudes.

3.9. Who gains, who loses

Chapter 2 indicated that equity and efficiency issues are not only hard to separate, but that equity concerns have often dominated discourse about social decisions. This suggests that any tabulation of costs and benefits must not only show the aggregate benefits and costs, following the rules outlined above, but should also show who gains and who loses. The "who" here may be different income groups, ethnic groups, geographical located groups and so on. Other forms of distributional incidence concern how benefits and costs might be allocated to business and consumer. The assumption is that the distributional analysis concerns the money value of benefits and the money value of costs. This in turn raises further issues of equity if benefits and costs are measured in terms of willingness to pay which is itself constrained by income The traditional way round this potential problem of unfairness is to weight the money values of benefits and costs by measures of "social deservingness", or equity weights. Chapter 15 discusses equity issues in detail.

3.10. Summary and guidance for decision-makers

Box 3.2 places the previous discussion in context by taking the cost-benefit equation and showing its various components.

Box 3.2. **The overall cost-benefit equation**

The overall CBA equation is shown below. For an initial screening of the contribution that the project or policy makes to social well-being to be acceptable, this equation must be positive, *i.e.* the present value of benefits must exceed the present value of costs. The equation is shown in its most comprehensive form, even though some of the factors affecting it have yet to be discussed in detail. For example, benefits and costs are shown to have "weights" (w). These reflect the social value attached to the money benefit (or cost) accruing to different people or groups (i). For example, poorer people may be given a higher weight than richer people. Chapter 15 looks at this "equity" weighting. For the purposes of this chapter, these weights have been set equal to unity. In which case the w's disappear. Similarly, the discount rate is shown as a function of time, *i.e.* as s(t) and not simply s. This reflects the possibility that s varies with time, an issue discussed in Chapter 13. As far as the current chapter is concerned, s is a constant so the formula would show s rather than s(t). Benefits are assumed to escalate at a rate e.y over time to reflect rising per capita incomes (rate of growth = y) and a positive income elasticity of willingness to pay (e). Note that e.y has nothing to do with inflation. The adjustment for rising unit willingness to pay is assumed not to be embodied in the value of B_t shown in the equation, *i.e.* it is applied to future benefits estimated without making any prior assumption about rising relative valuations. The circumflex over B and C indicates that these are expected values of benefits and costs or risk-adjusted benefits and costs (reflecting expected utility rather than expected value). Finally, T is the time horizon, i is the ith person affected, and N is the number of people whose benefits and costs "count". It was noted that there are no hard and fast rules for determining T or N.

$$\sum_{t,i}^{T,N} \frac{w_i.\hat{B}_{i,t}.(1+e.y_i)^t - w_i.\hat{C}_{i,t}}{(1+s(t))^t}$$

For the case where there is no real escalation of values of benefits, no equity weighting, and a constant discount rate, this equation reduces to the more familiar one:

$$\sum_{t,i}^{T,N} \frac{\hat{B}_{i,t} - \hat{C}_{i,t}}{(1+s)^t}$$

ANNEX 3.A1

Some Formal Statements About CBA

3.1. Optimal scale

Let the scale of a project or policy be given by Q. Q might be kilometres of road, micrograms per cubic metre of an air pollutant, level of biochemical oxygen demand in a river, etc. Then, B(Q) is the *benefit function* and C(Q) is the *cost function*. The aim of CBA in the context of scale considerations is to maximise net benefits, *i.e.*

$$\max B(Q) - C(Q) \tag{A3.1}$$

The condition for this maximum to be met is:

$$\frac{\partial B}{\partial Q} - \frac{\partial C}{\partial Q} = 0 \quad or \quad \frac{\partial B}{\partial Q} = \frac{\partial C}{\partial Q} \tag{A3.2}$$

i.e. marginal benefits must equal marginal costs.

3.2. Present values and annuities

It is usually preferable to present the summary costs and benefits in a CBA in present value form. To do this, all future costs and benefits must be discounted, usually by assuming a constant discount rate, and applying that rate to all years according to the formula:

$$NPV = \frac{B_1 - C_1}{(1+s)} + \frac{B_2 - C_2}{(1+s)^2} + \ldots + \frac{B_T - C_T}{(1+s)^T} \tag{A3.3}$$

where T is the end year. An alternative way to present the information is in terms of *annuities*. An annuity is simply a constant annual value which, when discounted and summed, produces the net present value given in A3.3. The formula for an annuity is:

$$NPV = \frac{A}{s}\left[1 - \frac{1}{(1+s)^T}\right] \tag{A3.4}$$

where A is the constant annual sum (the annuity) and T is the period over which discounting takes place. A3.4 can be rearranged as:

$$A = \frac{s.NPV}{1 - (1+s)^{-T}} \tag{A3.5}$$

For example, suppose the NPV at 5% and with T = 30 years in A3.4 comes to 120. What constant annual sum – the annuity – corresponds to this? Substituting in A3.5 gives:

$$A = \frac{(0.05)(120)}{1-(1.0.5)^{-30}} = \frac{6}{0.7} = 7.8$$

Hence, a constant annual sum of 7.8 for 30 years is the same as a present value of 120, given the time horizon and given the discount rate. Notice that the effective NPV is then:

$$NPV = A.\sum_t \frac{1}{(1+s)^t} \qquad \text{[A3.6]}$$

Discount tables usually give the sum of the discount factors (which is the sum of a geometric progression) so it is easy to convert NPVs into annuities using these tables. For example, the sum of an annual USD 1 discounted at 5% over 30 years is 16.37. This can be used to check the above calculation since 120/16.37 = 7.8.

Note that, unless the discount rate is zero, annuities always involve discounting because they are simply another way of expressing a present value. Box 3.1 showed an example of a study where costs and benefits were shown as constant annual sums, but without any indication of whether the sums were annuities or not (which they should be).

3.3. Rising relative valuations

A cost-benefit formula which computes the NPV of a stream of net benefits (NB = B – C) can be written as follows:

A cost-benefit formula which computes the NPV of a stream of net benefits (NB = B – C) can be written as follows:

$$NPV = \sum_t \frac{NB_t.(1+e.y)^t}{(1+s)^t} \qquad \text{[A3.7]}$$

This differs from a conventional CBA formula by including an expression on the top line to allow for rising relative valuations. In this case:

e = the income elasticity of willingness to pay, *i.e.* the percentage change in willingness to pay arising from a given percentage in real per capita income.

y = the rate of growth in per capital real incomes.

Evidence is only now emerging as to the likely size of e. It seems likely that, for environmental assets e is around 0.3 to 0.7 (Pearce, 2005). For any year t, then, and taking a mid estimate of 0.5 for e and a rate of growth of real incomes of, say, 2%, a given net benefit in that year needs to be multiplied by

1 + (0.5)(0.02)^t

If the year is 40 then this means year 40 benefits would be multiplied by 1.49. Including relative price changes can therefore make a potentially significant change to the outcome of a CBA.

3.4. Risk aversion

Risk aversion arises when the decision-maker has some preference for or against a specific distribution of benefits (or costs). That is, he or she is not solely concerned with the mean of the distribution (the expected value). A benefit utility function for someone who is risk averse takes on a concave shape – as the money value of benefits rise, utility rises but at a declining rate. This reflects *diminishing marginal utility* of money benefits. The utility function is shown as U(B) in the diagram below. Assume B_1 occurs with absolute certainty, then the expected utility at B_1 is given by $U(B_1)$. Similarly for B_2. Between these two extremes, consider any point, say B*. This is a probabilistic situation in which there is some probability (p) that B_1 will occur and some probability (1 – p) that B_2 will occur. So,

$$B^* = p.(B_1) + (1 – p).(B_2)$$

The line XY traces out the values of the *expected utility* of B* for various values of the probabilities that X_1 or X_2 will occur. For example, the expected utility of B* as shown in the diagram is EU(B*). Notice that EU(B*) is less than the utility value of B* if B* occurred with certainty, which is given by U(B*). One way of summarising this is to say that the utility of the expected value B* is greater than the expected value of the utility of B*. This tells us that the riskiness of the benefits imposes a cost on the decision-maker, known as the *cost of risk bearing*. Put another way, once the context is one of risk and risk aversion, the NPV of benefits minus costs will be less than where the context is one of certainty or one of risk-neutrality. Notice also that the expected utility of B* (which is the outcome of the probabilities in question) is the same as the utility from a lower level of benefit, B#. In other words, we can write:

$$EU(B^*) = U(B\#)$$

There are various ways of introducing this risk bearing cost into the CBA. The two main procedures are:

a) Deduct the cost of risk bearing from benefits (we have assumed costs are certain). In terms of the diagram this amounts to deducting B*-B# from recorded benefits.

b) Instead of recording benefits as they first appear, use the certainty equivalent of benefits. This is B# in the diagram.

There are formidable practical problems with these approaches – for a discussion see Pearce and Nash (1981, Chapter 5).

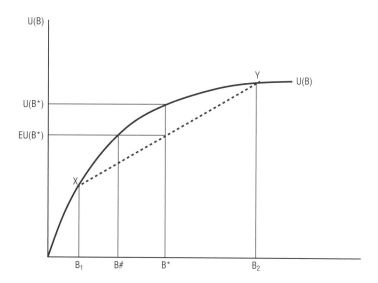

ISBN 92-64-01004-1
Cost-Benefit Analysis and the Environment
Recent Developments
© OECD 2006

Chapter 4

Decision Rules

Crucial to the final steps of a CBA is the decision rule. That is, the criterion whereby a particular project or policy can be recommended (or otherwise) on cost-benefit grounds. In this chapter it is noted that the correct criterion for reducing benefits and costs to a unique value is the net present value (NPV) or net benefits criterion. The correct rule is to adopt any project with a positive NPV and to rank projects by their NPVs. In certain cases, such as where budget constraints exist, the criteria for choosing projects or policies become more complex. This does not, however, alter the broad conclusion about the general primacy of the NPV rule.

4.1. Introduction

So far, it has been shown that cost-benefit analysis (CBA) proceeds on the explicit basis that a project or policy be deemed socially worth-while if its benefits exceed the costs it generates. The appropriate formula for expressing the social worth of a project has not been discussed in detail, nor have the guidelines been offered for assisting with the choice *between* alternative projects. This chapter looks in some detail at this problem.

4.2. The choice context

The necessary condition for the adoption of a project is that discounted benefits should exceed discounted costs. This rule can be stated as:

$PV(B) > PV(C)$

or,

$NPV > 0$

where $PV(B)$ refers to the (gross) present value of benefits, $PV(C)$ refers to the gross present value of costs and NPV refers to the net present value (or present value of net benefits) so that: $NPV = PV(B) – PV(C)$ with present values calculated at the social discount rate.

Formulated in this way, the "worth" of a project is expressible as a unique absolute magnitude, with costs and benefits measured in the same (money) units. In practice, the NPV rule will require some modification in the presence of: *a)* constraints on the objective function (*e.g.* see Chapter 16 on sustainability) and *b)* in the light of allowances for either distributional concerns (Chapter 15) or risk and uncertainty (Chapter 10).

The most basic types of choice facing the decision-maker can be classified as follows:

4.2.1. Accept-reject

Faced with a set of *independent* projects and no constraint on the number which can be undertaken, the decision-maker must decide which, if any, is worthwhile. The decision rule should enable a decision to be made about whether to accept or reject *each* individual project. That is, any project i for which benefits exceed costs should be accepted.

4.2.2. Ranking

If some input, such as capital, is limited in supply it may well be that all "acceptable" projects cannot be undertaken. In this case, projects must be ranked or ordered in terms of the objective function which, from the preceding discussion, might be inferred to mean in descending order of say net benefits. However, while we provide a simple illustration of this below, the decision rule for accept-reject situations cannot be so easily generalised to cover these situations.

Since constraints on the resources available for investment are always present in the public sector, it is worth looking a little closer at the effect of such constraints on the net present value rule. The problem is to rank projects in order of preference and to select the optimal combination of projects such that their total combined cost exhausts the budget. It is tempting to think that ranking the NPVs will achieve this result, but on this occasion it does not. Consider the following simple example in Table 4.1.

Table 4.1. **Ranking independent projects**

Project	Cost (C)	Benefits (B)	B – C	B/C
X	100	200	100	2.0
Y	50	110	60	2.2
Z	50	120	70	2.4

Suppose a capital constraint of 100 exists and that the constraint operates *only for the one year in which capital expenditure is incurred.* Ranking by NPV gives the ordering X, Z, Y so that X would be the only project selected, net benefits being 100 and the budget being exhausted. But inspection of the table shows that Y and Z could be adopted, with a combined NPV of 130 for the same cost. In the simple example in the table, it can be seen that ranking by benefit-cost ratios secures the correct combinations of projects, namely Y and Z. Thus, for single-period rationing of scarce resource inputs, projects can be ranked by their benefit-cost ratios. The decision-maker works down the list accepting projects, for which the benefit-cost ratio is greater than one, until the budget is exhausted. (However, while this reveals a useful role for the benefit-cost ratio in this instance, the relative worth of this indicator as the basis of a cost-benefit decision rule is, in general, far more limited – see Section 4.3.)

4.2.3. *Choosing between mutually exclusive projects*

Frequently, projects are not independent of each other. One form of interdependence exists when one project can only be undertaken to the exclusion of another project – *e.g.* these projects are two different ways of achieving the same objective. The projects are then "mutually exclusive" and the decision rule must enable the decision-maker to choose between the alternatives. For example, if the projects in Table 4.1 were actually mutually exclusive then the appropriate decision rule is to choose the project with the largest NPV (or the largest NPV and an outlay that does not exceed the budget constraint in the case of rationing).

An interesting and distinct case of mutual exclusion exists when any given project can be undertaken now or in a later period. There is a problem in choosing the appropriate point in time to start the project. This is the problem of "time-phasing" and, once again, the decision rule should offer guidance on this issue. There may be instances where say postponing a project for one period has a larger net benefit than starting the project now. For example, for a project which incurs construction costs in period 0 only and then enjoys benefits from periods 1 to n, it will be worth postponing the project if: i) the (discounted) return enjoyed on saved outlays over the period of postponement (i.e. $[s \times C]/[1 + s]$ where s is the return or social discount rate); *plus* ii) the (discounted) benefit enjoyed in the (new) final period of the project (i.e. $B/[1 + s]^{n + 1}$); *exceeds* iii) the benefit which is foregone by postponing (i.e. $B/[1 + s]$). Mishan (1988) questions the sense of taking this notion too far (that is, seeking to estimate the optimal starting date for projects). However, it may be that "on the margin" there is some practical worth to asking if a project should be started say this year or next.

Note that the rationale for postponement is based on a rather different consideration to that proposed in more recent discussions of the value of keeping options open. In the current example, costs and benefits streams are known with certainty (or at least their expected values are known). If, as we discuss in Chapter 10, there is uncertainty about the net benefit stream, and elements of irreversibility and scope for learning by delay, there is an option value attached to waiting or postponing the project until more is known about future states of nature.

4.3. Alternative decision rule criteria

4.3.1. Benefit-cost ratios

One of the most popular decision rules, particularly in the early years of applied cost-benefit analysis, was the use of benefit-cost ratios. The general rules become: *i*) accept a project if: $PV(B)/PV(C) > 1$; *ii*) in the face of rationing: rank by the ratio $PV(B)/PV(C)$; or, *iii*) in choosing between mutually exclusive projects: select the project with the highest benefit-cost ratio.

There are numerous and well-documented difficulties with using the benefit-cost ratio as a decision rule.

One fundamental point is that no rule should be sensitive to the classification of a project effect as a cost rather than a benefit, and *vice versa*. Thus, all costs can be treated as negative benefits and all benefits as negative costs. For the NPV rule it should be obvious that the outcome will be the same however the division is made. But the benefit-cost ratio will be affected by this division since it will affect the magnitudes which are entered as denominator and as numerator. Thus, if a project has (discounted) benefits of 10, 20 and 30 units and (discounted) costs of 10 and 20 it follows that the benefit-cost ratio is 2.0. But if the cost of 10 is treated as a negative benefit, the ratio becomes 50/20 = 2.5. On the other hand, discounted benefits minus costs (*i.e.* the NPV) remain the same, at 30 units, regardless of the transfer.

While it may seem superficially obvious what to count as a project cost and project benefit, perhaps on the basis of distinguishing clearly inputs (or outlays) and outputs, there are instances where this could conceivably be more complicated. For example, the provision of certain environmental amenities, such as changes in countryside landscape or the reintroduction into a wilderness of a locally extinct and charismatic but predatory wolf species, might represent, on the one hand, a good for some households and, on the other hand, a bad for other households. It is conceivable that those in the latter category might have a negative willingness for pay for this change – see Chapter 8. If the change goes ahead, these households will endure negative benefits. However, this impact might alternatively be thought of a cost of the project.

Apart from being sensitive to the classification of costs and benefits, the ratio rule is incorrect when applied to mutually exclusive contexts. Looking back at Table 4.1 assume now that these projects are mutually exclusive: for example, perhaps they describe alternative options for investing in sewer capacity so as to decrease the incidence of overflows of storm-water into a major river. Each option, X, Y and Z, is associated with its own construction and maintenance costs and so on just as each varies in terms of its effectiveness in reducing the harmful effects of breaches of sewer capacity. Thus, project X costing 100 units has benefits of 200 and so has a NPV of 100. This is to be preferred to both projects Y and Z which have NPVs of 60 and 70 respectively. But in ratio terms, X would be the least preferred option since it only has a ratio of 2.0 compared to say Y (2.2) and Z (2.4). However, selecting (mutually exclusive) option Z would entail losing the 30 units of net benefit that would have been enjoyed had the NPVs been used to guide the accept-reject decision rule.

In general, there is no defence for the use of benefit-cost ratios as a decision rule outside of the *rationing* context discussed in Section 4.2.2 above.

4.3.2. *Internal Rate of Return*

The net present value rule requires the use of some predetermined social discount rate rule to discount future benefits and costs. An alternative rule is to calculate the discount rate which would give the project a NPV of zero and then to compare this "solution rate" with the pre-determined social discount rate. In other words, the benefit and cost streams are presented in equation form,

$$B_0 - C_0 + \frac{B_1 - C_1}{(1+i)} + \frac{B_2 - C_2}{(1+i)^2} + ... + \frac{B_T - C_T}{(1+i)^T} = 0$$

where *i* is the rate of discount that solves the equation.

Once *i* is determined, the rule for accept-reject and for ranking of options is to adopt any project which has an internal rate of return (IRR) in excess of the predetermined social discount rate. As with the NPV rule, then, it remains essential to choose some acceptable discount rate.

An example of the use of the *IRR* is in project appraisal at the World Bank. Although the NPV rule is the main criterion the Bank uses to evaluate projects (Belli *et al.* 1998), many of the Bank's project documents make reference to the economic rate of return (which is equivalent to the IRR in a cost-benefit analysis as "economic" denotes a wider social interpretation of inputs and outputs than the narrower range which is the focus of financial or cash-flow analysis). Calculating IRR in an era of comparatively large computational capacity and user-friendly spreadsheet programmes, is a relatively straightforward task. This ease of estimation, while to be welcomed, is of course quite a different thing to asserting that the IRR is of value (relative say to NPV) as the basis of a decision rule for project analysis.

Arguments in favour of estimating the IRR include notions of acceptability and familiarity. It is often argued that the idea of a "rate of return" is a relatively familiar concept to decision-makers and, as a result, that the *IRR* is a more readily understandable summary statistic of a cost-benefit appraisal than the NPV. In addition, if the social discount rate – against which *i* (as defined above) is to be compared – is equivalent to the opportunity cost of capital then the IRR is, in effect, a test of whether the project earns a social return which exceeds what could be earned by investing economic resources elsewhere (*e.g.* Boardman *et al.* 2001). Of course, the net present value calculation provides this information as well but allied to the immediately preceding point, this might suggest that the IRR approach has something to commend it. These comments notwithstanding, this approach also suffers from a greater number of well-documented drawbacks.

One of the most notable shortcomings arises when comparing mutually exclusive projects as the following illustration shows. Table 4.2 gives an example of two projects X and Y, each with a life of 10 years (*i.e.* costs are incurred in the initial period of the project life and benefits enjoyed from the next period until the project's end). On the *IRR* rule, project X is preferred, but on the NPV rule, Y is preferred to X (for an assumed 8% social discount rate). The IRR rule is misleading here since it discriminates against Y because of the relative size of its capital outlay or cost. That is, choosing project X (and rejecting Y) will entail losing 2.72 units of net benefit.

Table 4.2. **Choosing projects using the IRR Rule**

Project	Cost	Benefit	IRR	NPV at 8%
X	2	0.40	14%	3.39
Y	4	0.75	12%	7.11
"Y – X"	2	0.35	10%	...

In such cases, a two part rule is required. This states that a project Y is preferable to project X if and only if: $i_Y > s$; and, $i_{(Y-X)} > s$, where i is the IRR and s the predetermined social discount rate. That is, this rule requires the calculation of the rate of return on the hypothetical project "Y – X" – i.e. on the differences in capital outlay. Since the IRR on Y – X is in excess of the predetermined social discount rate of 8% the larger project is to be preferred. In the (not atypical) case of choosing amongst more than two mutually exclusive options this two-part assessment becomes rather laborious. Project analysts may understandably conclude that a focus only on the NPV is an appropriate reaction to this. (Clearly, issues about budget constraints – rationing of scarce capital – raise distinct issues. However, this would amount to saying that certain projects may not be feasible options regardless of their NPV or IRR or benefit-cost ratio for that matter.)

Other disadvantages of the IRR approach to decision rules are sensitivity to economic life and timing of benefits.

In the former, where projects with different economic lives are being compared, the IRR approach will possibly inflate the desirability of a short-life project. This is because the IRR is a function both of the time periods involved and the size of capital outlay. Thus, USD 1 invested now has an IRR of 100% if it cumulates to USD 2 at the end of the year. Compare this to a USD 10 investment which cumulates to USD 15: i.e. an IRR of 50%. Thus, the IRR rule would rank the former project above the latter. However, given that these proposals have NPVs of USD 1 and USD 5 respectively, choosing the former will mean a sacrifice of USD 4 worth of net benefits.

In the latter, it is often the case that projects may not yield benefits for many years (e.g. infrastructure projects may entail long constructions periods before benefits come on-stream): that is, they have long "gestation" periods. The IRR will tend to be lower on such projects when compared to projects with a fairly even distribution of benefits over time, even though the NPV of the former may be larger. The problem here is essentially the same as in the above; the IRR will give high ranking to projects which "bunch" the benefits into the early part of their economic lives relative to other projects.

Another time-related issue concerns the possibility of time-varying discount rates. If the social discount rate changes over time then the calculation of the IRR does not permit an easy comparison. For the case of time-declining discount rates (see Chapter 13), if the IRR is 10% and the social discount declines from 8% to say 4% over the lifetime of the project then matters are relatively simple. However, if the social discount rate is 12% declining to 8% then no simple criterion of acceptability exists. The NPV rule does enable discount rate changes to be incorporated easily into the calculation.

Finally, a further complicating factor is that in computing the *IRR* it is possible to obtain more than one solution rate. In general, there are as many *IRR*s as there are changes in sign of the net benefit stream. If a project has two solutions say, 6% and 10% and the social discount rate of 8% then there appears to be no clear-cut criterion for acceptance or rejection. Clearly, this is a practical problem if such cases arise.

4.3.3. *Other considerations*

While the NPV rule is the key criterion for accepting or rejecting project alternatives, it is worth noting that the criterion only applies to actual project alternatives specified (a point made recently in Boardman *et al.* 2001). In other words, it applies only to those alternatives which are placed "on the table" to be considered by the cost-benefit analyst. This means that NPVs can be calculated – and the most efficient project chosen – only from those alternatives which the analyst is permitted to consider. While this point is on the surface self-evident, its significance lies in the possibility that the process of specifying project alternatives might itself be politically proscribed. Recognition of this is hardly a new development. Dasgupta and Pearce (1972), for example, distinguish between higher-level political objectives (regional balance, income equity, and so on) and other perhaps less socially desirable or merit-worthy objectives, which lead to the political screening out of certain project options. The extent to which this brings to the fore issues that need to be confronted by the project analyst itself raises contentious and conflicting advice as to the proper role of the analyst as "early" discussions in, for example, Dasgupta and Pearce, make clear. Perhaps not surprisingly modern cost-benefit texts appear largely to side-step, for better or worse, this arguably irresolvable *but* important debate (see Chapter 19).

4.4. Summary and guidance for decision-makers

The correct criterion for reducing benefits and costs to a unique value is the net present value or net benefits criterion. The correct rule is to adopt any project with a positive NPV and to rank projects by their NPVs. When budget constraints exist, however, the criteria become more complex. Single-period constraints – such as capital shortages – can be dealt with by a benefit-cost ratio ranking procedure. In other respects, the benefit-cost ratio has little to commend it as a decision rule for choosing projects. There is general agreement that the *IRR* should not be used to rank and select mutually exclusive projects. Where a project is the only alternative proposal to the status quo, the issue is whether knowing the *IRR* provides worthwhile additional information. Views differ in this respect. Some argue that there is little merit in calculating a statistic that is either misleading or subservient to the NPV. Others see a role for the *IRR* in providing a clear signal as regards the sensitivity of a project's net benefits to the discount rate. Yet, whichever perspective is taken this does not alter the broad conclusion about the general primacy of the NPV rule.

ISBN 92-64-01004-1
Cost-Benefit Analysis and the Environment
Recent Developments
© OECD 2006

Chapter 5

Policy and Project Costs

This chapter presents a range of challenges and responses facing practitioners in the task of measuring project and policy costs as accurately as possible. For example, the costs of complying with regulations and the costs of major projects are likely to be highly uncertain as well as have the potential to affect other costs and prices in the economy by a significant amount. In the case of the latter, for example, policy compliance costs ideally would be estimated using general equilibrium analysis, an approach which has its supporters and detractors. A distinct issue is that politicians are very sensitive about the effects of regulation on competitiveness and employment. Whether such concerns should be incorporated within a CBA needs careful consideration and can depend on the nature of the economy. Separate statements about say employment impacts instead may be advisable. Lastly, policies to address one overall goal may have associated effects in other policy areas (such as the case of climate gases and jointly produced air pollutants). While it is common practice to add benefits together, some experts have cast doubt on the validity of the procedure.

5.1. Dealing with costs and benefits: some terminology

It seems fair to say that CBA practitioners have paid more attention to the complex issues of valuing environmental benefits and damages than they have to the cost if implementing policies and projects. In part this is because "costing" appears to be more of an accounting exercise than an economic one, and in part because determining costs appears rather dry and uninteresting. In practice, however, it is of the utmost importance to get policy and project costs measured as accurately as possible.

At the outset it is useful to sort out some terminology, since it is easy to become confused. We focus attention on policies and projects with major environmental impacts. Where there are environmental losses arising from an environmental impact, those losses are known as "damage costs" or, more fully, "environmental damage costs". These costs will be assessed using the option of total economic value (TEV) to be introduced in Chapter 6. Essentially, TEV is the economic value attached to the environmental assets in question, as measured by the WTP to conserve those assets. A project or policy may have a negative impact on that TEV so we can write:

$$Damage\ Cost = -\Delta TEV \qquad\qquad [5.1]$$

where Δ simply means "change in". Where a project or policy *prevents a decline in an environmental asset* (avoids a reduction in its size or avoids a reduction in its quality), then the reduction in the damage cost is measured by the gain in TEV compared to what would have happened, *i.e.*:

$$Benefit = - Avoided\ Damage = + \Delta TEV \qquad\qquad [5.2]$$

In the same way, where a policy or project improves the existing scale or quality of an environmental asset, [5.2] also applies, *i.e.*:

$$Benefit = + \Delta TEV \qquad\qquad [5.3]$$

If a policy results in environmental damage, then the relevant loss in TEV is added to any other costs associated with the policy – this is case [5.1]. If [5.2] or [5.3] applies then the avoided damages or improvements in TEV define the environmental benefit side of the CBA equation. Unfortunately, in much of the literature the term "cost" appears without any qualification and the reader is sometimes left guessing whether what is being referred to is damage, a benefit or some other cost. Most of the confusion can be avoided by always prefixing "cost" with "damage" where what is referred to is environmental losses.

Policy (or project) costs will be the sum of:

- The resource costs of implementing the policy or project. These are usually referred to as "compliance costs" and compliance costs fall on the business sector and on households.

- Regulatory costs, if relevant, *i.e.* costs to government of implementing the policy.

- Any damage costs as defined above.

For the rest of this chapter the focus is on compliance costs and regulatory costs. Damage costs are dealt with in the chapters on benefit estimation (since avoided damage costs are a category of benefit).

5.2. Optimism and pessimism in cost estimation

Compliance costs are not necessarily straightforward to measure. In the first instance, they comprise the capital and operating costs of the project or policy. But the immediate costs may "spill over" to other agents in the economy, creating "general equilibrium" effects (Section 5.3). In principle, these additional costs need to be accounted for. Policies may also have the opposite effect – they may stimulate technological change that reduces compliance costs, if not immediately then in the future. Projecting these changes in future costs can be very difficult, and reflects the problem of "asymmetric information". This means that regulators and governments may not know what the real costs are likely to be of complying with a regulation simply because they do not possess the relevant information about what businesses or even households may do in order to comply. Often, compliance costs turn out to be much lower than might be thought. In part this is because the policy stimulates those who have to comply to search for cheaper approaches to compliance. In part it can be that firms and households deliberately exaggerate the likely costs of compliance in order to stop the policy being introduced. Once the policy is introduced, the "true" lower costs of compliance are revealed. If either or both of these factors are present, there is "cost pessimism": *ex ante* costs will be exaggerated. But it is also possible to cost optimism, *i.e.* likely costs may be understated *ex ante*. There are various reasons for this. In the context of projects, especially major public works, contractors may simply get their sums wrong. As it happens, they have little incentive to overstate costs since they may well lose out in the bid to achieve the project. They will then gamble on getting the project and arguing later about cost overruns. Quite a few major projects are also "one off" in the sense that they involve new technologies or activities for which there is no direct precedent. In that case, costs may often be best guesses rather than accurate statements.

Allowing for cost optimism and pessimism is not straightforward. Where contractors are involved, one approach is to check on their previous records – *i.e.* find out how often they have completed projects on time and to cost. Policy costs may be much more complex, especially where there is little history of similar policies to go on. One of the reasons for economists (general) preference for "market based instruments" (taxes, tradable permits etc.) is that they will tend to minimise compliance costs. In short, policies may often be accompanied by some requirements as to the policy instrument being adopted in an effort to keep compliance costs down.

5.3. General equilibrium analysis

Estimating compliance costs becomes complex when projects or policies are "non-marginal", *i.e.* cannot be embraced with partial-equilibrium frameworks of analysis. For marginal projects, the estimation of costs can be done in relatively narrow terms; that is, with reference to the (social) value of those costs that are directly incurred as a result of the proposal. However, for non-marginal or large projects, this notion of costs needs to include a wider range of impacts. For example, environmental policies such as the imposition of an energy tax will not just imply costs for those economic sectors upon which the tax is levied. Other sectors which, in turn, purchase energy inputs that are now subject to a higher price are also affected by this policy and so on. It is not hard to envisage that a wide range of environmental policies and programmes will have impacts which potentially extend far beyond those sectors directly targeted by these interventions. Whenever this is the case, it is important that these "spillovers" or indirect costs are also estimated if a fuller understanding of a project's impacts is to be accomplished.

What this means is that some way must be found of tracing all of the direct *and* indirect effects (whether these are gains or losses) of the change in relative prices that arise because of a given policy intervention. In some cases, this search could be circumscribed to those indirect impacts thought to be empirically significant. In other cases, however, an economy-wide focus may well be unavoidable along with the computational problems that this entails. Proposals that have sought to rise to this challenge unavoidably reflect the complexity of the task. Nevertheless, recent developments – as discussed later in this section – at least have allowed the impacts of non-marginal projects to be scrutinised in a routine and systematic fashion.

A prominent example is the growing use of computable general equilibrium (CGE) models. These are models of the national economy (or sub-sectors of that economy) which describe linkages between component sectors. A starting point for constructing such models is typically the input-output table (I-O) found in national accounts. An I-O table is a symmetrical matrix describing transactions between a wide range of economic sectors where the matrix columns indicate the purchase of inputs by a particular sector and the matrix rows indicate the sale of outputs by a particular sector. What a CGE model adds, to this mechanistic description of linkages between various parts of the economy, are standard assumptions about the economic behaviour of households, firms and government. Hence, it is a combination of these data on economic linkages and behavioural assumptions that drives the analysis of the wider response of the economy to, for example, some policy induced change.

The basic structure of this analysis is neatly described by Conrad (1999). Starting from a base scenario – indicating the actual values of economic variables in a base year – a given (non-marginal) policy change is modelled as an exogenous shock which leads to a change in relative prices faced by economic agents within an economy. Perhaps, for example, this reflects the introduction of some tax or regulation that has the effect of raising the price of fossil-fuel based energy. This leads to a new equilibrium with correspondingly new values for key variables which are endogenous to the model such as economic output. A comparison of the two sets of values (*i.e.* "before" and "after" the policy change) indicates the economic impact of the policy. An important feature of this estimate is that it reflects all of the (measurable) direct and indirect effects of the policy. As an illustration, a widely cited and pioneering application of CGE models to an environmental setting by Hazilla and Kopp (1990) investigated the economy-wide costs of the US Clean Air and Clean Water Acts. This study found that, while just over one-third of US economic sectors were affected *directly* by these programmes, all such sectors were affected *indirectly*. These indirect impacts included, for example, increases in production costs and corresponding decreases in productivity.

The strength of a CGE model is that it offers a meticulously detailed economic appraisal of the spillover effects of a given project or policy. As with any analytical approach there are also a number of possible disadvantages to consider as well.

First, CGE models are typically static, in the sense that the comparison of the pre- and post-policy equilibria takes place within a snap-shot of the economy at exactly the same point of time. However, this does not mean that insights about technological adaptations are necessarily absent or that more sophisticated models are incapable of introducing some dynamic element where a policy induces changes over time.

Second, it is important that such models reflect linkages between sectors in a realistic fashion. Of course, in practice, it is difficult to pin down or to interpret economic reality in any simple way such that divergences of the answers that different models offer may reflect existing uncertainties about key economic parameters. This is the problem of calibrating the CGE model, an important issue if the outputs of these models are to be seen as more than just an artefact of the assumptions that went into their construction.

Third, CGE models are a time-consuming and expensive addition to any cost-benefit appraisal. While this might be mitigated to some extent by the application of existing models to new policy questions, this particular concern almost inevitably gives rise to the question about when assessing general equilibrium effects is needed and when it is not. Unfortunately, as noted by Kopp *et al.* (1997), apart from a few general rules of thumb there is little specific guidance to be added here. For example, CGE models might be applied usefully when a proposal affects highly integrated sectors (where this integration reflects the purchase of a widely used intermediate good such as energy) or where direct costs are generally thought to be so large as to make empirically meaningful spillovers almost inevitable. Conrad (1999) notes, for example, that as environmental policies become more stringent, the likelihood is that the need for general equilibrium approaches becomes more pressing (if what is sought is a genuine understanding of the true costs of these interventions). Of course, CGE studies themselves can be a source of learning about the future need for this analysis by assessing the relative importance of direct and indirect effects across a variety of policy contexts.

5.4. Competitiveness impacts

Typically, traditional CBAs did not go beyond determining the scale of aggregate costs and benefits and, perhaps, their distributional incidence. Today, most governments have concerns about the impact of regulatory policies on competitiveness (the same concerns tend not to arise in the context of investment projects).

However, it is not always clear what the problem of competitiveness is meant to be. Krugman (1996) notes that most of the concerns about "competitiveness" are inconsistent with basic international trade theory:

"While influential people have used the word 'competitiveness' to mean that countries compete just like companies, professional economists know very well that this is a poor metaphor. In fact, it is a view of the world so much in conflict with what even the most basic international trade theory tells us that economists have by and large simply failed to comprehend that this is what the seemingly sophisticated people who talk about competitiveness have in mind."

While Krugman's remarks hold for nations, competitiveness has more meaning at the level of the firm. Several impacts may be differentiated. First, the policy measure itself may contribute to an increase in the monopoly elements in an industry. This will be true if the instruments increases barriers to new entrant – *e.g.* by making it very expensive to buy pollution abatement equipment or by allocating pollution emission permits to existing firms alone – or by encouraging firms to merge within the industry. Second, the policy may add costs to an industry without the same costs being imposed on foreign competitors. While many factors affect prices in the international trade market (*e.g.* exchange rate movements), governments tend to be very sensitive to these forms of cost increase. Overall, then, modern CBAs tend to be accompanied by a statement about the impacts on competitiveness. In general, any costs arising are not included in the CBA but, in principle, they could be.

5.5. Complementary benefits

CBA requires that all the benefits accruing to a policy or project be included in any measure of aggregate benefits. This is the "with/without" principle introduced in Chapter 3. However, an issue of "when to stop" arises in certain cases. For example, measures to tackle global warming will be directed at the emissions of greenhouse gases. The main one of these is carbon dioxide. But carbon dioxide is emitted from a very large number of installations and mobile sources: factories, houses and vehicles. Measures to reduce these emissions may necessarily reduce other environmentally or socially damaging activities at the same time. Examples would be an energy efficiency policy which reduces energy consumption which in turn reduces carbon dioxide emissions and sulphur oxide and particulate emissions. Thus, even apart from any savings in fuels costs, energy efficiency policies tend to take on a "multi-benefit" nature. In the circumstances, it seems quite correct to add the savings in energy costs, the reduced carbon dioxide (CO_2) emissions and the reduced sulphur emissions together to generate an aggregate benefit. Thus, while the prime motivation of a policy may be to save energy or reduce carbon emissions, there may be "complementary" or "ancillary" benefits that arise because other benefits are "jointly produced".

Box 5.1 illustrates the case of ancillary benefits for climate control policies in Europe.

But not all economists are convinced by the procedures for including ancillary benefits. Consider a further case where the policy to tackle climate change involves measures to reduce vehicle-kilometres travelled in a year, perhaps by raising fuel prices or the costs of vehicle use. Again, reducing CO_2 will also reduce other emissions from vehicles. But it may also reduce congestion which has a social cost. How far should the reduced congestion count as a benefit of the climate control policy? One of the problems is that while reduced congestion may be one of the ancillary effects, the relevant policy may be an inefficient way of securing the reduced congestion. Rather than raising fuel taxes, for example, it may be better to tackle congestion directly with a congestion charge. The issue is one of the extent to which one should credit a policy measure aimed at reducing climate change with the additional benefits of reduced congestion if those ancillary benefits could have been secured by an alternative, more cost-efficient policy. Perhaps because the issue of ancillary benefits has arisen mainly in the context of the climate policy debate, this more fundamental question has not been discussed.

5.6. Employment creation as a benefit

For many countries, the role that policies or projects can play in generating employment is important. As such, pressure may be placed on a cost-benefit analyst to "add in" these benefits on the benefit side of the CBA. In some cases this is a correct procedure, although it matters how it is carried out. In other cases, it is not a legitimate procedure and involves a risk of double-counting.

Box 5.1. **Ancillary benefits from climate change control policies**

One argument that has been used to provide additional justification for climate change policies is that such policies will tend to generate a wide array of ancillary benefits such as reduced air pollution, reduced congestion, lower accidents, and, when the policies involve helping developing countries to reduce emissions, a "warm glow" or "conscience relieving" effect (Markandya and Rübbelke, 2003). How far it is correct to credit all of these effects to climate change control policies is open to debate (see text). An additional complication is that of determining the "counterfactual", i.e. what would happen if the climate control policy had not been implemented. The process of crediting all ancillary benefits to the climate control policy implies that nothing would have happened without the climate policy, which, in most cases, is very unlikely. Moreover, this issue becomes complicated since the counterfactual policy to secure the benefits regarded as ancillary to the climate policy may well be cheaper than securing the ancillary benefits via the climate policy (Shogren, 1999). But it is common practice in climate change economics to credit those policies with ancillary benefits. Perhaps the best thing to say is that ancillary benefits should not be included in climate change policy CBA without first giving careful thought to the conceptual foundations of doing so.

How large might ancillary benefits be? In a survey of existing studies Pearce (2000) found the following results:

Country	Ancillary benefits as % of climate damage avoidance benefits	Comment
USA	7-670	Wide range due to a few outlier studies. Most studies in range 7-200
UK	100-430	Two studies both relying on same source
European Union	110-175	
Norway	230-320	

If correct, the studies appear to suggest substantial ancillary benefits associated with climate change control policy. Moreover, nearly all the studies focus on conventional air pollutants only.

The correct inclusion of employment benefits involves the *shadow pricing of labour* in contexts where there is fairly extensive unemployment. If it can be argued that the project or policy creates employment for labour that would *otherwise be unemployed*, the shadow price of that labour is below, and possibly well below, the wage paid to that labour once employed. The effect of shadow pricing in this context is to lower the costs of the project or policy to a level below that of the apparent money costs. This will make the net benefit figure larger and hence make it more likely that the project or policy will be adopted. It is in this way that employment effects are properly accounted for.

In a context where there is "full employment", i.e. some level of employment whereby employment creation in one area or sector tends to be at the cost of already employed labour elsewhere, the shadow pricing argument still applies but, in the limit, the effect will be to price labour at the ruling wage, producing no difference between the ruling wage and the shadow price of labour. The two are the same because every unit of labour "created" by the policy is at the cost of a unit of labour employed somewhere else.

If one expects labour to be more extensively unemployed in poorer countries and if there is "full employment" in richer countries, then the shadow pricing of labour is potentially important in the former context and unimportant in the latter case. But even where employment changes are judged not to be of relevance to the CBA strictly interpreted, impacts on employment are of interest to politicians, just as impacts of production costs are. Hence an overall "impact analysis" may well include a discussion and even quantification of employment effects directly arising from the policy or project. These need to be kept separate from the CBA as such, unless there is reason to involve the shadow pricing of labour at below market wage rates.

5.7. Summary and guidance for policy-makers

This section has looked at the issue of compliance costs and at selected impacts that tend not to be included in a CBA. The general messages are:

- It is unwise to assume that because costs may take the form of equipment and capital infrastructure their estimation is more certain than benefits. The experience is that costs of complying with regulations, and the costs of major projects, can be seriously over-stated or understated. In other words there may be cost pessimism or cost optimism. In light of this it is important to conduct sensitivity analysis, *i.e.* to show how the final net benefit figure changes if costs are increased or decreased by some percentage.

- Ideally, compliance costs would be estimated using general equilibrium analysis. In some cases such models are available for use by cost-benefit analysts. This is especially important if the project or policy is "discrete", *i.e.* has the potential to affect other costs and prices in the economy by a significant amount. In turn, general equilibrium analysis has its supporters and detractors. In favour of its use is that it avoids the obvious potential errors of omission in using partial equilibrium approaches. Against its use is the usually primitive assumptions that these models make about competitive markets and market clearing mechanisms.

- Politicians are very sensitive about the effects of regulation on competitiveness. This is why most Regulatory Impact Assessment procedures call for some kind of analysis of these effects. A distinction needs to be made between the competitiveness of nations as whole, and the competitiveness of industries. In the former case it is hard to assign much credibility to the notion of competitiveness impacts. In the latter case two kinds of effects may occur. The first is any impact on the competitive nature of the industry within the country in question – *e.g.* does the policy add to any tendencies for monopoly power? If it does then, technically, there will be welfare losses associated with the change in that monopoly power and these losses should be added to the cost side of the CBA, if they can be estimated. The second impact is on the costs of the industry relative to the costs of competing industries in other countries. Unless the industry is very large, it cannot be assumed that exchange rate movements will cancel out the losses arising from the cost increases. In that case there may be dynamic effects resulting in output losses.

- Policies to address one overall goal may have associated effects in other policy areas. The example of climate change and conventional air pollutants was cited. Reductions in climate gases may be associated with reductions in jointly produced air pollutants. Should the two be added and regarded as a benefit of climate change policy? On the face of it, yes, but care needs to be taken that the procedure does not result in double counting. To address this it is important to consider the counterfactual, *i.e.* what policies would be in place without the policy of immediate interest. While it is common practice to add the benefits together, some experts have cast doubt on the validity of the procedure.

● Finally, employment effects are usually also of interest to politicians and policy-makers. But the extent to which they matter for the CBA depends on the nature of the economy. If there is significant unemployment, the labour should be shadow priced on the basis of its opportunity cost. In turn this may be very low, *i.e.* if not used for the policy or project in question, the labour might otherwise be unemployed. In a fully employed economy, however, this opportunity cost may be such as to leave the full cost of labour being recorded as the correct value. Separate statements about employment impacts may well be advisable.

ISBN 92-64-01004-1
Cost-Benefit Analysis and the Environment
Recent Developments
© OECD 2006

Chapter 6

Total Economic Value

The notion of total economic value (TEV) provides an all-encompassing measure of the economic value of any environmental asset. It decomposes into use and non-use (or passive use) values, and further sub-classifications can be provided if needed. This chapter reviews this central concept which has been so important for properly understanding changes in well-being due to a project or policy that has environmental impacts.

6.1. The nature of total economic value

The net sum of all the relevant WTPs and WTAs for a project outcome or policy change defines the *total economic value* (TEV) of any change in well-being due to a project or policy. TEV can be characterised differently according to the type of economic value arising. It is usual to divide TEV into *use* and *non-use* (or *passive use*) values. Use values relate to actual use of the good in question (*e.g.* a visit to a national park), planned use (a visit planned in the future) or possible use. Actual and planned uses are fairly obvious concepts, but possible use could also be important since people may be willing to pay to maintain a good in existence in order to preserve the *option* of using it in the future. *Option value* thus becomes a form of use value. Non-use value refers to the willingness to pay to maintain some good in existence even though there is no actual, planned or possible use.[1] The types of non-use value could be various, but a convenient classification is in terms of *a)* existence value, *b)* altruistic value, and *c)* bequest value. Existence value refers to the WTP to keep a good in existence in a context where the individual expressing the value has no actual or planned use for his/herself *or for anyone else*. Motivations here could vary and might include having a feeling of concern for the asset itself (*e.g.* a threatened species) or a "stewardship" motive whereby the "valuer" feels some responsibility for the asset. Altruistic value might arise when the individual is concerned that the good in question should be available to others in the current generation. A bequest value is similar but the concern is that the next and future generations should have the option to make use of the good.

Figure 6.1 shows one characterisation of TEV by types of value. Stated preference techniques, in which respondents answer questions put to them by the analyst (see Chapters 8 and 9), are suited to eliciting all these kinds of value, although, in practice, it is usually not possible to disaggregate individual types of non-use value, nor is it usually relevant to a decision to secure that breakdown. But differentiating use and non-use values is important because the latter can be large relative to the former, especially when the good in question has few substitutes and is widely valued. In addition, non-use value remains controversial in some decision-making contexts, so that it is important to separate it out for presentational and strategic reasons.

6.2. TEV and valuation techniques

The valuation techniques developed by environmental economists (and others, especially health economists) can be used to measure the components of TEV. Figure 6.2 shows the various techniques and the TEV components they are best suited to measuring. Several observations are in order.

First, non-use values can only be estimated using stated preference techniques, *i.e.* techniques that are based on questionnaires given to respondents and which elicit the respondent's WTP (or WTA) directly or indirectly from respondent answers. Non-use values are likely to be especially important in contexts where the good being valued has few or no substitutes. Since use of a service or good leaves a "behavioural trail" revealed preference techniques – which work by seeking out markets in which the value of the good or service in question might be revealed – tend to be suited to eliciting use values. Stated preference techniques can also be used to elicit use values. But non-use value tends not to leave a behavioural trail, *i.e.* some behavioural change which affects a price or quantity which can be observed. Accordingly, revealed preference is unlikely to elicit non-use values.

Second, the central role of "dose-response functions" or "production functions" is observed. These functions link some change in the state of nature or a policy measure to some response. For example, air pollution would be a "dose" and a response might be an increased number of chronic bronchitis cases. Or there may be some change in medical care which improves patient well-being: the link is between the productive activity (medical care) and the output (patient well-being). These functions will invariably need to be estimated or derived from various kinds of literature. Economists have no particular expertise in this area and it will be important to ensure that research or policy analysis involving the use of such functions involves the relevant experts (epidemiologists, clinicians, technologists, etc.).

Figure 6.1. **Total economic value**

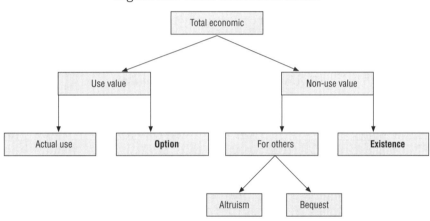

Third, the lower part of the diagram suggests that *benefits transfer* is one of the "goals" of valuation. Benefits transfer is a process of "borrowing" values that have already been estimated in some other study or context. Obviously, if it is a valid procedure, benefits transfer would save considerable time and effort in conducting "primary" valuation studies. Certainly, the more primary valuation research there is the more we can learn about benefits transfer. But benefits transfer is a subject within itself and it is far from clear that it is a valid procedure in many contexts (see Chapter 17).

6.3. A note on intrinsic value

Chapter 2 noted that critics of CBA sometimes reject the notion that individual preferences should be the yardstick of "value" preferring instead to speak of the intrinsic value of environmental assets, especially living assets. How is TEV related to the notion of *intrinsic value?* Intrinsic value is often regarded as being a value that resides "in" the asset in question, and especially environmental assets, but which is independent of human preferences. By definition, TEV relates to the preferences of individual human beings, so that if intrinsic value is defined to be independent of those preferences, TEV cannot encompass intrinsic values. However, notions of intrinsic value may well *influence* WTP and stated preference valuation techniques are particularly useful in eliciting such influences. Questionnaires should always seek to obtain information on the *motives* for stated WTP. These motives vary and may well include notions such as "a right to exist" for the asset in question. This is a fairly common motive when the asset is, for example, a living creature. Hence, TEV cannot embrace a *measure* of intrinsic value, but SP does help to make the motivations for WTP explicit, and those motives may well involve a concern "on behalf" of the object being valued.[2]

6.4. Summary and guidance for decision-makers

The notion of total economic value (TEV) provides an all-encompassing measure of the *economic value* of any environmental asset. It decomposes into use and non-use (or passive use) values, and further sub-classifications can be provided if needed. TEV does not encompass other kinds of values, such as intrinsic values which are usually defined as values residing "in" the asset and unrelated to human preferences or even human observation. However, apart from the problems of making the notion of intrinsic value operational, it can be argued that some people's willingness to pay for the conservation of an asset, independently of any use they make of it, is influenced by their own judgements about intrinsic value. This may show up especially in notions of "rights to existence" but also as a form of altruism.

Figure 6.2. **Total economic value**

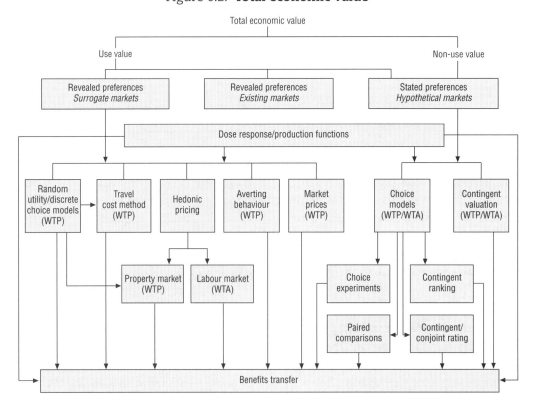

Notes

1. Freeman (2003) argues that non-use value is better defined as any value not measurable by revealed preference techniques. The attraction of this view is that it avoids some difficulties in defining what is meant by "use'".

2. We do not enter the debate on whether there is any meaning to the notion of intrinsic value. This is debated by philosophers. At the practical level, the problems of accounting for intrinsic value are formidable since it unclear how one determines what has intrinsic and what does not, and how one would trade-off this value against other values. One risk is that all trade-offs would be rejected, making decision-making impossible.

ISBN 92-64-01004-1
Cost-Benefit Analysis and the Environment
Recent Developments
© OECD 2006

Chapter 7

Revealed Preference Methods for Valuing Non-market Impacts

Many impacts of projects and policies are of an intangible nature and are not traded in actual markets. In some cases, discussed in this chapter, non-market goods and services may be implicitly traded. In such instances, revealed preference methods can be used to "tease out" their values embedded in observed prices. These techniques include the travel cost method, hedonic price method, averting behaviour and defensive expenditures and costs of illness/lost output approach. Each of these approaches has different conceptual bases, is often applicable to valuing different environmental goods (and bads) and has distinctive analytical problems. However, all share the common feature of using market information and/or behaviour to infer the economic value of an associated non-market impact. For some this makes the findings of market based studies a reliable indicator of peoples' preferences. The reality is somewhat more complicated and the superiority of these methods (relative to alternatives) cannot be straightforwardly generalised.

7.1. An introduction to revealed preference methods

An emergent theme in the appraisal of public policies is the desirability of quantifying in monetary terms the intangible impacts of these proposals (where relevant and practicable) on the well-being of the public. For example, within the domains of environmental or health policy, it is increasingly recognised that these intangible impacts are likely to comprise a meaningful component of the total benefits of policy interventions. However, many of these impacts are non-market goods (or bads). This means that the value that the public places on these impacts cannot simply be observed with reference to market information such as price and consumption levels. This has given rise to the proliferation of methods that have sought to uncover, in a variety of ways, the value of non-market goods. It is worth noting that some of the more prominent of these methods have been around for a number of years. Yet, their increasing use – most notably in environmental policy – has provided an additional impetus both in respect of, on the one hand, ever greater sophistication in application and, on the other hand, scrutiny regarding validity and reliability of these methods.

Table 7.1. **An overview of revealed preference methods**

Method	Revealed behaviour	Conceptual framework	Types of application
Hedonic pricing	Property purchased; choice of job	Demand for differentiated products	Property value and wage determinants
Travel cost	Participation in recreation activity at chosen site	Household production; complementary goods	Recreational demand
Averting behaviour/defensive expenditure	Time costs; purchases to avoid harm	Household production; substitute goods	Health: mortality and morbidity
Costs of illness	Expenditures to treat illness	Treatment costs	Health: morbidity

Source: Boyle (2003).

The unifying characteristic of *revealed preference methods* (RPMs) (also referred to as market-based methods) is the valuation of non-market impacts by observing actual behaviour and, in particular, purchases made in actual markets. To use the terminology of Russell (2001) these methods seek to quantify the market "footprint" of non-market goods (or bads). There are a number of different approaches that have been proposed to fulfil this objective. Boyle (2003) provides a recent review of the main four methods, summarised in Table 7.1: *i*) hedonic pricing; *ii*) travel cost; *iii*) averting or defensive behaviour; and *iv*) costs of illness.

Table 7.1 (Column 2) outlines the specific aspect or aspects of revealed economic behaviour that each method has sought to examine. This might entail the observation of purchases of durable goods such as property in the case of hedonic pricing or double-glazed windows in the case of defensive expenditure. In most cases, individual or household behaviour is the main focus. One exception is the costs of illness approach which also examines *social* provision of health services for those who fall ill as a result of, say, poor air quality. Behaviour in each of these markets is thought to reveal something about the implicit price of a related non-market good (or bad). However, the conceptual framework underpinning each approach is different (Table 7.1, Column 3). For example, the purchase of a property can be conceived of as buying a differentiated good whose price depends on a number of characteristics including the prevalence and quality of environmental amenities in the vicinity of the property. In the case of defensive expenditure, this could entail the purchase of a substitute market good such as double-glazed windows in order to compensate for the existence of a non-market bad such as road traffic noise.

RPMs have been applied in a variety of contexts (Table 7.1, Column 4). The strength of these approaches is that they are based on actual decisions made by individuals or households. This is in contrast to stated preference methods which ask people how they would hypothetically value changes in the provision of non-market goods. For some commentators this, in principle, makes the findings of market based studies the more reliable indicator of peoples' preferences. This is because they provide actual data on how much people are willing to pay to secure more of a non-market good or to defend themselves against the harm caused by a non-market bad. Of course, the reality is somewhat more complicated. For example, it is not necessarily straightforward to uncover these values in practice. Nor is it typically possible to test the behavioural assumptions upon which these methods rely. This is in contrast to stated preference methods where such tests are not only possible but commonplace (see Chapters 8 and 9). What this means then is that superiority of RPMs – relative to alternative valuation methods – in practice might better be considered on a case-by-case basis.

In this chapter, we provide an overview of the conceptual bases of a range of revealed preference approaches to the valuation of non-market economic impacts. We highlight the most important issues underpinning the theory of each approach, and implications for their practical application.

7.2. The hedonic price method

The hedonic price method (HPM) estimates the value of a non-market good by observing behaviour in the market for a related good. Specifically, the HPM uses a market good via which the non-market good is implicitly traded. The starting point for the HPM is the observation that the price of a large number of market goods is a function of a bundle of characteristics. For instance, the price of a car is likely to reflect its fuel efficiency, safety and reliability; the price of a washing machine might depend on its energy efficiency, reliability and variety of washing programmes. The HPM uses statistical techniques to isolate the implicit "price" of each of these characteristics.

Two types of market are of particular interest in non-market valuation: *a)* property markets; and, *b)* labour markets.

Starting with housing, we can describe any particular house by the qualities or characteristics of its structure, the number and size of rooms and so on, its location, the local environment and nearby amenities. The price of a house is determined by the particular combination of characteristics it displays, so that properties possessing more and better desirable characteristics command higher prices and those with larger quantities of bad qualities command lower prices.

For example, we might assume that, in general, people would prefer a quiet residential environment to a noisy one, but since no market exists for the amenity "peace and quiet", we have no direct market evidence on how much this amenity is valued where people live. However, peace and quiet can be traded implicitly in the property market. Individuals can express their preference for a quiet environment by purchasing a house in a quiet area. A measure of the value of peace and quiet is then the premium that is paid for a quieter house compared with a noisier but otherwise identical one.

The HPM is concerned with unbundling the contributions of each significant determinant of house prices in order to identify marginal willingness to pay for each housing characteristic. This involves collecting large amounts of data on prices and characteristics of properties in an area, and applying statistical techniques to estimate an "hedonic price function". This function is a locus of equilibrium prices for the sample of houses. These prices result from the interaction of buyers and sellers in the property market in question. If the array of housing characteristics in the market is approximately continuous, then we can say that buyers will choose levels of each characteristic so that its marginal implicit price is just equal to buyers' valuation of the characteristic. Then, the slope of the hedonic price function with respect to each characteristic is equal to the implicit price.

Hedonic studies of the property market have been used to identify the value of non-market goods (or bads) such as road traffic and aircraft noise, air pollution, water quality, proximity to landfill sites and planning restrictions on open spaces in and around urban areas. The HPM has also been used to estimate the value of avoiding risk of death or injury. It has done this by looking for price differentials between wages in jobs with different exposures to physical risk. That is, different occupations involve different risks (in that, for example, being a fire-fighter entails, on average, very much higher risks of injury or worse than does a desk-bound occupation). Employers must therefore pay a premium to induce workers to undertake jobs entailing higher risk. This premium provides an estimate of the market value of small changes in injury or mortality risks (Kolstad, 1999). Hedonic methods have thus been applied to labour markets in order to disentangle such risk premia from other determinants of wages (*e.g.* education, etc.).

Not surprisingly there are a number of issues surrounding the practical application of HPMs. For example, households/individuals might not have perfect information. In the case of wage-risk premia, this means that workers may not be fully aware of the accident risks they face in the workplace, so that their wage-risk choices do not accurately reflect their true valuation of risk. Estimates of the value of risk obtained from observing these choices will then be biased.

Another problem with the HPM estimation procedure is that of multicollinearity. Non-market characteristics tend to move in tandem: *e.g.* properties near to roads have greater noise pollution *and* higher concentrations of air pollutants. This means that it is frequently difficult to "tease out" the independent effect of these two forms of pollution on the price of the property (Day, 2001). In many cases, researchers have even tended to neglect the issue, omitting a potentially important characteristic from the analysis, and producing biased estimates as a result (although see Box 7.1).

Finally, care needs to be taken to specify the extent of the property market accurately. The extent of the market is defined for any one individual house buyer by that individual's search. If properties are included in the analysis which are outside of the individual's market, hedonic price estimates will be biased. If properties are excluded which are in the market, the resulting estimates will be unbiased but inefficient. Unfortunately, with many different individuals searching for property in a given locality, the resulting house purchase data are likely to be drawn from a large number of overlapping markets. In this case, it has

Box 7.1. **HPM and the impact of water quality on residential property values**

Leggett and Bockstael (LB) (2000) address the issue of multicollinearity directly in their study of the impact of varying water quality on the value of waterside residential property. Water pollution in Chesapeake Bay in the US can be produced by sewage treatment works and other installations which could also have a negative impact on visual amenity. The potential for bias thereby stems from the fact that properties closest to these installations could suffer both worse water quality and worse visual amenity, making it difficult to determine the price effect of each.

However, to overcome this potential problem, LB were able to take advantage of a natural feature of Chesapeake Bay. The Bay has a varied coastline, with many localised inlets and a diverse pollution-flushing regime. As a result, it was possible to find a property located on an inlet which suffered from poor water quality but with no direct line of sight to the associated pollution source, and hence no visual disamenity. Similarly, a property located close to a sewage treatment works would not necessarily suffer from poor water quality if the flushing regime in that particular inlet was benign. The natural features of Chesapeake Bay thereby broke the potentially collinear relationship between visual amenity and water quality, allowing both characteristics to be included in the estimation equation without causing statistical problems.

In hedonic property studies, as with most studies of the value of environmental resources, some consideration needs to be given of the appropriate way to measure the environmental variable of interest. For instance, laypeople often respond most readily to the visual appearance of water, tending to attach higher values to water of greater clarity. However, biological water quality – which reflects the ecological potential of a water body – is not necessarily related to water clarity. Further, chemical water quality is more important for determining whether a water body is suitable for swimming or other sports where contact with the water is a possibility. Chemical water quality might not be well understood by members of the public, however.

LB used reported faecal coliform levels as their measure of water quality. This indicates that it was in general the recreational value of being located close to Chesapeake Bay which was being estimated in their study. These data were advertised in local newspapers and at information points, and the limit at which beaches would be closed for public health reasons was also clearly stated. The authors also obtained good evidence for believing that existing and prospective Chesapeake residents took an active interest in local water quality, providing further support for the possibility of a positive relationship between property values and water quality.

LB found that standard locational variables had the expected signs in their estimated equation. Increased acreage, reduced commuting distance, and proximity to water all had positive impacts on property prices, compared with the average estimated USD 350 000 per one acre plot. The closer a property was to a pollution source, the lower the price would tend to be. Local faecal coliform levels were also negatively related to property prices. For every unit increase in median annual concentration reported at the nearest measuring station, property value was observed to fall by USD 5 000 (average concentration in the sample was one count per ml, with a range of 0.4-23/ml). This could be used as an estimate of the marginal value of small changes in water quality in the Chesapeake area, and elsewhere.

LB emphasise that their results cannot be used to estimate the value of significant changes in water quality (as might occur through the introduction of new environmental standards, for instance). This is because a significant change would constitute a shift in the supply of environmental quality to the Chesapeake Bay housing market, and hence would induce a shift in the hedonic price function, as buyers and sellers renegotiated to obtain new optimal house purchase outcomes. This is an important qualification to the policy use of non-market value estimates obtained via the HPM.

been argued that it is probably better to underestimate the extent of the market under study, rather than overestimate it (Palmquist, 1992).

7.3. The travel cost method

The travel cost method (TCM) has been developed to value the use of non-market goods, particularly geographical areas and locations used for recreational purposes. For example, natural areas are frequently the focus of recreational trips (*e.g.* parks, woodland, beaches, lakes etc.). Such natural areas, for a number of reasons, typically do not command a price in the market and so we need to find an alternative means of appraising their value. Before proceeding to a specific application, this section provides an overview of this method and draws extensively on Day (2001).

The basis of the TCM is the recognition that individuals produce recreational experiences through the input of a number of factor inputs. Amongst these factors are the recreational area itself, travel to and from the recreational area and, in some cases, staying overnight at a location and so on. Typically, the recreational area itself is an unpriced good, many of the other factors employed in the generation of the recreational experience do command prices in markets.

The TCM derives from the observation that travel and the recreational area are (weak) complements such that the value of the recreational area can be measured with reference to values expressed in the market for trips to the recreational area. To estimate the TCM, therefore, we need two pieces of information: *a)* the number of trips that an individual or household takes to a particular recreational area over the course of a year; and *b)* how much it costs that individual or household to travel to the recreational area. Such information is usually collected through surveys carried out at the recreational site.

The costs of travelling to a recreational area, in turn, include two elements: *i)* the monetary costs in return fares or petrol expenses, wear and tear and depreciation of the vehicle and so on; and *ii)* the cost of time spent travelling. Time is a scarce resource to the household. Time spent travelling could be spent in some other activity (*e.g.* working) that could confer well-being. In other words, the individual or household incurs an *opportunity cost* in allocating time to travel. Put more simply, demand for trips will be greater if it takes less time to travel to the recreational area, independently of the monetary cost of travel.

Of course to implement this procedure we require a value for the (shadow) price of time. One possible value for the price of time to an individual is their wage rate. If individuals can choose the number of hours they spend working then they will choose to work up to the point at which an extra hour spent at work is worth the same to them as an hour spent at leisure. At the margin, therefore, leisure time will be valued at the wage rate. In the real world, individuals can only imperfectly choose the number of hours they work and the equality between the value of time in leisure and the wage rate is unlikely to hold. Empirical work has been undertaken that has revealed that time spent travelling is valued at somewhere between a third and a half of the wage rate and travel cost researchers frequently use one or other of these values as an estimate of the price of time.

There are a number of problems in applying the TCM. One in particular is multiple purpose trips. Many recreational trips are undertaken for more than one purpose. For example, standard travel cost methods cannot easily be applied to trips undertaken by international tourists since such tourists will usually visit more than one destination. One

Box 7.2. **The recreational value of game reserves in South Africa**

Day (2002) provides a relatively sophisticated application of the travel cost method to four of South Africa's game parks. These internationally renowned games reserves – Hluhluwe, Umfolozi, Mkuzi and Itala – each cover vast land areas of roughly several hundred square kilometres and are managed by the KwaZulu-Natal Parks Board (KNPB).

The premise for Day's approach is that a visit to any one of these game reserves reflects a choice between four key cost determinants: i) the economic cost of travel to the site; ii) the cost of time while travelling; iii) the cost of accommodation at the site; and, iv) the cost of time whilst on-site. Most travel cost approaches have focused only on costs i) and ii). For many recreational sites this is sufficient. However, Day argues that overnight trips are an important feature of visits to the reserves that he examines in this study. In order to take account of this trip characteristic, Day extends a conceptual framework sometimes used in recreational contexts. Random utility models predict that an individual will choose to make a given visit to a particular site rather its alternatives because the chosen site provides that individual with the most utility (or well-being) from the options available. Such a model is thus ideally suited to explaining a visitor's decision with reference to the qualities of alternative sites (e.g. number and variety of fauna and flora) as well as the different costs of travelling to these sites. Day further extends this framework in order to take account of visitor choice of accommodation and length of stay at the site.

The data used in this study are based upon a (random) sample of 1 000 visitors to the four different reserves. For each of these visitors, this included information on, for example, length of stay, size of party and how much, in total, the visit cost each household. It is worth noting that this study did not need to use on-site surveys say of visitor total travel costs and demographic/socioeconomic characteristics. For example, with respect to physical distance travelled, this was calculated with reference to data on visitor addresses combined with a Geographical Information Systems (GIS) model in order to calculate the distance that each visitor travelled "door-to-door".

An interesting feature of Day's study is the determination of the money value to be assigned to an hour spent travelling relative to an hour spent on-site. Day demonstrates quite reasonably that an hour spent travelling is likely to be valued less highly than an hour spent on-site at the reserve. Furthermore, he argues that the former is likely to be valued more than time in general because there could be a significant disutility associated with time spent travelling. In other words, people enjoy time travelling a lot less than most other uses of time and so this activity has a high opportunity cost. By contrast, the latter is likely to be valued less than time in general because there could be a significant utility associated with time spent on-site. In terms of proportions of the wage rate, Day concludes that his analysis justifies valuing travel time at 150% of the household wage rate while on-site time is valued at 34% of the wage rate. Whereas the latter seems consistent with previous findings in the literature (see discussion above) the former is somewhat higher than conventionally assumed by travel cost practitioners.

Day uses assembled data on cost, trip duration and accommodation decision variables as well as other trip characteristics as inputs to a sophisticated statistical analysis of the determinants of the choice to take a given trip to a particular reserve. Ultimately, the findings of this detailed analysis can be used to derive policy relevant information on the benefits provided by the reserves. For example, Day calculates the amount of money that would have to be given to affected households in South Africa following the (hypothetical) closure of one of the reserves in order to fully compensate them for the loss of this recreational amenity.[*] A summary of these findings is presented in Table 7.2.

Box 7.2. **The recreational value of game reserves in South Africa** *(cont.)*

Table 7.2. **Per trip values for game reserves of KwaZulu-Natal, 1994/5**

Game reserve	Average per trip welfare loss (USD)	Total annual welfare loss (USD)
Hluhluwe	49.7	473 884
Umfolozi	30.5	290 448
Itala	20.4	194 169
Mkuzi	18.7	178 026
Hluhluwe and Umfolozi	105.6	1 006 208

Source: Day (2002).

Why are these data important? Day argues that one response to this question is that the KNPB is finding itself under increasing pressure to justify the substantial public funding that it receives. Demonstrating the monetary value of the recreational benefits provided by the KNPB might be one crucial way in which this body can make its case for public funds. Thus the values in Table 7.2 (Column 2) can be thought of as the per trip benefits attributable to the current management regime at each reserve. Alternatively, this is the (yearly) per trip loss of welfare or well-being in money terms, that occurs if the reserve were to be closed "tomorrow".

Column 3 in Table 7.2 illustrates the total annual welfare losses for each reserve: *i.e.* the per trip value multiplied by the number of trips which would no longer be taken over a year if the reserve was closed. In effect, this column provides policy-makers with one basis for assessing the dollar magnitude of the (non-market) recreational benefits generated by public expenditure on each reserve. Finally, it is interesting to note that the final row in Table 7.2 indicates that if both Hluhluwe and Umfolozi (*i.e.* the most highly valued) reserves were to close then the combined welfare loss is greater (than the sum of individual values in Column 3, Rows 2 and 3). The intuitive explanation for this is that these two parks are in close proximity to each other. Removing one or other would mean that many households would most likely just switch their visits to the remaining reserve. However, if both of these sites were to be no longer available for visits then the loss for households would be disproportionately greater reflecting the absence of remaining substitutes.

* Note then that these are the recreational losses that would be suffered by visitors living in South Africa. That is, these estimates do not include the welfare costs that would be associated with the loss of visitors from abroad.

solution to this problem has been to ask visitors (as part of the on-site survey) to estimate the proportion of the enjoyment they derived from their entire trip that they would assign to visiting the specific recreational area of interest. Total travel costs for the entire trip are multiplied by this amount and this can be used as the basis for assessing travel costs at the recreational site.

7.4. Averting behaviour and defensive expenditure

Methods based on averting behaviour take as their main premise the notion that individuals and households can insulate themselves from a non-market bad by selecting more costly types of behaviour. These behaviours might be more costly in terms of the time requirements they imply, or of the restrictions they impose on what the individual would otherwise wish to do. Alternatively, individuals might be able to avoid exposure to non-market bads via the purchase of a market good. These financial outlays are known as defensive expenditures. The value of each of these purchases represents an implicit price for the non-market good or bad in question.

There are numerous instances which provide an illustration of these methods to value non-market goods and bads. Garrod and Willis (1999) offer the example of households installing double-glazed windows to decrease exposure to road traffic noise. Essentially, double-glazing is a market good which, in this example, acts as a substitute for a non-market good (peace and quiet in the sense of the absence of road traffic noise). If noise levels decrease for other reasons – perhaps as a result of a local authority's implementation of traffic calming measures – then households will spend less on these defensive outlays. Changes in expenditures on this substitute good provide a good measure of households' valuations of traffic calming policies that decrease noise pollution (a bad) and, correspondingly, increase the supply of peace and quiet (a good).

Examples of defensive expenditure focus on the purchase of market goods which act as a substitute for a non-market good. However, individuals might change their behaviour in costly but perhaps less obvious ways in order to avoid an adverse impact on their well-being. Freeman (2003) uses the example of an individual who spends additional time indoors to avoid exposure to outdoor air pollution. In this case, the allocation of time to avoiding a non-market bad (i.e. the risk of adverse health impacts like asthma attacks, or coughing and sneezing episodes) is typically not observable and the substitute item is itself a non-market good (i.e. time that could have been used more productively). Nevertheless, the avoidance costs of spending time indoors could be evaluated by asking people directly about their time-use. Moreover, time use has a market analogue in the form of wages that would be paid to an individual if the time spent indoors could otherwise be spent working (see discussion of the travel cost method above).

A number of interesting complications arise in the practical application of averting behaviour and defensive expenditure approaches to valuing non-market goods. Two, in particular, are worth noting here. Firstly, defensive expenditures typically represent a partial or lower bound estimate of the value of the impact of the non-market bad on well-being. For example, in the double-glazing case, greater indoor tranquillity may be achieved, but gardens will still be exposed to road traffic noise at the same levels, so double-glazing will not help homeowners to avoid the costs of road traffic noise completely. Secondly, many avertive behaviours or defensive expenditures create joint products. For instance, time spent indoors avoiding air pollution is not otherwise wasted. This time can also be put to other productive uses that have value, such as undertaking household chores, indoor leisure activities or working from home (see Box 7.3). The double-glazing case also creates joint products – e.g. energy conservation. It is the net cost of the expenditure or change in behaviour – that is, the cost after taking account of the value of alternative uses of time, for instance, or energy savings – which is the correct measure of the value of the associated reduction in the non-market bad. However, distinguishing the determinant of behaviour that is of interest, and the costs of the various components, might not be an easy matter in practice.

Box 7.3. **Averting behaviour and air quality in Los Angeles**

Bresnahan, Dickie and Gerking (BDG) (1997) examine behaviour and changes in health risks. Specifically, these health risks arise from exposure to concentrations of ground-level ozone.[1] Acute health impairment particularly in response to peak concentrations of ozone has been documented in a number of epidemiological and medical studies. Moreover, BDG note that spending less time outdoors on bad air quality days – *e.g.* days when ozone concentrations exceed recommended standards – can effectively decrease exposure to pollution for certain at-risk groups. BDG seek to evaluate the extent of actual defensive expenditure and averting behaviour amongst members of these groups living in the Los Angeles area.

Data were drawn from repeated survey responses of a sample of (non-smoking) Los Angeles residents living in areas with relatively high concentrations of local air pollutants. In addition, the sample contained a high proportion of individuals with compromised respiratory functions. Respondents were asked a range of questions about, for example, their health status, purchase of durable goods that might mitigate indoor exposure to ground-level ozone, their outdoor behaviour in general and on bad air quality days in particular.

The findings of the BDG study were that two-thirds of their sample reported changing their behaviour in some meaningful way on days when air quality was poor. For example, 40% of respondents claimed either to re-arrange leisure activities or stay indoors during such days, and 20% of respondents increased their use of home air conditioning units. Furthermore, those respondents who experienced (acute) air pollution-related symptoms tended to spend less time outside on bad air quality days. Finally, BDG found tentative evidence that averting behaviour increases with medical costs that would otherwise be incurred if a respondent became ill.

In summary, bad air quality days appeared in this study to lead to significant changes in behaviour.[2] It is reasonable to speculate that these impose non-trivial economic costs on respondents. For example, these burdens might take the form of the purchase and running of air conditioning with an air purifying unit or the inconvenience imposed by spending time indoors. However, BDG do not attempt to put a monetary value on these actions. As Dickie and Gerking (2002) point out, this would not necessarily be a straightforward exercise. For example, and as we have already argued, time spent indoors avoiding exposure to air pollution is not necessarily time wasted. In other words, there is no simple way of valuing a person's time when time which an individual would have spent enjoying outdoor leisure activities is substituted for time spent enjoying indoor leisure activities.

1. Ground level ozone in cities can arise from a combination of certain pollutants (emitted as a result of energy generation and use of motor vehicles) with sunlight.
2. Note that these findings do not capture permanent decisions to take recreation indoors (regardless of air quality on particular days).

7.5. Cost of illness and lost output approaches

The cost of illness (COI) approach is similar to the defensive expenditures method described in the previous section in that it focuses on expenditure on medical services and products made in response to morbidity and other health effects of non-market impacts. For example, the costs of the health impacts of air pollution can be valued by looking at expenditure which affected individuals make on drugs to counter the resulting headaches, fever and other flu-like symptoms which some air pollutants are thought to cause. The difference between the COI and defensive expenditure approaches is that often the decision to incur these health care expenditures is not made by the individual alone, but by social administrators and ultimately the taxpayer. This can introduce uncertainties about what the COI approach is actually measuring. When the focus is expenditure made by the individual, we can be (reasonably) confident that these expenditure decisions reflect the preferences of the individual for reduced negative impacts. If an individual's expenditure rises, this reflects his assessment that the negative impact has got worse (whether in absolute physical terms, or as judged by the individual in relative terms). However, expenditure decisions made by social administrators, politicians and so on might reflect other considerations, including politics and ethics. A decision to increase expenditure in a particular area might then appear to have made the problem worse (since costs of illness have increased), even though an individual's real health status might actually have improved.

The difficulty with the COI approach can be that changes in expenditure on treatments of the health impacts of air pollution, for instance, are often not observed directly with ease. This can be the case for a number of reasons, including the fact that the link between health and air pollution is stochastic, and that air pollution tends to cause health impacts which can arise for a range of other reasons. In these cases, the costs of illness are often calculated using an approach similar to that used for calculating lost output. The lost output approach is related to the COI/defensive expenditure approaches since it uses observed or estimated market prices as the measure of value. Examples are agricultural prices for changes in agricultural yields, or wages rates for changes in labour supply.

However, unlike COI, the approach does not require an actual transaction to take place whereby costs are incurred or expenditures made. Rather, the existence of an observed or estimated price is taken as evidence that such a transaction would have occurred had the non-market impact not had an effect. An example relating again to air pollution serves to illustrate the approach. Emissions of air pollution by road transport have been linked with increased concentrations of ground-level ozone. Increased concentrations of ground-level ozone have in turn been linked with reductions in the yields of some agricultural crops. This negative pollution impact can be valued by estimating the resulting reduction in yield, and applying the observed market price for the agricultural product in question.* In this way, it is not necessary to estimate directly the reduction in agricultural revenues resulting from elevated ozone levels, which is likely to be infeasible anyway given the complexity of the pathway whereby ozone can have negative economic impacts. Rather, the lost output approach breaks down that impact pathway into manageable relationships, and thereby "constructs" the economic impact by estimating the successive impacts along the relevant pathway.

Clearly, this approach requires information on the various relationships which contribute to the economic impact we are interested in. In the examples above, this means information on the link between ozone levels and crop yields, and on air pollution levels and health impacts. These types of relationships are often estimated scientifically in the form of "exposure-response" relationships. The translation of an estimated physical response into an economic impact often requires detailed information on what the economic implications of the estimated physical response actually are. With commodities like agricultural products, the translation can be relatively straightforward, since changes

---

* In fact, given the widespread intervention in agricultural markets, it could be argued that agricultural prices no longer reflect the true economic opportunity cost of agricultural production. Hence, a strict economic approach might adjust observed prices to take account of this intervention, to obtain a "shadow price" which better reflects the true economic value of agricultural outputs.

in yields have direct economic impacts themselves. With other impacts such as those relating to health effects, the translation might be less obvious.

For instance, air pollutants have been linked with a higher prevalence of respiratory illnesses. These can range from relatively mild impacts (such as coughing or chest tightness), which cause some minor temporary discomfort but nothing more, to more disruptive impacts such as flu-type symptoms which lead to an individual spending a couple of days at home in bed. They can also be linked with even more serious impacts, such as breathing difficulties which require hospital admission, and in the limit, premature mortality. For an impact such as a hospital admission for respiratory illness, an individual might require complex medical treatments over a number of days, as well as a significant period of convalescence at home, restricting the individual's ability to work or otherwise continue his/her life normally. Conventionally, the costing of health treatments and lost work time is a conceptually and often practically simple procedure. However, in this case the issue is further complicated by the fact that pollution-related health impacts are more likely to be experienced by elderly people with pre-existing medical conditions, who no longer work and who might have few economic resources with which to express a "willingness to pay".

In practice, many of these economic valuation issues can be overcome through careful characterisation of the effects of a given impact on an individual's well-being and capability. Often, the greater difficulty arises because of a lack of good evidence on "exposure-response" or other relationships relating to physical impacts or quantities. Economic valuation using the lost output approach is greatly hindered, and often made impossible, by an absence of this type of evidence.

7.6. Summary and guidance for decision-makers

Economists have developed a range of approaches to estimate the economic value of non-market or intangible impacts. Those which we have considered in this chapter share the common feature of using market information and behaviour to infer the economic value of an associated non-market impact.

These approaches have different conceptual bases. Methods based on hedonic pricing utilise the fact that some market goods are in fact bundles of characteristics, some of which are intangible goods (or bads). By trading these market goods, consumers are thereby able to express their values for the intangible goods, and these values can be uncovered through the use of statistical techniques. This process can be hindered, however, by the fact that a market good can have several intangible characteristics, and that these can be collinear. It can also be difficult to measure the intangible characteristics in a meaningful way.

Travel cost methods utilise the fact that market and intangible goods can be complements, to the extent that purchase of market goods and services is required to access an intangible good. Specifically, people have to spend time and money travelling to recreational sites, and these costs reveal something of the value of the recreational experience to those people incurring them. The situation is complicated, however, by the fact that travel itself can have value, that the same costs might be incurred to access more than one site, and that some of the costs are themselves intangible (*e.g.* the opportunity costs of time).

Averting behaviour and defensive expenditure approaches are similar to the previous two, but differ to the extent that they refer to individual behaviour to avoid negative intangible impacts. Therefore, people might buy goods such as safety helmets to reduce accident risk, and double-glazing to reduce traffic noise, thereby revealing their valuation of these bads. However, again the situation is complicated by the fact that these market goods might have more benefits than simply that of reducing an intangible bad. Averting behaviour occurs when individuals take costly actions to avoid exposure to a non-market bad (which might, for instance, include additional travel costs to avoid a risky way of getting from A to B). Again, we need to take account of the fact that valuing these alternative actions might not be a straightforward task, for instance, if time which would have been spent doing one thing is instead used to do something else, not only avoiding exposure to the non-market impact in question, but also producing valuable economic outputs.

Finally, methods based on cost of illness and lost output calculations are based on the observation that intangible impacts can, through an often complex pathway of successive physical relationships, ultimately have measurable economic impacts on market quantities. Examples include air pollution, which can lead to an increase in medical costs incurred in treating associated health impacts, as well as a loss in wages and profit. The difficulty with these approaches is often the absence of reliable evidence, not on the economic impacts, but on the preceding physical relationships.

ISBN 92-64-01004-1
Cost-Benefit Analysis and the Environment
Recent Developments
© OECD 2006

Chapter 8

Stated Preference Approaches I: Contingent Valuation Method

Stated preference methods offer a direct survey approach to estimating willingness to pay for changes in provision of (non-market) goods. In this chapter, the most prominent example – the contingent valuation (CV) method – is discussed. The CV method is applicable to almost all non-market goods, to ex ante and ex post valuations and it is one of the few available methodologies able to capture all types of benefits from a non-market good including those unrelated to current or future use. There remain concerns about the validity and reliability of the findings of CV studies. Indeed, much of the research in this field has sought to construct rigorous tests of the robustness of the methodology across a variety of policy contexts and non-market goods and services. Much more is now known about the circumstances in which these methods work well and where problems can be expected. Such findings have had an important bearing on progressing best practice in how to design a CV questionnaire.

8.1. Introduction

A startlingly common feature of modern cost-benefit analysis has been the broadening of economic appraisals beyond those costs and benefits, which can be measured using data from actual markets. This has been an important development because many goods and services arising from public projects, programmes and policies are of an *intangible* nature and are not traded in actual markets. That is, changes in their quality or quantity cannot be measured using market data. That does not mean they do not have an economic value, but simply that analysts have to resort to more sophisticated methods for uncovering these values. In some cases, as discussed in the preceding chapter, non-market goods and services may be implicitly traded. In such instances, revealed preference methods can be used to "tease out" their values embedded in observed prices. However, a range of costs and benefits – such as some of the categories of value of environmental resources – cannot be straightforwardly inferred in this way. Indeed, in such cases, analysts are increasingly resorting to stated preference methods. In this chapter we discuss one prominent example: the contingent valuation method. In Chapter 9, we turn our attention to other stated preference methods, which are broadly grouped under the heading of "choice modelling" approaches.

Stated preference approaches are survey-based and elicit people's intended future behaviour in constructed markets. By means of an appropriately designed questionnaire, a hypothetical market is described where the good in question can be traded (Mitchell and Carson, 1989). This contingent market defines the good itself, the institutional context in which it would be provided, and the way it would be financed. A random sample of people is then directly asked to express or reveal, in some way, their maximum willingness to pay (or willingness to accept) for a hypothetical change in the level of provision of the good. Respondents are assumed to behave as though they were in a real market. One of the strengths of stated preference methods lies in their flexibility. For example, the contingent valuation method is applicable, in principle, to almost all non-market goods, to *ex ante* and *ex post* valuations and it is one of the few available methodologies able to capture *all* types of benefits from a non-market good or service including those unrelated to current or future (*i.e.* so-called non-use values).

The contingent valuation method is perhaps the dominant stated preference method or survey-based technique. Particularly from the 1990s onwards, this method has been extensively applied to the valuation of environmental impacts both in developed and developing countries. The range of environmental issues addressed is wide: water quality, outdoor recreation, species preservation, forest protection, air quality, visibility, waste management, sanitation improvements, biodiversity, health impacts, natural resource damage and environmental risk reductions to list but a few. Carson *et al.* (1995) produced a bibliography of contingent valuation published and unpublished studies: even back in 1995 their list had over 2 000 entries from more than 40 countries.

Although still controversial, this direct survey approach to estimating individual or household demand for non-market goods has been gaining increased acceptance amongst both academics and policy makers as a versatile and complete methodology for benefit estimation. Much of the impetus to this acceptance were the conclusions of the special panel appointed by the US National Oceanic and Atmospheric Administration (NOAA) in 1993 (Arrow *et al.* 1993) following the Exxon Valdez oil spill in Alaska in 1989. The panel concluded that, subject to a number of recommendations, contingent valuation studies could produce estimates reliable enough to be used in a (US) judicial process of natural resource damage assessment.

It is now over a decade since the NOAA deliberations and it is no exaggeration to say that a discussion of interim developments in the field of stated preference methods and contingent valuation in particular, could command a volume in itself. Indeed, recent important developments have included the publication of "official" guidelines for using stated preference research to inform UK public policy (Bateman *et al.* 2002) and state-of-the-art guidance on most aspects of non-market (environmental) valuation for the US (Champ *et al.* 2003). Developments have not been restricted only to the application of these tools in the field of environmental economics. There has also been important cross-fertilisation with, for example, health economics and, more recently, cultural economics. Most promisingly, much more is now known about in what circumstances stated preference methods work well – in terms of resulting in valid and reliable findings – and where problems can be expected. Such findings have had an important bearing on progressing best practice in how to design say a contingent valuation questionnaire. In this chapter, we have sought to distil some of the important developments of each of these elements.

The rest of this chapter is organised as follows. Section 8.2 discusses and evaluates a number of key points that guide good survey design, on the basis that valid and reliable estimates of non-market values are far more likely to emerge from studies which draw on the wealth of experience that can be gleaned from the literature on contingent valuation. Section 8.3 outlines issues related to divergences between mean and median WTP – an issue of particular importance in aggregating the findings from stated preference studies. Section 8.4 discusses how evidence of validity and reliability can be confirmed (or otherwise) in studies and considers a number of potential problems and biases that have been cited as being amongst the most important challenges facing contingent valuation practitioners. Finally, Section 8.4 offers some concluding remarks and policy guidance.

8.2. Designing a contingent valuation questionnaire

As with other survey techniques, a key element in any contingent valuation (CV) study is a properly designed questionnaire: *i.e.* a data-collection instrument that sets out, in a formal way, the questions designed to elicit the desired information (Dillon *et al.* 1994). Questionnaire design may seem to be a trivial task where all that is required is to put together a number of questions about the subject of interest. But this apparent simplicity lies at the root of many badly designed surveys that elicit biased, inaccurate and useless information, possibly at a great cost. In fact, even very simple questions require proper wording, format, content, placement and organisation if they are to elicit accurate information.[1] Moreover, any draft questionnaire needs to be adequately piloted before it can said to be ready for implementation in the field. In this context, Mitchell and Carson (1989, p. 120) note that:

> "the principal challenge facing the designer of a CV study is to make the scenario sufficiently understandable, plausible and meaningful to respondents so that they can and will give valid and reliable values despite their lack of experience with one or more of the scenario dimensions."

This section introduces the basics of contingent valuation questionnaire design, the typical aim of which is to elicit individual preferences, in monetary terms, for changes in the quantity or quality of a non-market good or service. The questionnaire intends to uncover individuals' estimates of how much having or avoiding the change in question is worth to them. Expressing preferences in monetary terms means finding out people's maximum willingness to pay (WTP) or minimum willingness to accept (WTA) for various changes of interest. In other words, a CV questionnaire is a survey instrument that sets out a number of questions to elicit the monetary value of a change in a non-market good. Typically, the change described is hypothetical (but could credibly be implemented with policy).

There are three basic parts to most CV survey instruments.

First, it is customary to ask a set of attitudinal and behavioural questions about the good to be valued as a preparation for responding to the valuation question and in order to reveal the most important underlying factors driving respondents' attitudes towards the public good.

Second, the contingent scenario is presented and respondents are asked for their monetary evaluations. The scenario includes a description of the commodity and the terms under which it is to be hypothetically offered. Information is also provided on the quality and reliability of provision, timing and logistics, and the method of payment. Then respondents are asked questions to determine how much they would value the good if confronted with the opportunity to obtain it under the specified terms and conditions. The elicitation question can be asked in a number of different ways as discussed later in this chapter. Respondents are also reminded of substitute goods and of the need to make compensating adjustments in other types of expenditure to accommodate the additional financial transaction.

Finally, questions about the socio-economic and demographic characteristics of the respondent are asked in order to ascertain the representativeness of the survey sample relative to the population of interest, to examine the similarity of the groups receiving different versions of the questionnaire and to study how willingness to pay varies according to respondents' characteristics.

Econometric techniques are then applied to the survey results to derive the desired welfare measures such as mean or median WTP (and are used to explain what are the most significant determinants of WTP).

In the remainder of this section we focus on the second part of a CV questionnaire referred to above. This itself comprises three interrelated stages. Specifically, this involves: i) identifying the good to be valued; ii) constructing the hypothetical scenario; and iii) eliciting the monetary values.

8.2.1. *What is the policy change being valued?*

Before starting to design the questionnaire, researchers must have a very clear idea of what policy change they want to value, *i.e.* which quality or quantity change(s) is of interest and of what particular non-market good(s) or service(s). This is in essence the formulation of the valuation problem. But as fundamental as this is, formulating the problem to be valued may not be straightforward. First, there may be scientific uncertainty surrounding the physical effects of particular changes. Second, it may be unclear how physical changes affect human well-being. Third, the effects of some changes may be difficult to translate into terms and sentences that can be readily understood by respondents. Fourth, some changes are very complex and multidimensional and cannot be adequately described within the timeframe and the means available to conduct the questionnaire. Fifth, textual descriptions of some changes may provide only a limited picture of the reality (*e.g.* changes in noise, odour, or visual impacts). Table 8.1 presents examples of changes that may be difficult to define.

Table 8.1. **Possible valuation topics and potential problems**

Change to be valued	Problems
Damages caused in a river from increased water abstractions	Scientific uncertainty surrounding the physical changes caused by increased abstractions.
	Difficulty in describing a wide range of changes in the fauna, flora, visual amenity, water quality and recreational potential, without causing information overload.
	Difficulty in isolating abstraction impacts in one river from impacts in other rivers.
	The damages may be different in different stretches of the river and in different periods of the year.
Reduced risk of contracting a disease or infection	Risk and probability changes are not easily understood.
	Difficulties in conveying the idea of small risk changes.
	Difficulties in isolating pain and suffering impacts from the cost of medication or of lost wages.
Damages caused by traffic emissions on an historical building	Difficulties in isolating the impact of traffic related air pollution and other sources of air pollution.
	Difficulty in explaining the type of damage caused (*e.g.* soiling of the stone vs. erosion of the stone).
	Difficulty in conveying the visual impacts of the change if visual aids are not used.
Damages caused by the introduction of a plant pest	Limited scientific information may not permit full identification of the wide range of environmental impacts caused by plant pests.
	Difficulty in explaining in lay terms the idea of damages to biodiversity and ecosystems.
	The impacts of a pest may be too complex to explain in the limited time that the questionnaire lasts.

8.2.2. *Constructing the hypothetical scenario*

As with all surveys, CV surveys are context dependent. That is, the values estimated are contingent on various aspects of the scenario presented and the questions asked. While some elements of the survey are expected to be neutral, others are thought to have a significant influence on respondents' valuations. These include the information provided about the good, the wording and type of the valuation questions, the institutional arrangements and the payment mechanism. Hence, the design of the hypothetical scenario and the payment mechanism is of crucial importance for the elicitation of accurate and reliable responses.

A hypothetical scenario has three essential elements:

1. A description of the policy change of interest.

2. A description of the constructed market.

3. A description of the method of payment.

Description of the policy change of interest

For single impact policies the description of the policy change to be valued entails a number of steps. Clearly, there must be a description of the attributes of the good under investigation in a way that is meaningful and understandable to respondents. Some of those issues outlined in Table 8.1 arise in this context, as it forces complex and potentially overwhelmingly large amounts of information to be translated into a few meaningful "headline indicators". The description of available substitutes for the good (its degree of local, national or global uniqueness) and of alternative expenditure possibilities may affect respondents' values and should also be part of the scenario description. Lastly, the scenario should include a description of the proposed policy change and of how the attributes of the good of interest will change accordingly.[2] In particular the *reference* (*status quo* or baseline level) and *target levels* (state of the world with the proposed change) of each attribute of interest needs to be clearly described.

If a multidimensional policy is to be appraised, then this provides extra challenges in terms of questionnaire design. For example, if the specific change being valued is part of a more inclusive policy that comprises a number of other changes occurring simultaneously (*e.g.* protecting the white tiger when protection of black rhinos, blue whales, giant pandas and mountain gorillas are also on the agenda) then it is fundamental to present the individual change as part of the broader package. This provides respondents with a chance to consider all the possible substitution, complementarity and income effects between the various policy components, which would have been impossible had the policy component been presented in isolation (which would have led to possible embedding effects and an overestimation of the value of the policy component – see Section 8.4).

One such approach is to follow a top-down procedure, whereby respondents are first asked to value the more inclusive policy and then to partition that total value across its components. There is an obvious limitation to the number of components that can be valued in such a way: as one tries to value an increasing number of policy changes, the description of each becomes necessarily shorter, reducing the accuracy of the scenario, while respondents may also become fatigued or confused. It should be noted that while contingent valuation is in theory applicable to value multidimensional changes, as described above, a more efficient way of dealing with such changes might be to adopt a choice modelling approach (see Chapter 9).

Description of the constructed market

The constructed market refers to the social context in which the hypothetical CV transaction, *i.e.* the policy change, takes place. A number of elements of the constructed market are important.

The *institution* that is responsible for providing the good or change of interest. This can be a government, a local council, a non-governmental organisation or NGO, a research institute, industry, a charity and so on. Institutional arrangements will affect WTP as respondents may hold views about particular institutions level of effectiveness, reliability and trust. *The technical and political feasibility of the change* is a fundamental consideration in the design of the questionnaire. Respondents can only provide meaningful valuations if they believe that the scenario described is feasible.

Conditions for provision of the good includes respondents' perceived payment obligation and respondents' expectations about provision. Regarding the former, there are several possibilities: respondents may believe they will have to pay the amounts they state; they may think the amount they have to pay is uncertain (more or less than their stated WTP amount); or they may be told that they will pay a fixed amount, or proportion of the costs of provision. Regarding the latter, the basic question is whether respondents believe or not that provision of the good is conditional on their WTP amount. Both types of information are important as each different combination evokes a different type of strategic behaviour (Mitchell and Carson, 1989). In particular, it is important to provide respondents with incentives to reveal their true valuations, *i.e.* to design an *incentive compatible* mechanism. We return to this issue, at various points, later in this chapter (see in particular Box 8.2).

The timing of provision – when and for how long the good will be provided – also needs to be explicitly stated. Given individual time preferences, a good provided now will be more valuable than a good provided in 10 years' time. Also, the amount of time over which the good or service will be provided can be of crucial importance. For example, the value of a programme that saves black rhinos for 20 years might only be a fraction of the value of the same programme where protection is awarded indefinitely.

Description of the method of payment

A number of aspects of the method of payment should be clearly defined in CV questionnaires. Most fundamentally, the choice of benefit measure is a fundamental step in any CV survey. Discussion of the types of measure that can be elicited as well as the choice between WTP and WTA is conducted elsewhere in this volume (see Chapter 11) and so we only note the importance of these issues in the current context. However, Box 8.1 notes a further issue regarding the possible existence and elicitation of negative WTP in situations where some respondents could just as conceivably value the *status quo*.

With regards to the payment vehicle – how the provision of the good is to be financed – the basic choice is between voluntary or coercive payments. Coercive payment vehicles include taxes, rates, fees, charges or prices. Voluntary payments are donations and gifts. The payment vehicle forms a substantive part of the overall package under evaluation and is generally believed to be a non-neutral element of the survey. Mechanisms such as income taxes and water rates are clearly non-neutral and it is relatively common to find respondents refusing to answer the valuation question on the grounds that they object in principle to paying higher taxes or water rates, in spite of the fact that the proposed change is welfare enhancing. The use of taxes also raises issues of accountability, trust in the government, knowledge that taxes are generally not hypothecated, excludes non-tax payers from the sample and may not be credible when the scenario is one of WTA, *i.e.* corresponding to a tax rebate. Voluntary payments on the other hand might encourage free-riding, as respondents have an incentive to overestimate their WTP to secure provision, with a voluntary later decision on whether or not to purchase in the future (see Box 8.2). The use of prices also poses problems as respondents may agree to pay more but simply adjust the quantities consumed so that the total expenditure remains the same.

Although there seems to be some consensus that voluntary payment vehicles should generally be avoided due to the insurmountable problem of free-riding, ultimately, the choice of the payment vehicle will depend on the actual good being studied and the context in which it is to be provided. Credibility and acceptability are important considerations here. A simple

Box 8.1. **Eliciting negative WTP**

Policy-makers often are concerned with choosing between a proposed environmental change – or number of proposed changes – and the *status quo*. To help in making such a decision, stated preference survey techniques such as the CV method may be employed to gauge the size of the welfare benefits of adopting each one of the proposed changes. In the case of changes in the provision in, for example, rural landscapes opinion could be split with some respondents favouring the change, whilst others wishing to indicate a preference for the *status quo*. In such cases, CV practitioners might consider designing a survey to allow respondents to express either a monetary value of their welfare gain or welfare loss for any particular change.

A number of studies have sought to examine this problem of *negative* WTP including Clinch and Murphy (2001) and Bohara *et al.* (2001). One example of the issues that can arise is illustrated in Atkinson *et al.* (2004). In this CV study of preferences for new designs for the towers (or pylons), which convey high voltage electricity transmission lines, opinion on the new designs was divided. Some respondents favoured a change, whilst others indicated a preference for the *status quo*. Indeed, for some respondents, a number of the new designs were considered sufficiently unsightly that they felt the landscape would be visually poorer for their installation.

For those respondents preferring a new design to the current design, WTP was elicited using the payment vehicle of a one-off change of the standing charge of their household electricity bill. For those people preferring the current design to some or all of the new tower designs, the procedure was less straightforward. Respondents could be asked for their willingness to accept a reduced standing charge as compensation for the disamenity of viewing towers of the new design. This reduction, for example, could be explained as reflecting reductions in the maintenance costs of the newer design. Here a particular respondent might prefer one change to the *status quo* whilst "dispreferring" another. Yet, within the context of seeking separate values for each of a number of different changes, this would require respondents to believe a scenario in which preferred changes happened to trigger increases in bills but less preferred changes resulted in reductions in bills. Whether respondents would find this credible or not was a question that was considered by the authors.

As an alternative, respondents were asked instead to state which of a number of increasingly arduous tasks they would perform in order to avert the replacement of the current towers with towers of a new design. These tasks are described in the first column in Table 8.2 and involved signing petitions, writing complaint letters or making donations to protest groups. Each intended action can then be given a monetary dimension by relating it to the associated value of time lost (writing letters, signing petitions) or loss of money (donations).

Table 8.2. **Translating intended actions into WTP estimates**

Intended action	Assumed WTP to retain the current design
I wouldn't do anything as I don't really care	$WTP = 0$
I would sign a petition complaining to my MP and local council	$0 < WTP < c$
I would sign a petition and independently write to my local council and/or MP and/or electricity company in order to complain	$c \leq WTP < £10 + c$
As well as signing a petition and writing letters of complaint I would be prepared to donate £10 to a group coordinating protest	$£10 + c \leq WTP < £230 + c$
As well as signing a petition and writing letters of complaint I would be prepared to donate £30 to a group coordinating protest	$WTP \geq £230 + c$

Note: c is the value in money terms of the time, effort and expense involved in writing a letter of complaint.

Source: Atkinson *et al.* (2004).

Box 8.1. **Eliciting negative WTP** (cont.)

The second column in Table 8.2 describes the results of imputing WTP values to each of the possible actions to avoid replacing the current design where the value in money terms of the time, effort and expense involved in writing a letter of complaint is described by c. A respondent who indicated that he/she would not do anything was assumed to be stating indifference, i.e. a zero WTP to retain the current design. A respondent stating that they would sign a petition but not go as far as writing a letter to their MP was assumed to be indicating that they were not indifferent but would not suffer a sufficient welfare loss to invest the time, effort and expense in writing a letter. Hence, their WTP was larger than zero but less than c. A respondent stating they would write a letter but would not pay GBP 10 to a protest group was indicating that their welfare loss lay in the interval between c (inclusive) and c + GBP 10 (exclusive). Respondents stating they would write a letter and pay GBP 10 to a fighting fund but not pay GBP 30 were indicating that their welfare loss lay in the interval above or equal to c + GBP 10 but below c + GBP 30. For those willing to donate GBP 30, it can be inferred that their maximum WTP is above or equal to c + GBP 30.

Given that c is of an unknown magnitude, the assumption was made that it takes an hour to produce and mail such a letter. Put another way, c is the value the household places on one hour of its time. Following some frequently used assumptions concerning the value of non-labour time, c is calculated from the annual after-tax income. Specifically, the value of time is taken as a third of the wage rate, which is approximated as a two-thousandth of the annual after-tax income of the household.

Box 8.2. **Coercion vs. voluntarism and WTP for a public good**

Carson, Groves and Machina (1999) have analysed extensively the conditions under which CV respondents have incentives to free-ride. They conclude that the provision of a public good by means of voluntary contributions is particularly troublesome as there is a strong incentive to overstate WTP in the survey context (if stated WTP is perceived to be unrelated to actual payment). This is because overstating hypothetical WTP increases the chances of provision of the desired public good without having to pay for it. Conversely, respondents may choose to free-ride (state a lower WTP value than they would pay in reality) if stated values were perceived to translate credibly into actual contributions. The implication is that voluntary contribution mechanisms should generally be avoided in CV surveys, as that seems to be the cause of the bias rather than the hypothetical nature of the method. Incentive compatible payment methods should be used to minimise the risk of strategic behaviour.

A study by Champ et al. (2002) has sought to test some of these ideas. The authors examined three types of payment vehicle, which they used to elicit WTP for the creation of an open space in Boulder County, Colorado: (A) voluntary individual contribution to a trust fund; (B) voluntary individual contribution to a trust fund, which would be reimbursed in full if the open space project did not go ahead; and, (C) one-off tax on residents based on the results of a referendum. Assuming that respondents believed their WTP values could form the basis of the charge they would actually face to finance the project, it was hypothesised that theory (as just described) would predict that:

1. WTP (C) ≤ WTP(A)

2. WTP(C) ≤ WTP(B)

3. WTP(A) ≤ WTP(B)

> ### Box 8.2. **Coercion *vs.* voluntarism and WTP for a public good** *(cont.)*
>
> Put another way, the authors reckoned that the relatively coercive form(s) of payment vehicle would be less likely to encourage free-riding than the relatively voluntary form(s). The findings of this study appear to confirm this in part as strong evidence was detected for the first prediction. That is, WTP in form of a tax (C) was significantly greater than WTP in the form of voluntary contributions (A). While there was less strong evidence (if any) for the remaining two hypotheses, these findings, nevertheless, provide some support for the conjecture that coercive payment vehicles reduce implicit behaviour that might be interpreted as having some strategic element. However, as the authors note this is just one desirable criterion of a payment vehicle and, in practice, the credibility of any payment medium will also play a large part in determining its relative merits.

guideline is to use the vehicle, which is likely to be employed in the real world decision: *i.e.* if water rates are the method by which the change in provision will be affected then there should be a presumption in favour of using water rates or charges in the contingent market. A caveat to this guide arises where this causes conflict with certain of the criteria set out above. For example, a study by Georgiou *et al.* (1998) found considerable resistance to the use of a water rates or charge vehicle in the immediate aftermath of the privatisation of the public water utilities in the UK. As a practical matter, in such cases, the use of a different payment vehicle (if credible) might well be justified.

Eliciting monetary values

After the presentation of the hypothetical scenario, the provision mechanism and the payment mechanism, respondents are asked questions to determine how much they would value the good if confronted with the opportunity to obtain it, under the specified terms and conditions.

The elicitation question can be asked in a number of different ways. Table 8.3 summarises the principal formats of eliciting values as applied to the case of valuing changes in landscape around Stonehenge (a UK World Heritage Site) (Maddison and Mourato, 2002). The examples in the table all relate to the elicitation of WTP but could easily be framed in terms of WTA.

The direct *open-ended* elicitation format is a straightforward way of uncovering values: it does not provide respondents with cues about what the value of the change might be, is very informative as maximum WTP can be identified for each respondent and requires relatively straightforward statistical techniques. Hence, there is no anchoring or starting point bias: *i.e.* respondents are not influenced by the starting values and succeeding bids used. However, CV practitioners due to a number of problems have progressively abandoned it. Open-ended questioning leads to large non-response rates, protest answers, zero answers and outliers and generally to unreliable responses (Mitchell and Carson, 1989). This is because it may be very difficult for respondents to come up with their true maximum WTP, "out of the blue", for a change they are unfamiliar with and have never thought about valuing before. Moreover, most daily market transactions involve deciding whether or not to buy goods at given prices, rather than stating maximum WTP values.

The *bidding game* was one of the most widely used technique used in the 1970s and 1980s. In this approach, as in an auction, respondents are faced with several rounds of discrete choice questions, with the final question being an open-ended WTP question. This iterative format was reckoned to facilitate respondents' thought processes and thus encourage them to consider their preferences carefully. A major disadvantage lies in the possibility of anchoring or starting point bias. It also leads to large number of outliers, that is unrealistically large bids and to a phenomenon that has been labelled as "yea-saying", that is respondents accepting to pay the specified amounts to avoid the socially embarrassing position of having to say no.

Payment card approaches were developed as improved alternatives to the open-ended and bidding game methods. Presenting respondents with a visual aid containing a large number of monetary amounts facilitates the valuation task, by providing a context to their bids, while avoiding starting point bias at the same time. The number of outliers is also reduced in comparison to the previous methods. Some versions of the payment card show how the values in the card relate to actual household expenditures or taxes (benchmarks). The payment card is nevertheless vulnerable to biases relating to the range of the numbers used in the card and the location of the benchmarks.

Single-bounded dichotomous choice or referendum methods became increasingly popular in the 1990s. This elicitation format is thought to simplify the cognitive task faced by respondents (respondents only have to make a judgement about a given price, in the same way as they decide whether or not to buy a supermarket good at a certain price) while at

Table 8.3. **Examples of common elicitation formats**

Format	Description
Open ended	*What is the maximum amount that you would be prepared to pay every year, through a tax surcharge, to improve the landscape around Stonehenge in the ways I have just described?*
Bidding game	*Would you pay GBP 5 every year, through a tax surcharge, to improve the landscape around Stonehenge in the ways I have just described?* If Yes: Interviewer keeps increasing the bid until the respondent answers No. Then maximum WTP is elicited. If No: Interviewer keeps decreasing the bid until respondent answers Yes. Then maximum WTP is elicited.
Payment card	*Which of the amounts listed below best describes your maximum willingness to pay every year, through a tax surcharge, to improve the landscape around Stonehenge in the ways I have just described?* 0 GBP 0.5 GBP 1 GBP 2 GBP 3 GBP 4 GBP 5 GBP 7.5 GBP 10 GBP 14.5 GBP 15 GBP 20 GBP 30 GBP 40 GBP 50 GBP 75 GBP 100 GBP 150 GBP 200 > GBP 200
Single-bounded dichotomous choice	*Would you pay GBP 5 every year, through a tax surcharge, to improve the landscape around Stonehenge in the ways I have just described?* (the price is varied randomly across the sample)
Double-bounded dichotomous choice	*Would you pay GBP 5 every year, through a tax surcharge, to improve the landscape around Stonehenge in the ways I have just described?* (the price is varied randomly across the sample) If Yes: *And would you pay GBP 10?* If No: *And would you pay GBP 1?*

the same time providing incentives for the truthful revelation of preferences under certain circumstances (that is, it is in the respondent's strategic interest to accept the bid if his WTP is greater or equal than the price asked and to reject otherwise, see Box 8.2 for an explanation of incentive compatibility). This procedure minimises non-response and avoids outliers. The presumed supremacy of the dichotomous choice approach reached its climax in 1993 when it received the endorsement of the NOAA panel (Arrow *et al.* 1993). However, enthusiasm for closed-ended formats gradually waned as an increasing number of empirical studies revealed that values obtained from dichotomous choice elicitation were significantly and substantially larger than those resulting from comparable open-ended questions. Some degree of yea-saying is also possible. In addition, dichotomous choice formats are relatively inefficient in that less information is available from each respondent (the researcher only knows whether WTP is above or below a certain amount), so that larger samples and stronger statistical assumptions are required. This makes surveys more expensive and their results more sensitive to the statistical assumptions made.

Double-bounded dichotomous choice formats are more efficient than their single-bounded counterpart as more information is elicited about each respondent's WTP. For example, we know that a person's true value lies between GBP 5 and GBP 10 if she accepted to pay GBP 5 in the first question but rejected GBP 10 in the second. But all the limitations of the single-bounded procedure still apply in this case. An added problem is the possible loss of incentive compatibility due to the fact that the second question may not be viewed by respondents as exogenous to the choice situation and the added possibility of anchoring and yea-saying biases.

Recent developments in elicitation formats includes Hanemann and Kanninen's (1999) proposal of a *one and a half bound dichotomous choice* procedure whereby respondents are initially informed that costs of providing the good in question will be between X and Y (X < Y), with the amounts X and Y being varied across the sample. Respondents are then asked whether they are prepared to pay the lower amount X. If the response is negative no further questions are asked; if the response is positive then respondents are asked if they would pay amount Y. Conversely respondents may be presented with the upper amount Y initially and asked about amount X if the former is refused.

Key problems arising for each elicitation format are summarised in Table 8.4. Of course, these weaknesses need to be scrutinised in the light of the strengths that each approach possesses. Hence, considering the pros and cons of each of the approaches above, contributions such as Bateman *et al.* (2002) and Champ *et al.* (2003) typically recommend dichotomous choice approaches and, to some extent, payment cards. The latter are more informative about respondents' WTP, cheaper to implement than the former and are superior to both direct open-ended questions and bidding games. The former may be incentive compatible and facilitates respondents' valuation task.[3] The new variants

Table 8.4. **Elicitation formats – some stylised facts**

Elicitation format	Main problems
Open-ended	Large number of zero responses, few small positive responses
Bidding game	Final estimate shows dependence on starting point used
Payment card	Weak dependence of estimate on amounts used in the card
Single-bounded dichotomous choice	Estimates typically higher than other formats
Double-bounded dichotomous choice	The two responses do not correspond to the same underlying WTP distribution

Source: Carson *et al.* (2001).

Box 8.3. **Value uncertainty and WTP**

It seems plausible that some individuals may not have precise preferences for changes in the provision of certain non-market goods. Within stated preference studies this might manifest itself in respondent difficulty in expressing single and exact values. If so, then it might be worthwhile to allow respondents to express a range of values within which, for example, their WTP would most likely reside. A few studies have attempted to allow respondents in CV surveys to be able to express this uncertainty. For example, Dubourg *et al.* (1997) and Hanley and Kriström (2003) both adapt a payment card elicitation format in order to assess the significance of this uncertainty.

The latter study describes a CV survey of WTP for improvements in coastal water quality in two locations in Scotland. A payment card (see Figure 8.1) with values ranging from GBP 1 to GBP 125 was presented to those respondents in their sample of the Scottish population around these locations – who had indicated that their WTP for the improvement was positive. In order to test whether these particular respondents were uncertain about their exact WTP, the authors posed the valuation question in two ways.

First, respondents were asked if they would definitely pay the lowest amount on the card (*i.e.* GBP 1) for improving coastal water quality. If the answer was "yes" then the respondent was asked whether they would definitely pay the second lowest amount on the card (*i.e.* GBP 2) and so and on and so forth with successively higher amounts being proposed until the respondent said "no" to a particular amount.

Second, in addition to this conventional way of eliciting WTP using a payment card, respondents were then asked to consider whether the highest amount on the payment card (*i.e.* GBP 125) was too much for them to pay. If "yes" then the respondent was asked whether the second highest amount on the card (*i.e.* 104) was too much to pay and so on and so forth with successively lower amounts being proposed to the respondent until the respondent stated that they were not sure that a particular amount was too much.

Figure 8.1. **Payment card in CV study of improvements in Scottish coastal waters**

£ per annum	A: I would devinitely pay per year (✓)	B: I would NOT devinitely pay per year (✗)
1	✓	
2	✓	
5	✓	
10	✓	
13	✓	
15	✓	
20	✓	
26	✓	
34	✓	
40		✗
52		✗
60		✗
65		✗
70		✗
93		✗
104		✗
125		✗

Source: Adapted form Hanley and Kriström (2003).

> Box 8.3. **Value uncertainty and WTP** (*cont.*)
>
> An illustration of the end of this process is described in Figure 8.1. This describes the notion of uncertainty that was captured by this way of posing the WTP question. It is the difference between the ticks and crosses on this payment card that indicates how uncertain respondents are about their exact WTP. That is, the respondent would definitely not pay GBP 60 but is not sure whether amounts ranging between GBP 34 and < GBP 60 are too much. Understanding more about the source of this uncertainty – *e.g.* it may stem from a number of candidate explanations – and whether it varies depending on the non-market good being valued are clearly important questions for future research of this kind.

described (the one and a half bound approach and the randomised card sorting procedure) also show potential although further research is needed before they become established.[4] A final consideration is that while it is of utmost importance to find out which elicitation format is the more valid and reliable, some degree of variety in use of formats should be expected. For example, as Box 8.3 illustrates certain types of elicitation format are better suited for answering particular methodological issues than others.

8.3. Mean *versus* median willingness to pay

In using the findings of a cost-benefit analysis (CBA), a decision-maker accepts measures of individuals' preferences, expressed as WTP sums, as valid measures of the welfare consequences of a given change in provision of say some public good. Generally, no account is taken of how ability to pay might constrain those WTP sums (*i.e.* the present distribution of income is taken as given) and those expressing a higher WTP are considered as simply reflecting their higher preferences for the good. (However, see Chapter 15 for a discussion of ways in which to take account of the distribution). In this system, mean WTP is preferred to median WTP as a more accurate reflection of the variance in preferences across the mass of individuals whose aggregation is considered to represent society's preference.

For a number of CV studies of environmental and cultural goods, a not uncommon finding is that the distribution of WTP is skewed. For example, there is a very small number of respondents bidding very large values and a very large number of respondents bidding very small (or even zero) values. In other words, the problem in such cases is that *mean* WTP gives "excessive" weight to a minority of respondents who have strong and positive preferences. While mean WTP is the theoretically correct measure to use in CBA, median WTP is arguably the better predictor of what the majority of people would actually be willing to pay (when there is a wide distribution of values). From a practical viewpoint this is important if a decision-maker wishes to capture some portion of the benefits of a project in order to recover the costs of its implementation. As median WTP reflects what the majority of people would be willing to pay, passing on no more than this amount to individuals should have a correspondingly greater degree of public acceptability than seeking to pass on an amount which is closer to a mean WTP, which has been overly influenced by a relatively few very large bids. However, this argument, between the dominance of preference values or a referendum, is an ongoing debate within environmental economics, which has yet to be resolved. In short, if mean and median measures deserve consideration in contemporary decision-making then there is a corresponding need for CV studies to report both measures.

8.4. Validity and reliability

Despite numerous methodological improvements and a widespread application particularly in the field of environmental economics, the contingent valuation method still raises substantial controversy. One of the main areas of concern regards the ability of the method to produce valid and reliable estimates of WTP. A number of factors may systematically bias respondents' answers. These factors are not specific to CV studies but are common to most survey based techniques and are mostly attributable to survey design and implementation problems. Mitchell and Carson (1989) provide an extensive review.

Possible types of bias include: hypothetical bias (umbrella designation for problems arising from the hypothetical nature of the CV market); strategic behaviour (such as free-riding); embedding/scope problems (where the valuation is insensitive to the scope of the good); anchoring bias (where the valuation depends of the first bid presented see Section 8.2.2 above); and, information bias (when the framing of the question unduly influences the answer). We discuss several of these biases in more detail in what follows.

It is not straightforward to assess the validity (*i.e.* the degree to which a study measures the intended quantity) and reliability (*i.e.* the degree of replicability of a measurement) of the estimates produced by contingent valuation studies for the obvious reason that actual WTP is unobserved. Nevertheless it is possible to test indirectly various aspects of validity and reliability.

One obvious test is to check whether CV results conform to the predictions of economic theory. This corresponds to the concept of *theoretical validity*. In general, theoretical validity tests examine the influence of a number of demographic, economic, attitudinal and locational variables, thought to be WTP determinants, on some measure of the estimated WTP. The test is normally formulated by regressing estimated WTP on these variables and checking whether the coefficients are significant with the expected sign and size. These tests are now standard CV practice and most studies report them. A common theoretical validity test (for say dichotomous choice formats) is to check whether the percentage of respondents willing to pay a particular price falls as the price they are asked to pay increases. This is similar to a negative price elasticity of demand for a private good and is generally tested by checking whether the price coefficient is negative and significant. The condition is almost universally observed in CV studies (Carson *et al.* 1996).

Another test involves observing whether WTP increases with the size of the quantity or quality of the good being offered. Compliance of CV estimates with this scope test is one of the most controversial points in the CV validity debate. Insensitivity to scope is often called the "embedding effect". Scope tests can be internal: whereby the same sample is asked to value different levels of the good. Or these tests can be external: where different but equivalent sub-samples are asked to value different levels of the good. Internal tests of scope typically reject the embedding hypothesis. The focus of the controversy has been based on the more powerful external scope tests.

In two widely cited studies, Kahneman and Knetsch (1992) and Desvousges *et al.* (1993) found that individuals' CV responses did not vary significantly with changes in the scope and coverage of the good being valued. A number of explanations were advanced for this phenomenon. For the environmental example, Kahneman and Knetsch (1992) argued that, because individuals' do not possess strongly articulated preferences for environmental goods, they tend to focus on other facets of the environment, such as the moral satisfaction associated with giving to a good cause. This "warm glow" effect would be independent of the size of the cause. Others have argued that embedding is more an artefact of poor survey design (for example, Smith, 1992). Another suggestion is that, to make valuation and financial decisions easier, people think in terms of a system of expenditure budgets, or "mental accounts", to which they allocate their income (Thaler, 1984). For environmental improvements, if the amount allocated to the "environment account" is quite small, then this might result in an inability to adjust valuations substantially in response to changes in the size and scope of an environmental good. Essentially, embedding might be a result of valuations' being determined by an income constraint which is inflexible and relatively strict compared with assessments of an individual's total (or full) income.

To assess the empirical importance of this phenomenon, Carson (1998) undertook a comprehensive review of the literature on split-sample tests of sensitivity to scope. This showed that, since 1984, 31 studies rejected the insensitivity hypothesis while 4 did not. Another way of looking at this issue involves comparing different studies valuing similar goods. A meta-analysis of valuation of air quality improvements (Smith and Osborne, 1996) also rejected the embedding hypothesis and showed that CV estimates from different studies varied in a systematic and expected way with differences in the characteristics of the good. Hence, it seems that early conclusions about the persistence of insensitivity to scope can partly be attributed to the lack of statistical power in the test used to detect differences in values.

Many practitioners have concluded that insensitivity to scope – to the extent that it exists – is normally a product of misspecified scenarios or vague and abstract definitions of the policy change that can lead respondents not to perceive any real difference between impacts of varying scope (Carson and Mitchell, 1995). A clear, detailed and meaningful definition of the scope of the proposed policy change is therefore required. Nevertheless, there are instances where describing the scope of policy changes is particularly difficult. A typical example is the presentation of small changes in health risks where insensitivity to scope has consistently been found, despite researchers efforts to convey the information in simple and "respondent-friendly" ways (see Box 8.4).

Another common theoretical validity test consists of analysing the relationship between income and WTP. If the environmental good being valued is a normal good, then a positive and significant income coefficient is to be expected. A positive income elasticity of WTP that is significantly less than one is the usual empirical finding in CV studies of environmental goods. The small magnitude of this income elasticity has been the focus of some of the criticism directed at contingent values: since most environmental commodities are generally regarded as luxury goods rather than necessity goods, many authors expected to find larger than unity income elasticities of WTP. However, as Flores and Carson (1997) point out, CV studies yield income elasticities of WTP for a fixed quantity, which are different from income elasticities of demand, a measure based on varying quantity. The authors show that a luxury good in the demand sense can have an income elasticity of WTP which is less than zero, between zero and one or greater than one. They also analyse the conditions under which the income elasticity of WTP is likely to be smaller than the corresponding income elasticity of demand.

Box 8.4. **Risk insensitivity in stated preference studies**

Past evidence has indicated that respondent WTP, in stated preference surveys, might be insufficiently sensitive to the size of the reduction in risk specified and that this is particularly the case for changes in very small baseline risks (Jones-Lee *et al.* 1985; Beattie *et al.* 1998). In a comprehensive review, Hammitt and Graham (1999) concluded that: *"Overall, the limited evidence available concerning health-related CV studies is not reassuring with regard to sensitivity of WTP to probability variation"* (p. 40). Interestingly, however, Corso *et al.* (2000) found that, on the one hand, there was evidence of risk insensitivity when risk reductions were only communicated *verbally* to respondents but, on the other hand, there was significant evidence of risk sensitivity when risk changes were also communicated *visually*.

This particular visual variant has been used successfully in a study, of the preferences of individuals for reductions in mortality risks in Canada and the US, by Alberini *et al.* (2004). Respondents were asked – in the a dichotomous choice format – for their WTP to reduce this risk by *either* 1 in 1 000 or 5 in 5 000: *i.e.* an external scope test. In order to assist them to visualise these small changes, the authors used the type of risk communication mechanism recommended by Corso *et al.* (2000), which in this case was a 1000 square grid where red squares represented the prevalence of risks (used along side other devices to familiarise respondents with the idea of mortality risk). Initial questions to respondents sought to identify those who had grasped these ideas and those who apparently had not. For example, respondents were asked to compare grids for two hypothetical people and to state which of the two had the higher risk of dying. Interestingly, roughly 12% of respondents in both the US and Canada failed this test in that they (wrongly) chose the person with the lower risk of dying (*i.e.* fewer red squares on that hypothetical person's grid).

The point of this, and other screening questions that the authors used, was to identify those respondents in the sample who "adequately" comprehended risks – in the sense of readiness to answer subsequent WTP questions – and those who did not. The authors' expectations were that the responses of those in the former group were more likely to satisfy a test of scope (*e.g.* proportionality of WTP with the size of the change in risk) than those "contaminated" by the responses of those in the latter group. However, while the authors find that restricting the analysis to those who passed risk tests leads to significantly different WTP amounts for the 1 in 1 000 and 1 in 5 000 risk reductions, this does not result in the sort of proportionality that many demand of this particular scope test: *i.e.* is WTP for the 5 in 1 000 risk change (about) 5 times WTP for the 1 in 1 000 risk change?

Table 8.5. **A scope test for mortality risks (Median WTP, USD)**

Risk reduction	Canada median WTP		US median WTP	
	More confident	Less confident	More confident	Less confident
5 in 1 000	USD 414	USD 268	USD 205	USD 445
1 in 1 000	USD 126	USD 136	USD 23	USD 236
Ratio	3.3	2.0	8.9	1.9

Source: Alberini *et al.* (2004).

What seems to make a difference in this study is a subsequent self-assessment question based on how confident a respondent felt he (she) was about his (her) WTP response. The results are summarised in Table 8.5. More confident respondents, on balance, appear to state WTP amounts, which pass the stricter scope test of proportionately. (The ratios of median WTP are not exactly 5 in either the US or Canadian case. However, the important thing here is there numbers are not significantly different from this value.) The median WTP values based only on those respondents who were not so confident about their WTP answers, by contrast, did not pass this particular scope test. In other words, these findings appear to provide some important clues in the understanding of WTP and risk insensitivity.

A common claim of CV critics is that WTP estimates, obtained in this way, represent gross overestimates of respondents' true values (*e.g.* Cummings *et al.* 1986). One indirect way of addressing the importance of this validity issue is to compare the estimates derived from a CV study with values for the same good derived from alternative valuation methods based upon revealed preferences. This corresponds to testing for *convergent validity*. Carson *et al.* (1996) conducted a meta-analysis looking at 616 estimates from 83 studies that used more than one valuation method. The authors concluded that, in general, contingent valuation estimates were very similar and somewhat smaller than revealed preference estimates, with both being highly correlated (with 0.78-0.92 correlation coefficients). This finding lends support to the claim that the values estimated by CV studies provide reasonable estimates of the value of environmental goods, very similar to those based on actual observed behaviour, in spite of the hypothetical nature of the method. The usefulness of convergent validity testing is however restricted to quasi-public goods as only estimates of use values can be compared due to the limited scope of revealed preference techniques. Hence, values for pure public goods cannot be analysed in this way.

A somewhat different concept is that of reliability, which can cast light on this particular issue, a measure of the stability and reproducibility of a measure. A common test of reliability is to assess the replicability of CV estimates over time (test-retest procedure). McConnell *et al.* (1997) reviewed the available evidence on temporal reliability tests and found a high correlation between individuals WTP over time (generally between 0.5 and 0.9), regardless of the nature of the good and the population being surveyed, indicating that the contingent valuation method appears to be a reliable measurement approach. In addition, the original state-of-the-art Alaska Exxon Valdez questionnaire (Carson *et al.,* 2003) was administered to a new sample two years later: the coefficients on the two regression equations predicting WTP were almost identical (Carson *et al.,* 1997). (See Chapter 17 for a discussion of reliability and benefits transfer.)

Arguably, an even more powerful and direct way of checking the validity and accuracy of contingent values is to compare contingent valuation hypothetical values with "true" or "real" values, when these can be discerned in actual behaviour. These *criterion validity* tests analyse the extent to which the hypothetical nature of the CV systematically biases the results, when all other factors are controlled for. This is the most difficult validity test to perform as is not feasible for many types of good. Indeed, many of the criterion validity tests have been conducted in a laboratory setting, using simulated, "real money" transactions and most have been undertaken with private goods. An interesting and novel extension of this experimental work is described in Box 8.5.

Foster *et al.* (1997) conducted a review of the literature in this area covering both field and laboratory experiments. Voluntary payment mechanisms are typically used. The empirical evidence shows that there is a tendency of hypothetical CV studies to exaggerate actual WTP. Most calibration factors (*i.e.* ratios of hypothetical to actual WTP) were found to fall in the range of 1.3 to 14. In order to explain what accounts for this discrepancy between real and hypothetical values, Foster *et al.* (1997) also conducted an experiment comparing data on actual donations to a fund-raising appeal for an endangered bird-species with CV studies focusing on similar environmental resources. The main finding was that the divergence between the data on real and hypothetical valuations might be due as much to free riding behaviour – because of the voluntary nature of the payment mechanism – as to the hypothetical nature of the CV approach.

Box 8.5. **Hypothetically speaking: Cheap talk and contingent valuation**

A small but growing number of studies have sought to investigate the impact on hypothetical biasof adapting "cheap talk" (CT) concepts (defined as the costless transmission of information) in CV-like experiments. These studies include the pioneering experiments of Cummings and Taylor (1999) and Brown *et al.* (2003).

Hypothetical bias is described in these studies as the difference in what an individual says s/he would pay in a hypothetical setting *vis-à-vis* what s/he pays when the payment context is real. CT adds an additional text/script to the (hypothetical) question posed explaining the problem of hypothetical bias and asking respondents to answer as if the payment context was real. Put another way, the objective of this approach to see if people can be talked out of behaving as if the experiment was hypothetical.

Although, there are a number of psychological concerns about the effect that this CT information will have on respondents – will it bias them the other way and/or be too blatant a warning? – the results from these studies have been both interesting and important. For example, Cummings and Taylor (1999) only use one bid level which participants are asked to vote "yes" or "no" to. They find the CT-script to work well in reducing hypothetical biasthat in bringing stated WTP amounts more in line with actual payments. Brown *et al.* (2003) vary the bid-level across respondents and still find that CT works well on the same terms as just mentioned.

Most of these studies are based on experiments using (paid) university students; *i.e.* not based on applications in the field amongst the public. This enables the CT-script to be on the long side. One concern is that the script would have to have much shorter if this method was to be widely applied and the impacts of script-shortening on survey success do not appear to be encouraging in experiments (Loomis *et al.* 1996) or in the field (Poe *et al.* 1997).

8.5. Conclusions and guidance for policy makers

Although controversial in some quarters, the contingent valuation method has gained increased acceptance amongst many academics and policy makers as a versatile and powerful methodology for estimating the monetary value of non-market impacts of projects and policies. Stated preference methods more generally offer a direct survey approach to estimating individual or household preferences and more specifically WTP amounts for changes in provision of (non-market) goods, which are related to respondents' underlying preferences in a consistent manner. Hence, this technique is of particular worth when assessing impacts on non-market goods, the value of which cannot be uncovered using revealed preference methods. However, it is worth noting that contingent valuation methods are often being used even where a revealed preference option is available.

This growing interest has resulted in research in the field of contingent valuation evolving substantially over the past 10 to 15 years or so. For example, the favoured choice of elicitation formats for WTP questions in contingent valuation surveys has already passed through a number of distinct stages, as previously discussed in this chapter. This does not mean that uniformity in the design of stated preference surveys can be expected any time soon. Nor would this particular development necessarily be desirable. The discussion in this chapter has illustrated findings from studies that show how, for example, legitimate priorities to minimise respondent strategic bias by always opting for incentive compatible payment mechanisms must be balanced against equally justifiable concerns about the credibility of a payment vehicle. The point is the answer to this problem is likely to vary across different types of project and policy problems.

There remain concerns about the validity and reliability of the findings of contingent valuation studies. Indeed, much of the research in this field has sought to construct rigorous tests of the robustness of the methodology across a variety of policy contexts and non-market goods and services. By and large, the overview provided in the latter part of this chapter has struck an optimistic note about the use of the contingent valuation to estimate the value of non-market goods. In this interpretation of recent developments, there is a virtuous circle between translating the lessons from tests of validity and reliability into practical guidance for future survey design. Indeed, many of the criticisms of the technique can be said to be imputable to problems at the survey design and implementation stage rather than to some intrinsic methodological flaw. Taken as a whole, the empirical findings largely support the validity and reliability of CV estimates. There are exceptions to this positive assessment. Chapter 11, for example, discusses in detail the view that WTP/WTA disparities are far being an artefact of the way in which say CV questions are asked.

On the whole, developments in CV research overwhelmingly point to the merits (in terms of validity and reliability) of good quality studies and so point to the need for practitioners to follow, in some way, guidelines for best practice. While the NOAA guidelines continue to be a focal point, there are a number of more recent guidelines (*e.g.* Bateman *et al.* 2002 which is intended to guide official applications of stated preference methods in the UK and Champ *et al.* 2003 for the US), which also provide useful and state-of-art reference points for practitioners.

Notes

1. Clearly, there are general principles for writing valid questions and of questionnaire form and layout as well as guidelines in the context of stated preference research. Guidelines as regards these general issues can be found in a number of sources (see, for example, Tourangeau *et al.* 2000).

2. Describing the good and the policy change of interest may require a combination of textual information, photographs, drawings, maps, charts and graphs.

3. It is worth mentioning some adjustments that have to be made in the arguments presented above when WTA is used rather than WTP. First, contrary to what happens when WTP is used, under a WTA format, open-ended elicitation procedures will produce higher average values than dichotomous choice procedures. Open-ended elicitation may also yield very large outliers. In this case, dichotomous choice is the conservative approach. Given that WTA measures are not constrained by income, respondents may have a tendency to overbid. Attention may have to be given to mechanisms to counteract this tendency.

4. Whatever the elicitation format adopted respondents are reminded of substitute goods and of their budget constraints and the related need to make compensating adjustments in other types of expenditure to accommodate the additional financial transaction implied by the survey. The former reminds respondents that the good in question may not be unique and that this has implications upon its value, the latter reminds respondents of their limited incomes and of the need to trade-off money for environmental improvements. Once the WTP elicitation process is over, debriefing and follow-up questions can help the analyst to understand why respondents were or were not willing to pay for the change presented. These questions are important to identify invalid (*e.g.* protest) answers: that is, answers that do not reflect people's welfare change from the good considered.

ISBN 92-64-01004-1
Cost-Benefit Analysis and the Environment
Recent Developments
© OECD 2006

Chapter 9

Stated Preference Approaches II: Choice Modelling

Widely used in the market research and transport literatures, choice modelling (CM) (which is actually a family of survey-based methodologies) has only relatively recently been applied to the environment. A clear strength of CM lays in this ability to value environmental changes which are multidimensional. What this means is that an environmental asset affected by a policy often will give rise to changes in component attributes each of which command distinct valuations. CM approaches are able to quantify marginal or unit values of each attribute or dimension that comprise some environmental change. On one interpretation, CM is most useful as a stated preference method where an environmental problem is complex or multidimensional and proposed policy options are not only numerous but also provide different combinations of these multiple dimensions. However, CM studies reflecting intricate environmental changes are themselves complex to design and to analyse. With regards to the validity of responses, the cognitive difficulty of choosing between options in (multiple) choice sets is a prominent concern.

9.1. Introduction

There is general acceptance amongst both practitioners and policy makers that the contingent valuation method is the most versatile and powerful methodology for estimating the monetary value of changes in non-market goods. However, as the previous chapter showed, the embrace of this method does not mean that its problems are no longer acknowledged. And while contingent valuation is the most familiar valuation technique based on stated preferences, there has been growing interest in choice modelling (CM) approaches.[1] While CM has been widely used in the market research and transport literatures (*e.g.* Green and Srinivasan, 1978; Henscher, 1994) it has only relatively recently been applied to other areas such as the environment.

In the environmental context, at least some of this emerging interest in CM has arisen as a response to the problems of contingent valuation. Some of the arguments behind claims that CM can overcome certain of these problems are largely, at this time, a matter of speculation. However, a clear strength of CM lies in its ability to value changes which are multidimensional: that is, entailing changes in a number of attributes of interest. (Indeed, the conceptual microeconomic framework for choice modelling lies in Lancaster's [1966] characteristics theory of value which assumes that consumers' utilities for goods can be decomposed into utilities for composing characteristics.) Contingent valuation, typically, would be used to uncover the value of the total change in a multi-dimensional good. If policy-makers require measures of the change in each of the dimensions or attributes of the good then some variant of choice modelling might be considered.

Regarding the specifics of these approaches, CM is a family of survey-based methodologies for modelling preferences for goods, where goods are described in terms of their attributes and of the levels that these attributes take. Respondents are presented with various alternative descriptions of a good, differentiated by their attributes and levels, and are asked to rank the various alternatives, to rate them or to choose their most preferred. By including price/cost as one of the attributes of the good, willingness to pay (WTP can be indirectly recovered from people's rankings, ratings or choices. As with contingent valuation, CM can also measure all forms of value including non-use values.

This chapter is organised as follows. Section 9.2 contains a descriptive analysis of the main CM techniques. Section 9.3 then summarises the advantages and disadvantages of CM and compares its performance with contingent valuation. Section 9.4 then offers concluding remarks and guidance.

9.2. Choice modelling techniques

A typical choice modelling (CM) exercise is characterised by a number of key stages. These are described in Table 9.1. Individual preferences can be uncovered in CM surveys by asking respondents to rank the options presented to them, to score them or to choose their most preferred.

Table 9.1. **Stages of a choice modelling exercise**

Stage	Description
Selection of attributes	Identification of relevant attributes of the good to be valued. Literature reviews and focus groups are used to select attributes that are relevant to people while expert consultations help to identify the attributes that will be impacted by the policy. A monetary cost is typically one of the attributes to allow the estimation of WTP.
Assignment of levels	The attribute levels should be feasible, realistic, non-linearly spaced, and span the range of respondents' preference maps. Focus groups, pilot surveys, literature reviews and consultations with experts are instrumental in selecting appropriate attribute levels. A baseline "status quo" level is usually included.
Choice of experimental design	Statistical design theory is used to combine the levels of the attributes into a number of alternative scenarios or profiles to be presented to respondents. *Complete factorial designs* allow the estimation of the full effects of the attributes upon choices: that includes the effects of each of the *individual* attributes presented (main effects) and the extent to which behaviour is connected with variations in the *combination* of different attributes offered (interactions). These designs often originate an impractically large number of combinations to be evaluated: for example, 27 options would be generated by a full factorial design of 3 attributes with 3 levels each. *Fractional factorial designs* are able to reduce the number of scenario combinations presented with a concomitant loss in estimating power (*i.e.* some or all of the interactions will not be detected). For example, the 27 options can be reduced to 9 using a fractional factorial. These designs are available through specialised software.
Construction of choice sets	The profiles identified by the experimental design are then grouped into choice sets to be presented to respondents. Profiles can be presented individually, in pairs or in groups. For example, the 9 options identified by the fractional factorial design can be grouped into 3 sets of four-way comparisons.
Measurement of preferences	Choice of a survey procedure to measure individual preferences: ratings, rankings or choices.
Estimation procedure	Ordinary least squares (OLS) regression or maximum likelihood estimation procedures (logit, probit, ordered logit, conditional logit, nested logit, panel data models, etc.). Variables that do not vary across alternatives have to be interacted with choice-specific attributes.

These different ways of measuring preferences correspond to different variants of the CM approach. There are four main variants – choice experiments, contingent ranking, contingent rating and paired comparisons – summarised in Table 9.2. As will be shown in the remainder of this section, these techniques differ in the quality of information they generate, in their degree of complexity and also in their ability to produce WTP estimates that can be shown to be consistent with the usual measures of welfare change.[2] The conceptual details of these approaches are outlined in Appendix 9.1. In what follows, we discuss the main elements of each approach.

Table 9.2. **Main choice modelling alternatives**

Approach	Tasks	Welfare consistent estimates?
Choice experiments	Choose between two or more alternatives (where one is the *status quo*)	Yes
Contingent ranking	Rank a series of alternatives	Depends
Contingent rating	Score alternative scenarios on a scale of 1-10	Doubtful
Paired comparisons	Score pairs of scenarios on similar scale	Doubtful

9.2.1. *Choice experiments*

In a choice experiment (CE) respondents are presented with a series of alternatives, differing in terms of attributes and levels, and asked to choose their most preferred. A baseline alternative, corresponding to the *status quo* or "do nothing" situation, is usually included in each choice set. (As is discussed below, this inclusion of a baseline or do-nothing option is an important element of CE approaches as it permits the analysts to interpret results in standard [welfare] economic terms.) The conceptual framework for CE assumes that consumers' or respondents' utilities for a good can be decomposed into utilities or well-being derived from the composing characteristics of the good. More specifically, in the CE approach, the (indirect) utility function for each respondent is made up of two parts. One of these elements is a function of the attributes or characteristics of the different alternatives in the choice set. The other element is made up of unobservable influences on individual choice.

Figure 9.1 presents an example used in a recent study of options to clean-up the River Thames. In this study, described in detail in Box 9.1, the good is reducing the amount of stormwater (sewage) overflows that end up in the River Thames. This good itself can be defined in terms of its attributes such as fewer fish deaths, less days when exposure to the river water is a health risk and decreased visual disamenity. Each respondent is asked a sequence of these questions.[3]

Figure 9.1. **Illustrative choice experiment question**

WHICH OPTION FOR REDUCING STORMWATER OVERFLOWS INTO THE THAMES WOULD YOU PREFER, GIVEN THE OPTIONS DESCRIBED BELOW?

	Current situation	Option A	Option B
Sewage litter	Some items visible (10% of total litter)	Items almost never visible (1% of total litter)	Not present (0% of total litter)
Other litter	Present	Present	Present
Water sports/health risk	120 days/year of increased health risk	4 days/year of increased health risk	0 days/year of increased health risk
Fish population	8 potential fish kills per year	0 potential fish kills per year	< 1 potential fish kills per year
Annual cost	GBP 0 per year	GBP 15 per year	GBP 36 per year
Preferred option			

The probability that any particular respondent prefers say Option A to alternative options, can be expressed as the probability that the *utility* or *well-being* associated with Option A exceeds that associated with all other options. As previously mentioned, the main observable elements determining choices would be expected to be the attributes of each option (*e.g.* column 1 in Figure 9.1). Socio-economic and demographic characteristics of the respondent may also influence choice and this can also be quantified in the analysis although needs to be done in a particular way (*i.e.* interacted with choice specific attributes: see Annex 9.A1).

Parameter estimates for the attributes and characteristics can be obtained by appropriate statistical analysis of respondents' choices. From these findings the analyst can obtain estimates of WTP. Consider the following example, which is based on the River Thames example used so far (and in Box 9.1). This might entail the analyst assuming that utility or well-being (of the ith respondent for the j different alternatives in the choice set) depends simply (and linearly) on the attributes of the choices presented to respondents and unobserved factors as follows,

$$U_{ij} = b_1(SEWAGE)_{ij} + b_2(HEALTH)_{ij} + b_3(FISH)_{ij} + b_4(COST)_{ij} + e_{ij}$$

where "SEWAGE" is the proportion of sewage litter in the river, "HEALTH" is the days when there is a (minor) health risk to being exposed to the river water, "FISH" is the number of significant fish-kills, "COST" is the cost of an option and "e" are unobserved factors. Now suppose that the analyst has estimated this relationship and found the following coefficient values:

$$\Rightarrow b_1 = -0.035; \ b_2 = -0.007; \ b_3 = -0.029; \ b_4 = -0.019$$

The coefficients on these attributes are all negative as having more of any of these particular things decreases utility or well-being. WTP to reduce each unit of incidence of

Box 9.1. **Choice experiments and a cleaner river Thames**

Combined sewage overflows in the Thames Tideway cause raw sewage and sewage litter to enter the river, degrading water quality and causing disamenity. Indeed, in the summer of 2004 an unseasonably severe rainstorm on the 4th August led to exactly this outcome as about 600 000 tonnes of sewage was released into the Thames. While this particular episode generated a large amount of national and regional media coverage, it is reckoned that a large number of these incidents occur each year along the Thames Tideway. More generally, there is concern that London's 19th Century sewer system – while an impressive feat of Victorian engineering – can no longer take the strain of the rainfall that the city typically experiences in the face of an ever-increasing populace. This has led to the consideration of a number of proposals for construction of a "super-sewer" to decrease the number of these incidents each year. Various investment options exist and at least 9 have been seriously considered by Thames Water plc (the company responsible for implementing this project). Each is associated with different costs as well as distinct levels of provision of various benefits. Analysing each of these investment options using the contingent valuation method would be a complicated and long-winded process (each option would require its own scenario). In such a situation, a choice modelling approach is a useful alternative.

The objective of a study by EFTEC (2003) was to measure people's preferences for the benefits of engineering solutions to reduce sewage litter and improve water quality in the river using a choice experiment approach. Respondents asked to make choices between potential river improvement scenarios. Scenarios were described using attributes, described in Table 9.3, which took on different levels across scenarios where one of the attributes is cost to households. In the final choice sets, 8 choice cards were presented per person where each card contained the baseline plus two improvement scenarios or options. These choices presented to respondents all involved trade-offs such as those described in Figure 9.1 above. The main survey consisted of face-to-face interviews with a sample of 1 214 Thames Water customers throughout London and the South East.

The implicit (unit or marginal) prices of three attributes, which it was reckoned would improve if some investment option were undertaken, were sought. These prices can be interpreted as the mean willingness to pay (WTP) of households per year to reduce: *a)* sewage litter (SEWAGE); *b)* health risk days (HEALTH); and, *c)* fish population deaths (FISH), by one unit (*e.g.* one per cent, one day and one fish death episode respectively).

Table 9.3. **River attributes and levels**

Attribute	Description	Levels
Sewage litter	As % of total litter	*10%*, 3%, 1%, 0%
Water sports/health risk	Number of days per year when water sports are not advisable due to increased health risk (minor illness)	*120*, 60, 10, 4, 0
Fish population	Potential fish kills per year	*8*, 4, 2, less than 1, 0
Annual cost	Increase in annual water bills	*0*, GBP 5, GBP 15, GBP 23, GBP 36, GBP 47, GBP 77, GBP 115

Notes: Values in italic bold indicate baseline/*status quo* levels.

> Box 9.1. **Choice experiments and a cleaner river Thames** (cont.)
>
> These implicit prices corresponded to: WTP_{SEWAGE} = GBP 1.84; WTP_{HEALTH} = GBP 0.38; and, WTP_{FISH} = GBP 1.51. These unit values can be aggregated to evaluate the total benefits of a given option to reduce stormwater overflows. That is, if the physical reduction in health risks days (from the baseline) is known then this can be multiplied by the implicit price for that attribute. For example, for an option that eliminated wholly any sewage discharges into the Thames, the total benefits per household of this policy is calculated as follows:
>
> | SEWAGE | HEALTH | FISH | TOTAL |
> |---|---|---|---|
> | [GBP 1.84 × (10 – 0)] + | [GBP 0.38 × (120 – 0)] + | [GBP 1.51 × (8 – 0)] | = GBP 76 |
>
> Thus, it was estimated that the average (annual) WTP of each household to eliminate stormwater overflows altogether was roughly GBP 76. If it is reckoned that all of the 5.6 million households in the Thames Water area (on average) would be willing to pay this amount, then this household value would be multiplied by this total equating to just over GBP 400 million per year. The present value of these total benefits could then be compared with the present value of capital costs of this "ideal" option in order to calculate its net benefits.

the first three attributes can be estimated by dividing the coefficient of each attribute (*e.g.* SEWAGE, HEALTH or FISH) by the coefficient on the COST (*i.e.* b_4). This gives the following implicit prices for each of these attributes.

$$WTP_{SEWAGE} = b_1/b_4 = -0.0346/-0.0190 = GBP\ 1.82$$

$$WTP_{HEALTH} = b_2/b_4 = -0.0073/-0.0190 = GBP\ 0.38$$

$$WTP_{FISH} = b_3/b_4 = -0.0287/-0.0190 = GBP\ 1.51$$

Before we turn to consider alternative choice modelling approaches, it is worth noting that choice experiments are consistent with utility maximisation and demand theory, at least when a *status quo* option is included in the choice set. If a *status quo* alternative is not included in the choice set, respondents are effectively being "forced" to choose one of the alternatives presented, which they may not desire at all. If, for some respondents, the most preferred option is the current baseline situation, then any model based on a design in which the baseline is not present will yield inaccurate estimates of consumer welfare. This is an important consideration for evaluating other choice modelling approaches.

9.2.2. Contingent ranking

In a contingent ranking (CR) experiment respondents are required to rank a set of alternative options, characterised by a number of attributes, which are offered at different levels across options. As with CE, a *status quo* option is normally included in the choice set to ensure welfare consistent results. An example is provided in Figure 9.2. In this example, a baseline option is included. As discussed in Section 9.2.1 this is important if the results are to be interpreted on standard welfare economic terms. If no baseline option were offered to respondents then this interpretation strictly speaking would not be valid. For the illustration in Figure 9.2, if a respondent chooses the baseline alternative then (given that subsequent choices tell us nothing further about a respondent's real demand curve) any subsequent rankings should be discarded from the estimation procedure.

Figure 9.2. **Illustrative contingent ranking question**

PLEASE RANK THE ALTERNATIVES FOR REDUCING STORMWATER OVERFLOWS INTO THE THAMES BELOW
ACCORDING TO YOUR PREFERENCES, ASSIGNING 1 TO THE MOST PREFERRED, 2 TO THE SECOND MOST
PREFERRED, 3 TO THE LEAST PREFERRED

	Current situation	Option A	Option B
Sewage litter	Some items visible (10% of total litter)	Items almost never visible (1% of total litter)	Not present (0% of total litter)
Other litter	Present	Present	Present
Water sports/health risk	120 days/year of increased health risk	4 days/year of increased health risk	0 days/year of increased health risk
Fish population	8 potential fish kills per year	0 potential fish kills per year	< 1 potential fish kills per year
Annual cost	GBP 0 per year	GBP 15 per year	GBP 36 per year
Ranking			

The CR approach shares many conceptual characteristics with the CE approach outlined in Section 9.2.1. The major difference between the two approaches is that the former provides information about how alternatives are *fully* ranked by respondents. CR can be seen as a series of choices in which respondents face a sequential choice process, whereby they first identify their most preferred choice, then, after removal of that option from the choice set, identify their most preferred choice out of the remaining set and so on. In other words, one can decompose a contingent ranking exercise into a set of choice experiments (Chapman and Staelin, 1982). WTP values can therefore be estimated as in the choice experiment example. Ranking data provides more statistical information than choice experiments, which leads to tighter (*i.e.* smaller) confidence intervals around the parameter estimates and so might result in more precise implicit prices or measures of WTP.

One of the limitations of this approach lies in the added cognitive difficulty associated with ranking choices with many attributes and levels. Previous research in the marketing literature by Ben-Akiva *et al.* (1991), Chapman and Staelin (1982), and Hausman and Ruud (1987) found significant differences in the preference structure implicit across ranks. In other words, choices seem to be unreliable and inconsistent across ranks. A possible explanation is that responses may be governed by different decision protocols according to the level of the rank. An alternative interpretation is that these results could indicate increasing noise (random effects) with the depth of the ranking task as, in general, lower ranks seem to be less reliable than higher ranks. Box 9.2, later in this chapter, describes one particular study that has sought to investigate this important issue about the logical consistency of respondents' choices.

9.2.3. Contingent rating

In a contingent rating exercise respondents are presented with a number of scenarios and are asked to rate them individually on a semantic or numeric scale. Rating data have been analysed within frameworks, which permit ratings to be transformed into a utility scale. In this context, the utility that an individual receives from an option is assumed, in some way, to be related to the individual's rating of that option. In the context of valuing options in monetary terms, Roe *et al.* (1996) have shown how to estimate compensating variation measures from ratings data. This is based on ratings differences and involves subtracting a monetary cost from income until the ratings difference is made equal to zero.

Figure 9.3. **Illustrative contingent rating question**

ON THE SCALE BELOW, PLEASE RATE YOUR PREFERENCES FOR REDUCING STORMWATER OVERFLOWS
INTO THE THAMES FOR THIS OPTION

	Option A
Sewage litter	Items almost never visible (1% of total litter)
Other litter	Present
Water sports/health risk	4 days/year of increased health risk
Fish population	0 potential fish kills per year
Annual cost	GBP 15 per year

1	2	3	4	5	6	7	8	9	10
Very low preference									*Very high preference*

Despite its popularity amongst marketing practitioners, ratings exercises have a number of drawbacks, which might limit their applicability in economic benefit assessments. For example, in marketing applications, the analysis of ratings has typically implied a strong assumption about the cardinality of the ratings scale (*e.g.* a rating of 8 implies say twice as much utility is enjoyed than if a rating of 4 was chosen). An alternative, and less demanding, approach is to assume that the ratings only have an ordinal significance. In either case, there remains the implicit assumption that ratings are comparable across individuals, which may not be valid. In general, there is concern that contingent rating exercises do not produce welfare consistent value estimates, which clearly is a drawback in an economic assessment.

9.2.4. *Paired comparisons*

In a paired comparison exercise respondents are asked to choose their preferred alternative out of a set of two choices and to indicate the strength of their preference in a numeric or semantic scale. This format is also known as graded or rated pairs. Figure 9.4 provides an example.

Figure 9.4. **Illustrative paired comparisons question**

WHICH OPTION WOULD YOU PREFER FOR REDUCING STORMWATER OVERFLOWS INTO THE THAMES, GIVEN
THE TWO OPTIONS DESCRIBED BELOW?

	Option A	Option B
Sewage litter	Items almost never visible (1% of total litter)	Not present (0% of total litter)
Other litter	Present	Present
Water sports/health risk	4 days/year of increased health risk	0 days/year of increased health risk
Fish population	0 potential fish kills per year	< 1 potential fish kills per year
Annual cost	GBP 15 per year	GBP 36 per year

1	2	3	4	5	6	7	8	9	10
Strongly prefer Option A									*Strongly prefer Option B*

The graded pairs approach is an attempt to get more information than simply identifying the most preferred alternative and, as such, combines elements of choice experiments (choosing the most preferred alternative) and rating exercises (rating the strength of preference). If the ratings are re-interpreted as providing an indication about choices only, then this approach collapses into a choice experiment and the comments and procedures described previously also apply in this case. (Note, however, that previous comments still apply that a *status quo* option must always be present in the pairs for the resulting estimates to be interpreted on welfare economic terms.) Yet, this variant creates a conundrum in that if only choice information is used from the ratings then why not specify the choice as a CE in the first place? By contrast, if instead information supplied responses to the rating scale are used, the resulting data can be analysed in a similar fashion to the case of contingent rating. However, some of the caveats described in Section 9.2.3 would also become relevant.

9.3. Advantages and problems of choice modelling

9.3.1. *Advantages*

As several authors have pointed out, CM approaches possess some advantages relative to the standard contingent valuation (CV) technique. Principal among the attractions of CM are claimed to be the following:

i) CM is particularly suited to deal with situations where changes are multi-dimensional and trade-offs between them are of particular interest because of its natural ability to separately identify the value of individual attributes of a good or programme, typically supplied in combination with one another. Whilst in principle CV can also be applied to estimate the value of the attributes of a programme, for example by including a series of CV scenarios in a questionnaire or by conducting a series of CV studies, it is a more costly and cumbersome alternative. Hence CM does a better job than CV in measuring the marginal value of changes in various characteristics of say environmental programmes. This is often a more useful focus from a management/policy perspective than focussing on either the gain or loss of the good, or on a discrete change in its attributes. Useful here might mean more generalisable, and therefore more appropriate from a benefits transfer viewpoint (for encouraging evidence on the use of CM in benefits transfer, see Morrison *et al.* 1998: see also Chapter 17 for a discussion of benefits transfer and cost-benefit analysis more generally).

ii) Some CM variants such as choice experiments are arguably more informative than discrete choice CV studies as respondents get multiple chances to express their preference for a valued good over a range of payment amounts. For example, if respondents are given 8 choice pairs and a "do nothing" option, they may respond to as many as 17 bid prices, including zero. In fact, the choice experiment format has been viewed by some as a generalisation of discrete choice contingent valuation concerning a sequence of discrete choice valuation questions where there are two or more goods involved.

iii) CM generally avoids an explicit elicitation of respondents' willingness to pay by relying instead on ratings, rankings or choices amongst a series of alternative packages of characteristics from where willingness to pay can be indirectly inferred. As such, for example, CM may minimise some of the response difficulties found in CV studies covered in Chapter 8. We return to this point in Section 9.3.3 below.

9.3.2. *Problems*

Experience with CM in economic appraisals in, for example, environmental contexts is still fairly limited. However, these approaches have been very widely applied in the fields of transport and marketing. Several problem areas seem to be important:

i) Arguably, the main disadvantage of CM approaches lies in the cognitive difficulty associated with multiple complex choices or rankings between bundles with many attributes and levels. Both experimental economists and psychologists have found ample evidence that there is a limit to how much information respondents can meaningfully handle while making a decision. One common finding is that the choice complexity or depth of a ranking task can lead to greater random errors or at least imprecision in responses (see Box 9.2). More generally, since respondents are typically presented with a large number of choice sets there is scope for both learning and fatigue effects and an important issue is which – on average – will predominant and when. Handling repeated answers per respondent also poses statistical problems and the correlation between responses in such cases needs to be taken into account and properly modelled (Adamowicz, Louviere and Swait, 1998).

This implies that, whilst the researcher might want to include many attributes and so on, unless very large samples are collected, respondents will be faced with daunting choice tasks. The consequence is that, in presence of complex choices, respondents use heuristics or rules of thumb to simplify the decision task. These filtering rules lead to options being chosen that are good enough although not necessarily the best, avoiding the need to solve the underlying utility-maximisation problem (*i.e.* a satisficing approach rather than a maximising one). Heuristics often associated with difficult choice tasks include maximin and maximax strategies and lexicographic orderings (Tversky, 1972; Foster and Mourato, 2002). Hence, it is important to incorporate consistency tests into CM studies in order to detect the range of problems discussed above (see, for example, Box 9.2).

In order to estimate the total value of a public programme or a good using a CM approach as distinct from a change in one of its attributes, it is necessary to assume that the value of the whole is equal to the sum of the parts (see Box 9.1). This raises two potential problems. First, there may be additional attributes of the good not included in the design, which generate utility (in practice, these effects can be captured in other ways). Second, the value of the "whole" may not be simply additive in this way. Elsewhere in economics, objections have been raised about the assumption that the value of the whole is indeed equal to the sum of its parts (see Chapter 12).

In order to test whether this is a valid objection, values of a full programme or good obtained from CM could be compared with values obtained for the same resource using some other method such as contingent valuation, under similar circumstances. In the transport field, research for London Underground and London Buses among others has shown clear evidence that values of whole bundles of improvements are valued less than the sum of the component values, all measured using CE (SDG, 1999, 2000). Foster and Mourato (2003) found that the estimates from a choice experiment of the total value of charitable services in the UK were significantly larger than results obtained from a parallel contingent valuation survey.

ii) It is more difficult for CM approaches to derive values for a sequence of elements implemented by policy or project, when compared to a contingent valuation alternative. Hence, valuing the sequential provision of goods in multi-attribute programmes is probably better undertaken by contingent valuation.

iii) As is the case with all stated preference techniques, welfare estimates obtained with CM are sensitive to study design. For example, the choice of attributes, the levels chosen to represent them, and the way in which choices are relayed to respondents (*e.g.* use of

Box 9.2. **Testing the cognitive burden of choice modelling**

Contingent ranking is a choice modelling approach to valuation whereby respondents are required to rank a set of alternative options. Each alternative is characterised by a number of attributes, which are offered at different levels across options. However, the ranking task imposes a significant cognitive burden on the survey population, a burden which escalates with the number of attributes used and the number of alternatives presented to each individual. This raises questions as to whether respondents are genuinely able to provide meaningful answers to such questions. A recent study by Foster and Mourato (2002) looks at three different aspects of logical consistency within the context of a contingent ranking experiment: dominance, rank consistency, and transitivity of rank order. Each of these concepts are defined below before we proceed to outline the findings of this study:

Dominance: One alternative is said to dominate a second when it is at least as good as the second in terms of every attribute. If Option A dominates Option B, then it would clearly be inconsistent for any respondent to rank Option B more highly than Option A. Dominant pairs are sometimes excluded from contingent ranking designs on the grounds that they do not provide any additional information about preferences. However, their deliberate inclusion can be used as a test of the coherence of the responses of those being surveyed.

Rank consistency: Where respondents are given a sequence of ranking sets, it also becomes possible to test for rank-consistency *across* questions. This can be done by designing the experiment so that common pairs of options appear in successive ranking sets. For example, a respondent might be asked to rank Options A, B, C, D in the first question and Options A, B, E, F in the second question. Rank-consistency requires that a respondent who prefers Option B over Option A in the first question, continues to do so in the second question

Transitivity: Transitivity of rank order requires that a respondent who has expressed a preference for Option A over B in a first question, and for Option B over C elsewhere, should not thereafter express a preference for Option C over A in any other question. There are clearly parallels here with the transitivity axiom underlying neo-classical consumer theory.

The data set which forms the basis of the tests outlined in Foster and Mourato (2002) is a contingent ranking survey of the social costs of pesticide use in bread production in the United Kingdom. Three product attributes were considered in the survey, each of them offered at three different levels: the price of bread, together with measures of the human health – *annual cases of illness as a result of field exposure to pesticides* – and the environmental impacts of pesticides – *number of farmland bird species in a state of long-term decline as a result of pesticide use*. An example choice card for this study is illustrated in Figure 9.5.

Figure 9.5. **Sample contingent ranking question from pesticide survey**

	Process A	Process B	Process C	Process D
Price of bread	60 pence per loaf	85 pence per loaf	85 pence per loaf	GBP 1.15 per loaf
Health effects on general public	100 cases of ill health per year	40 cases of ill health per year	40 cases of ill health per year	60 cases of ill health per year
Effects on farmland birds	9 bird species in decline	2 bird species in decline	5 bird species in decline	2 bird species in decline
Ranking				

Notes: Process A: current technology for wheat cultivation. Process B: B-D: alternative environmentally friendly options for wheat cultivation.

Box 9.2. **Testing the cognitive burden of choice modelling** (cont.)

The basic results of the authors' tests for logical consistency are presented in Table 9.4. Each respondent was classified in one of three categories: i) "no failure" means that these respondents always passed a particular test; ii) "occasional failures" refers to those respondents who pass on some occasions but not on others; while, iii) "systematic failures" refers to those respondents who fail a test on every occasion that the test is presented.

The results show that on a test-by-test basis, the vast majority of respondents register passes. More than 80% pass dominance and transitivity tests on every occasion, while two thirds pass the rank-consistency test. Of those who fail, the vast majority only fail occasionally. The highest failure rate is for the rank-consistency test, which is failed by 32% of the sample, while only 13% of the sample fails each of the other two tests. Systematic failures are comparatively rare, with none at all in the case of transitivity.

Table 9.4. **Comparison of test failures**

Per cent

	No failures	Occasional failures	Systematic failures
Dominance	83	13	4
Rank consistency	67	32	1
Transitivity	87	13	0
ALL	54	41	5

Note: The overall percentage of occasional failures reported in the final row of the table is net of all individuals who systematically failed anyone of the test.

When the results of the tests are pooled, Table 9.4 indicates that only 5% of the sample makes systematic failures. The overall "no failure" sample accounts for 54% of the total. The fact that this is substantially smaller than the "no failure" sample for each individual test indicates that *different* respondents are failing *different* tests rather than a small group of respondents failing *all* of the tests. Yet, this finding also indicates a relatively high rate of occasional failures among respondents with nearly half of the sample failing at least one of the tests some of the time.

Results such as these could have important implications for the contingent ranking method and perhaps choice modelling more generally. The fact that a substantial proportion of respondents evidently find occasional or persistent difficulty in providing coherent responses to contingent ranking problems arguably raises some concerns about the methodology, when the ultimate research goal is to estimate coefficient values with which to derive valid and reliable WTP amounts.

photographs *vs.* text descriptions, choices *vs.* ranks) are not neutral and may impact on the values of estimates of consumers' surplus and marginal utilities.

9.3.3. Does choice modelling solve any of the main problems of CV?

Contingent valuation has been criticised as a means of eliciting environmental preferences by many authors, most famously perhaps by Kahneman and Knetsch (1992) and by Hausman (1993). Moreover, practitioners have been very open about areas of sensitivity in applying the method. Some of the main areas in which difficulties have been encountered include the following:

i) "Hypothetical" bias: From early on in the history of the CV, there has been a concern that, for example, the hypothetical nature of CV responses might lead respondents to overestimate their true valuations (*e.g.* see Chapter 8). There are very few similar tests at present for CM. However, given that *e.g.* CE is in effect a generalisation of discrete choice CV, there is little reason to suppose, a priori, that it performs any better than CV in this regard.

ii) Sensitivity to scope: One advantage of CM is that it provides a natural internal scope test due to the elicitation of multiple responses per individual. The internal test is however weaker than the external test in as much as the answers given by any particular individual are not independent from each other and thus sensitivity to scope is to some extent forced.

iii) Sensitivity of estimates to study design: a common finding in CV studies is that bids can be affected by design choices, for example in terms of the choice of payment mechanism, the amount and type of information provided, and the rules of the market.[4] However, design issues are as important in CM as in CV studies.

iv) Protest responses: a percentage of respondents in contingent valuation studies typically refuse to "play the game" and protest to some aspect of the contingent market such as payment vehicle (*e.g.* higher taxes) and so on. Such responses are usually treated as protests and are typically excluded from the analysis. Certain prominent types of protests may be sensitive to the type and amount of monetary payment requested. If so, CM might reduce the incidence of protesting as that the choice context can be less "stark" than direct elicitation of willingness to pay. However, this point – while interesting – has yet to be proven.

v) Expense: CV studies can be hugely expensive, especially when large probabilistic samples and personal interviews are used. If split-samples are required, for example to evaluate various components of a given programme, then the costs can quickly become prohibitive. When valuing multi-attribute programmes, CM studies can reduce the expense of valuation studies, because of their natural ability to value programme attributes in one single questionnaire and because they are more informative than discrete choice CV surveys.

9.4. Summary and guidance for decision-makers

Many types of environmental impact are multidimensional in character. What this means is that an environmental asset that is affected by a proposed project or policy often will give rise to changes in component attributes each of which command distinct valuations. This is not unlike the conceptual premise underlying the hedonic approach, a revealed preference method discussed in Chapter 7, where the value of particular goods such as properties can be thought of comprising consumers' valuations of bundles of characteristics, which can be "teased out" using appropriate statistical analysis. In contrast, however, the suite of stated preference methods collectively known as choice modelling (or CM) discussed in this chapter must estimate respondents' valuations of the multiple dimensions of environmental goods, when the good's total value is not itself observable because no market for it exists. Indeed, it is this information about the (marginal) value of each dimension that is subsequently used to estimate the total value of the change in provision of the environmental good.

The application of CM approaches to valuing multidimensional environmental problems has been growing steadily in recent years. Indeed, choice modelling is now routinely discussed alongside the arguably better-known contingent valuation (CV) method in state-of-the-art manuals regarding the design, analysis and use of stated preference studies. While there are a number of different approaches under the CM umbrella, it is arguably the choice experiment variant (and to some extent contingent ranking) that has become the dominant CM approach with regard to applications to environmental goods. In a choice experiment, respondents are asked to choose their most preferred from a choice set of at least two options one of which is the *status quo* or current situation. It is this CM approach that can be interpreted in standard welfare economic terms, an obvious strength where consistency with the theory of cost-benefit analysis is a desirable criterion.

Much of the discussion in Chapter 8 about, for example, validity and reliability issues in the context of CV studies is likely to apply in the context of the CM. While it is likely that on some criteria, CM is likely to perform better than CV – and *vice versa* – the evidence for such assertions is largely lacking at present. Moreover, while those few studies that have sought to compare the findings of CM and CV appear to find that the total value of changes in the provision of the same environmental good in the former exceeds that of the latter, the reasons for this are not altogether clear. Intellectual curiosity doubtless will ensure that more research emerges to cast light about both of these sources of uncertainty about the relative merits of CM and CV. However, whether the two methods should be seen as always competing against one another – in the sense of say CM being a more general and thereby superior method – is debatable. Both approaches are likely to have their role in cost-benefit appraisals and a useful contribution of any future research would also be to aid understanding of when one approach should be used rather than the other.

One circumstance in which CM is a highly useful approach can be best described by way of an example. For this purpose, we return to the case study of options to clean up the River Thames discussed earlier in this chapter. In that example, there were at least 9 alternatives to the current situation for decision-makers to consider. Moreover, each of these options was characterised by different levels of provision of the attributes of a cleaner River Thames. Applying the CV method to this problem typically would entail the design of 9 contingent markets separately describing each proposed change. Applying CM, by contrast, can achieve this end – *via* a rather more economical route – because it estimates unit values for each attribute of interest. The total value of each project or policy option is obtained in two steps. First, multiply the unit value of each attribute by that option's quantity (or quality) change for the relevant attribute. Second, sum the component changes in attribute values. Complicating factors – where, for example, valuations are not simply a linear function of some change in an attribute level – can be also accommodated within this analysis where needed.

On this interpretation, CM is most pertinent as a stated preference method where an environmental problem is relatively complex – *i.e.* multidimensional – and proposed policy options are not only numerous but also provide different combinations of these multiple dimensions. There are, as we have discussed a number of known disadvantages to the CM approach. CM studies reflecting complex environmental changes are themselves complex to design and to analyse. With regards to the validity of responses, the cognitive difficulty of choosing between options in (multiple) choice sets is a prominent concern. In both respects, CV could be said to be the more straightforward approach. However, echoing our earlier comment, what this means is that CM should be used when the circumstances demand. In other words, is it important to know the marginal or unit values of each of dimensions that comprise some environmental change of interest? As the answer to this question on occasion will be in the affirmative, CM is very much an important part of the cost-benefit analyst's portfolio of valuation techniques.

Notes

1. This approach is also sometimes known as "conjoint analysis".

2. See Louviere *et al.* (2000) and Morrison *et al.* (1999) for further information on these techniques.

3. This standard practice of giving respondents a series of choice cards is not without its problems. Typically, analysts treat the response to each card as a separate data point. In other words, responses for each of the choice sets presented to each respondent are regarded as completely independent observations. This is most probably incorrect, since it is likely that there will be some correlation between the error terms of each group of sets ranked by the same individual. The data thus is effectively a panel with "time periods" corresponding to the choice sets faced by each individual. Hence, standard models that ignore this over-estimate of the amount of information contained in the dataset. There are procedures to deal with this problem. In some cases – such as the most preferred alternative model – an *ex post* correction can be made by multiplying the standard errors attached to the coefficients for each attribute by the square root of the number of questions administered to each respondent. Other types of model used to estimate CM data – such the random parameters logit model – automatically correct for this bias within the estimation procedure.

4. This sensitivity is desirable in some cases, as it mirrors the picture for market goods: for example, we expect WTP to change when respondents' information sets change (Munro and Hanley, 1999).

ANNEX 9.A1

Conceptual Foundations of Choice Modelling

9.1. Choice experiments

The choice experiment approach was initially developed by Louviere and Hensher (1982) and Louviere and Woodworth (1983). Choice experiments share a common theoretical framework with dichotomous-choice contingent valuation in the Random Utility Model (Luce, 1959; McFadden, 1973), as well as a common basis of empirical analysis in limited dependent variable econometrics (Greene, 1997). According to this framework, the indirect utility function for each respondent i (U) can be decomposed into two parts: a deterministic element (V), which is typically specified as a linear index of the attributes (X) of the j different alternatives in the choice set, and a stochastic element (e), which represents unobservable influences on individual choice. This is shown in equation (A9.1).

$$U_{ij} = V_{ij}(X_{ij}) + e_{ij} = bX_{ij} + e_{ij} \qquad \text{[A9.1]}$$

Thus, the probability that any particular respondent prefers option g in the choice set to any alternative option h, can be expressed as the probability that the utility associated with option g exceeds that associated with all other options, as stated in equation (A9.2).

$$P[(U_{ig} > U_{ih}) \; \forall h \neq g] = P[(V_{ig} - V_{ih}) > (e_{ih} - e_{ig})] \qquad \text{[A9.2]}$$

In order to derive an explicit expression for this probability, it is necessary to know the distribution of the error terms (e_{ij}). A typical assumption is that they are independently and identically distributed with an extreme-value (Weibull) distribution:

$$P(e_{ij} \leq t) = F(t) = \exp(-\exp(-t)) \qquad \text{[A9.3]}$$

The above distribution of the error term implies that the probability of any particular alternative g being chosen as the most preferred can be expressed in terms of the logistic distribution (McFadden, 1973) stated in equation (A9.4). This specification is known as the conditional logit model:

$$P(U_{ig} > U_{ih}, \forall h \neq g) = \frac{\exp(\mu V_{ig})}{\sum_{j} \exp(\mu V_{ij})} \qquad \text{[A9.4]}$$

where μ is a scale parameter, inversely proportional to the standard deviation of the error distribution. This parameter cannot be separately identified and is therefore typically assumed to be one. An important implication of this specification is that selections from the choice set must obey the Independence from Irrelevant Alternatives (IIA) property (or Luce's Choice Axiom; Luce, 1959), which states that the relative probabilities of two options being selected are unaffected by the introduction or removal of other alternatives. This property follows from the independence of the Weibull error terms across the different options contained in the choice set.

This model can be estimated by conventional maximum likelihood procedures, with the respective log-likelihood functions stated in equation (A9.5) below, where y_{ij} is an indicator variable which takes a value of one if respondent j chose option i and zero otherwise.

$$\log L = \sum_{i=1}^{N} \sum_{j=1}^{J} y_{ij} \log\left[\frac{\exp(V_{ij})}{\sum_{j=1}^{J} \exp(V_{ij})}\right] \qquad [A9.5]$$

Socio-economic variables can be included along with choice set attributes in the X terms in equation (A9.1), but since they are constant across choice occasions for any given individual (*e.g.* income is the same when the first choice is made as the second), they can only be entered as interaction terms, *i.e.* interacted with choice specific attributes.

Once the parameter estimates have been obtained, a WTP compensating variation welfare measure that conforms to demand theory can be derived for each attribute using the formula given by (A9.6) (Hanemann, 1984; Parsons and Kealy, 1992) where V^0 represents the utility of the initial state and V^1 represents the utility of the alternative state. The coefficient b_y gives the marginal utility of income and is the coefficient of the cost attribute.

$$WTP = b_y^{-1} \ln\left\{\frac{\sum_i \exp(V^1{}_i)}{\sum_i \exp(V^0{}_i)}\right\} \qquad [A9.6]$$

It is straightforward to show that, for the linear utility index specified in (A9.1), the above formulae can be simplified to the ratio of coefficients given in equation (A9.7) where b_C is the coefficient on any of the attributes. These ratios are often known as implicit prices.

$$WTP = \frac{-b_C}{b_y} \qquad [A9.7]$$

Choice experiments are therefore consistent with utility maximisation and demand theory, at least when a *status quo* option is included in the choice set.

Notice however that specifying standard errors for the implicit price ratios is more complex. Although the asymptotic distribution of the maximum likelihood estimator for the parameters b is known, the asymptotic distribution of the maximum likelihood estimator of the welfare measure is not, since it is a non-linear function of the parameter vector. One way of obtaining confidence intervals for this measure is by means of the procedure developed by Krinsky and Robb (1986). This technique simulates the asymptotic distribution of the coefficients by taking repeated random draws from the multivariate normal distribution defined by the coefficient estimates and their associated covariance matrix. These are used to generate an empirical distribution for the welfare measure and the associated confidence intervals can then be computed.

If a violation of the IIA hypothesis is observed, then more complex statistical models are necessary that relax some of the assumptions used. These include the multinomial probit (Hausman and Wise, 1978), the nested logit (McFadden, 1981) and the random parameters logit model (Train, 1998). IIA can be tested using a procedure suggested by Hausman and McFadden (1984). This basically involves constructing a likelihood ratio test around different versions of the model where choice alternatives are excluded. If IIA holds, then the model estimated on all choices should be the same as that estimated for a sub-set of alternatives (see Foster and Mourato, 2002, for an example).

9.2. Contingent ranking

In a contingent ranking experiment respondents are required to rank a set of alternative options, characterised by a number of attributes, which are offered at different levels across options. As with CE, a *status quo* option is normally included in the choice set to ensure welfare consistent results.

As before, the random utility model provides the economic theory framework for analysing the data from a ranking exercise. Under the assumption of an independently and identically distributed random error with a Weibull distribution, Beggs, Cardell and Hausman (1981) developed a rank-order logit model capable of using all the information contained in a survey where alternatives are fully ranked by respondents. Their specification is based on the repeated application of the probability expression given in equation (A9.4) until a full ranking of all the alternatives has been obtained. The probability of any particular ranking of alternatives being made by individual i can be expressed as:

$$P_i(U_{i1} > U_{i2} > ... > U_{iJ}) = \prod_{j=1}^{J} [\frac{\exp(V_{ij})}{\sum_{k=j}^{J} \exp(V_{ik})}] \qquad [A9.8]$$

Clearly, this rank ordered model is more restrictive than the standard conditional logit model in as much as the extreme value (Weibull) distribution governs not only the first choice but all successive choices as well. As before, the RD model relies critically on the IIA assumption, which in this case is what permits the multiplication of successive conditional logit probabilities to obtain the probability expression for the full ranking.

The parameters of the utility function can be estimated by maximising the log-likelihood function given in equation (A9.9).

$$\log L = \sum_{i=1}^{N} \sum_{j=1}^{J} \log[\frac{\exp(V_{ij})}{\sum_{k=j}^{J} (\exp V_{ik})}] \qquad [A9.9]$$

Contingent ranking can be seen as a series of choices in which respondents face a sequential choice process, whereby they first identify their most preferred choice, then, after removal of that option from the choice set, identify their most preferred choice out of the remaining set and so on. In other words, one can decompose a contingent ranking exercise into a set of choice experiments (Chapman and Staelin, 1982; Foster and Mourato, 2002). Welfare values can therefore be estimated as in the choice experiment example. Ranking data provides more statistical information than choice experiments, which leads to tighter confidence intervals around the parameter estimates.

9.3. Contingent rating

In a contingent rating exercise respondents are presented with a number of scenarios and are asked to rate them individually on a semantic or numeric scale. This approach does not involve a direct comparison of alternative choices and consequently there is no formal theoretical link between the expressed ratings and economic choices.

Rating data have been analysed within the framework of the random utility model with ratings being first transformed into a utility scale. In this context, the indirect utility function is assumed to be related to an individual's ratings via a transformation function:

$$R_{ij}(X_{ij}) = \phi[Vj_{ij}(X_{ij})] \tag{A9.10}$$

where R represents the rating of individual i for choice j and ϕ is the transformation function. In marketing applications these data are typically analysed using OLS regression techniques which imply a strong assumption about the cardinality of the ratings scale. An alternative approach, which allows the data to be analysed in a random utility framework, is to use ordered probit and logit models that only imply an ordinal significance of the ratings. However, there remains the implicit assumption that ratings are comparable across individuals.

Roe *et al.* (1996) have shown how to estimate compensating variation measures from ratings data based on ratings differences. The approach consists in subtracting a monetary cost from income until the ratings difference is made equal to zero:

$$R^1_{ij}(W^1_{ij}, M - WTP) - R^0_{ij}(X^0_{ij}, M) = 0 \tag{A9.11}$$

where V^0 is the rating of the baseline choice, V^1 the rating attributed to the alternative choice, and M is income.

ISBN 92-64-01004-1
Cost-Benefit Analysis and the Environment
Recent Developments
© OECD 2006

Chapter 10

(Quasi) Option Value

Costs and benefits are rarely known with certainty, but uncertainty can be reduced by gathering information. Any decision made now and which commits resources or generates costs that cannot subsequently be recovered or reversed, is an irreversible decision. In this context of uncertainty and irreversibility it may pay to delay making a decision to commit resources. The value of the information gained from that delay is the option value or quasi-option value. This chapter explains how option value arises and addresses some of the terminological confusions that have arisen in the literature.

10.1. Some terminology

Intuitively, most people would argue that a decision that involves the irreversible loss of an asset should be made more cautiously than one where the asset is lost but can be recreated if it is later judged that there has been a mistake. The argument seems especially relevant when there is uncertainty about the future benefits of the asset. Environmental assets are good examples of assets about which we have only limited information: for example, many millions of species have not been screened for their full information, no-one is sure what exists in the canopy of rain forests, or in coral reefs. In such contexts, the CBA rules do not seem quite appropriate: benefits are uncertain, their loss may be irreversible and the scale of the loss could be substantial. CBA appears to ignore the combination of uncertainty and irreversibility. There may also be irreversibility on the cost side. We can imagine an investment decision that requires us to commit resources to the investment such that, if conditions change, there is little or nothing to be done to reverse the investment costs. This will be the case, for example, with "dedicated" investment expenditures – expenditures on capital equipment which has only one specific use and which cannot be readily converted to other uses. In the natural resources literature, the example of fishing fleet investments is often cited. So, both benefit streams and investment or policy costs may be irreversible.

In fact the CBA decision rule can be reformulated to take account of the combination of uncertainty and irreversibility, so long as there is also a third element present – the opportunity for learning more, i.e. gathering new information.[1] This involves the notion of *quasi-option value* (QOV), which was introduced and developed by Arrow and Fisher (1974) and Henry (1974). QOV is the value of information gained by delaying a decision to commit to some irreversible action. Confusingly, in the financial and investment literature, this concept of QOV is called *option value*, or *real option value* (Dixit and Pindyck, 1994). Fisher (2000) argues that these two concepts – QOV and "real" OV – are the same and relate to a context in which there is uncertainty, irreversibility, and where a decision can be delayed such that learning occurs during the period of delay.

It is advisable to retain the terminology of QOV in order to distinguish it from yet another notion of OV in the environmental economics literature. This other concept is the difference between *option price* and the *expected value of consumer's surplus*. Option price is the maximum willingness to pay for something in a risky world in which one does not know for sure what the outcomes will be. Option price is an *ex ante* concept, i.e. a willingness to pay now for a future state of affairs which is uncertain. This option price can differ from the expected value of the consumer surplus, and the difference is known as option value. Note that option price and option value arise in contexts where individuals are risk-averse. As we shall see, QOV arises in contexts of both risk aversion and risk neutrality. In general:

$$OP = E\,(CS) + OV$$

Technically, OV can be positive or negative. In other words, using E(CS), which is what CBA does in practice, could introduce an error in CBA estimates. The problem is that OV cannot be estimated without some knowledge of the underlying structure of preferences of the individuals in question (their *utility functions*). In practice, it is unclear that the error is significant, *i.e.* making assumptions about the nature of preference structures, the evidence suggests that no major errors are introduced by using E(CS) alone.

We do not consider this notion of OV any further. It may be important in some contexts, but the focus is on the QOV = real OV concept since this is more likely to affect the way CBA is conducted.

To summarise:

- OV in environmental economics tends to refer to the difference between option price and the expected value of consumer's surplus.

- QOV in environmental economics refers to the value of information secured by delaying a decision where outcomes are uncertain, where one or more benefits (or costs) is uncertain, and where there is an opportunity to learn by delay.

- OV or real OV in the financial literature refers to the value of information secured by delaying uncertain and irreversible investments, *i.e.* it is the same as QOV in the environmental economics literature.

10.2. A model of QOV[2]

Most expositions of the QOV concept are intricate and involved. Here we attempt to understand the basics.

Consider a forested area which can either be preserved or converted to, say, agriculture. Call the conversion process "development". Let the current period be 0 and the future period be 1, *i.e.* for simplicity, there are just two periods. It is immediately obvious that if the forest is converted now, period 0, it cannot be preserved in period 0 or in the future period 1. But if the forest is preserved now it still leaves open the choice of converting or preserved in period 1. Suppose that the agricultural development benefits are known with certainty, but the preservation benefits are not known with certainty. This seems fairly realistic – we can be fairly sure what the forest land will produce by way of crops but we still do not know much about the nature and value of ecological services from forests. By converting now, certain benefits of D_0 and D_1 are secured (D_0 and D_1 can be thought of as present values). By preserving now, there is a conservation value of V_0, plus an uncertain conservation value of V_1 in period 1. Keeping the analysis simple, let these uncertain values in period 1 be V_{high} and V_{low}. V_{high} might correspond to some very valuable genetic information in the forest. V_{low} would arise if that information turns out to be very much less valuable. Let the probabilities of V_{high} and V_{low} be p and $(1 - p)$ respectively. The expected value (*i.e.* probability weighted) of preservation benefits (EP) in both periods, arising from the decision to conserve now, is therefore:

$$EP = V_0 + pV_{high} + (1 - p) V_{low} \qquad [10.1]$$

A moment's reflection shows that if the forest is converted in 0 the expected value of development benefits will be the same as the certain value of the development benefits:

$$ED = D_0 + D_1 \qquad [10.2]$$

If the decision to preserve or develop has to be taken now, then a simple comparison of [10.1] and [10.2] will suffice. Thus, the forest would be developed if:

$$ED > EP, \text{ or, } [D_0 + D_1] > [V_0 + pV_{high} + (1 - p)V_{low}] \qquad [10.3]$$

This is how most cost-benefit studies would proceed: the expected value of the development (which, in this case, is certain) would be compared with the expected value of preservation. The relevance of QOV is that it changes the cost-benefit rule by allowing for postponing a decision. While political factors may dictate an immediate decision, it is often possible to postpone decisions, *i.e.* to wait before making the final choice of preservation or development. To see the possible choices, it helps to construct a *decision tree* such as the one shown in Figure 10.1.[3] A decision tree shows each stage of the decision process assuming certain events occur and certain choices are made. In Figure 10.1 the "trunk" of the tree is connected to various "branches" via *decision nodes* (marked as a square and *probabilistic occurrences* (marked by circles). The analysis begins with a decision node which is either to decide now ("commit") or wait. The decision to commit involves either developing now or preserving now and forever. If the choice is to develop, then the outcome is clearly net benefits of $ED = D_0 + D_1$. If the choice is to preserve then the expected value of benefits is $EP = V_0 + pV_{high} + (1 - p)V_{low}$. In other words, committing now is formally equivalent to the comparison of the two expected values, which we noted was how cost-benefit analysis normally proceeds.

Now consider the decision to wait. This involves moving down the right hand side of Figure 10.1. Waiting means that the decision to develop or preserve is postponed until period 1. Benefits of V_0 this occur in period 0. What happens next depends on whether "high" or "low" preservation benefits occur. Under either scenario, the decision is whether to preserve or develop in period 1. Hence there are 2×2 possibilities: if the high preservation benefits occur, developing in 1 will produce a sequence of $V_0 + D_1$ and preserving will produce sequence $V_0 + V_{high}$; if the low preservation benefits occur, the two sequences will be $V_0 + D_1$ and $V_0 + V_{low}$. Notice that we have ruled out the option of development in 0 and preservation in 1. This is because development is regarded as being *irreversible*: once it occurs, it cannot be reversed. This is a useful way of thinking about many problems, but, in practice, there are many gradations of irreversibility. The destruction of a primary forest through agricultural conversion does not, for example, necessarily rule out the recreation of a secondary forest which may well look just like the lost primary forest, although with different ecological features. And, one day, the *Jurassic Park* scenario of recreating extinct species may be realisable.

To see which option is best – from the point of view of expected values – it is convenient to attach some hypothetical numbers to the probabilities and outcomes in Figure 10.1. This avoids "getting lost" in the elaborate equations that otherwise emerge.

Let: $V_0 = 20$, $V_{high} = 300$, $V_{low} = 40$, $p = 0.4$, $(1 - p) = 0.6$, $D_0 = 60$, $D_1 = 120$.

Compare waiting and committing.

Waiting entails

a) $V_0 + D_1 = 20 + 120 = 140$, or

b) $V_0 + V_{high} = 20 + 300 = 320$, or

c) $V_0 + V_{low} = 20 + 40 = 60$

Committing entails

d) $D_0 + D_1 = 60 + 120 = 180$, or

e) $V_0 + V_{high} = 20 + 300 = 320$,

f) $V_0 + V_{low} = 20 + 40 = 60$.

Note that outcomes *e)* and *f)* are the same as outcome *b)* and *c)*.

Figure 10.1. **A decision tree**

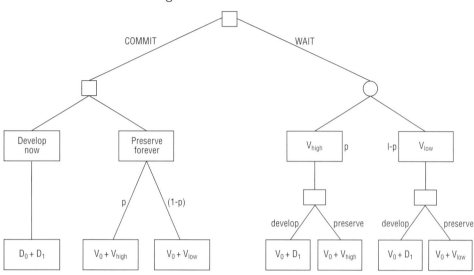

Which is the best decision? The analysis needed to answer this question is in two stages. Ultimately, the optimal choice requires a comparison of the expected values obtained by committing to immediate development (ED), the expected value obtained by immediately committing to preservation for all time (EP), and the expected value obtained by waiting (EW). However, to calculate EW we must first consider the optimal course of action after we decide to wait. What is the best decision after deciding to wait? It depends on whether V_{high} or V_{low} occurs. If V_{high} occurs, the decision should be *wait and preserve* because 320 > 140, but if V_{low} occurs the decision should be *wait and develop* because this decision produces 140 compared to 60 from wait and preserve. But how do we know if high or low preservation values will emerge? The point about waiting is that it gives us the chance to *find out* which of the two preservation values will occur. Put another way, waiting (postponing) generates *information* and this information can greatly improve the efficiency of decision-making: it reduces the uncertainty of the benefits of preservation. QOV links these important features of decision-making in many environmental contexts:

a) uncertainty,

b) irreversibility,

c) waiting and learning.

Notice throughout that the decision rule is still based on expected values.

It is often argued that decisions about global warming control should be postponed because the science of global warming is advancing rapidly. Postponing decisions could prevent the irreversible commitment of resources to controlling global warming, resources that could be used perhaps to more social benefit elsewhere. Control decisions could be made later when information has improved. In fact the global warming context is more complex than this. While decisions are postponed, and if warming is a proven fact, then warming increases and any damage associated with it increases. Hence it is necessary to build into the decision tree the likelihood that the waiting option will increase damage if warming turns out to be a genuine phenomenon. There are two irreversibilities here – unrecoverable costs of action, and irreversible warming. The decision theory approach appears capable of making allowance for this aspect of the decision. The other feature of global warming is that we have very little idea of the probabilities of the outcomes. For example, catastrophic events may be uncertain in their scale, the probability of their occurrence and the time when they might occur. Hence decision-making may have to take place in the context of "pure uncertainty", uncertainty associated with no known probabilities. Even here, waiting may enable better information about those probabilities to be revealed, so the QOV framework remains relevant if this is the case.[4] Overall, it should be easy to see that QOV approaches improve the decision-making procedure compared to the simplistic comparison of expected values of costs and benefits in the "no waiting" – i.e. commitment – case. How far such approaches encompass the full range of problems embraced by uncertainty and irreversibility remains open to question, however.

It is possible now to write an expression for the expected value of waiting (EW). This is:

$$EW = V_0 + pV_{high} + (1-p)D_1 \qquad\qquad [10.4]$$

To understand this expression, inspect Figure 10.1 again. EW is the value of waiting in period 0 and then choosing the best option in period 1. Waiting clearly secures V_0 in period 0. The numerical example tells us that $V_{high} > D_1 > V_{low}$. V_1 is random – it can be "high" or "low" – and is the value of preservation in period 1. If high preservation values occur we opt for preservation because $D_1 > V_{high}$. If "low" preservation values occur, we develop anyway since $D_1 > V_{low}$. Hence in period 1 the expected value is the weighted average of the high preservation value and the development value: $pV_{high} + (1-p)D_1$ which, when added to V_0 in period 0 gives us the expected value of waiting shown in [10.4].

In terms of the numerical values in the hypothetical example, we have:

$$EW = 20 + 0.4(320) + 0.6(140) = 232$$

The value for EW (232) is higher than the value for $EP = V_0 + pV_{high} + (1-p)V_{low} = 20 + 0.4(320) + 0.6(40) = 172$

Hence, in this example, EW >EP. In fact, it is always better to wait than to commit to preservation forever, so long as $D_1 > V_{low}$. This is because by waiting one can always secure the value of EP since waiting involves preservation in period 0 and this leaves open the option of preserving in period 1. Thus waiting allows a flexible choice: preserve in period 0 and preserve in period 1, and preserve in period 0 and develop in period 1.

The previous argument establishes that, under the conditions stipulated, it is better to wait than commit forever to preservation. What of waiting *versus* outright development? This requires that we compare EW with ED. We know that EW = 232 and $ED = D_0 + D_1 = 180$, so the expected value of waiting exceeds the expected value of outright development.

There are now two "rules" by which development and preservation can be compared. The first emerges from the previous analysis, the second from the conventional cost-benefit approach. Immediate development is justified if either ED > EW or ED > EP. As long as EW > EP, the former rule will be harder for an advocate of development to meet. *Thus, allowing for waiting makes the irreversible development option more difficult to achieve (recall that"conventional"CBA would simply compare ED and EP).*

The final stages of the analysis permit us to identify the meaning of QOV more precisely. First, we rewrite EW as:

$$EW = V_0 + EV_1 + Emax(D_1 - V_1, 0) = EP + Emax(D_1 - V_1, 0) \qquad\qquad [10.5]$$

The proof of this is shown in the Annex to this chapter. The term $Emax(D_1 - V_1, 0)$ is to read as follows: it is the expected value of the maximum of $D_1 - V_1$ and 0 as seen from the standpoint of period 0. So, if $D_1 - V_1$ exceeds zero, the expected value of this is entered into equation [9.5] (recall that we do not know V_1 when in period 0, so it is random. We do know it when we move to period 1).

The condition for developing the land immediately was that $ED > EW$ and we observed that this was a stricter condition than simply comparing the two expected values of development and preservation, as would be the case in the conventional cost-benefit case. We can rewrite the condition $ED > EW$ in terms of the expression for EW in [10.5], so that development immediately is only justified if:

$$(D_1 - D_2) > EP + \text{Emax}(D_1 - V_1, 0) \tag{10.6}$$

In slightly different form, this is the equation derived in Arrow and Fisher (1994).

Since we have gone through a lot of derivation, it is as well to summarise the basic finding:

- "conventional" cost-benefit analysis would follow a rule that, for development to be justified, $ED > EP$;
- the "options" approach requires a stricter rule, namely that $ED > EW$;
- EW and EP differ by an amount $\text{Emax}(D_1 - V_1, 0)$;
- So EP *understates* the "true" value of preservation by the amount $\text{Emax}(D_1 - V_1, 0)$.

How should QOV be interpreted? In some analyses QOV would be identified with the last expression above – i.e. $\text{Emax}(D_1 - V_1, 0)$. *But it is more precise to think of QOV as the increase in expected value of benefits from waiting.* The expression for this would be:

$$QOV = EW - \max(ED, EP) \tag{10.7}$$

That is, QOV is the difference between the expected value of waiting and whichever is the larger of ED and EP. Equation 10.5 implies that if $ED < EP$ then QOV and $\text{Emax}(D_1 - V_1, 0)$ are the same. But if, as in the example above, $ED > EP$ then QOV is *less* than $\text{Emax}(D_1 - V_1, 0)$.

10.3. How large is QOV?

In some ways, asking about the "size" of QOV is not very sensible. What matters is whether consideration of waiting and learning will change the nature of the decision made to commit resources to some policy or project. If that process results in a changed decision relative to the "baseline" of making decisions as if delay was not an option, then QOV may be large relative to the resources committed to the decision. It is in this sense that the financial literature argues that what we have called QOV, and what in that literature is known as the value of an option,[5] can be large (Dixit and Pindyck, 1995). In the financial literature, investing irreversibly "kills" the option because the decision cannot be reversed and the option of waiting for new information is also forgone. As a result:

> "This lost option value is an opportunity cost that must be included as part of the cost of the investment" (Dixit and Pindyck, 1994, p. 6).

Finding examples of estimated QOV in environmental economics applications is far harder. Box 10.1 outlines one study of forest conversion. Wesseler (2000) has suggested that QOV has a positive value in the context of postponing the introduction of genetically modified farm crops in Europe.

The discussion should be sufficient to underline an important feature of QOV: *it is not a component of total economic value (TEV)*. Rather, it is a reminder that decisions should be

Box 10.1. **Quasi option value and tropical forest conversion**

Tropical forests are rich testing grounds for determining the importance of "quasi option value" (QOV). QOV measures the value of information secured by postponing a decision that has irreversible consequences. Conversion of primary tropical forest land to agriculture would be one example of a loss that tends to be irreversible – while forests often do grow back as secondary forest, the biodiversity profile of the new forest may be different to that of the old one. QOV arises because there is uncertainty about the value of the forest. Delay in converting the forest improves the chances of improving information about the value of forest functions.

In a study of Costa Rica's tropical forests, Bulte *et al.* (2000) concluded on cost-benefit grounds that Costa Rica has "too much" forest: the social returns to conversion exceed the social returns to conservation. But the authors' model was "deterministic" – *i.e.* it assumed that future costs and benefits were known with certainty. In a later paper, Bulte *et al.* (2002), some of the authors show that once uncertainty ad irreversibility are included, Costa Rica has "too little" tropical forest cover.

The best way to appreciate the analysis is to set up their model in three stages. In each case, the (net present value, NPV) benefits of a sustainable forestry regime (B_F = "conservation") is compared to the benefits of converting the land to agriculture, which involves wholesale deforestation (B_A = "conversion").

Stage I: compare $NPV(B_F)$ with $NPV(B_A)$. The computation of B_F involves estimating the total economic value (see Chapter 6) of the forest under a sustainable forest regime. The authors estimate this value with and without global externality benefits. Global externalities here include what the rest of the world might be willing to pay Costa Rica for biodiversity benefits and for carbon sequestration.

Stage II: compare $\alpha NPV(B_F)$ with $NPV(B_A)$. The α here denotes a multiplier ($\alpha > 1$) to reflect a rising relative valuation of forest ecological services. In terms of Chapter 3, α reflects the income elasticity of the willingness to pay for environmental quality, multiplied by the trend rates of growth of per capita incomes. Bulte *et al.* (2002) set $\alpha = 2.5\%$ p.a. which is fairly arbitrary. In fact they could have borrowed a central estimate of the income elasticity of WTP from the literature of about 0.5. Multiplied by per capita income growth in Costa Rica of about 2.8% p.a. (1990-2001), the value of α would then be 1.4%, little more than half the Bulte *et al.* "guesstimate".

Stage II is equivalent to replacing the standard discount rate, s, with a "net" discount rate of $s - \alpha$. This "relative valuation effect" was noted in the early literature on irreversibility (Krutilla and Fisher, 1975; Porter, 1982).

Stage III: compare $\beta \alpha NPV(B_F)$ with $NPV(B_A)$. The β is a further adjustment, this time for uncertainty about B_F. β is essentially the value of QOV. Bulte *et al.* acknowledge that the value of β is not known. They therefore estimate "critical values" that would make agricultural conversion a better option than conservation. They show that uncertainty about forest values justifies more forest conservation than in the case where values are known with certainty. The size of QOV varies with the area of land converted to agriculture, as one would expect. The more forest is converted, the lower the marginal value of converted land.

One outcome of the study is that QOV (β) turns out to be considerably less important for the forest conservation/conversion decision than the rising relative valuation (α). This finding is consistent with another study that sought to elicit QOV (Albers *et al.* 1996). Bulte *et al.* note that what matters for the decision are *a*) the value of α, and *b*) the presence of global externalities. Indeed, if global externalities are ignored, and if $\alpha < 2.5\%$, which we indicate above is almost certainly the case for Costa Rica, then optimal forest stocks might be less than the current stock – more deforestation would be economically justified. Once the global values are included, however, the balance shifts strongly to favouring conservation over conversion. They conjecture that QOV remains unimportant relative to these other considerations

"If this result is confirmed by other studies, much simpler models that capture only trend [what we have called α] but ignore uncertainty may be sufficient for policy analysis" (Bulte *et al.*, 2002, p. 156).

made rationally. Despite this, QOV often does appear in the literature as if it is a component of TEV. This is not correct. Freeman (2003) sums it up well:

"Quasi-option value is not a component of the values individuals attach to resource changes. Even if individuals' utility functions were known, quasi-option value could not be estimated separately and added into a benefit-cost equation. Quasi-option value is a benefit of adopting better decision-making procedures. Its magnitude can only be revealed by comparing two strategies where one of the strategies involves optimal sequential decision-making to take advantage of information obtained by delaying irreversible resource commitments. The decision-maker who knows how to use an optimal sequential decision-making strategy has no reason to calculate quasi-option value. The calculation would be redundant because the best decision is already known" (p. 250-251).

10.4. Summary and guidance for decision-makers

The notion of quasi option value was introduced in the environmental economics literature some three decades ago. In parallel, financial economists developed the notion of "option value". Somewhat confusingly, environmental economists also developed a concept of option value that was unlinked to either QOV or the OV of the financial literature. In the end, QOV was recognised as being the same as the financial literature's OV.

QOV is not a separate category of economic value. Rather it is the difference between the net benefits of making an optimal decision and one that is not optimal because it ignores the gains that may be made by delaying a decision and learning during the period of delay. Usually, QOV arises in the context of irreversibility. But it can only emerge if there is uncertainty which can be resolved by learning. If the potential to learn is not there, QOV cannot arise.

Can QOV make a significant difference to decision-making? Potentially, yes. It is there to remind us that decisions should be made on the basis of maximum feasible information about the costs and benefits involved, and that includes "knowing that we do not know". If this ignorance cannot be resolved then nothing is to be gained by delay. But if information can resolve it, then delay can improve the quality of the decision. How large the gain is from this process is essentially an empirical question since QOV is the difference in the net benefits of an optimal decision and a less than optimal one. The financial literature suggests that this difference can be large relative to the scale of resources being committed to a decision. Further study is needed in the environmental context to see if similar results hold. Examples to date are limited.

Notes

1. Which is the more important of these features is open to debate. Some have argued that it is uncertainty and the opportunity for learning that matter most and that irreversibility is of limited consequence. Nonetheless, the literature has generally proceeded on the basis of there being irreversibility in either the commitment of resources or some of the benefits forgone.

2. This section has been adapted from material kindly supplied by Dr. Joseph Swierzbinski of the Department of Economics, University College London and largely comprises a simplification of the original article by Arrow and Fisher (1994).

3. Decision trees are one of the basic constructs of *decision analysis* (*e.g.* see Merkhofer, 1987).

4. Dixit and Pindyck (1994, pp. 395-6) advocated the use of their "real options" approach to global warming policy evaluation. For an application see Ulph and Ulph (1997).

5. There are also analogies with financial call options in the financial literature – see Dixit and Pindyck (1994).

ANNEX 10.A1

Deriving the Expected Value of Waiting

Equation [10.5] in the text was written as

$$EW = V_0 + EV_1 + \text{Emax}(D_1 - V_1, 0) = EP + \text{Emax}(D_1 - V_1, 0) \qquad \text{[A10.1]}$$

This is derived from the first expression for EW (Equation 9.4 in the text) as follows:

$$EW = V_0 + pV_{high} + (1 - p)D_1 \qquad \text{[A10.2]}$$

Add $(1 - p)V_{low}$ and then subtract it from [A9.2] to give

$$EW = V_0 + V_{high} + (1 - p)V_{low} + (1 - p)(D_1 - V_{low}) \qquad \text{[A10.3]}$$

or

$$EW = EP + (1 - p)(D_1 - V_{low}) \qquad \text{[A10.4]}$$

High preservation benefits occur in period 1 with a probability of p, so the maximum of $D_1 - V_1$ and 0 is 0 since the development value in period 1 is below the high preservation value. Low preservation benefits in period 1 occur with a probability $(1 - p)$ and the maximum of $D_1 - V_1$ and 0 is then $D_1 - V_{low}$ since the development value exceeds the low preservation value. Hence:

$$\text{Emax}(D_1 - V_1, 0) = + (1 - p)(D_1 - V_{low}) + p.0 = (1 - p)(D_1 - V_{low}, 0) \qquad \text{[A10.5]}$$

Hence [A10.4] can be written:

$$EW = EP + \text{Emax}(D_1 - V_1, 0) \qquad \text{[A10.6]}$$

which is equation [10.5] in the main text.

ISBN 92-64-01004-1
Cost-Benefit Analysis and the Environment
Recent Developments
© OECD 2006

Chapter 11

Willingness to Pay *vs.* Willingness to Accept

Until recently, CBA has worked with concepts of willingness to pay (WTP) and willingness to accept compensation (WTA). Which concept is used depends on the assumption about property rights. If there is no right to the benefit of a project or policy, then WTP is the correct measure. If there is a right to the benefit, then WTA compensation to forego the benefit is the correct measure. Which is chosen would not matter if, in practice, they are empirically very similar. This was the assumption until stated preference analysis showed that WTA appears systematically to exceed WTP. This chapter reviews the empirical evidence and looks at various theories designed to explain the marked disparity between WTP and WTA. Which measure is used can make a substantial difference to a CBA outcome.

11.1. Conventional procedures for economic valuation

CBA requires that benefits and costs be valued in money terms, as far as is possible. Technically, a benefit is measured by the willingness to pay to secure it (WTP) and a cost by the willingness to accept compensation for the loss (WTAC or WTA for short). But these rules conceal an issue of just what the correct basis is for measuring gains and losses in money terms. Moreover, even these rules are not usually followed in conventional practice. The costs of a project, for example, usually consist of the actual capital and operating costs of the investment, plus any external costs. The former are measured in financial terms (see Chapter 5) and this financial cost is taken as an approximation of the opportunity cost of the project, *i.e.* the benefits that could have been earned had the money been used in its next best use. This equation of financial costs with opportunity costs is at best an approximation of true opportunity cost. Similarly, any external costs tend to be measured by individuals' WTP to avoid the relevant losses, rather than their WTA compensation to bear the losses. The practice of CBA thus tends to mix approximations to WTP with some direct measures of WTP, and WTA tends to get only a limited treatment. This would not matter if, for all practical purposes, WTP and WTA are roughly the same. The problem is that a considerable body of empirical analysis suggests they are not the same. If this is true, and if there are valid reasons for the disparity between WTP and WTA, then it will matter in practice which concept is used to measure gains and which to measure losses.

11.2. Consumer's surplus for quantity changes

Hicks (1943) showed that the Marshallian measure of consumer's surplus (the area under a conventional demand curve bounded from below by the prevailing price) is not in fact a true measure of the benefit of a price change. The essential reason for this is that the Marshallian measure holds *income* constant, whereas for a true measure of welfare change it is *welfare* (utility, well-being) that needs to be held constant. The issue then is what the reference point is for holding welfare constant. It could be the welfare achieved *before* the change (i.e. before the policy or project) or *after* the change. Hicks produced four measures of welfare change in the context of a *price change*, two of which hold welfare constant at the pre-change level, and two of which hold welfare constant at the post-change level. But there are two contexts for each measure: one in which prices decrease and one in which they increase. Hence, for the context of a price change, no less than eight notions of surplus emerge. These concepts are analysed in the annex to this chapter.

While the four measures (five, including the Marshallian measure) were developed by Hicks for *price changes*, they also apply to *quantity* changes. The relevant quantity-based measures were first developed by Mäler (1971, 1974). Quantity change tends to be more relevant for environmental policy and investments which generally change quantities rather than the prices of environmental goods. The relevant measures of surplus in this context are *compensating and equivalent surplus* measures since these constrain the individual to certain quantities of the goods (Randall and Stoll, 1980), the feature noted for quantity-constrained measures of surplus arising from price changes.

Figure 11.1 translates these measures in terms of demand curves. There are now three demand curves:

H_{new} is the Hicksian demand curve for the new level of welfare, *i.e.* where the relevant reference point is the level of welfare that would arise in the situation after a policy change.

H_{orig} is the Hicksian demand curve for the original level of welfare, *i.e.* where the relevant reference point is the level of welfare that pertains in the original, pre-change, situation.

M is the Marshallian demand curve.

The strictly correct demand curves are the Hicksian ones, also known as *compensated demand curves*. They are correct because their reference point is a constant level of welfare, whether it is before or after the change in question. The Marshallian demand curve holds income constant, not welfare. Depending on the magnitude of the difference between these demand curves, which one is chosen could matter for cost-benefit analysis. There is one situation in which the curves all coincide, and this is:

Figure 11.1. **Demand curve representations of consumer's surplus**

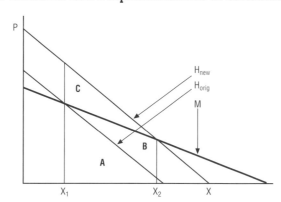

where the marginal utility of income is constant, *i.e.* the consumer gets the same amount of welfare from an extra unit of income regardless of how much income he/she has.

Figure 11.1 shows a situation in which the quantity of good X changes from X_1 to X_2. The relevant measures of consumer's surplus are as follows:

Area A + B = Marshallian surplus (MS)

Area A = compensating surplus (CS)

Area A + B + C = equivalent surplus (ES)

Note that the following relationships hold for a quantity *increase*:

ES > MS > CS

and

ES < MS < CS for a quantity decrease.

Following Mitchell and Carson (1989), the measures of surplus for both quantity changes and for price changes can be summarised as in Table 11.1. The table also shows the links to willingness to pay and willingness to accept. The measures in bold are the ones most likely to be relevant to environmental contexts where quantities change but prices do not.

Table 11.1. **Summary of surplus measures**

	WTP	WTA
Quantity increase	CS	ES
Quantity decrease	ES	CS
Price increase	ES, EV	CS, CV
Price decrease	CS, CV	ES, EV

Mitchell and Carson suggest that the two CS measures fit most contexts. They argue that the context for policy is usually one where benefits are measured relative to the *current* state of individuals' welfare. For an improvement in environmental quality or quantity, CS is the maximum WTP for that improvement whilst maintaining the pre-policy level of welfare (*i.e.* the individual is just as well off with the improvement as without it). For any decrease in environmental quality or quantity, CS is the minimum compensation the individual is willing to accept to tolerate the reduce quality. In short:

CS (q+) = maxWTP

CS (q–) = min WTA

(where q+ is the quantity increase and q- the quantity decrease.)

11.3. Property rights

The implicit assumption in Mitchell and Carson's recommendation of CS is that individuals have a (property) right to the *initial* situation. They have no right to the benefit brought about by the policy in question and hence the relevant magnitude is their willingness to pay. But they have a right not to have their existing situation worsened, hence the relevant magnitude if this is the context is their willingness to accept compensation.

But it is feasible to argue that individuals have some right to the "new" quantity of the environmental good, *i.e.* the post-policy level. Indeed, this idea is very much at the heart of environmental debates. First, many environmentalists would argue that there are basic "rights" to clean air, etc. If this is accepted, then it is sensible to retain the notions of ES as well as CS, since ES relates to the context where there is a "right" to the change. Second, reflection on the nature of some environmental legislation suggests that much of it confers rights to future states of the environment. Consider, for example, an extensive piece of legislation like the Clean Air Act in the USA or the Water Framework Directive in the European Union. The former implies that there is a legal obligation to secure a future state of air quality which is an improvement over the level of quality at the time of the legislation.[1] The second requires that all European Union water bodies secure "good ecological status" which will generally involve improving water quality compared to its current state. In both cases, it could be argued that a legal "right" has been assigned to a future state of the environment. If so, it could be argued that WTA to forego that right is the relevant valuation concept.

In practice, determining these property rights is not straightforward. Consider the EU Water Framework Directive again. It requires a widespread improvement in water quality but it does allow for "derogations", *i.e.* exceptions to the rule which arise in contexts of "disproportionate cost". Simply put, if it is "too expensive" to secure the water quality improvement, that quality change need not come about. What derogation clauses of this kind do is to confer a separate set of rights, effectively on taxpayers, to the effect that they have a right not to have their tax payments used in contexts where the costs of quality improvements are regarded as being, in some sense, disproportionate to the benefits. The Water Framework Directive could, therefore, be argued to embody a *prima facie* right to a future, improved state of the environment, while at the same time attenuating that right if taxpayers' interests are deemed to be disproportionately affected.

The basic rule for the practice of CBA, then, is that the analyst needs always to consult with legislators and interest groups as to precisely what the property rights regime is, or is thought to be. These deliberations should then set the context for deciding which valuation concept, WTP or WTA (or both), might be used. As we see later, there may be reasons for adopting WTP even when WTA is the "right" notion.

Table 11.2 is an alternative way of presenting the information in Table 11.1 and summarises the all-important connections between the various equivalent and compensating measures, WTP and WTA. For convenience, the CS and ES measures are omitted for price changes, and a minus sign is placed in front of CS and ES for the "policy worse" cases. Note that in all cases:[2]

$$WTA - WTP = ES - CS$$

Table 11.2. **Summary links between WTP, WTA and equivalent and compensating measures**

PROPERTY RIGHTS:	POLICY MAKES INDIVIDUAL WORSE OFF: PRICE INCREASE or QUANTITY DECREASE	POLICY MAKES INDIVIDUAL BETTER OFF: PRICE DECREASE or QUANTITY INCREASE
RIGHT TO THE STATUS QUO	WTA TO TOLERATE LOSS CV −CS	WTP TO SECURE GAIN CV CS
RIGHT TO A NEW SITUATION	WTP TO AVOID LOSS EV −ES	WTA TO FOREGO THE BENEFIT EV ES

11.4. Do WTP and WTA differ in practice?

The previous excursion into the theoretical foundations of benefit and cost measurement would be "academic" if WTP and WTA do not differ much in practice. But more and more empirical work is finding that WTP and WTA do differ, and sometimes by considerable amounts. This information comes from stated preference studies (see Chapters 8 and 9) based on some questionnaires in which respondents are asked for both their WTP and their WTA. Many of these studies have been analysed in a very useful study by Horowitz and McConnell (2002).

Horowitz and McConnell find 45 usable studies reporting WTP and WTA. The ratio of mean WTA to mean WTP ("the ratio") was regressed on the following explanatory variables:

● Private or public good.

● Hypothetical or real valuation questions (real means actual money was involved).

● Elicitation technique (open ended questions, payment cards, etc.).

● Respondents: students or non-students.

● Number of observations.

They find that the further away the good being valued is from being an ordinary private good, the higher is the ratio. Table 11.3 shows the results:

Table 11.3. **WTA/WTP for types of goods**

Type of good	Ratio	Standard error
Public or non-market	10.4	2.5
Health and safety	10.1	2.3
Private goods	2.9	0.3
Lotteries	2.1	0.2
Timing*	1.9	0.2
All goods	7.2	0.9

* Time at which a good is supplied.

Source: Horowitz and McConnell (2002).

The closer the good gets to money itself, the narrower the ratio. Table 11.4 shows a further breakdown of the results for public goods, since these are most relevant to environmental contexts. Horowitz and McConnell also found that surveys using real goods showed no lower ratios than surveys with hypothetical goods. This suggests that the disparity between WTP and WTA is not peculiar to the hypothetical contexts that characterise stated preference studies, one of the explanations sometimes advanced for the disparity. They also found that surveys with high incentive compatibility (truth-telling) do not produce lower ratios. There is a widespread suggestion that strategic behaviour on the part of respondents will impart greater disparity on the WTA-WTP relationship, but the study found no evidence for this. However, they did find that elicitation methods – i.e. the type of WTP/WTA question asked – may or may not affect the disparity.

Table 11.4. **Ratio of WTA to WTP for public goods**

Type of good	Ratio	Standard error
Miscellaneous public/non-market goods	27.6	7.5
Hunting	10.5	5.3
Visibility	7.4	2.3
Siting	4.1	1.8
Sucrose octa-acetate*	4.0	0.5

* Bitter but harmless substance used in several experiments.

Source: Horowitz and McConnell (2002).

Horowitz and McConnell are clear in their conclusions that a) the disparities are real, b) they are generally not due to questionnaire-related features, and c) they matter most for precisely the kinds of areas characterised by environmental policy.

11.5. Why do WTP and WTA diverge?

A substantial literature has emerged which attempts to explain the observed divergence between WTP and WTA. The details of the arguments are not of concern here (see Pearce, 2003a), but a brief summary of the arguments is in order. Explanations matter because, if for some reason the disparity is an artefact of questionnaire design or respondent behaviour, then it would not be correct to adopt those values for policy purposes. In turn, this would mean that the WTA vs. WTP debate would not be relevant for the practice of CBA. Rather, the policy strategy might be to adopt a more conservative approach to value selection. If, however, the disparities reflect genuine features of the goods being valued, or genuine features of individuals' preference structures, then there is a case for looking again at the way in which cost-benefit appraisal and benefit assessment is carried out.

Table 11.5 tries to summarise the central points. It is not easy to derive any central conclusion because the debate continues and, while individual contributors may be clear as to what they think is the dominant explanation, any independent assessment must conclude that there are strong features to most of the arguments presented. In short, it remains the case that "the jury is out".

Table 11.5. **Summary of factors affecting the WTA-WTP disparity**

Explanation	Context	
	WTA > WTP for quantity gains (or losses)	WTA for a quantity loss > WTP for a quantity gain
Income effect	WTA-WTP must be small due to income effect: Randall and Stoll (1980); Diamond (1996). Observed WTA – WTP disparities too high to be accounted for by income effects	
Income and substitution effect	WTA-WTP could be large if substitution effect small Hanemann (1991, 1999)	
Substitution effect		WTA-WTP could be large Hanemann (1999)
Questionnaire design	Possible biases to "open ended" WTA and WTP answers such that WTA-WTP widens (Hanemann, 1999). No firm evidence (Horowitz and McConnell, 2000)	
Reference dependency: endowment effect alone		Bateman et al. (1997) and others find endowment effects. Moral commitment as source of reference point? Boyce et al. 1992, and others
Mixed substitution and endowment effects		Morrison (1996, 1997) finds endowment effect plus substitution effect
Uncertainty about preferences, and effects of learning	Imprecise preferences can understate WTP and overstate WTA. Kolstad et al. 1999. Repeated trials may tend to reduce disparity to point where WTA ≈ WTP Shogren et al. 2001 (contra Horowitz and McConnell). "Real options" approach: uncertainty about value of good, plus significant transactions costs of reversing the decision, leads to a desired delay to get more information. If forced to state a value now, respondent will give a lower value of WTP now, or a higher value of WTA (Zhao and Kling, 2001).	

Table 11.5 suggests various explanations for the disparity. Two contexts are differentiated. The first is where what is compared is two measures of gain or two measures of loss. That is, WTP for a gain is compared to WTA to forego the gain, or WTP to avoid a loss is compared to WTA the loss. The second context is where what is compared is a gain (WTP) with a loss of an equivalent quantity (WTA).

11.5.1. *Income effects*

The first explanation for the disparity rests on an income effect, *i.e.* on the fact that real income changes in a different way according to whether the individual has to pay or receives compensation. The bigger the income elasticity of demand for the good in question, the bigger the disparity between WTA and WTP. This suggests that the disparity could be small or big. However, in an influential article, Willig (1976) argued that the disparity must be small, so much so that nothing is lost by adopting the *Marshallian* measure of surplus rather than a measure based on compensated demand curves. Willig showed how to use information on the income elasticity of demand to "bound" the differences between EV and CV for a price change. Any error in using the Marshallian measure of surplus is proportional to the income elasticity of demand and consumer surplus as a fraction of income. For most realistic cases, Willig argued, the errors are small and of a few percentage points only. By and large, then, income effects cannot explain the substantially different estimates of WTP and WTA. Some authors believe that this implication is sufficient to cast doubt on the observed disparity between WTP and WTA, *i.e.* observed differences must be due to some artefact of the procedures used to derive the estimates, namely stated preference studies (*e.g.* Diamond, 1996). The consensus point, however, is that income effects cannot explained the observed disparities between WTA and WTPO. Hence those disparities are either artefacts or something else is happening.

11.5.2. *Substitution effects*

Hanemann (1991, 1999) shows that the *substitution effect* is capable of explaining the WTA-WTP difference. Intuitively, if environmental goods have few substitutes then very high levels of compensation will be required to tolerate a reduction in their quantity. More technically, the ratio of WTA to WTP depends on the ratio of the income effect to the substitution effect. If the latter is very small relative to the income effect, the disparity will be wide.[3]

11.5.3. *Endowment effects*

Now consider the context where WTP for a gain is being compared to WTA for a loss, the quantity of the gain and loss being equal. This case has produced a substantial literature and has given rise to notions of "loss aversion" and "reference dependency" which, if correct, would have major implications for cost-benefit analysis. The basic idea behind reference dependency and loss aversion is that losses are weighted far more heavily than gains, where loss and gain are measured equally in terms of quantities. The point of reference for the loss and gain is an *endowment point* which is often the bundle of goods, or the amount of a specific good, already owned or possessed, but could be some other point, *e.g.* an aspiration level. The reference dependency model is owed mainly to Tversky and Kahnemann (1991) and builds on the earlier "prospect theory" work of Kahnemann and Tversky (1979). Many of the seminal works on reference dependency are collected together in Kahnemann and Tversky (2000).

The features of reference-dependency then are that valuations of gains and losses are always *relative* to the reference or endowment point, losses are valued more heavily than gains, and the valuation function exhibits diminishing marginal valuation the further away from the reference point one gets. The effect is to produce the result that that WTA > WTP and, depending on the degree of loss aversion, WTA could greatly exceed WTP. The explanation of reference dependency is essentially psychological: advocates of the approach argue that it is an observed feature of many gain/loss contexts, so that theory is essentially being advanced as an explanation of observed behaviour.

Whether substitution effects *alone* or an endowment effect *alone* explains WTA > WTP would now appear to be an empirical issue. Shogren *et al.* (1994) claimed to show that only the substitution effect is present in contexts where WTA > WTP, thus rejecting the endowment effect. Their argument was essentially as follows:

● WTP and WTA are likely to converge for marketed goods with close substitutes (high elasticity of substitution).

● The empirical evidence was consistent with this proposition.

● WTA was found to be greater than WTP for goods with low substitutability.

● If there is an endowment effect, it should show up as WTA > WTP regardless of the degree of substitutability.

● But as close substitutes showed WTA and WTP to be similar, there could be no endowment effect.

Adamowicz *et al.* (1993) designed an experiment concerning tickets to a hockey game. Part of the sample was informed that the game would be broadcast and part that it would not. The former thus believed there was a substitute and the latter than there was no substitute on offer. Respondents were given WTP questions (how much WTP to purchase a ticket) and how much WTA compensation to sell the ticket. The ratio of WTA to WTP fell from 1.9 in the no-substitute case, to 1.7 in the substitute case, which offers some evidence for the effects o substitution for a familiar, everyday private good. Some authors (*e.g.* Morrison, 1996; 1997; Knetsch, 1989; Knetsch and Sinden, 1984) have argued that both an endowment effect and a substitution effect explain WTA > WTP. Effectively, loss aversion magnifies the substitution effect by shifting the indifference curve.

11.5.4. Uncertainty

Zhao and Kling (2001) offer one of several explanations for the WTA/WTP disparity based on the presence of uncertainty. In their argument, irreversibility is also present. When irreversibility and uncertainty combine with the opportunity for learning, there are incentives to delay decisions – this is the essence of quasi-option value (see Chapter 10). Now add the presence of transactions costs such that it is costly to reverse any decision actually made. The sequence is then as follows:

● The respondent to a questionnaire is asked to state a WTP or a WTA.

● The respondent is unsure about the value of the good in question but he/she knows it will be costly to reverse the decision.

● He/she therefore prefers to wait and gather information before offering a bid price or agreeing to a price posed by the questioner.

● If forced to state a WTP *now*, it will be *lower* than in a world of certainty because the respondent wants to be compensated for having to take the decision now and to forego the value of the information derived from delay.

● If forced to state a WTA now, it will be *higher* than otherwise on the same argument, *i.e.* compensation is needed to forego the value of information.

The Zhao-Kling arguments are ingenious in bringing together the option value approach (Chapter 10) and the various welfare measures. They also claim that some experimental work (notably Bateman *et al.* 1997) supports their conjecture.

11.6. Why do the competing explanations for WTA > WTP matter?

The brief review of the explanatory literature is important for the practice of CBA.

First, if WTA > WTP is an observed and significant discrepancy then the use of one or the other in a CBA framework will significantly affect the outcome of the CBA. A CBA using WTP for benefits and costs, for example, would probably produce a very different result from one using WTA for benefits and costs (Carson *et al.* 2001). The extent of the difference would depend on the nature of the good being considered, as the Horowitz-McConnell survey suggests.

Second, while the conventional literature has proceeded as if the assignment of property rights in a CBA always favours rights to the status quo but not to improvements, this is hard to square with the nature of much environmental legislation which appears to confer rights to future, improved states of the environment. Offsetting this, if the legislation observes notions such as "disproportionate cost" it suggests that there is a mix of property rights between beneficiaries and losers.[4] Either way, the importance of "sorting out" the property rights in a CBA context is important.

Third, if the discrepancy between WTP and WTA is an artefact of the way the results are obtained (recall that the discrepancy comes from observations in stated preference studies about which there is a separate controversy), then there is no issue to be debated: WTP and WTA are similar, as some of the traditional theory would predict.

Fourth, if the discrepancy is real and due to substitution effects, conventional approaches to CBA are preserved but the analysts would have to consider using WTA regardless of whether the context is one of property rights to the status quo (an argument that would be widely accepted) or the improved context (which would be more debated).

Fifth, if the discrepancy is real but is due to an endowment effect independently of the substitution effect, there are far more serious implications for CBA. These are not explored here, but effectively amount to a questioning of the underlying theory of demand and willingness to pay.

11.7. Practical reasons for using WTP

In the wake of the controversy over the use of contingent valuation to assess damages in the *Exxon Valdez* case,[5] in 1992 the US National Oceanic and Atmospheric Administration (NOAA) set up an expert panel to evaluate the "validity" of contingent valuation. While the Panel endorsed the use of contingent valuation in liability contexts, it issued a number of Guidelines that it considered should be met in the conduct of future studies (Arrow *et al.* 1993). One of those Guidelines relates to the value elicitation format and states that:

> "The willingness to pay format should be used instead of compensation required because the former is the conservative estimate" (Arrow *et al.* 1993, p. 51).

It is easy to understand the concern for "conservatism" in valuation estimates since the *Exxon Valdez* case was controversial precisely because the resulting WTP values were already large (they also related mainly to "passive" or "non-use" values, which added to the controversy). Use of WTA values may well have made them much larger. However, it can be argued that there is no particularly logical case for espousing "conservatism". What matters is the agreed nature of property rights and the degree of uncertainty associated with the valuation estimates. In the *Exxon Valdez* case, liability for damage related to the status quo, not to any improvement, so the property rights issue was ultimately fairly straightforward. But liability contexts are just one of many contexts in which economic valuation is required. The Arrow *et al.* recommendations are really specific to the liability context where the property rights are indeed to the status quo and where damage has been done to that status quo. As noted earlier, there is no real argument that, in this context, WTP is the correct notion of economic value. It is not at all clear that this presumption carries over to regulatory contexts.

11.8. Summary and guidance for decision-makers

Traditionally, economists have been fairly indifferent about the welfare measure to be used for economic valuation: WTP and WTA have both been acceptable. By and large, the literature has focused on WTP. However, the development of stated preference studies has, fairly repeatedly, discovered divergences, sometimes substantial divergencies, between WTA and WTP. These differences still would not matter if the nature of property rights regimes were always clear. WTP in the context of a potential improvement is clearly linked to rights to the status quo. Similarly, if the context is one of losing the status quo, then WTAC for that loss is the relevant measure. By and large, environmental policy tends to deal with improvements rather than deliberate degradation of the environment, so there is a presumption that WTP is the right measure. The problems arise when individuals can be thought of as having some right to a future state of the environment. If that right exists, their WTP to secure that right seems inappropriate as a measure of welfare change, whereas their WTAC to forego that improvement seems more relevant. In practice, the policy context may well be one of a mixture of rights, *e.g.* a right to an improvement attenuated by the rights of others not to pay "too much" for that improvement.

Finding out why, empirically, WTA and WTP differ also matters. If there are legitimate reasons to explain the difference then the preceding arguments apply and one would have to recommend that CBA should always try to find both values. The CBA result would then be shown under both assumptions. But if the observed differences between WTA and WTP are artefacts of questionnaire design, there is far less reason to be concerned at the difference between them. The fallback position of their approximate equality could be assumed. Unfortunately, the literature is undecided as to why the values differ. This again suggests showing the CBA results under both assumptions about the right concept of value.

Notes

1. Space forbids a detailed discussion but the US Supreme Court has ruled that the cost of achieving the CAA goals is not a relevant consideration in achieving those goals. Contrast this with the EU Water Framework Directive where cost considerations are quite explicitly accounted for.

2. This requires recalling the minus signs. For the quantity gain WTA – WTP is obviously ES-CS. For the quantity loss, however, WTA – WTP = –CS–(–)ES = ES – CS.

3. Technically, in the case of a price change it is the income effect that explains the difference between WTP and WTA. For a quantity change, which is more relevant to the environmental context, both substitution and income effects are present – see Carson *et al.* (2001).

4. Note that such notions are widespread in environment policy, *e.g.* "best available technology not entailing excessive cost" (BATNEEC), "as low as is reasonably achievable" (ALARA), etc.

5. The oil tanker *Exxon Valdez* ran aground in Bligh Reef, Alaska in 1989, discharging a large quantity of oil. Contingent valuation was used to value the resulting damage (or, more technically, the WTP to avoid a similar incident).

ANNEX 11.A1

Hicks's Measures of Consumer Surplus for a Price Change

11.1. Hicks's four consumer's surpluses when the price of X changes

Compensating variation (CV)

Consider a price *decrease*. The individual is better off with the price decrease than without it. CV is then the maximum sum that could be taken away from the individual such that he is indifferent between the post-change (new) situation and the pre-change (original) situation. The reference point is the *original* level of welfare.

Consider a price *increase*. The individual is worse off with the price increase than without it. CV is then the compensation required by the individual to make him indifferent between the new and old situations. The reference point is again the *original* level of welfare

The CV measures relate to a context in which the change in question takes place. In this case they relate to the situation in which the price falls. CV in the context of a price fall thus measures the individual's *maximum willingness to pay* rather than relinquish the price reduction. In the context of a price rise, CV is the *minimum amount the individual is willing to accept* by way of compensation to tolerate the higher price. Note that the implicit assumption about property rights with CV is that the individual is entitled to the pre-change situation.

Equivalent variation (EV)

Consider a price *decrease*. The individual is better off with the price decrease than without it. EV measures the sum of money that would have to be given to the individual in the original situation to make him as well off as he would be in the new situation. The reference point is the level of welfare in the *new* situation.

Consider a price *increase*. EV is now the individual's willingness to pay to avoid the price increase, *i.e.* to avoid the decrease in welfare that would arise in the post-change situation. The reference point is the level of welfare in the *new* situation.

The EV measures relate to a context in which *the price change does not take place*. EV for a price fall is the *minimum willingness to accept* to forego the price fall. EV for a price rise is the *maximum willingness to pay* to avoid the price rise. Note that the implicit assumption about property rights with EV is that the individual is entitled to the post change situation.

Compensating surplus (CS)

The compensating surplus, CS, and equivalent surplus (ES) measures relate to contexts in which the individual is constrained to consume either the new quantity of X (CS) or the old quantity of X (ES) arising from the price change. CS is then defined as the sum that would make the individual indifferent between the original situation and a situation in which he is constrained to buy the quantity of X that results from the price change. If the context is a price *decrease*, then CS is a measure of the *willingness to pay* to secure that decrease. If the context is one of a price *increase*, then CS is a measure of the *willingness to accept* compensation for the price increase.

Equivalent surplus (ES)

ES is similarly quantity-constrained and is defined as the sum that would make the individual indifferent between the new situation (with the price change) and the old situation if the individual is constrained to buy the quantity of X in the original situation. If the context is a price *decrease*, then ES is a measure of the *willingness to accept* compensation to forego the benefit of the price decrease. If the context is one of a price *increase*, then ES is a measure of the *willingness to pay* to avoid the increase.

The concepts can be shown diagrammatically, as in Figure A11.1 which shows the situation for a price fall. The following relationships hold for equivalent price changes:

● CV price fall = –EV price rise.

● EV price fall = –CV price rise.

● EV = CV if the income elasticity of demand for X is zero.

● EV > CV for a price decrease if the income elasticity of demand is positive.

● EV < CV for a price increase if the income elasticity of demand is positive.

● The higher the income elasticity of demand for X, the greater the disparity between CV and EV.

Figure A11.1. **Hicks's four consumer's surpluses for a price fall**

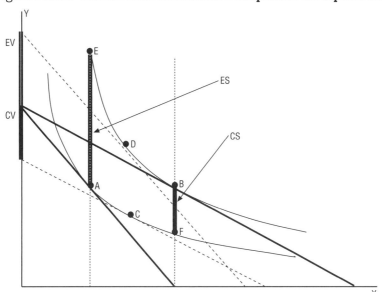

Note that Figure A11.1 shows the four measures of surplus for a price fall. The same notions will apply to a price rise, giving eight measures in all.

ISBN 92-64-01004-1
Cost-Benefit Analysis and the Environment
Recent Developments
© OECD 2006

Chapter 12

The Value of Ecosystem Services

Ecosystems function like other capital assets – they generate a flow of services through time, and the capital can be held intact if the services are consumed in a sustainable fashion. Moreover, any ecosystem tends to generate many such services. This chapter analyses ecosystems from this multi-functional perspective, making a clear distinction between the total value of the ecosystem as an asset and the value of small or discrete changes in its service flow. The valuation issues are illustrated with reference to the debated benefits of ecosystems as providers of genetic value for pharmaceutical research.

12.1. Ecosystem services

All life is embedded in various categories of *ecosystems*, where ecosystems are defined at life forms ("biota") and their abiotic environments. Thus, a forest or a wetland is an ecosystem, as are coral reefs, deserts, estuaries and rivers. All ecosystems generate *services* which are extensive and pervasive. Those services essentially maintain life on Earth so, in one sense, all ecosystem services are economic services – they have an economic value based on the benefits human beings receive from those ecosystems. An ecologist might select the following services as being of considerable importance, but would probably define them without necessarily having the focus on how humans benefit, which tends to be the economist's perspective. Here we select some services that have obvious human benefit. Ecosystems provide:

- Purification services: for example, wetlands filter water and forests filter air pollution.

- Ecological cycling: for example, growing vegetation takes in ("fixes" or "sequesters") carbon dioxide, and stores it in the biomass until the death of the vegetation, the carbon then being transferred to soil. Since carbon dioxide is a greenhouse gas, growing biomass reduces those gases in the atmosphere.

- Regulation: natural systems have interacting species such that pests are controlled through natural processes, reducing the need for artificial controls. Ecosystems may regulate watershed and weather behaviour, reducing risk of floods.

- Habitat provision: habitats are stores of biological diversity which in turn may be linked to processes that reduce the risks of ecosystem collapse ("resilience"), even apart from providing sources of food, scientific information, recreational and aesthetic value.

- Regeneration and production: ecosystems "grow" biomass by converting light, energy and nutrients. This biomass provides food, raw materials and energy. Ecosystems ensure pollination and seed dispersal take place, ensuring that the systems are themselves renewed. It is estimated that some 30% of the world's food crops are dependent on natural pollination.

- Information and life support. Ecosystems are the products of evolution and hence embody millions of years of information. This information has scientific value but is also a source of wonder and life support.

While much of the focus is on "natural" ecosystems, the reality is that few ecosystems are unmodified by human behaviour, either deliberately – as with conversion of forest land to agriculture, or inadvertently through pollution or the introduction of non-endemic biological species ("biological invasions"). The challenge for cost-benefit analysis is to secure some kind of measure of these various ecological-cum-economic values for both natural and semi-natural ecosystems. If such an exercise were possible, and was reasonably accurate, we would have a far better idea of what is being sacrificed when ecosystems degrade in face of constant threats to convert them to simpler, less diverse systems (*e.g.* homogeneous agriculture). In terms of Chapter 6, we would know more about the total economic value (TEV) of ecosystems.

In recent years considerable efforts have been made to identify these ecosystem service values (*e.g.* Daily 1997). There are also increasing efforts to gather some idea of the sum of the values of the individual services – for forests see Pearce and Pearce (2001), for wetlands see Brouwer *et al.* (1999) and Woodward and Wui (2001). In the case of forests, for example, progress has been made on measuring the economic values associated with timber and non-timber products, carbon sequestration and storage, recreation, and watershed regulation. Some limited progress has been made in estimating the non-use values of forests. Far more elusive are the informational values – although a lively debate exists on the value of genetic material in forests for pharmaceutical research (for a survey, see Pearce 2004c) – and the wider ecological values, especially "resilience" to shocks and stresses.

But there are major methodological issues to be addressed. First, it is not clear that the "bottom-up" approaches whereby each type of service is valued separately and then the values are added to get some idea of the TEV of the ecosystem, are capturing the "whole" value of the ecosystem. Put another way, the value of the system as a whole may be more than the value of the sum of its parts. Ecosystems have interactive processes, a variable potential to adapt to exogenous change, and the relevant changes are often non-linear (Arrow *et al.* 2000). The bottom-up valuation procedure could therefore be misleading. A small economic value for one service might suggest it could be dispensed with, yet its removal could reverberate on the other services through complex changes within the ecosystem. The second problem arises from non-linearity. A cost-benefit analysis that fails to account for thresholds, for example, might dictate the conversion of part of an ecosystem for more direct human use. The assumption would be that conversion of this part of the ecosystem would not affect the remaining ecological services. Non-linearity means that this assumption is suspect. The third problem is that there is both uncertainty about the nature of the services themselves and, even more so, about their interactions. Converting a natural system may therefore produce unanticipated effects. And those effects may be irreversible. Chapter 10 looked at one way of approaching this problem in terms of (quasi) option value. We return to this approach shortly.

It follows that "ecosystem valuation" is not a straightforward exercise and it seems fair to say that the literature has progressed only a limited distance in tackling these issues.

12.2. Marginal *vs.* total valuation

Economists are clear that when they value an environmental asset they are valuing a very small ("marginal") change in the asset, or a discrete change. In the former case, consumer and producer surplus (see Chapter 2) are negligible. In the latter case they need to be estimated using the valuation techniques described in Chapter 7-9. A moment's reflection shows that it is not sensible to speak of the "total" value of a type of ecosystem and even less sensible to speak of the total value of all ecosystems. Unfortunately, some of the recent literature on ecosystem valuation claims to do just this (*e.g.* Costanza *et al.* 1997; Sutton and Costanza 2002). To see the issues, consider Figure 12.1. On the vertical axis we measure economic value in dollars. On the horizontal axis we measure the flow of ecosystem services (ES) which we assume can be conflated into a single measure for purposes of exposition.

The first construct is a demand curve for ecosystem services $D_{ES, M}$. This is a demand curve for the *commercial*, or *marketed*, services of ecosystems, *i.e.* those services that have associated with already established markets in which formal exchange takes place using the medium of money. Thus, if we have an ecosystem producing timber or fuelwood or wildmeat, and, say, tourism, and if these products have markets, then the demand for these products would be shown by $D_{ES, M}$. Another name for a demand curve is a "marginal willingness to pay" curve (mWTP) because the curve shows how much individuals are willing to pay for incremental amounts of the good in question, ES. While it is tempting to think of D_{ES} as a demand curve for *all* services of *all* ecosystems, we see later than this is a risky interpretation. For the moment it is best to think of ES in Figure 12.1 as covering a single ecosystem, say tropical forests.

The second construct is another demand curve but this time for all services from the given ecosystem, regardless of whether they currently have markets or not. This is $D_{ES, MNM}$ which is the demand curve for marketed (M) and non-marketed (NM) ecosystem services. As noted above, there are various non-market services such as watershed protection, carbon sequestration and storage, scientific knowledge, the aesthetics of natural ecosystems, and so on.

We know that $D_{ES, MNM}$ lies everywhere above $D_{ES, M}$. This is because, historically, ES have been abundant and hence there has been only a limited incentive for humans to establish property rights over them. As humans systematically expand their "appropriation" of ecosystems, however, there is an incentive to establish property rights because ES become scarce relative to human demands on them. A widely quoted indicator of this appropriation is that of Vitousek *et al.* (1997) who estimate that humans already appropriate around 30-40% of the net primary product (NPP) on land. Net primary production is the energy or carbon fixed in photosynthesis less the energy (or carbon) used up by plants in respiration. NPP is like a surplus or a net investment after depreciation (what is required for maintenance of function).

The two demand curves shown in Figure 12.1 are downward sloping, as we would expect. The more ES there are the less humans are likely to value an *additional unit* of ES. We have no reason to suppose that ES are any different in this respect to other goods and services: they should obey the "law of demand". But notice what happens if we have a very low level of ES. Imagine a world with very few forests, very little unpolluted oceans, a much reduced stock of

Figure 12.1. **Stylised costs and benefits of ecosystem service provision**

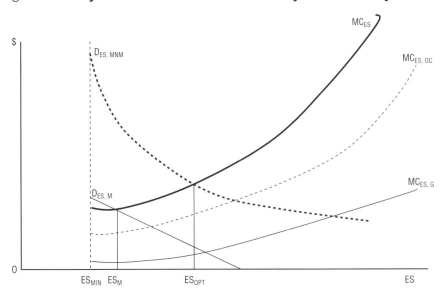

coral reefs, an atmosphere with a very much higher concentration of carbon dioxide and other greenhouse gases. In the limit, if there were no unpolluted oceans, no forests, extremely high concentrations of greenhouse gases, then the willingness to pay for one more unit of ES would be extremely high, perhaps on the way to infinity. Simply put, while a few may survive in some kind of artificial Earth bubble, humans would, by and large, disappear. For this reason, $D_{ES, MNM}$ bends sharply upwards as we go to points closer to the origin on the horizontal axis. Essentially, $D_{ES, MNM}$ is unbounded. There is some irreducible minimum ES below which marginal WTP would rise dramatically. Some suggest that at ES_{MIN} the demand curve would become infinitely elastic (see Turner *et al.* 2003), but as long as it is a (marginal) willingness to pay curve, this cannot strictly be correct since incomes and wealth would still be bounded. It is technically more correct to say that there is no meaning to the notion of economic value in the unbounded area of Figure 12.1.

Left alone, ecosystems might continue to provide the same ES year after year. After all, they have been doing this for millennia. But in order to maintain ES of value to humans we know that certain costs are incurred. Figure 12.1 shows the first category of these costs as $MC_{ES, G}$ – the marginal costs of managing ES. In the absence of any very strong evidence about the shape of $MC_{ES, G}$, we show it as a gently rising line. The second category of costs is of considerable importance and comprises the opportunity costs of providing ESs. The assumption is that ESs are best secured by conserving the ecosystems that generate them. This is not consistent with using the ecosystem for some other purpose, *e.g.* agriculture. Hence, a potentially significant cost of having ES is the forgone profits (more technically, the forgone social value) of the alternative use of the ecosystem. We refer to this as $MC_{ES, OC}$ – *i.e.* the marginal opportunity cost of ecosystem conservation. It is formally equivalent to the forgone net benefits of ecosystem conversion, *i.e.*"development" as we tend to call it. The sum of $MC_{ES, G}$ and $MC_{ES, OC}$ = MC_{ES} gives us the overall marginal cost of conservation.

Figure 12.1 is simplistic. For example, it ignores the possibility that ES might be largely maintained while serving some development function. Agro-forestry might be one example of this "symbiotic" development. But, in general, we know that there is a long-run trend towards ecosystem conversion with the nature of the conversion meaning that many ES are lost. It also ignores the possibility, realistic in practice, that the conversion process may be very inefficient. Ecosystems may be converted only for the development option not be realised because of mismanagement of the conversion process or of the development option. Thus some converted land becomes sterile, serving neither development nor ES purposes. In what follows we ignore these qualifications in order to focus on the basic messages from the analysis.

Figure 12.1 shows various points of interest.

First, since the true *aggregate* costs of maintaining a given level of ES are given by the area under the overall MC_{ES} curve, and since the true global benefits of ES provision are given by the area under the $D_{ES, MNM}$ curve, the point ES_{OPT} shows the economically optimal level of ES provision.

Second, any point to the left of ES_{OPT} has benefits of ES (area under $D_{ES, MNM}$) greater than the overall costs of their supply. But all such points also have an interesting feature. Unless we arbitrarily confine attention to points between ES_{MIN} and ES_{OPT}, all points to the left of ES_{OPT} have apparently *infinite* total benefits and this arises from the fact that the demand curve for ES is unbounded. As noted above, others may prefer to reformulate the issue and say that the idea of cost and benefit comparison for going below ES_{MIN} has no meaning.

Third, while $D_{ES,\,MNM}$ reflects the true global benefits of ES provision, it is not an "operational" demand curve. This means that unless the WTP is captured by some form of market, or unless the evidence on WTP is used to formulate some quantitative restrictions on ecosystem conversion (bans, restrictions on type of conversion etc.), the demand curve that matters is curve $D_{ES,\,M}$. Figure 12.1 shows the real possibility that failure to reflect true WTP in actual markets results in a serious under-provision of ES. Here we see the importance of the dual process of economic valuation (determining the location of $D_{ES,\,MNM}$) and capturing those values through forms of market creation.

Figure 12.1 can be used to explain why it is not possible to measure the *total* economic value of all ecosystems. This value would be the area under $D_{ES,\,MNM}$), but, as noted above, this area cannot be defined. If the view is taken that $D_{ES,\,MNM}$ becomes infinitely elastic at ES_{MIN}, then, the relevant area measuring total value would be infinite. This explains, perhaps, why one economist referred to Costanza *et al.*'s estimate of the total value as "a serious underestimate of infinity" (Toman 1998). Similar critiques of efforts to estimate the total value of all ecosystems, or even the value of a single global ecosystem, can be found in Pearce (1998b) and Bockstael *et al.* (2000).

The focus of ecosystem valuation, therefore, must be on small changes in the size or functioning of the ecosystems. However, if non-linearity is a serious issue, one should not rule out the possibility that small changes might lead to much larger levels of damage.

12.3. Finding ecosystem values

It is clear that ecosystems are "multi-functional" or "multi-product" – they generate an array of ecological-economic services. Unlike a multi-product firm, however, it was noted above that the "products" of ecosystems are usually not known with the level of certainty that would apply to a firm produces an array of market products. The products in question will also range from being purely private goods (*e.g.* fuelwood, clean water) through to being localised public goods (watershed protection) and finally to being global public goods (carbon sequestration and the non-use value of the ecosystem). Table 12.1 provides a simple typology to remind us of the array of products and services, and their probable associated property rights.

If the examples of products and services given in Table 12.1 were independent of each other, then, while the last of valuing changes in their provision would be huge, it is in

Table 12.1. **Economic characteristics of ecosystem products and services**

Examples	Private goods	Public goods		
		Local	Regional	Global
Forest	Fuelwood, water, rattan, food	Watershed protection	Air pollution reduction	Carbon storage and sequestration; Non-use values
Wetland	Fish	Soil erosion control	Storm protection	Carbon storage and sequestration; Non-use values
Corresponding property regime	Open access or common property	Open access or common property	Open access	Open access[1]

1. International agreements such as the Convention on Biological Diversity and the Framework Convention on Climate Change and its first Protocol (Kyoto) can be thought of as partial measures to turn global open access assets into global common property assets.

principle something that can be done using the array of valuation techniques available. In the cases of forests and wetlands, for example, numerous studies exist on the individual services provided. The real difficulty, however, arises from the interdependencies between the services. In terms of valuation this means that the economic value of any one service may depend on its relationship to the other services. Recall that what valuation is doing is to value *changes* in the ecosystem, so the valuations are themselves dependent on how everything changes, not just the services we might want to focus on. (This is, incidentally, another reason why estimating "total" value is not feasible – as one, say, decreases the ecosystem dramatically, everything will change). As Arrow *et al.* (2000) note, this makes the task of valuing ecosystem services extremely complex, and it underlines the necessity to simplify simply to make valuation tractable. But simplification comes at a cost.

To summarise, the following issues arise in ecosystem valuation:

● Identifying ecosystem service and products in a context where we are usually uncertain about how ecosystems behave and what they "do".

● Focusing on marginal or discrete changes, not the value of the "total ecosystem".

● Determining the degree of irreversibility in ecosystem change.

● Establishing the geographical scope of the benefits generated, from local to global.

● Establishing the property rights regime for the resource in question.

● Valuing the products and services as if they are independent of each other.

● Analysing, in simplified form, the interactions between services to see, as far as possible, how this might modify the "sum of independent values" approach outlined above.

12.4. Valuing an ecosystem product: genetic information for pharmaceuticals

This section briefly reviews one set of attempts to place an economic value on one ecosystem product – the information that resides in tropical forests and which might be used to produce new drugs. Early excitement about the economic values embodied in forests arose primarily from the view that, since pharmaceutical companies have huge billion dollar sales of drugs based on natural materials, the value of those materials must similarly be huge. For example, world markets in products derived from genetic resources are estimated to be valued at USD 500-800 billion (ten Kate and Laird, 1999). Hence it appears that, provided "bioprospectors" could be induced to pay for access to genetic material, the subsequent cash flows should be substantial.

But this approach does not conform to the relevant economic magnitude being sought: the willingness to pay to search for and utilise the relevant information. There are various factors that determine this willingness to pay. First, there are technological developments that are likely to reduce the need of bioprospectors to have access to natural organisms, notably the ability to use synthetic and combinatorial chemistry, and biotechnology using human genes. Second, technological change is increasing the ability to exploit further existing collections of seeds, reducing the need for access to new genetic resources. Third, search processes are becoming very selective, favouring particular areas with known prior information, and thus reducing the demand for access to new areas as a whole. Fourth, paralleling the demand for organic foods, there is a growing demand for "natural" products that require direct access to genetic material. Fifth, legal and institutional difficulties in securing access may well deter bioprospectors. Sixth, the supply of genetic material is vast. At best, bioprospectors can be expected to "demand" only a tiny fraction of what is available, so that most natural areas will be very unlikely to benefit from bioprospecting. Seventh, international patent law still discriminates against worldwide protection for natural materials.

These variable forces affecting supply and demand should show up in the price received for genetic material. No consistent tabulation of contract prices appears to be available (for limited information see ten Kate and Laird, 1999), but various efforts have been made to estimate what a bioprospector would be willing to pay for forest genetic material, especially Simpson *et al.* (1996), Craft and Simpson (2001), Rausser and Small (2000) and Costello and Ward (2003).

These studies correctly try to estimate the economic value of the *marginal species*, *i.e.* the contribution that one more species makes to the development of new pharmaceutical products.

The fundamental equation elicited by Simpson *et al.* (1996) is given below.

$$\max WTP = \frac{\lambda.(R-c)e^{\frac{-R}{R-K}}}{r(n+1)} \qquad [12.1]$$

where

λ = expected number of potential products to be identified = 10.52

n = number of species that could be sampled = 250 000

c = cost of determining whether a species will yield a successful product = USD 3 600

r = discount rate = 10% = 0.1

e = natural logarithm = 2.718

K = expected Research and Development cost per new product successfully produced = USD 300 million.

R = revenues from new product net of costs of sales but gross of R and D costs = USD 450 million.

Note the very large sums for K and R: developing new drugs is extremely expensive, and the revenues from successful ones are potentially extremely large. One implication is that pharmaceutical companies may find paying for prospecting rights easy so long as such rights are small fractions of the very large development costs. But, as noted above, if there are alternative routes to finding the genetic material, making prospecting difficult through bureaucratic procedures and high transactions costs, the prospecting companies may well take them.

Substituting the estimates above into equation [12.1] gives a maximum willingness to pay (WTP) of USD 9410 for the marginal species. However, WTP for the marginal species is not a concept with which it is easy to identify. Accordingly, the literature tends to translate these values into WTP for land that is subject to the risk of conversion. This is done as follows. First, the "species-area" relationship is given by

$$N = \alpha A^Z \qquad [12.2]$$

where n is the number of species, A is area, α is a constant reflecting the species richness potential of the area, and Z is a constant equal to 0.25. Species-area equations of this kind are widely used to estimate the number of species likely to be present on a given area of land. Second, the economic value V of land area A is given by

$$V[n(A)] \qquad [12.3]$$

Equation [12.3] refers to the value of a collection of species, n, likely to be found in area A. Third, the value of a change in land area A is given by differentiating [12.3]:

$$\frac{\partial V}{\partial A} = \frac{\partial V.\partial n}{\partial n.\partial A}$$

[12.4]

The expression $\frac{\partial V}{\partial n}$ is the marginal value of the species, for example the USD 9410 derived above. The expression $\frac{\partial n}{\partial A}$ is the change in the number of species brought about by a small change in the land area.

Differentiating [12.2] gives:

$$\frac{\partial n}{\partial A} = Z\alpha A^{Z-1} = \frac{Z.n}{A} = Z.D$$

[12.5]

where D = n/A is the density of species. Hence, the bioprospecting value of marginal land is given by:

$$\frac{\partial V}{\partial A} = \frac{\partial V}{\partial n}.Z.\frac{n}{A}$$

[12.6]

or, simply, the value of the marginal species multiplied by 0.25 multiplied by the density of species.

The resulting values derived by Simpson *et al.* are given in the second column of Table 12.2. The overwhelming impression is of the very small values that emerge. The essential reasons for the low values are *a)* that biodiversity is abundant and hence one extra species has low economic value; *b)* that there is extensive "redundancy" in that, once a discovery is made, finding the compound again has no value. Each additional "lead" is likely to be non-useful or, if useful, redundant. Either way, low values result.

Table 12.2. **Estimates of the pharmaceutical value of "hot spot" land areas**

Max WTP USD per hectare

Area	Simpson *et al.* (1994) WTP of pharmaceutical companies per ha	Simpson and Craft (1996) "Social value" of genetic material per ha	Rausser and Small (1998a) WTP of pharmaceutical companies per ha
Western Ecuador	20.6	2 888	9 177
South-western Sri Lanka	16.8	2 357	7 463
New Caledonia	12.4	1 739	5 473
Madagascar	6.9	961	2 961
Western Ghats of India	4.8	668	2 026
Philippines	4.7	652	1 973
Atlantic Coast Brazil	4.4	619	1 867
Uplands of western Amazonia	2.6	363	1 043
Tanzania	2.1	290	811
Cape Floristic Province, S. Africa	1.7	233	632
Peninsular Malaysia	1.5	206	539
South-western Australia	1.2	171	435
Ivory Coast	1.1	160	394
Northern Borneo	1.0	138	332
Eastern Himalayas	1.0	137	332
Colombian Choco	0.8	106	231
Central Chile	0.7	104	231
California Floristic Province	0.2	29	0

Source: Simpson *et al.*, 1996; Simpson and Craft, 1996; Rausser and Small, 2000.

The third column of Table 12.2 also shows later estimates by Simpson and Craft (1996). The basic difference between the Simpson *et al.* (1996) estimates and the Simpson and Craft (1996) estimates is that the former assume either perfect substitutability between species or no relationship between species, whereas the latter estimates assume that species are "differentiated" such that one is not a perfect substitute for the other. The result is that the new estimates relate to "social surplus", *i.e.* the sum of profits and consumer surplus and this is higher than the original estimate of the marginal value of a species. Simpson and Craft (1996) illustrate the outcome of their estimation procedure by assuming a 25% loss in the number of species. The result is a social loss of some USD 111 billion in net present value terms. The policy implications of the earlier work by Simpson *et al.* are modified to some extent by the Simpson and Craft work. Whereas economic values of (effectively) zero to USD 20 per hectare are extremely unlikely to affect land conversion decisions, the larger "social" values could be relevant to changing land use in some areas. The Simpson and Craft paper of 1996 is modified by a later paper – Craft and Simpson (2001) – which shows that "social" values could be very different to private values, depending on the degree of complementarity presumed among new products. On one model, the social value could actually be negative due to excessive entry into the market for differentiated products. On another model, social values always exceed private values. The essential feature of these later models is that allow for competition between derived products as well as for the scarcity or otherwise of the natural resource. Social values become "model-dependent and parameter-specific" (Craft and Simpson, 2001, p. 13).

The general import of the Simpson *et al.* work remains that private prospecting values are very small, whilst social values may or may not be significantly different. But the result that private values are very small is challenged by Rausser and Small (2000). The fourth column of Table 12.2 shows Rausser and Small's estimates. Rausser and Small argue that the Simpson studies characterise the pharmaceutical companies' search programme as one of randomly selecting from large numbers of samples. Each sample is then as good as any other since each is assumed to contribute equally to the chances of success. This random sequential testing does not in fact describe a cost-minimising approach to selection. Rather, samples are selected on a structured basis according to various "clues" about their likely productivity. "Leads" showing high promise are therefore of significant value because they help to reduce the costs of search overall. Such leads are said to command "information rents", *i.e.* an economic value that derives from their role in imparting information. In effect, samples cease to be of equal "quality" with some samples having much higher demand because of their information value. Clues to that value may come from experience, knowledge of particular attributes, even indigenous use of existing materials. Rausser and Small (2000) argue that the information value attached to a lead arises from the costs of search and the probability of a success, with the value of the successful drug being relatively unimportant. The effect of having different probabilities of success, argue Rausser and Small, is that an equation like [12.1] no longer applies. The Rausser-Small estimates confer greater value on biodiversity than do the Simpson-Craft estimates and substantially more than the Simpson *et al.* values. Rausser and Small (2000) conclude that "The values associated with the highest quality sites – on the order of USD 9000/hectare in our simulation – can be large enough to motivate conservation activities". The basic difference, it appears, is that the Rausser-Small has "informed search" while the Simpson *et al.* models have "random search".

Costello and Ward (2003) test for the likely differences in value from informed search as compared to random search by conducting a numerical experiment. Their finding is that the Rausser-Small values hardly change if random search is substituted for optimal search. Indeed, the values are not very different if search is conducted perversely, *i.e.* by taking the lowest probabilities of success first. This suggests that the differences in the estimates have very little to do with the search assumption. Rather, it is assumptions about parameter values that mainly explain the differences. For example, Equation [12.2] above set $Z = 0.25$ where Z is the exponent in the species-area relationship. But Rauuser-Small have an implicit assumption that $Z = 1$. Similarly, the value of n (the number of species) is far higher in Simpson *et al.* than in Rausser and Small, lowering the value in the former case and raising it in the latter.

By shifting the focus to parameter estimates, the Costello-Ward analysis changes the debate. Previously, the search model seemed to explain the difference between optimism and pessimism about bioprospecting. In that case, it is comparatively easy to argue about which search model is the more realistic. Now that the difference seems to be explained mainly by parameter values, the issue becomes one of choosing the "right" values. The problem is that the plausibility of these values has not been tested. Just as Craft and Simpson (2001) showed that *social* values are model and parameter dependent, the situation now appears to be that *private* values are also parameter dependent.

How far does the bioprospecting literature illuminate the policy dimension? If *private* prospecting values are high, as Rausser-Small would suggest, then there appears to be no role for social policy, *i.e.* there is no need for a policy instrument to encourage prospecting. However, social policy might be focused on ensuring that prospectors pay what they are alleged to be willing to pay, rather than treating genetic material as a *de facto* open access resources. To this end, the Convention on Biological Diversity would be right in its urging of host countries to extract their share of the rent through binding contracts. If values are small, as suggested by Simpson *et al.*, then we would not expect to see significant prospecting activity, nor would there be a rationale for encouraging it since the values to be captured would be small. Again, however, there would be case for encouraging host countries to extract their "share" of the benefits, small as they may be. The more positive role for instruments to encourage prospecting comes if social and private values diverge significantly. The problem at the moment is that we have no real idea what this divergence is. What appeared to be significant differences in some cases now appears to be highly dependent on models and parameters. Perhaps the best that can be said is that the early, largely unqualified optimism for bioprospecting, cannot be sustained, at least until the assumptions about models and parameter values are better developed. But the analyses to date also show just how difficult it is to estimate ecosystem values, even without allowing for the various kinds of ecological interdependence discuss earlier.

12.5. Actual and potential economic value

Ecosystems are self-evidently important, so important that without them human and other life would not exist. The economic issue is one of measuring what is being lost when parts of given global ecosystems are lost or degraded. The central problem is one of uncertainty – the basic fact is that we do not know what these losses are likely to be. Efforts at valuation are therefore important but are unlikely to inform us of the scale of "tolerable" change. Moreover, if decisions are made and they turn out to be extremely costly, little can be done to reverse them. Finally, if ecologists are right and the systems have thresholds and other non-linearities, maybe the consequences of losing even modest ecosystem areas could be large. Ecosystem loss thus combines several features:

● A potential large "scale" effect;

● irreversibility;

● uncertainty.

Economists have long known that this combination dictates a "precautionary" approach (*e.g.* Dasgupta 1982). To these features we need to add another:

● Few ecosystems undisturbed by human activity exist.

The relevance of this last point is that the world no longer has a "reserve" of ecosystems subject only to natural variation and to which it could turn for genetic and other information. In effect, the information stored over millions of years of evolution is at risk. Moreover, the impacts of human intervention in these systems are not known. One reason for this is that intervention may appear to leave the ecosystem "intact", say in terms of geographical coverage, but may change the species composition of the system. In particular, interventions frequently reduce the *diversity* of the system. It is widely argued that ecosystem productivity – the amount of biomass generated within an ecosystem – depends on that diversity, and that the resilience of the ecosystem to shocks and stresses also depends on diversity (Tilman and Polasky, n.d.). The implications for ecosystem valuation are that the goal of maximising the economic value of ecosystems might be served by not just "conserving" ecosystems but by managing them for their diversity. Rather like an economic "production function" ecosystems as they are may not be producing maximum economic value. Arguably, if undisturbed by humans and left only to the forces of natural variation, "ecosystem worth" would be maximised. But since nearly all ecosystems are not undisturbed, there is likely to be a potentially large degree of "inefficiency" in the services they do provide. In terms of valuation, care needs to be taken to value the potential rather than what is actually generated.

12.6. Cost-benefit analysis and precaution

Chapter 10 observed that there are two ways in which to conduct CBA. The first approach – the one that is most commonly used – operates either in a world of low uncertainty or in a context of uncertainty where the appropriate decision might be made in terms of expected values. The second takes more account of uncertainty and also takes explicit account of irreversibility either because funds committed cannot be "uncommitted" or because other effects of the policy cannot be reversed (or both). This was described as the "real options" approach to CBA. On the real options approach considerable attention would be paid to the opportunities for learning, and thus reducing uncertainty, by delaying irreversible decisions. It seems clear that the entire issue of ecosystem change fits the real options approach: there is uncertainty, irreversibility and a major chance to learn through scientific progress in understanding better what ecosystems do and how they behave. It is in this sense that real options give rigorous content to a notion like "the precautionary principle". Note that, on this interpretation of the precautionary principle, there would be far more caution about losing ecosystems, but benefits and costs would still be traded off.

Another contender for a precautionary approach would be the "safe minimum standard" (Ciriacy-Wantrup 1968; Bishop 1978). On this approach ecosystem conversion or loss would not be countenanced unless the opportunity costs – *i.e.* the value of the forgone "development" – were intolerably high. What the safe minimum standards approach does is to reverse the onus of proof, away from assuming that development is justified unless the costs to the environment are shown to be very high, to a presumption that conservation is the right option unless its opportunity costs are very high. But determining what is meant by "intolerable costs" is not easy. The level of "tolerance" might be determined by the political process, by reference to some notional benchmark – perhaps a percentage of GNP, or by a more extreme indicator – *e.g.* the forgone development causes severe hardship or poverty.

Finally, others argue that the precautionary principle acts like the strong sustainability principle discussed in Chapter 16. To anticipate the concept, it argues that no further degradation or loss of ecosystems would be tolerated. In a very extreme form it would argue that no existing ecosystem should be degraded. In less extreme form it would argue that any loss has to be offset by the creation of a like asset.

Thus "precaution" could enter into decision-making in several ways:

- As a strong sustainability constraint. In this case CBA remains valid but it operates within this sustainability constraint – see Chapter 16.

- As a safe minimum standard. In this case the trade-off between costs and benefits still exists but, in effect, a substantial premium is added to the benefits of conservation of ecosystems. Put another way, the benefit-cost ratio for deciding to degrade or lose the ecosystem is much higher than unity.

- As an option value approach. In this case the development option must be debited with the potential forgone costs of not waiting to learn more about the conservation benefits.

12.7. Summary and guidance for decision-makers

Research into the value of ecosystem services has evolved to the point where efforts are being made to estimate the total economic value of ecosystem change. This needs to be distinguished from misconceived efforts to value "all" ecosystems. The problems with valuing changes in ecosystem services arise from the interaction of ecosystem products and services, and from the often extensive uncertainty about how ecosystems function internally, and what they do in terms of life support functions. Considerable efforts have been made to value specific services, such as the provision of genetic information for pharmaceutical purposes. But even that literature is still developing, and it does not address the interactive nature of ecosystem products and services.

Once it is acknowledged that ecosystem functioning may be characterised by extensive uncertainty, by irreversibility and by non-linearities that generate potentially large negative effects from ecosystem loss or degradation, the focus shifts to how to behave in the face of this combination of features. The short answer is that decision-making favours precaution. But just what precaution means is itself a further debate. The suggestions here are that real options (Chapter 10), safe minimum standards and strong sustainability (Chapter 16) are all contenders.

ISBN 92-64-01004-1
Cost-Benefit Analysis and the Environment
Recent Developments
© OECD 2006

Chapter 13

Discounting

Critics of CBA often focus on the use of positive "discounting " – the procedure whereby a lower weight is put on the future than on the present. This chapter shows how discount rates have traditionally been determined and raises the issue of whether a constant discount rate is justified. Not only are discount rates that vary negatively with time observable in practice, but there are various theoretical justifications for such rates. The justifications centre on uncertainty about the discount rate itself, on uncertainty about the future of the economy, and on ethical precepts requiring that the present should not dominate the future nor the future the present. The effect of time-varying discount rates is to raise the weight given to future impacts and this is likely to be especially important for environmental impacts such as global warming and biodiversity loss.

13.1. Introduction

Few issues in CBA excite more controversy than the use of a discount rate. Discounting refers to the process of assigning a lower weight to a unit of benefit or cost in the future than to that unit now. The further into the future the benefit or cost occurs, the lower the weight attached to it. It is comparatively easy to illustrate the moral dilemma in discounting. Let the weight that is attached to a gain or loss in any future year, t, be w_t. Discounting implies that $w_t < 1$. Moreover, discounting implies that the weight attached to, say, 50 years hence should be lower than the weight attached to 40 years hence. The discounting formula is then:

$$w_t = \frac{1}{(1+s)^t}$$

Inspection of this equation shows that it is simply compound interest upside down. This is why the approach is often called "exponential discounting". The weight w_t is the *discount factor* and s is the *discount rate*. It is important to distinguish the two, as we will see. The discount factor is often represented as a fraction, and the discount rate as a percentage. For example, is s = 4%, then the discount factor for 50 years hence would be:

$$w_{50} = \frac{1}{(1.04)^{50}} = 0.14$$

In practical terms, this would mean that a gain or loss 50 years hence would be valued at only 14% of its value now. The arithmetic illustrates the alleged "tyranny" of discounting. Keeping to the 4% discount rate, environmental damage 100 years from now would be valued at just one fiftieth of the value that would be assigned to it if it occurred today. Imagine a cost of USD 1 billion 100 years from now. The use of discounting means that this loss would appear as just GBP 20 million in any appraisal of the costs and benefits of environmental damage control. Discounting appears to be inconsistent with the rhetoric and spirit of "sustainable development" – economic and social development paths that treat future generations with far greater sensitivity than has hitherto been the case.

The problem addressed in a number of recent analyses of discounting is thus: given that discounting appears to have a very strong theoretical rationale, how can this be made consistent with the moral objections that arise when discounting is applied in practice? One response, of course, is that the moral objections should be overridden, *i.e.* the rationality of discounting is morally superior to the objections about intergenerational fairness or equity. This view would be favoured by some economists. Another response would be to argue that discounting simply is not consistent with such moral concerns. If those concerns have superior moral status, then one should not engage in discounting. This view would be embraced by a significant number of philosophers, and also some economists (*e.g.* Broome, 1992). As we note below, however, "not discounting" is the same as discounting at 0% rate of discount and this has its own problems. The main focus of this chapter is on a suggested "middle way", *i.e.* on an approach that is consistent (in the main) with the theoretical underpinnings of CBA but which greatly reduces the "tyranny" of discounting. The essence of this approach is that the weight, w_t, no longer reflects a *constant* discount rate s, but rather s varies negatively with t. Thus, s becomes a "time-declining discount rate".

13.2. Zero discounting

What is meant by "not discounting" is that the discount rate is zero. In terms of the discounting equation, if s = 0, w_t = 1 and everyone is "equal" now and in the future. This outcome would not matter much for the debate but for some very unnerving implications of using zero discount rates. The first is transparently simple. Zero discounting means that we care as much for someone not just one hundred years from now as we do for someone now, but also someone one thousand years from now, or even one million years from now. It seems at least legitimate to ask: *do* we care about someone one million years hence (we already know we do not), and *should* we care about someone one million years from now? If the answer is "yes" then zero discounting has a moral rationale. If the answer is "no", it does not.

A more involved argument that rejects zero discounting goes as follows. As long as interest rates are positive, zero discounting implies that there are situations in which current generations should reduce their incomes to subsistence levels in order to benefit future generations. The effect of lowering the discount rate towards zero is to increase the amount of saving that the current generation should undertake. The lower the discount rate, the more future consumption matters, and hence more savings and investment should take place in the current generation's time period. Thus, while lowering the discount rate appears to take account of the well-being of future generations, it implies bigger and bigger sacrifices of current well-being. Indeed, Koopmans (1965) showed that, however low the current level of consumption is, further reductions in consumption would be justified in the name of increasing future generations' consumption. The logic here is that there will be a lot of future generations, so that whatever the increment in savings now, and whatever the cost to the current generation, the future gains will substantially outweigh current losses in foregone consumption. The implication of zero discounting is the impoverishment of the current generation (Olson and Bailey, 1981). This finding would of course relate to every generation, so that, in effect each successive generation would find itself being impoverished in order to further the well-being of the next. The Rawls criterion (Rawls, 1972) – that we should aim to maximize the well-being of the poorest individual in society – would reject such a policy of current sacrifice, since the sacrifice would be made by the poorest generation. Thus zero discounting has its own ethical implications that few would find comforting or acceptable. "Not discounting" appears not to be an answer to the discounting dilemma.

13.3. Time declining rates: a practical rationale

The logic of CBA rests on the value judgment that individuals' preference count in a normative sense (see Chapter 2). One way of dealing with the discount rate controversy, then, is simply to find out how people discount the future and adopt whatever weighting procedure emerges from this empirical observation. The standard approach to discounting assumes that people have a "constant" discount rate. But, until recently, few studies made any attempt to find out how people *actually* discount the future. It was simply *assumed* that they engaged in activities consistent with the discounting formula set out above. There are good reasons why the assumption of a constant discount rate has been made and they have to do with a complex issue of "dynamic time consistency" which we address shortly. But there is nothing in the assumption that means this is how people actually have to behave. A significant body of evidence now exists to suggest that people do not behave as if their own discount rates are a constant (Frederick *et al.* 2002). Rather, their discount equations are "hyperbolic" (to contrast them with the former equation which behaves exponentially). Simply put, individuals' discount rates are likely to decline as time goes on. Discount rates are said to be "time varying". Instead of "s" in the previous equation, we need to write s_t to signal that the value of s will change with the time period. Moreover, s will fall the larger is t.

Although it is fair to say that the empirical evidence is not overwhelming, hyperbolic discounting emerges as an empirical discovery, a description of how people actually behave. If this form of discounting reflects preferences, then hyperbolic discounting could legitimately be used in policy and investment appraisal. The effect of hyperbolic discounting is generally to raise the initial discount rate relative to the exponential rate (the constant value of s) and then lower the rate in later years. By observing how people choose between options located in different future periods, it is possible to estimate the rate at which such rates decline. Of course, the social discount rate is a *normative* construct – it tells us what we should do. Deriving a normative rule from an empirical observation contradicts David Hume's dictum that "ought" cannot be derived from "is". However, if what people do (the "is") reflects preferences and preferences count, then, what is becomes relevant to what ought to be.

13.4. Time declining rates: a theoretical rationale based on uncertainty about interest rates

Weitzman (1998, 1999) and Gollier (2002) have produced separate but related rationales for time-declining discount rates. While the details of these approaches quickly become extremely complex, it is possible to gain some idea of the resulting revolution in thinking about discounting. For both Weitzman and Gollier, the clue lies in how we treat uncertainty about the future. For Weitzman, that uncertainty is reflected in uncertainty about future interest rates. For Gollier, the uncertainty is about the state of the economy.

Interest rates provide relative valuations of the future relative to the present. But these relative valuations are uncertain. Formally, this uncertainty shows up in the lack of certainty about the weights to be attached to future time. One approach to uncertainty is to take a probability-weighted average (an expected value) of the likely weights. But the discussion above showed that the weights are the discount *factors*, w_t. Rather than averaging likely future discount *rates* what should be averaged are the probabilistic discount *factors*. Somewhat counter-intuitively, this process produces discount *rates* that decline with time. A numerical example shows this – see Table 13.1.

In Table 13.1, there are ten potential scenarios, and each scenario has an equal probability of occurring: $p_1 = p_2 = \ldots = p_{10} = 0.1$. Consider the first cell where t = 10 and the discount rate is 1%. The corresponding discount factor is 0.9053, shown in Table 13.1 in rounded form as 0.91. Computing the relevant discount factors for all the discount rates and time periods shown produces the rest of the entries in the main body of the table. Now take the average of these discount *factors* for any given time period. Since we have assumed equal probabilities of occurrence a simple average produces, for example, a value of

0.61 for the t = 10 column. This value of 0.61 is what Weitzman calls the "certainty equivalent discount factor". Notice that this declines as t gets bigger. We now want the discount *rate* that corresponds to the averaged discount factor and this is shown in the final row of Table 13.1. For example, for t = 10, we would get a "certainty equivalent discount rate", s*, given by the equation

$$\frac{1}{(1+s*)^{10}} = 0.61$$

to give a value of s* of 4.73%. It is easy to see that the certainty-equivalent discount rate approaches the lowest discount rate of the ten scenarios considered, 1%. In year 200 the rate has fallen to 1.16%, and by year 500 this rate has fallen 1.01%. This is Weitzman's key result – in the limit, as t goes to infinity, the discount rate converges on the lowest possible discount rate – 1% in this example.

Table 13.1. **Numerical example of Weitzman's declining certainty-equivalent discount rate**

Interest rate scenarios	Discount factors in period *t*				
	10	50	100	200	500
1%	0.91	0.61	0.37	0.14	0.01
2%	0.82	0.37	0.14	0.02	0.00
3%	0.74	0.23	0.05	0.00	0.00
4%	0.68	0.14	0.02	0.00	0.00
5%	0.61	0.09	0.01	0.00	0.00
6%	0.56	0.05	0.00	0.00	0.00
7%	0.51	0.03	0.00	0.00	0.00
8%	0.46	0.02	0.00	0.00	0.00
9%	0.42	0.01	0.00	0.00	0.00
10%	0.39	0.01	0.00	0.00	0.00
Certainty-equivalent discount factor	0.61	0.16	0.06	0.02	0.00
Certainty-equivalent discount rate	4.73%	2.54%	1.61%	1.16%	1.01%

Source: Adapted from Pearce *et al.* (2003).

13.5. Time declining rates: a theoretical rationale based on uncertainty about the economy

Weitzman's result follows from a very reasonable assumption that we are uncertain about the future. In his case, it is interest rates themselves that are uncertain. The contribution of Gollier (2002) is to treat uncertainty about the future of the economy in general. Gollier's work is complex and the results depend on various factors some of which are never likely to be capable of estimation in practice. The central result can be found by looking at the "normal" way in which the theory of social discounting is presented.

The notion of a social discount rate is usually presented in the form of the following equation, known as a Ramsey equation (after Ramsey (1928)):

$s = \rho + \mu.g$

The social discount rate, s, is equal to the sum of two factors: ρ which is the "pure" rate of time preference, reflecting people's impatience; and the product of μ – to be explained – and g, the growth rate of future (per capita) consumption. μ is known as the elasticity of the marginal utility of consumption, the percentage change in the welfare derived from a percentage change in consumption (or income). The intuition behind μ is that it expresses individuals' aversion to fluctuations in their income levels. While there is a substantial debate about the value of μ, recent reviews suggest that it takes a convenient value of about 1.0 (Cowell and Gardiner, 1999). Notice that there is a simple intuition behind $\mu.g$. People in the future will (almost certainly) be richer and hence the "utility" they attach to one more dollar of income is likely to be lower than that attached to the same dollar today. Effectively, then, discounting is justified simply by the fact that future people will be better off than people today.

Rates of impatience are also notoriously difficult to estimate, but recent work suggests a value of, at most, 0.5% (Pearce and Ulph, 1999). So, for an economy growing at 2% per annum, the Ramsey formula suggests a discount rate of, say, 2.5%. But the Ramsey formula says nothing about the effects of the kind of uncertainty that Gollier (and Weitzman) are interested in. What Gollier shows is that, once we recognize that future income is uncertain, there will be two effects rather than the single effect shown by μ in the Ramsey formula. Whereas μ is picking up individuals' aversion to uncertainty about future income (the *wealth effect*), there is a second effect not in the formula, namely precautionary saving. Where people are unsure about future income they will save for a "rainy day", what Gollier calls a *prudence effect*. What Gollier shows is that this prudence effect lowers the discount rate, whereas the bigger is μ, the higher the discount rate. Two effects now compete for an influence on the overall discount rate: the desire to "smooth" fluctuations in income, and attitudes to risk.

In a situation in which economic growth rates are similar across time periods, the rationale for declining social optimal discount rates is driven by the preferences of the individuals in the economy, rather than expectations of growth. Gollier derives the conditions under which the discount rate declines under different assumptions concerning the likelihood of economic recession (negative growth). When there is no risk of recession, the discount rate will decline as individuals exhibit decreasing relative aversion to risk as wealth increases. Many studies have found empirical evidence to show that people have such preferences. For example, the share of wealth invested in risky assets increases with income in most developed countries. However, these observations are insufficient for the result to hold when the risk of recession is introduced. Indeed, the conditions on individual preferences required for the economy to exhibit discount rates which decline with time become increasingly complex, non-intuitive, and empirically difficult to test.

The wealth effect; and the prudence effect act in opposition to one another in determining the discount rate. When individuals in the economy are prudent (that is, their response to uncertainty is to save more), the wealth effect is offset, and the optimal discount rate is lowered. Gollier (2002) recommends that, given growth is an uncertain phenomenon, the long-run discount rate should decline, due to the cumulative effects of risk over time. He goes on to recommend using the risk free rate for medium term horizons (5% in the case of France), dropping to 1.5% for costs and benefits that accrue in the very long run, *e.g.* 200 years.

13.6. Social choice and declining discount rates

A third approach to time-declining rates derives from the analysis of the "tyranny" problems as a "social choice" problem. The social choice approach simply says that such tyranny is not acceptable and that the discount rate issue should be determined by specific axioms that make tyranny impossible. The contributions of Chichilnisky (1996) and Li and Löfgren (2000), while different in approach, show that a declining discount rate (more specifically, the ρ in the Ramsey equation above) is consistent with a rule whereby current (future) generations must always take into account the well-being of future (current) generations. Out another way, there must be no "dictatorship" of one generation over another. In the Chichilnisky approach, current day decision-makers adopt a mixed goal: maximizing the discounted value of net benefits, and a "sustainability" requirement that effectively amounts to a requirement to consider future generations' well-being. The Li and Löfgren approach assumes that society consists of two individuals, a utilitarian and a conservationist, each of which makes decisions over the inter-temporal allocation of resources. The important difference between these two decision-makers is that they are assumed to discount future utilities at different rates: the utilitarian discounting at a higher rate than the conservationist who may, for example, have a zero discount rate. What generates the time-declining discount rate from this situation are a) the fact that there are two different discount rates, and b) the weights to be attached to the conservationist and the utilitarian, i.e. the degree of power that each has to influence the final outcome. In a manner that parallels the Weitzman result, the long run discount rate for society as a whole tends towards the lowest discount rate held by any party, in this case the conservationist.

13.7. The problem of time-inconsistency

The major advances in the theory of discounting is easily summarized. Once uncertainty about the future – whether about interest rates or economic prospects – is introduced, there are realistic situations in which the socially correct discount rate, to be used by governments in investment and policy appraisal, is one that declines with time. Not only is there a theoretical rationale for time-varying discount rates, but their practical use does much to overcome the "tyranny" of discounting which is so widely noted by philosophers and environmentalists. But time-varying discount rates have their own problems and chief among them is "time inconsistency".

Time inconsistency, or "incongruence", refers to a situation where plans that are made at one point in time are contradicted by later behaviour. The identification of this possibility is usually credited to Strotz (1956). Time consistency requires that generation A chooses a policy, and generation B acts in accordance with it. Generation B does not revise what generation A planned. If generation A's plans are revised by generation B, then generation A will not have optimised its behaviour – what it intended for generation B will turn out to have been wrong. So, as fast as time-declining discount rates solve the "tyranny" issue, they create another problem.

But how serious is time-inconsistency? Henderson and Bateman (1995) see the process of changing the discount rate as time moves on as legitimate. People, they say, do not see themselves living in absolute, but in relative time. Revising and re-evaluating plans as time moves on is consistent with psychological and behavioural studies, and with the value judgment that what ought to be done by way of discounting should reflect what people actually prefer. If we should not expect individuals to behave consistently, we should not expect it of societies – the general theory of preference aggregation shows that societies usually satisfy weaker rationality conditions than individuals. Heal (1998) argues that from a social choice perspective, time consistency is a "most unnatural requirement".

Unless government can make a once-and-for-all self-binding commitment to a policy rule, private sector agents will expect government to "re-optimise" at later dates. In other words, private sector agents anticipate that government will deviate from the policy rule even in the absence of external shocks to the economy. When faced with such dynamic inconsistency, a government without a commitment mechanism can formulate policy in a "naïve" or "sophisticated" manner. The "naïve" government behaves as though it is unaware of its time-inconsistent preferences, while the "sophisticated" government is aware. Neither situation is satisfactory. The sophisticated government takes into account the fact that private agents will anticipate the government's incentive to deviate from its optimal (committed) policy, and must therefore formulate policy which is less than optimal. In other words, the government makes policy, which is the best response to successive government's best responses. For the "naïve" government, which presses ahead regardless with dynamically inconsistent policy, the consequences might be particularly severe. For instance, Hepburn (2003) shows that a naïve government employing a hyperbolic (declining) discount rate in the management of a renewable resource may unwittingly manage the resource to extinction. Time inconsistency does seem to matter.

There is no easy resolution of this issue. Heal (1998) proves that almost all types of declining discount rates result in time-inconsistency, so the problem is not easy to avoid. As a practical matter, however, the dynamic inconsistency inherent in declining discount rates may not be any more troubling than policy inconsistencies and changes that are prompted by external shocks or political shifts. Ultimately, few, if any policies are "optimal" in an unqualified sense.

13.8. Conclusions and guidance for decision-makers

Recent advances in discounting have largely been prompted by the alleged "tyranny of discounting" – the fact that discounting has a theoretical rationale in the underlying welfare economics of CBA, but with consequences that many seem to find morally unacceptable. This unacceptability arises from the fact that distant future costs and benefits may appear as insignificant present values when discounting is practised. In turn, this appears to be inconsistent with notions of intergenerational fairness. Current activities imposing large costs on future generations may appear insignificant in a cost-benefit analysis. Similarly, actions now that will benefit future generations may not be undertaken in light of a cost-benefit analysis.

The weakness of the conventional approach, which assumes that one positive discount rate is applied for all time, is that it neither incorporates uncertainty about the future nor attempts to resolve the tyranny problem. Additionally, the assumption of a constant discount rate is exactly that – an assumption. The "escapes" from the tyranny problems centre on several approaches:

- Observing that, very often (but not always), people actually discount "hyperbolically", *i.e.* people actually do use time-declining discount rates. If what people do reflects their preferences, and if preferences are paramount, there is a justification for adopting time-declining discount rates.

- Introducing uncertainty about future interest rates: here it can be shown that uncertainty about the temporal weights – *i.e.* the *discount factor* – is consistent with a time declining certainty equivalent *discount rate*.

- Introducing uncertainty about the state of the economy more generally: here it can be shown that time-declining rates can emerge if certain conditions are met.

- Positing the tyranny problem as a social choice problem in which neither the present nor the future dictates outcomes. The adoption of reasonable ethical axioms can be shown to produce time-declining rates.

- In terms of the uncertainty and social choice approaches, the time-path of discount rates could be very similar with long term rates declining to the "lowest possible" rates of, say, 1%.

But time-consistency problems remain and some experts would regard any time-declining discount rate as being unacceptable because of such problems. Others would argue that the idea of a long-run optimising government that never revises its "optimal" plan is itself an unrealistic requirement for the derivation of an optimal discount rate.

ISBN 92-64-01004-1
Cost-Benefit Analysis and the Environment
Recent Developments
© OECD 2006

Chapter 14

Valuing Health and Life Risks[1]

The last few decades have seen major developments in the theory and practice of giving economic values to premature mortality and to morbidity. The traditional concept of a "value of a statistical life" remains valid but has been brought into question by analyses showing that, in rich countries, risk-reducing policies may alter life chances only moderately. Where the time of death is reduced by only a few weeks or months it may be inappropriate to adopt values of statistical life. Instead, a value of a "life year" may be preferred. Empirical studies have also provided insights into the factors determining the valuation of life risks – income, risk level, age and latency have been particularly studied. Special problems arise with the valuation of childhood risks since children cannot articulate willingness to pay for risk reduction. Morbidity values have been studied to a lesser extent but the empirical basis for this is gradually being built up.

14.1. Introduction: the importance of health effects in CBA

Environmental policy affects human health in a number of ways. First, by reducing environmental risks to lives, it may "save lives", *i.e.* reduce premature *mortality*. Second, it may improve the health of those living with a disease, *e.g.* a respiratory illness. This is a *morbidity* benefit. Third, it may reduce the stresses and strains of living and thus improve *mental health*. By and large, environmental economics has focused on the first two types of benefit, and has paid relatively little attention to the third effect, although some would argue that these effects are generally captured by individuals' willingness to pay to reduce stress – *e.g.* from noise.

One very important reason for focusing on human health benefits is that, in practical terms, they often dominate cost-benefit studies. Inspection of European Union studies relating to air pollution reveals that health benefits account for a minimum of one-third and a maximum of nearly 100% of overall benefits from pollution control (Holland and Krewitt, 1996; AEA Technology, 1998a, 1998b; 1998c, 1998d, 1999; Krewitt *et al.*, 1999; IVM, NLUA and IIASA, 1997; Olsthoorn *et al.*, 1999). Moreover, in most cases these benefits exceed the costs of control by considerable margins. Health benefits therefore "drive" positive benefit-cost results. Nor is this outcome peculiar to the European Union. The US EPA's retrospective and prospective assessments of the Clean Air Act produce extremely high benefit-cost ratios, *e.g.* 44 for the central estimate of benefits and costs (US EPA, 1997; 1999). Moreover, EPA regards these as probable underestimates. In turn, the benefits are dominated by health benefits (99% if damage to children's IQ is included).

If health benefits are so important in the analysis of environmental policy, it matters a great deal that the underlying theory and empirical procedures are correct.

14.2. Valuing life risks: the VOSL

By and large, the procedure for valuing risks to life, *i.e.a mortality risk*, have involved an estimation of the willingness to pay to secure a risk reduction arising from a policy or project, or the willingness to accept compensation for tolerating higher than "normal" risks. The former studies have involved use of stated preference techniques (see Chapters 8 and 9) and avertive behaviour approaches (see Chapter 7). The latter have involved hedonic wage risk studies (see Chapter 7). The procedure involves taking the risk change in question and dividing this into the WTP for the risk reduction, to secure a "value of statistical life" (VOSL).[2] CBA tends to mix objective and subjective aspects of life risks. Thus, the usual procedure is to take an "objective" measure of risk arising from some change in an environmental variable, say pollution. This is shown as a *dose-response* or *exposure response function*. The dose-response function is used to estimate numbers of premature mortalities, and it is these mortalities that are multiplied by the VOSL to give an aggregate measure of benefit.

The Annex to this chapter shows the standard derivation of the VOSL expression for the simplest case. The final equation is:

$$VOSL = \frac{dW}{dp} = 1 = \frac{u_a(W) - u_d(W)}{(1-p).u'_a(W) + p.u'_d(W)} \qquad [14.1]$$

where W is wealth, p is the probability of dying in the current period (the "baseline risk"), (1 – p) is the probability of surviving the current period, u is utility, "a" is survival, and "d" is death. The utility function u_d allows for bequests to others on death. The numerator thus shows the difference in utility between surviving and dying in the current period. The denominator shows the marginal utility of wealth (which is usually measured empirically as income) conditional on survival or death. The expected relationships between VOSL, p, W and expected health status on survival are discussed in Annex 14.A1. Another potentially important issue is age of the individual at risk, and exposure risks that occur now but with effects in T years time ("latent" risks). Again, the expected theoretical relationships with VOSL are discussed briefly in Annex 14.A1. The issue of "dread" is discussed later, as there may be grounds for supposing that the risks of certain types of death (notably from cancer) should attract a premium over the "standard" VOSL.

Figure 14.1 illustrates the link between WTP and risk levels. VOSL is a *marginal* WTP and hence Figure 14.1 shows MWTP against the risk level. The status quo risk level is usually referred to as the initial or baseline risk level. Policy usually involves *reducing* risks so as the risk level declines so does MWTP, as shown in Figure 14.1, and as risk rises so MWTP is expected to rise.

Suppose the policy measure in question reduces risk levels from P2 to P1 in Figure 14.1. Then the WTP for that risk reduction is seen to be equal to the area under the MWTP curve between P2 and P1. Notice that MWTP may be fairly constant at low levels of risk (to the right of the diagram). Small differences in the initial (baseline) risk level are therefore usually assumed to have little effect in VOSL studies.[3]

Figure 14.1. **Risk and willingness to pay**

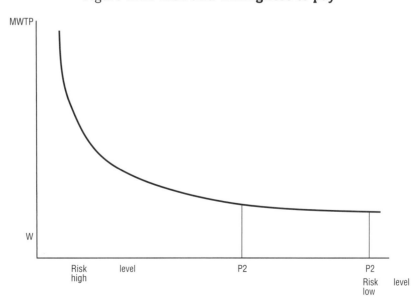

Suppose now a policy promises to reduce risks from 5 in 10 000 to 3 in 10 000, a change of 2 in 10 000 (Δr). Suppose the mean WTP to secure this risk reduction is USD 50. Then the VOSL is usually computed as

$$\frac{WTP}{\Delta r} = \frac{50 \times 10,000}{2} = 250\,000 \qquad [14.2]$$

The VOSL would be USD 250 000.

It tends to be assumed that the quality of the period survived affects WTP, *i.e.* WTP to reduce risks should be higher if the individual anticipates being in good health (apart from the risks in question), and lower if the individual expects to be in poor health. The equation implies that WTP rises with wealth since *a)* it is assumed that the marginal utility of wealth is greater for survival than as a bequest when dead, and *b)* there is aversion to financial risk. The former makes the numerator increasing in wealth.

The equation does not say anything about *latent risks, i.e.* situations in which exposure now does not produce death until a later period. The usual procedure here is to look at the risk reduction in the future period. Following Hammitt (2000), suppose this is 1 in 100 000, *i.e.* 0.00001 in 20 years time. Suppose the individual is WTP GBP 50 in 20 years time to secure that risk reduction. The relevant WTP now is the discounted value of USD 50, *e.g.* at 3% it is about USD 27. In turn, this should be multiplied by the probability of surviving the next 20 years, so the final WTP now will be less than GBP 27. Note that the *future* VOSL is USD 50/0.00001 = USD 5 million.

In the same way, the equation does not tell us if WTP (and hence VOSL) varies with age. Age is usually thought to have two potentially offsetting effects: *a)* the older one gets, the fewer years are left so the benefit of any current reduction in risk declines – we would expect VOSL to decline with age; *b)* the opportunity cost of spending money on risk reduction declines as time goes by because savings accumulate, so WTP for risk reduction may actually rise with age.

Several debates have occurred in recent years. These are briefly discussed below and relate to:

- the way in which VOSL varies with underlying determinants. To a considerable extent, these analyses are attempts to test the *validity* of VOSL. For example, one would expect the WTP for risk reduction to pass a "scope test" which means that higher risk changes should be associated with higher WTP.

- The size of the VOSL.

- The relevance of VOSL to all risk contexts. By and large this has involved assessing whether VOSLs derived in accident contexts (especially road accidents and workplace accidents) are equally applicable to pollution contexts, and whether VOSL should be replaced by a related notion of the "value of a life year" (VOLY or VLY).

14.3. The sensitivity of VOSL to risk levels

There are two types of risk that may affect VOSL. The first is background or initial risk, *i.e.* the risks of "dying anyway". The second is the risk change brought about by the policy or project in question, and for which the VOSL is usually sought.

14.3.1. Background risk

Most VOSL studies do not consider the issue of background risk. The VOSL is usually derived by considering only the WTP for a risk change and the size of the risk change itself (basically, VOSL is the WTP divided by the risk change). The issue arises of whether WTP is likely to be influenced by other risks not considered in this simple equation. Eeckhoudt and Hammitt (2001) investigate this issue. The expectation is that a "competing risk", *i.e.* some other risk to life independent of the risk being addressed by the policy measure, will reduce the WTP for the policy-related risk because of the "why bother" effect. That is, the competing risk reduces the chance that the individual will benefit from the policy-related risk. But, in general, the effect will be very small. Eeckhoudt and Hammitt (2001) cite the example of a male worker aged about 40 in the USA. The mortality risk for that age group is 0.003 and this translates directly into a reduction in VOSL of just 0.3 of a percentage point. However, risks of death from air pollution are highest for the elderly whose background risks are very high, *i.e.* they are at high risk of death from other causes. The "why bother" effect comes into play in a significant fashion.

If the effect is significant, we would expect it to show up in expressed WTP for those who have high competing risks, notably *a)* those who are in poor health anyway, and *b)* the aged. The extent to which the empirical literature picks up this effect is discussed in the sections below dealing with health states and age.

14.3.2. Policy-related risk

The theory of the VOSL requires that WTP varies directly with the size of the policy-related risk. Hammitt and Graham (1999) conduct a comprehensive review of contingent valuation studies of WTP for risk reduction, with the explicit goal of seeing if WTP varies with risk in the manner predicted by economic theory. In particular they test for two predicted relationships: *a)* that WTP should vary directly with the size of the risk reduction, and *b)* for low probabilities (probability being their chosen measure of risk), WTP should be virtually proportional to the change in risk. Thus, if WTP for a change in risk ΔX (where X is small) is W, WTP for $\alpha\Delta X$, should be αW. They also look at "baseline risk", *i.e.* the level of risk from which ΔX deviates (the background risk as outlined above). Of the 25 studies they review (up to 1998), only 10 contain sufficient information to test scope sensitivity within sample (internal validity). In general, those 10 studies confirm the first hypothesis that WTP varies with risk reduction, but not the second. Proportionality is not observed. Even in the former case, a significant minority of respondents report the same WTP regardless of the size of risk change, or ΔX. External validity (across sample scope tests) assessments showed a similar pattern, but with even the first hypothesis receiving only weak support. They replicate a previous study by Johansson *et al.* (1997) on WTP in Sweden for a one year "blip" in the change in mortality (after which risks return to their "normal" levels) and again find that the theoretical expectations are not fulfilled. Finally, they report new CV studies for automobile risks (air bags) and food contamination risks. While some improvements in meeting theoretical expectation is secured by adopting a different approach to the WTP question in the surveys, the general result is again that theoretical expectations are not met. They conclude that:

> "… our review of the prior published literature, including the replication of Johansson *et al.* (1997), suggests that many of the stated WTP estimates reported in the literature on health risk do not represent economic preferences" (p. 58, Hammitt and Graham, 1999).

They suggest that their innovations in the automobile and food risk studies secured some improvement, holding out the possibility that scope insensitivity may be the result of questionnaire and study design rather than an engrained impossibility of getting sensible WTP results for risk changes. However, the latter pessimistic conclusion would be consistent with some of the psychological literature. Moreover, strict scope sensitivity was also not observed in the Chilton *et al.* (2004) study and the Markandya *et al.* (2004) study. Similarly, Alberini *et al.* (2004) use two contingent valuation studies for the USA and Canada and find that there is scope sensitivity for risk changes, both mean and median estimate of WTP being larger for higher risk reductions. The stricter requirement that WTP be *proportional* to risk reduction is not, however, met. The same result occurs in Krupnick *et al.* (1999) for Japan.

Reasons why scope insensitivity may occur include, for stated preference studies, the notable problems of communicating low risk levels to respondents, low risks being the ones that typically define environmental contexts. In wage-risk studies any lack of a WTP-risk relationship may be due to "self-selection", where higher risk tolerant workers may be selecting the more hazardous employment. Meta-analyses of wage-risk studies also produce somewhat more mixed results. As risk increases, one would expect WTA (since what is measured is the premium on wages to accept higher risks) to vary directly with risk levels. On the other hand the self-selection effect may mean that less risk-averse workers gravitate to higher risk occupations. Mrozek and Taylor (2002) find both effects, *i.e.* a rising WTA at first followed by a reduction thereafter. This "risk loving" effect has been noted in other occupational studies as well (for a summary, see Hammitt, 2002). On the other hand, Viscusi (2004) finds that wage premia vary directly with death risks and with injury risks in occupations, and Viscusi and Aldy's (2003) meta-analysis of wage risk studies for the USA finds VOSL that vary directly with risk reduction but with only a minor effect of high risk on VOSL (the implied VOSL is USD 12-22 million for low risks and a tenfold increase in risks changes this to USD 10-18 million).

The implications of the risk scope sensitivity analyses for environmental CBA are not easy to discern. Some of the work suggests that WTP or WTA is not sensitive to risk levels or, if sensitive, fails a test of proportionality. If so, considerable caution is needed in using VOSL estimates based on such exercises. It may be that, in the context of stated preference studies, the nature of risk changes associated with environmental policy are simply too small for people to identify with. In the context of wage-risk studies there is some evidence that compensation levels reverse as more risk-loving workers occupy riskier positions.

14.4. VOSL and the income elasticity of willingness to pay

WTP should vary directly with income. Indeed, it is widely considered that sensitivity to income and to absolute risk are the two basic tests of the validity of any preference-based technique for measuring the VOSL. As noted above, while there is usually sensitivity to absolute risk change, the requirement of strict proportionality is rarely met.

Most studies find that WTP varies with income. Apart from the requirement that WTP should vary with income as a theoretical validity test, the link between income and WTP is of interest for other reasons. Often in valuation exercises there is the need to account for rising relative valuations of benefits and costs over time. This means ascertaining the likelihood that a given benefit or cost is likely to have a higher (or lower) real unit WTP in the future. For example, suppose that the willingness to pay to save a statistical life rises faster than the rate of inflation (which is always netted out in CBA). Then it would be correct to include that rising real valuation in the CBA formula.

Several recent studies have attempted to estimate the income elasticity of WTP for mortality risk reduction. One of the most detailed meta-studies, by Viscusi and Aldy (2003), replicates previous meta-studies, and finds point estimates of the elasticity of WTP of between 0.5 to 0.6 and certainly less than unity. These estimates are very similar to those obtained judgementally by Pearce (2005) for environmental quality (in the range of 0.37 to 0.4). In a meta-study of transport risks, de Blaeij *et al.* (2003) find an elasticity of 1.33, considerably higher than the Viscusi-Aldy estimates. The only available time-series study, by Costa and Kahn (2002) for the USA, suggests that the VOSL has risen considerably in the period 1940-1980, with an implied elasticity of VOSL with respect to per capita GDP of 1.5 to 1.7.

While uncertainty surrounds the estimates of income elasticity, the coverage of the studies varies, making comparisons difficult. As a working hypothesis and on grounds of comprehensiveness, it seems safe to adopt the Viscusi-Aldy elasticity of 0.5-0.6. In terms of the concept of the net discount rate (s-n) (see annex for more detail) such an elasticity (say, 0.5) would produce the following values for different values of the discount rate, s, growth of income, y, and growth in WTP, n:

s	y	n	s-n
0.03	0.01	0.005	0.025
	0.02	0.010	0.020
	0.03	0.015	0.015
0.04	0.01	0.005	0.035
	0.02	0.010	0.030
	0.03	0.015	0.025

14.5. The size of VOSL

Assuming that VOSL estimates are accepted for policy purposes, two major issues arise: *a)* how large is the VOSL and *b)* can a VOSL estimated in one context, say road accidents, be applied to another context, say environmental pollution? We refer to these as the *size issue* and the *transferability issue*.

Various countries adopt single values for the VOSL and use them in policy appraisal. Usually, estimates are not varied by context but recent work has begun to investigate the extent to which the transferability of single values is valid. Similarly, several major recent studies have looked at the likely size of VOSL. Table 14.1 reports on the main studies. Note that VOSLs should vary with the policy induced risk change so that values are not always directly comparable if different risk levels have been assumed.

Table 14.1 suggests that VOSLs of around USD 2 million would be justified for the UK, and around USD 3-5 million for the USA. The figure for Japan appears to be very different, for reasons that are not clear.

The Beattie *et al.* (1998) study is shown in Table 14.1 but the main conclusion of that study was that serious embedding, sequencing and framing effects were present in the contingent valuation responses (see Chapter 8 for the importance of these problems). Hence the results of this study need to be treated with considerable caution. Instead, the second stage of this work, Carthy *et al.* (1999), which involves a mixed approach – contingent valuation and standard gamble – is to be preferred. This study elicits a value for

Table 14.1. **Recent estimates of the VOSL**

Study	Country	Type of study	Risk Context	VOSL USD million (year prices)
Costa and Kahn 2002	USA	Wage risk time series	Fatality rates over time	1980: 4.2 – 5.3 (1990)
Viscusi and Aldy 2003	USA	Wage risk meta analysis	Various occupational risks	2000: 7.0 (2000)[1]
Viscusi 2004	USA	Wage risk	Occupational-industry risk measure	1997: 4.7 (2000)
Hammitt 2000	USA	Various	Various	1995: 3.0 – 7.0 (1990)
Alberini *et al.* 2004	USA	Contingent valuation	Context free reduction in mortality risk between ages of 70 and 80	2000: 1.5 – 4.8 (2000)[2]
	Canada	Contingent valuation		2000: 0.9 – 3.7 (2000)[2]
Krupnick *et al.* 1999	Japan	Contingent valuation	Context free reduction in mortality risk between ages of 70 and 80	1998: 0.2 – 0.4 (1998)
Persson *et al.* 2001	Sweden	Contingent valuation	Road traffic risks	1999: 2.64 (1999)
Markandya *et al.* 2004	UK	Contingent valuation	Context free reduction in mortality risk between ages of 70 and 80	1.2 – 2.8 0.7 – 0.8 0.9 – 1.9 (2002)[3]
Chilton *et al.* 2004	UK	Contingent valuation	Mortality impacts from air pollution	0.3 – 1.5 (2002)[3,4]
Chilton *et al.* 2002	UK	Contingent valuation	Roads (R), Rail (Ra), Domestic fires (Fd) and public fires (Fp)	Ratios: Ra/R=1.003 Fd/R=0.89 Fp/R=0.96[6]
Beattie *et al.* 1998	UK	Contingent valuation	Roads (R) and domestic fires (F)	5.7 14.8 8.5 (2002)[3]
Carthy *et al.* 1999	UK	Contingent valuation/ standard gamble	Roads	1.4 – 2.3 (2002)[3,5]
Siebert and Wei 1994	UK	Wage risk	Occupational risk	13.5 (2002)[3]
Elliott and Sandy 1996	UK	Wage risk	Occupational risk	1996: 1.2 (2000)[3]
Arabsheibani and Marin 2000	UK	Wage risk	Occupational risk	1994: 10.7 (2000)[3]

1. Median of the studies reviewed.
2. Range varies with risk reduction level, lower VOSLs for larger risk reductions.
3. GBP converted to USD using PPP GNP per capita ratio between UK and US. Range reflects different risk reductions.
4. Based on WTP to extend life by one month assuming 40 years of remaining life.
5. Based on trimmed means.
6. This study sought respondents' relative valuations of a risk relative to a risk of death from a road accident. Numbers reported here are for the 2000 sample rather than the 1998 sample. Between the two sample periods there was a major rail crash in London.

a non-fatal injury (VNFI) and then uses a standard gamble approach to compute a ratio, r, of a the value of a prevented fatality (VPF) to the value of the non-fatal injury. Hence:

$$VPF = r.VNFI \qquad [14.3]$$

Chilton *et al.* (2002) is one of the few studies that attempts to test for the effect of risk context on valuations. The study directly sought valuations of risks in rail and fire contexts relative to risks in road accidents. The general conclusion is that context makes little difference. Perhaps, at best, domestic fires are valued about 10% less than a road accident, probably reflecting the degree of control individuals feel they have over domestic fire. If the lower value in Carthy *et al.*(1999) is taken as the VOSL in a road context, then domestic fires might have a VOSL of, say, GBP 0.9 million. Rail and road deaths would be valued the same at around GBP 1.0 million. The work of Chilton *et al.* (2004) suggests air pollution values of some GBP 1.1 million, so, again, context appears not to have a significant effect on valuation.

Table 14.1 suggests that, provided stated preference studies only are considered, VOSL is largely invariant with context and consensus numbers tend to emerge for each country. However, if wage-risk studies are considered, this consensus appears to disappear. In the UK case, for example, VOSLs are very much higher other than in the Elliott and Sandy case which converges on the contingent valuation estimates. However, there are at least two reasons why one might expect hedonic risk studies to produce higher values than stated preference studies in public accident contexts. First, occupational risks tend to be higher than public risks. If valuations are reasonably proportional to risk levels, as the theory predicts, then one would expect higher values from occupational studies. Second, hedonic risk studies measure WTA, not WTP. While the relationship between WTP and WTA is still debated (see Chapter 11), a number of reasons have been advanced for supposing that WTA will exceed WTP, perhaps by significant ratios. One suggestion, then, is that, whilst interesting, the hedonic wage studies do not "transfer" readily to the public accident context, as several authors have concluded (*e.g.* see Dionne and Lanoie, 2004).

Other factors of relevance are as follows. While hedonic wage risk studies are based on observed behaviour, it is typically assumed in these studies that the workers' perceptions of risk of death are commensurate with actual risk estimates. In addition, through the hedonic wage approach it can be difficult to measure the effect of covariates such as income, age and health status primarily due to difficulty in isolating the Marginal WTP function from the marginal hedonic wage function. Indeed, virtually all hedonic wage studies stop at the stage where the hedonic wage estimate is derived. In contrast, the hypothetical nature of CV enables the effect of covariates to be identified more readily. Moreover, it is possible to ascertain via testing in the questionnaire whether or not individuals comprehend the changes in the magnitude of risks to mortality, *i.e.* does WTP change proportionately with changes in risk – discussion of which follows.

The contingent valuation approach also permits context free testing and the valuation of health benefits that occur in future years from pollution reduction policies implemented currently, an approach taken by Krupnick *et al.* (1999), Alberini *et al.* (2004) and Markandya *et al.* (2004). In fact, these three studies use the same survey instrument and valuation scenario which seeks to elicit respondent WTP for *a)* a reduction in mortality impact that accrues over a 10 year period and *b)* a reduction in the probability of death between age 70 and 80. In the CV exercise, respondents are informed of their baseline mortality risk over the next 10 years, and then asked whether they would be willing to purchase a "product", at a stated price, that would reduce this risk by either 1 in 1 000 (amounting to 1 in 10 000 annually) or 5 in 1 000 (amounting to 5 in 10 000 annually). The product is paid for annually during the 10 year period.

14.6. Age and VOSL

Much debate in the VOSL literature has focussed on how the age of an individual matters in relation to different risk contexts. By and large this has involved assessing whether VOSLs derived in accident contexts (especially road accidents and workplace accidents) are equally applicable to pollution contexts, and whether VOSL should be replaced by a related notion of the "value of a life year" (VOLY or VLY). The basic issue here is that accidents tend to affect people of much lower average age than pollution which tends to have a "harvesting" effect among older people. A neglected issue, until recently, is the appropriate procedure where mortality may have a significant incidence among children – the issue of valuing children's lives. Theoretically, the literature suggests that WTP should vary non-linearly with age, with an upside-down "U" curve that probably peaks around age 40 (Shepard and Zeckhauser, 1982; Arthur, 1981). Whilst widely accepted in the literature, this relationship is far from robust. First, the theoretical grounds for this form of non-linearity is not strong (Johansson, 2002). (The arguments are complex and are not repeated here). Second, the empirical evidence is far from conclusive on this issue.

Early studies of the VOSL made little or no reference to the age of the individuals at risk. This appears to be because the studies focused on either road accident or occupational risks where the mean age of the person at risk is fairly constant. However, once the VOSL discussion is placed in the context of environmental policy it is quite possible that age matters in a potentially significant way. This is because pollution control policy tends to "save" lives of older people, or, to put it another way, pollution has the effect of "harvesting" the older population (Pope *et al.*, 1995; Krupnick *et al.*, 1999). The question naturally arises as to whether someone aged, say, 70 years of age has the same WTP to avoid a mortality risk as someone of 35 years of age. More critically, environmental policies may save a disproportionate number of lives in the "very old" category, *i.e.* saving lives that would have terminated perhaps just months, weeks or even days later without the policy. The issue, then, is whether WTP varies with age.

Two risk contexts need to be kept separate: immediate and future risks. The *immediate risk* would be relevant to, say, road or occupational accidents. What is sought in this context is the WTP to avoid that risk which could occur tomorrow or in the next few years, *i.e. acute risks*. Now consider an air pollution context. Here the risk may well still be immediate for older people since we know that it is older people who tend to be most affected by air pollution, *i.e.* the risks they face are still acute. Older persons' WTP to reduce the immediate risk is still relevant. But for younger people the risk of immediate premature mortality will be considerably less. The

Table 14.2. **Recent studies of the age-WTP relationship**

Study	Nature of risk	WTP and age
UK		
Carthy *et al.* 1999	Risk generally	VOSL constant up to age 70 but rapidly declining thereafter. 85 year old would have a WTP 35% of that of a 70 year old.
Chilton *et al.* 2004	Risk generally	WTP declines with age
Markandya *et al.* 2004	Context free	No effect of age on WTP
Japan		
Krupnick *et al.* 1999	Context free	No effect of age on WTP
USA		
Alberini *et al.* 2004	Context free	No effect of age on WTP
Hammitt and Graham 1999	Transport risk and food risk	WTP declines with age
Dillingham *et al.* 1996	Occupational risk	WTP for remaining worklife declines with age. 50 yrs = 0.5 x 30 years
Canada		
Alberini *et al.* 2004	Context free	Post 70 WTP falls by 25% compared to 40-69 group
Sweden		
Johannesson *et al.* 1997	Trade-off between saving current and future lives	WTP rises with age

benefit of reducing pollution will accrue to this younger group when they are much older. What is relevant for this younger group is the WTP now to reduce a *future* risk. The vast majority of WTP studies deal only with immediate, acute risks and very few look at WTP for a future risk reduction. Growing exceptions in the pollution context are Johannesson *et al.* (1997) for Sweden, Alberini *et al.* (2004) for the USA and Canada, Krupnick *et al.* (1999) for Japan, Markandya *et al.* (2004) and Chilton *et al.*, (2004) for the UK.

Table 14.2 summarises the available information from recent studies of age and WTP. The results are clearly very mixed. In terms of policy guidance, the best that can be said is that for immediate risks the relevant WTP (VOSL) is that relevant for each age group. If age does not affect WTP, then immediate risks can be valued using a "standard" VOSL as has been the practice in the past. If age does affect WTP, it becomes important to elicit WTP by age group and to use the age-related WTP (VOSL).

The issue changes if the context is one of both immediate and future risks. This is far more likely to be the case for environmental policies which tend to change the "average" levels of pollution or risk in general through time. In this case the VOSL of older people for an immediate risk is still the relevant measure as far as that age group is concerned. But the relevant VOSL for younger people will tend to be their WTP to avoid a future risk. Hence the evidence on this WTP is needed.

14.7. Latent risks

An environmental policy that lowers the average level of pollution also lowers the average exposure over a lifetime and exposure to the peaks in acute episodes. As noted above, for younger people the relevant WTP is now the WTP to reduce a future risk. Few studies have attempted to value this WTP.

Johannesson and Johansson (1996) report a contingent valuation study in Sweden where adults are asked their WTP for a new medical programme or technology that would extend expected lifetimes conditional on having reached the age of 75. Respondents are told that on reaching 75 they can expect to live for another 10 years. They are then asked their WTP to increase lifetimes by 11 years beyond 75, *i.e.* the "value" of one extra year. The results suggest average WTP across the age groups of slightly less than SEK 10 000 using standard estimation procedures and SEK 4 000 using a more conservative approach. In 2002 pound sterling terms, this is roughly about GBP 400-GBP 1 000 for a one year increase in expected life, and in dollar terms about USD 600-1 500 for one year increase in expected life. WTP actually *increases* with age, although not dramatically; on the standard basis, SEK 8 000 (GBP 800) for the 18-34 age group, 10 000 (GBP 1 000) for the 35-51 age group and 11 700 (GBP 1 160) for the 51-69 age group. Johannesson and Johansson suggest these values are consistent with "normal" VOSL of USD 30 000 to USD 110 000 (GBP 19 000-GBP 69 000), substantially less than the VOSL reported in the literature (usually several million dollars) as shown in Table 14.1. Finally, they argue that these lower valuations are consistent with findings in Sweden and the USA on social attitudes to allocating resources to life saving (*e.g.* survey respondents tend strongly to favour life saving programmes which save the lives of young people rather than old people). Earlier work by Johannesson and Johansson (1995) found that Swedish attitudes were similar, and that expectations about the future quality of life at old age play a significant role (regardless of what the actual quality of life is).

Alberini *et al.* (2004) for the USA and Canada, Krupnick *et al.* (1999) for Japan, Markandya *et al.* (2004) and Chilton *et al.* (2004) for the UK report findings for the WTP to reduce future risks. The Alberini, Krupnick and Markandya studies use a standardised format for comparability purposes, asking respondents for their WTP each year for the next ten years for a risk change that occurs between the ages of 70-80. Respondents are reminded there is a chance that they may not survive to the age of 70. The results are shown in Table 14.3 along with the implied VOSL for immediate or acute risk for purposes of benchmarking. Taking the mean values, Table 14.3 suggests that for the USA, Canada and Japan future risks are valued at around 50% of immediate risks and at 40% in the UK. Table 14.3 also shows a result from Hammitt and Liu for Taiwan where the implied ratio is 74%, depending on the type of health effect. All in all, the studies provide some support for the view that latency will result in lower VOSLs, perhaps in the range 50-80% for 20 year latency periods.[4]

Table 14.3. **Valuing future risks and immediate risks (GBP)**

Study	Country	VOSL for future risk (5/1000)		VOSL for immediate risk (5/1000)		Ratio of mean WTP for future risk to mean WTP for immediate risk
		Mean	Median	Mean	Median	
Krupnick *et al.* 1999	Japan	180 000	23 750	344 375	120 625	0.52
Alberini *et al.* 2004	USA	438 038	211 456	962 500	437 000	0.46
Alberini *et al.* 2004	Canada	307 500	78 750	583 125	316 250	0.52
Markandya *et al.* 2004	UK	377 880	138 820	920 000	484 440	0.41
Hammitt and Liu 2004	Taiwan[1]	–	–	–	–	0.74

1. VOSLs vary by type of mortality cause. For lung cancer, the relevant values in USD million are 1.6 (latent) and 2.1 (acute); for liver cancer the respective numbers are 0.8 and 1.0; for lung non-cancers 1.1 and 1.6 and for liver non-cancers 0.6 and 0.8.

Source: adapted from VOSL and WTP data in sources cited.

14.8. VOSL and VOLY

14.8.1. *From VOSL to VOLY: rules of thumb*

The preceding discussion suggests that VOSL is relevant for acute deaths and for "latent" deaths. For chronic health effects, however, life-years appear to be more relevant. Largely because of doubts about the wisdom of transferring VOSL estimates from studies of workplace accidents (which tend to affect healthy, middle-aged adults), and road accidents (which tend to affect median age individuals) to environmental contexts, efforts have been made recently to impute a "value of a life year" (or VOLY). The argument is that someone with, say, 40 years of life remaining and facing an immediate risk would tend to value "remaining life" more than someone with, say, 5 years of remaining life. Table 14.2 above brings this assumption into question since, if it was true, we would expect WTP to vary inversely with age, and only some studies observe this. The theoretical rationale for supposing that WTP varies with life expectancy comes from the lifetime consumption model whereby the WTP to reduce the probability of dying is equal to the present value of expected utility of consumption for the remaining years of life. Arguably though, this model ignores the scarcity value of time itself, *i.e.* fewer years left results in a higher WTP for the remaining years.

The unease about using VOSL in contexts where remaining years may be few for the affected individuals has led to the use of "life year" valuations derived from VOSL. The simplest conversion is to divide the VOSL of someone of a given age, say 40, by the remaining years of life expectancy, say 38. Each "life year" would then be valued at:

$$VOLY = \frac{VOSL_A}{T - A}$$ [14.4]

where T is age at the end of a normal life and A is current age. In keeping with the lifetime consumption model, however, it is usually argued that the remaining life-years should themselves be discounted, so that the calculation becomes:

$$VOLY = \frac{VOSL_A}{\sum_t \frac{1}{(1+s)^{T-A}}}$$ [14.5]

As an example, someone aged 40, with a life expectancy of 78 and VOSL of GBP 5 million would have a VOLY of GBP 131 579 on the simple approach, and GBP 296 419 on the discounted approach.[5] While attractive in principle (because of its simplicity), securing a VOLY in this way from a VOSL rests on substantial assumptions. First, as noted, the life time consumption model may not itself be capturing the features relevant to valuing remaining life years. Second, the resulting VOLY is very sensitive to the assumption made about the discount rate. Note that discount rates are not directly observed in this approach but are superimposed by the analyst. These criticisms suggest that what is needed is the remaining context of valuation, i.e. WTP for future risks.

14.8.2. Direct estimation of VOLY

Chilton et al. (2004) sought a direct estimate of a VOLY in the UK context, using the contingent valuation method. Fatality values were divided into "acute" deaths, defined as a death brought forward when in poor health ("P"), and "chronic" effects, defined as reduced life expectancy due to long-term exposure but with the individual being in normal health ("N"). The questions asked sought values of N and P, (V_N, V_P), these states being defined in the CV scenario. For N and P the "good" was defined as 1, 3 or 6 months extra "life" in normal and poor health respectively.

Summary per person values from the study are shown below. The units are current GBP per person for one year extra life expectancy in the case of N and P. The values for V_N and V_P can be thought of as "values of a life year" (VOLY). Consideration is given later to how these might be compared to a VOSL.

Table 14.4. **Direct estimates of the VOLY (GBP) – Chilton et al. (2004) for the UK**

	V_N	V_P
1 month sample	630 27	280 7
Likelihood adjusted[1]	–	280 14
3 months sample	430 9	600 1
6 months sample	040 6	290 1

1. Adjusted for the likelihood of the poor health state coming about.

Reading *across* the columns for V_N and V_P the lower values for P compared to N fit with intuition, i.e. extra "life" in poor health is valued significantly less than extra "life" in normal health. Reading *down* the columns reveals a *scope sensitivity* problem since one would expect the value of 6 months extra "life" to be worth proportionately more than 3 months' extra life and more again than 1 month of extra life. Here, budget constraints may be playing a part. Specifically that a 6 month life extension would be seen as non-marginal and hence it is difficult for respondents to imagine the kinds of budget adjustments they would need to make. On this basis, the 1 month sample may be the most relevant.

On reason for optimism about the 1 month result for V_N is that, if applied to someone at the average age of a road accident, it would imply a VOSL of GBP 27 630 × 40 = GBP 1.105 million, which is very close to the VOSL (VPF) of GBP 1.2 million used by UK Department for Transport (DfT).[6] Indeed, the Chilton *et al.* study concludes that "There is no strong evidence from the present study for using a figure which is either significantly higher, or else significantly lower, than the road safety value" (p. 44). Cautions about this conclusion arise from *a)* the scope insensitivity problem, and *b)* prior expectations, noted above, as to why pollution values should differ from accident values.

14.8.3. Indirect estimation of VOLY

In contrast to Chilton et al, the Markandya *et al.* (2004) study estimates VOSLs for the UK. To derive VOLYs from the reported VOSL estimates requires further steps. This is done by taking the WTP for the given risk change, say 5 in 1000. Thus, the median WTP for this risk change is GBP 242.22. On the basis of work by Rabl (2002), this is found to correspond to 40 days of increased life expectancy given the average age of the respondents. The corresponding VOLY is then:

$$\text{GBP } 242.22*365/40*10 = \text{GBP } 22\,080 \qquad [14.6]$$

where 10 allows for the fact that the risk change is spread over 10 years. The resulting VOLYs are presented in Table 14.5.

Table 14.5. **Indirect estimates of the VOLY (GBP) – Markandya *et al.* (2004)**

	5/1000 risk change	1/1000 risk change
Mean	41 975	94 334
Median	22 080	25 149

Markandya *et al.* (2004) argue that the 5/1000 risk change is more reliable. They also expressed a preference for using the median values, but for policy purposes the mean value is the more relevant.

Table 14.6 brings together the two sets of estimates of the VOLY. The Markandya *et al.* study produces GBP 41 975 for the 5/1000 risk change (and using the mean), whereas the Chilton *et al.* study secures GBP 27 630. The difference here probably partly reflects the procedure used in the Markandya study for working out the VOLY from the VOSL. Alternatively, differences in the average age of respondents in the two studies might help to explain the difference. Table 14.6 summarises the comparisons of the mean estimates.

Table 14.6. **Comparison of VOLYs and VOSLs**

Study	Estimate of VOLY	VOSL	VOLY
Chilton *et al.*	Direct	GBP 1.11 million	GBP 27 632
Markandya *et al.*	Inferred	GBP 0.92 million	GBP 41 975

14.9. Implied "values of life"

While there are often vociferous criticisms of economists' "value of life" estimates, it is useful to bear in mind that all decisions involving tolerance, acceptance or rejection of risk changes imply such valuations. The reason is very simple: risk reductions usually involve expenditure of resources, so that not spending those resources implies a sum of VOSLs less than the resource cost. Conversely, spending the resources implies a sum of VOSLs greater than the resource cost. Several reviews in the USA have sought to measure the implied VOSLs by taking the costs of regulatory actions and computing the likely lives saved by the regulations (Morrall, 1986; Tengs, 1995). Morrall has recently updated his survey (Morrall, 2003). Covering 76 regulations, Morrall derives implied VOSLs ranging from USD 100 000 for a regulation covering childproof lighters, through USD 500 million for sewage sludge disposal regulations, and up to USD 100 *billion* for solid waste disposal facility criteria. Taking a USD 7 million "cut-off" point, Morall finds that nearly all regulations aimed at safety pass a cost-benefit test, but less than 20% of regulations aimed at reducing cancers pass such a test. Finally, by employing "risk-risk" or "health-health" analysis, Morrall shows that USD 21 million of public expenditure gives rise to one statistical death.[7] Hence any measure that implies a VOSL of more than USD 21 million "does more harm than good", *i.e.* it generates more deaths than lives saved. 27 of the 76 regulations studies fail this test.

Studies of implied VOSLs serve several purposes. First, and perhaps least important, they remind us that there is no "escape" from the valuation of life risks. Second, they serve as a measure of consistency across public agencies: the implied VOSL for, say, transport risks should not be significantly different to the implied VOSL for pollution reduction, unless there is a reason to suppose that the risks should be valued differently. Third, even if there is no consensus on "the" VOSL, the Morall (2003) exercise shows that some policy measures are not credible in terms of their stated goal of cost-effectively saving lives. On the basis Morall's analysis, it is not possible to argue that lives should be saved at a cost of USD 100 billion per life.

14.10. Valuing children's lives[8]

14.10.1. Why should we pay attention to children?

The relationship between environment and children's health has been the subject of an increasing interest these last ten years. This interest has resulted in a growing number of epidemiological studies aiming at establishing a causal link between environmental pollution and the health of children. However, the valuation of children's health strongly differs from the valuation of adults' health in several respects and constitutes a real challenge for analysts as well as for decision-makers. On the one hand, one can note a difference in terms of risk between adults and children. From their daily behavioural pattern, adults and children are exposed neither to the same environmental risks, nor to the same level of risk. Also, from a metabolic point of view, children are more receptive and more sensitive to pollution than adults, as their bodies are still developing. Thus, even though they are exposed to the same environmental risk and to a level *a priori* identical to that of adults, the body of a child can be more affected than that of an adult by this form of pollution. Recent epidemiological studies highlight the particular susceptibility of children to environmental pollution (Tamburlini, 2005).

The valuation of children's health may have significant methodological implications that should be taken into account to obtain reliable estimates of benefits in the context of the design and development of environmental and/or health policies. Three valuation differences may be particularly problematic: the elicitation of children's preferences, the valuation context, and the difficulties associated with age, latency and discounting (Scapecchi, 2005). Their methodological implications are examined below.

14.10.2. Elicitation of children's preferences

Whose preferences count?

Three distinct perspectives can be used to elicit children's preferences. The first approach is referred to as the "societal perspective", and consists in asking a representative sample of the population, including all adults, *i.e.* both parents and non-parents. An alternative is the "children perspective" where the children are directly asked about the value they place in reducing a risk affecting them directly. Finally, the "parental perspective" can be used: parents (or caregivers) are asked about the value they place on their children's health.

The first perspective may be substantially affected by altruism and the difficulty in distinguishing between altruism towards own children and altruism towards children in general. The second perspective is rendered inappropriate by the lack of well defined preferences and budget constraints for children. The third perspective appears as the most relevant approach: various theoretical economic models suggest that parents' choice are the appropriate proxy for children's preferences and constitute a reliable source of information (Viscusi *et al.*, 1987). Even though altruism is likely to remain a major concern, this approach has the advantage of asking the persons who are actually directly affected by the risk reduction and who have the interests of the child at heart.

Methodological implications

The parental perspective, however, raises two major methodological problems. The first one refers to *decision-maker's autonomy*: most important decisions concerning children are taken by their parents or their caregivers, on behalf of their children. In addition, children are not always able to express their preferences through their own behaviour. This may have serious implications for most of the valuation methodologies relying on decision-maker's choices and preferences.

The second problem is related to the potential effect of *risk perception* on the estimates. Society and parents are known to be more risk averse to risks experienced by children than to those experienced by adults. Reasons for such a behaviour could include risk aversion and attributes of risk, such as the voluntariness of risk, risk uncertainty and dread issues (Fischhoff *et al.*, 1978; Slovic, 1987; Viscusi *et al.*, 1991), and altruism (Dickie and Gerking, 2005). These factors may alter risk perception and therefore bias WTP estimates.

These fundamental complications in valuing children's health benefits may conflict with the usual assumptions of neoclassical consumer theory. In this case, we cannot rely on children's own evaluation of a change in their own welfare and we have to rely on the most sensible proxy: their parents (or caregivers).

14.10.3. Valuation context

The valuation of children's health does not take place in the traditional individual context (where someone is asked to state a WTP for his/her own risk reduction), but rather in a household (*i.e.* collective) context where someone (*e.g.* a parent) is asked to evaluate a risk reduction for another member of his/her household (*e.g.* his/her child). As a consequence, the choice of the intra-household allocation model and household-related factors may have a substantial impact on the WTP estimates.

Choice of the social welfare model

Two types of household allocation model can be used: a unitary model in which the household is treated as a unit and financial resources are pooled, or a collective model in which the individual utility functions of each household member (at least the adults) are pooled to obtain a collective decision, taking account of the differences in household members' preferences. These two types of household allocation models differ according to two criteria: whether children are treated as independent decision-makers, and whether the family is assumed to maximise a single utility function. Generally, children are considered as passive participants in family decision-making. But what happens when the child becomes adolescent and is in a better position to express his/her preferences? What about two parents having different preferences concerning their own children? Alternative approaches that could fit better these particular contexts should also be considered and examined. For further details on the various household allocation models, see Dickie and Gerking (2005).

Influence of household-related factors

In a household decision context, household-related factors may affect children's health estimates. As an example, the family structure and composition affect resource allocation and health outcomes experienced (Dickie and Ulery, 2001). Some studies have highlighted differences between children according to their health status, gender or age (Pitt and Rosenzweig, 1990; Hanushek, 1992; Liu *et al.*, 2000). Finally, altruism from parents toward their children may significantly affect the estimates and be a source of disparity between adults' values and children's values (Dickie and Ulery, 2001). These results suggest that applying a unique value for all children would lead to unreliable estimates of children's health.

14.10.4. Difficulties related to age, latency and discounting

A number of issues when valuing children's health have been identified and include difficulties related to age, latency and discounting. They affect the valuation of adults' health and thus may be of greater concern when considering the case of children given the differences between adults and children.

Some of the empirical evidence related to adults' health valuation highlights a potentially large influence of age on WTP values: young adults do not have the same WTP values to reduce fatal risks than middle-aged or older adults (Johannesson *et al.*, 1997). Therefore, we could reasonably expect that age would matter more for children relative to adults. There is no consensus based on empirical evidence but many economic studies have found that the VOSL for children is at least as great as the VOSL for adults. For a review of the literature, see Scapecchi (2005). See also Dickie and Gerking (2005).

Many environmental health risks involve a time lag between exposure and the onset of illness or death: *i.e.* the issue of latency – see Section 14.7. For example, exposure to some heavy metals and chemicals (especially in childhood) is known to result in health impairments later in life. A reduction in exposure today, therefore, would result in risk reductions to be experienced later in life. As Section 14.7 showed, it is thus necessary to know the present WTP of people for a risk reduction to be experienced in the future. Latency is a major concern for the valuation of environmental health risks to children, because of their particular vulnerability to environmental pollutants and given their longer lifespan. In addition, trade-off decisions that involve latent health effects may be influenced by the perceptions of future health states and preferences. This increases the uncertainty associated with the valuation of children's health and thus adds complexity (Hoffmann *et al.*, 2005).

Discounting is particularly important when health effects are long-lived such as those concerning children. In a context of discounting children's health, we must refer to the preferences of parents. It is not known then whether parents discount their own future health benefits at the same rate as they discount future health benefits to their children. The unfamiliarity with this sort of decision-making, the uncertainty associated with future health events, the cognitively demanding task and the meaning of the description of future health events make it difficult to elicit parents' preferences (Cairns, 2005). Moreover, it is of common practice to use a constant discount rate over time and across individuals. However, results from recent empirical studies suggest that non-constant discount rates and more generally hyperbolic discounting may be better appropriate than traditional exponential discounting when dealing with health effects – see Chapter 13.

14.10.5. *Review of the literature*

Little is known about the valuation of children's health, but experience with research on adults' health suggest that WTP could be considered as the best way to evaluate risk reductions on children's health. The results of recent studies estimating WTP to reduce risks to children's health are presented below (see Table 14.7).

Table 14.7. **Studies valuing children's health**

Study	Country	Valuation method	Benefits measure used	Value (in USD)
Mortality				
Mount, Weng, Schulze and Chestnut (2000)	US	Averting behaviour model – Automobile safety purchases data (1995 survey)	WTP to reduce fatality risks for different age groups	VOSL (in USD million) 7.3 (child) 7.2 (adult) 5.2 (elderly)
Jenkins, Owens and Wiggins (2001)	US	Averting behaviour model – Child bicycle helmets market data (1997survey)	Parental WTP to reduce fatality risks to children	VOSL (in USD million) 2.9 (child of 5-9) 2.8 (child of 10-14) 4.3 (adult)
Acute morbidity				
Liu *et al.* (2000)	Taiwan	Contingent valuation survey	Mother's WTP for preventing a cold to her and to her child	USD 57 (child) USD 37 (mother)
Agee and Crocker (2001)	US	Contingent valuation survey	Parental WTP for a 1% reduction of their child's daily exposure to environmental tobacco smoke	USD 10.2 (child exposure to environmental tobacco smoke)
			WTP for a 10% increase of the health status of the child and the respondent	USD 452 (for the child health status) USD 249 (for the respondent health status)
Dickie and Ulery (2001)	US	Contingent valuation survey	Parental WTP to avoid acute illnesses	USD 50 (to avoid one symptom for 1 day)
			WTP to avoid seven days of one symptom	USD 150 to USD 350 (child) USD 100 to USD 165 (adult)
			WTP to avoid one-week incident of acute bronchitis	USD 400 (child) USD 200 (adult)
Dickie and Brent (2002)	US	Contingent valuation survey	WTP to avoid one day of first symptom	USD 94 (child) USD 35 (adult)
Chronic morbidity				
Maguire, Owens and Simon (2002)	US	Hedonic model – Baby food market data	Price premium to avoid pesticide residues in baby food	USD 0.012 per jar
Dickie and Gerking (2001)	US	Contingent valuation survey	Parental WTP for a 1% point reduction in non-melanoma skin cancer risk	USD 3.18 (child) USD 1.29 (adult)

COST-BENEFIT ANALYSIS AND THE ENVIRONMENT: RECENT DEVELOPMENTS – ISBN 92-64-01004-1 – © OECD 2006

The number of empirical studies that have considered the valuation of a reduction of health risks to children is limited. Most studies do not consider a health risk reduction in an environmental context but provide nonetheless useful results for further empirical work. The estimates are rather incomplete, and only a few studies provide estimates for acute effects. Concerning the valuation of a reduction of the mortality risk among children, the results are mixed, though the majority tends to suggest that the VOSL for a child is greater, or at least not less, than that of an adult.

14.10.6. Conclusion on valuing children's lives

Empirical evidence on the valuation of children's environmental health is limited. The lack of available data specific to children precludes an evaluation of the health impacts of existing environment-related health policies. More data are necessary, and more particularly data on specific health endpoints comparable to those for adults, such as chronic morbidity risk and asthma morbidity. Therefore, priority should be given to the collection and assessment of epidemiological data to implement valuation studies to provide meaningful policy advice. However, improved epidemiological data of this sort is not sufficient. Ignoring valuation differences between adults and children could lead to biased estimates of health benefits associated with a reduction of environmental risk and therefore to inefficient policies. In order to be able to correctly compare children and adults values of health benefits, estimates should be obtained from a consistent valuation approach.

In addition, analysts tend to transfer values when credible values are lacking. In the case of valuation of children's environmental health, where so few studies are available, benefits transfer may be particularly hazardous – see Chapter 17. One possibility would consist of inferring a marginal rate of substitution, defined as the ratio of adults' values for their own health and adults' values for their children's health, as suggested in the literature – see Dickie and Gerking (2005). However, benefit transfer through the use of a generic marginal rate of substitution has no justification if the estimates to be transferred are not reliable. Given that this marginal rate of substitution may vary across different health risks or different demographic groups, estimating children's health benefits as any constant multiple of adult benefit may be misleading. Similarly, transferring estimates for adults to children on a 1-to-1 basis may lead to an underestimation of children's health benefits.

Policy implications

Policymakers have been forced to make decisions and set priorities on the basis of very limited evidence and limited information. This raises a question on the validity of policies currently in place: do they reflect the differences between adults and children? Are they (still) appropriate?

Three related "policy failures" can be identified. First, environmental standards are based on their impacts on adults, which are quite different from those for children. Proper valuation of impacts on children would result in standards which are different, probably more stringent. Second, policy priorities across different environmental health impact areas are based on adult responses, and so are often inappropriate for children. In such cases, governments are not allocating investments so as to avoid loss of lives or ill-health in an optimal manner. Third, the allocation of resources between the environmental (*ex ante*) and the health (*ex post*) public policy fields may be imbalanced – with too much focus on "cleaning up" the health impacts generated by environmental problems, rather than on preventing the environmental problems in the first place. While limited, existing evidence seems to indicate that the resources devoted toward children's health are too low.

Given the lack of available data and the methodological complexities involved, valuation of children's environmental health impacts is likely to be even more fraught with difficulties. In the light of previous considerations on valuing children's lives, further research would be necessary to determine the most relevant measure of health outcomes (*e.g.* WTP or QALYs) and the most appropriate valuation technique (stated preferences vs. revealed preferences techniques). Valuation differences may affect both measures but the order of magnitude is still to be determined. In addition, it would be necessary to better understand how the VOSL differs with the characteristics of individuals. Finally, given regional disparities, comparative economic studies carried out in different countries would contribute to the generation of more credible values.

14.11. Valuing morbidity

The previous sections have been concerned with the valuation of premature mortality. Also important in environmental contexts is morbidity, *i.e.* non-fatal ill health.

An extensive study on morbidity in the European Union (plus Norway) is reported in Ready *et al.* (2004a, 2004b). This study undertook contingent valuation surveys in Portugal, the Netherlands, Norway, Spain and the UK for health effects that were thought to be associated with air pollution, specifically respiratory illness. In each country, WTP to avoid episodes of certain illnesses was elicited. An explicit effort was made to test for the effects of *context* by eliciting values for health end points without any reference to context, and repeating the exercise for the same endpoints but with some contextual material added to the questionnaire. In addition, the study tested the validity of benefits transfer (BT) by estimating WTP in any one "policy" country on the basis of the values derived in the other (study site) countries – for more detail see Chapter 17. Comparison of the BT estimate with the actual value derived from the contingent valuation study in the "policy" country provides a measure of validity of BT. The resulting error (E) was defined as:

$$E = \frac{(WTP_T - WTP_{CV})}{WTP_{CV}} \qquad [14.7]$$

Where WTP_T is the transferred WTP value and WTP_{CV} the original CV estimate. Table 14.8 provides the central estimates for five countries and the pooled European average.

Table 14.8. **Values for morbidity in Europe: GBP WTP to avoid an episode**

Illness episode	Pooled	Netherlands	Norway	Portugal	Spain	UK
Hospital	306 (490)	283 (453)	301 (482)	300 (480)	426 (682)	164 (262)
Casualty	158 (253)	128 (205)	239 (382)	185 (296)	146 (234)	131 (210)
Bed	97 (155)	71 (114)	119 (190)	88 (141)	113 (181)	83 (133)
Cough	27 (43)	28 (45)	36 (58)	28 (45)	39 (62)	20 (32)
Eyes	35 (56)	40 (64)	31 (50)	70 (112)	53 (85)	14 (22)
Stomach	35 (56)	–	–	61 (98)	–	26 (42)

Notes: Bracketed values are EURO conversion. GBP converted to EURO at 1.6:1.
Hospital = hospital admission for the treatment of respiratory diseas.
Casualty = emergency room visit for relief from respiratory illness.
Bed = 3 days spent in bed with respiratory illness.
Cough = one day with persistent cough.
Eyes = one day with itchy, watering eyes.
Stomach = one day of persistent nausea or headache.
Source: Ready *et al.* 2004a.

The illness categories in Table 14.8 relate to respiratory illnesses; however the valuations were designed to be "context free" in the sense that the causes of the illness were not identified. Further analysis showed that the introduction of "context" made no statistical difference to the estimates of WTP. In principle, then, these WTP could be transferred from one location to another regardless of context, since the values are context-free (and context is arguably not an influence). The reliability of such a transfer exercise partly rests on whether all contexts are accounted for. The study tested for context in the contingent valuation surveys by adopting different questionnaires: one in which context was absent, and one in which the causal context was cited. In the UK survey a further contextual dimension was added, namely the policy context, with a description of policies that would reduce air pollution. By and large, the "causal" context does not affect WTP, although the Portuguese survey found a lower WTP when context was cited. The more detailed UK survey also found that policy did influence WTP, with WTP being significantly higher in the "with policy" case. As will be discussed shortly, context takes on many different aspects.

In relation to the validity of transferring WTP values between countries, the average value of the transfer error (E) was 0.36 (*i.e.* there would be an average 36% error involved in transferring estimates to a country outside the five countries studied). Most probably, this is an acceptable degree of error in cost-benefit studies and could easily be incorporated in sensitivity analysis. For the within-sample, errors were as small as 2% for "hospital" in Norway (*i.e.* taking the WTP for hospital from the other four countries and applying it to Norway) but as high as 111% for the UK for hospital, and 235% for "eyes". As a general proposition, transferring estimates *to* the UK appears particularly error-prone (a range of 23% to 235%).

The transferability of the morbidity WTP estimates thus appears fairly safe in principle, provided the values sought are context free. In the case where WTP for proposed policy changes is sought, one might add a premium to the context-free estimates, but more research would be needed to establish what this premium (or discount) is according to different policy contexts.

A final point of interest from Table 14.8 is that WTP to avoid states of illness appears not to be correlated with income, *e.g.* the WTP to avoid illness is highest, or second highest, in Spain for hospital, bed, cough and eyes. This probably reflects the different forms of health care available in the different countries. For the within-country studies, WTP was found to be correlated with income and WTP was *positively* associated with age (see the comparable discussion about age and VOSL above).

Table 14.9 compares the Ready *et al.* EU study estimates with those of ExternE (CEC DGXII 1995; CEC DGXII 1998) and Maddison (2000).

The ExternE values relate reasonably well to Ready *et al.* for casualty and stomach, but bed, cough and eyes all appear to be underestimated in the ExternE procedure. The Maddison (2000)[9] estimates are relevant because they are derived from a form of meta-analysis in which an overall transfer function is derived. Maddison follows the analysis of Reed Johnson (1996; see also Desvousges *et al.*, 1998) by integrating "quality of well-being" (QWB) indexes with WTP estimates. QWB estimates are cardinal indicators of well-being

Table 14.9. **Comparison of morbidity values in Ready *et al.* (2004a)
and those in ExternE and Maddison (2000) (GBP)**

Illness episode	Pooled values from Ready *et al.* 2004a	ExternE values	Maddison 2000
Hospital	306 (490)	4919 (7870)	n.a.
Casualty	158 (253)	139 (223)	n.a.
Bed	97 (155)	47 (75)	122 (195)
Cough	27 (43)	5 (7.5)	45 (72)
Eyes	35 (56)	5 (7.5)	38 (61)
Stomach	35 (56)	47 (75)	76 (121)

Notes: Bracketed values are EURO conversion. GBP converted to EURO at 1.6:1. Categories are not identical in the studies. Hospital and casualty are the same. A respiratory bed day is taken to be the same as restricted activity day in ExternE but the bed-day may be more restricted. Cough and eyes are minor restricted activity days and correspond to the ExternE minor restricted days. Stomach is a day of work lost and does not have a direct counterpart in the ExternE study, so it is taken here to be a restricted activity day. "Stomach" is also assumed to be equivalent to Maddison's restricted activity day. All of Maddison's values relate to an episode of one day's duration.

based on a 0 to 1 scale, death to perfect health. Maddison adds some Norwegian data to the US data used in Reed Johnson and derives the following meta-equation:

$$\ln WTP = 1.76 - 4.80.\ln QWB + 0.49\ln DAYS \qquad [14.8]$$

where DAYS is the duration of the illness. Note that as QWB falls, WTP increases sharply. While there are few estimates to compare, Maddison's results do not seem far removed from those derived from the original contingent studies reported in Table 14.8.

Vassanadumrongdee *et al.* (2004) conduct a meta-analysis of contingent valuation morbidity valuations in air pollution contexts. Their analysis covers sixteen separate studies with a wide international geographical coverage. Morbidity states range from coughs, to angina attacks, respiratory illness, asthma and respiratory hospital admissions. The studies include an early version of the EU studies described above. Like Maddison (2000) and Reed Johnson *et al.* (1996), this meta analysis integrates the QWB score for each health state, *i.e.* the various health end states are assigned Quality of Well-being scores which are bounded by zero (death) and perfect health (unity). WTP for the avoided health state is then regressed on the various factors assumed to influence WTP, including the QWB score, income, age etc. The basic form of the regression equation is:

$$WTP = f(QWB, DAYS, POP, STUDY) \qquad [14.9]$$

where DAYS refers to the duration of the illness, POP refers to population characteristics (age, gender, education and income), and STUDY refers to the features of the contingent valuation study (geographical location, elicitation format, and survey method). Various econometric techniques and functional forms are used. The general results are:

- QWB and DAYS are highly correlated with WTP and a broad scope test is passed, *i.e.* WTP increases the more severe the health state and the longer it lasts. A strict scope test is not met – *i.e.* there is no strict proportionality between WTP and the health state and duration, a finding consistent with that for the VOSL studies.

- There is a diminishing marginal WTP for improved health, *i.e.* as health improves, one further unit of improvement is valued positively but at a declining rate.

- Age and income have strong explanatory power for WTP. Note that the strong effect of age contrasts with the ambiguous results obtained for the link between age and VOSL.

● WTP studies in developing countries produce lower WTP than in developed countries, as one would expect.

The researchers select what they regard as their "best" model and then use this to predict WTP for a given health state (avoidance of coughing). The predicted value can then be compared to actual WTP for locations where primary studies have been carried out. By and large, predicted and actual WTP were similar (the comparison is across countries). The general suggestion is that, despite the wide geographic variation in primary studies, WTP for avoiding ill-health can be estimated on the basis of a meta-equation of the kind outlined above.

14.12. Cancer premia

It is widely believed that there may be a higher WTP to avoid cancers than other diseases. This is because of the "dread" effect of such a serious illness. Fatal cancers could be valued at the relevant VOSL (see previous discussions above), although in a context where there is prior knowledge of the likely cause of death, the "dread" factor could increase WTP. Non-fatal cancers (NFCs) may attract values that are unique to those illnesses. It is somewhat surprising that the valuation literature has comparatively little to say about the values attached to cancers. Table 14.10 summarises the results from studies that have looked at NFCs.

Rowe *et al.* (1995) adopt a value based on the US costs of treating cancers ("cost of illness", COI) and then multiply this by 1.5 on the basis that, where COI and WTP studies are available, WTP appears to be 1.5 times the COI. This procedure is clearly not satisfactory, as there are few studies that estimate COI and WTP. Moreover, the Rowe *et al.* COI value dates from the mid-1970s. Their valuation is some 6% of the VOSL they use. ExternE uses a figure of USD 450 000 for an NFC (*i.e.*, some 15% of the VOSL), but it is unclear how this sum has been derived.

Table 14.10. **Economic valuation of NFCs (GBP 1999)**

Study	Country	Value	Comment
Rowe *et al.* 1995	USA	116 250	NFCs generally, based on COI
ExternE	Europe	281 250	Source unknown
Viscusi, 1995	USA	1 218 750	Lymph cancers
Aimola, 1998	Italy (Sicily)	31 250	Lung cancer
		56 250	Uterine cancer
		312 500	Prostate cancer
		456 250	Leukaemia

Viscusi (1995) conducts a computer experiment in which respondents are able to trade off ill health against risk of death in an automobile accident. His results (for the USA) suggest that a curable lymph cancer would be valued at some 63% of the VOSL, which, in this case, would give a value of about four times the suggested ExternE figure.

Murdoch and Thayer (1990) estimate WTP for skin cancer avoidance using a "defensive expenditures" approach, *i.e.* by looking at changes in expenditure on sun protection products. They find that the total damages from anticipated increases in non-melanoma cancers are about one-half of the COI measure used by the US Environmental Protection Agency at the time. In undiscounted form, their estimates can be shown to result in a value per case of around USD 30 000.[10] However, most of the cases occur well into the future.

Values for skin cancer are clearly not comparable to those for pollution or radiation-induced cancers, since the vast majority of skin cancers are operable with only slight effects. Aimola (1998) uses the CV method to elicit cancer risk valuations from a small sample of the population in Sicily. The cancers in question were prostate, uterus, leukaemia and lung cancers.

It is difficult to derive a clear conclusion from the studies but it seems clear that values for avoiding NFCs are fractions of a VOSL, as would seem correct. Since individuals are likely to believe that some cancers are more life-threatening than others, one might expect individuals to respond with higher WTP to avoid those NFCs. Arguably the table lends some support to this view in respect of the values for leukaemia and prostate cancer.

Finally, if NFC values are less than VOSLs but with values being proportional to some "dread" factor, one would also expect VOSL to vary with type of disease causing death. Hammitt and Liu (2004) find evidence that there is a cancer premium which they estimate to be about one-third, *i.e.* VOSL for avoiding a cancer risk is 1.3 times that of a VOSL for some other disease.

We can conclude that there is a case for assigning some premium to VOSLs according to the type of disease causing death. Where cancers are non-fatal, some fraction of VOSL should be used, perhaps with the fraction varying by the nature of the NFC.

14.13. Summary and guidance for decision-makers

Considerable strides have been made in recent years in terms of clarifying both the meaning and size of the "value of a statistical life" (VOSL). One of the main issues has been how to "transfer" VOSLs taken from non-environmental contexts to environmental contexts. Non-environmental contexts tend to be associated with immediate risks such as accidents. In contrast, environmental contexts are associated with both immediate and future risks. The futurity of risk may arises because the individual in question is not at immediate risk from *e.g.* current levels of pollution but is at risk in the future when there is greater vulnerability to risk. Or futurity may arise because the risk is latent as with diseases such as asbestosis or arsenicosis. All this suggests *a)* that valuations of immediate risk might be transferred to environmental immediate risk contexts (provided that the perception of the risk is the same[11]) but *b)* future risks need to be valued separately.

In terms of practical guidelines, the age of the respondent who is valuing the risk matters. Age may or may not be relevant in valuing immediate risks – the literature is ambiguous. The general rule, then, is to ensure that age is controlled for in any primary valuation study. For "benefits transfer" the rule might be one of adopting a default position in which immediate risks are valued the same regardless of age (*i.e.* the VOSL does not vary with age), with sensitivity analysis being used to test the effects of lower VOSLs being relevant for older age groups. Age is very relevant for valuing future risks. Thus a policy which lowers the general level of exposure to pollution should be evaluated in terms of the (lower than immediate VOSL) valuations associated with younger people's valuations of future risks, plus older persons' valuation of that risk as an immediate risk.

Some environmental risks fall disproportionately on the very young and the very old. The valuations of older people are discussed above, but a complex issue arises with valuing risks to children. The calculus of willingness to pay now seems to break down since children may have no income to allocate between goods, including risk reduction, may be ill-informed about or be unaware of risks, and may be too young to articulate preferences anyway. The result is that adults' valuations of the risks *on behalf of* children need to be estimated. The literature on which to base such judgements is only now coming into existence. Preliminary findings suggest that the resulting values of WTP may be higher for adults valuing on behalf of children than they are for adults speaking on behalf of themselves. The safest conclusion at this stage is that bringing the effects on children into the domain of CBA is potentially important, with a default position being to use the adult valuations of "own" life risks for the risks faced by children.

Notes

1. This chapter is necessarily selective in its coverage since the literature on valuing human health impacts is now extremely large. We focus only on issues that have occupied attention in the recent literature.

2. Terminology varies: VOSL is also known as a "value of a prevented fatality" (VPF) and, despite the warnings of economists about this phrase, "value of life".

3. Terminology can be confusing. The initial or baseline risk level needs to be distinguished from the change in the risk level brought about by the policy in question.

4. Note that several effects are present. Discounting the future will lower the WTP for avoiding a delayed health effect, but income growth will raise WTP according the income elasticity of WTP. See Hammitt and Liu (2004) for the full model.

5. The issue arises of whether individuals have already discounted the future when providing their WTP response if the approach used is a stated preference study. If so, the simple approach is relevant. If not, the discounted approach is more relevant.

6. The same "scaling up" from a VOLY to a VPF cannot be done for V_P since this value relates to an elderly person in poor health. For argument's sake, however, one might assume, say 5-10 years life expectancy without the acute pollution effect, in which case the VPF for this category would be (GBP 7280 – 14280)*(5 – 10), or GBP 36 400 to GBP 142 800 for an "acute" VPF. However, this issue was not discussed at the Workshop and the suggestion should be treated with some caution.

7. All policies cost money which ultimately comes from taxation, reducing the disposable income of taxpayers. Some of that forgone income would have been spent on life-saving measures. Hence all government expenditure causes life loss. Comparable studies exist for Sweden where the cut-off point is USD 6.8 – 9.8 million – see Gerdtham and Johannesson (2002) and the UK, where the cut-off is around USD 8 million (Whitehurst, 1999).

8. This section was written by Pascale Scapecchi of the OECD Environment Directorate. It builds on OECD work on the valuation of environmental health risks to children – see Scapecchi (2005a).

9. Maddison's estimates cover a wider range of health effects but not casualty and hospital. Other effects are major asthmatic attack (GBP 107), lower respiratory infection (GBP 45), respiratory symptoms (GBP 45), acute bronchitis (GBP 106), chest discomfort (GBP 60), minor RAD (restricted activity day) (GBP 45), phlegm (GBP 26).

10. Estimated by taking their estimated 2.96 million extra cases and an undiscounted defensive expenditure of USD 87.7 billion.

11. Space forbids a discussion of this issue, but some studies make it clear that the nature of the risk may matter as well as the level of risk. For example, a risk of cancer may be perceived quite differently to the same probability of disability from an accident.

ANNEX 14.A1

Deriving the Value of a Statistical Life

The standard approach to the VOSL is to assume that an individual's utility function for wealth (W) and mortality risk (p) is expressed in the utility function:

$$U(p, W) = (1 - p).u_a(W) + p.u_d(W) \qquad [A14.1]$$

where U is (expected) utility, $u_a(W)$ is the utility conditional on surviving – i.e. the utility of being alive – and $u_d(W)$ is the utility conditional on dying. It is assumed that $u'_a < 0$ and $u''_a < 0$. The former assumption says that marginal utility of wealth is increasing in wealth, and the second says that the individual is averse to gambles with expected value of zero, i.e. individuals are averse to financial risk.

This is a one-period model, and for the sake of simplicity, $u_d(W)$ can be interpreted as including bequests etc., so that it is not necessarily equal to zero, i.e. $u'_d \geq 0$. It is further assumed that:

$$u_a(W) > u_d(W) \text{ and}$$

$$u'_a (W) > u'_d (W) \qquad [A14.2]$$

The second condition simply means that more wealth provides more utility if the individual survives than if he/she dies. Put another way, additional wealth yields more utility in life than as a bequest.

The corresponding indifference curve is:

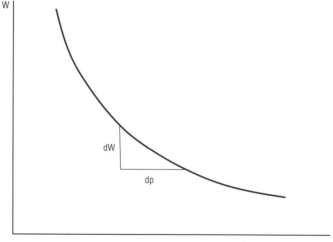

Differentiating A14.1 whilst holding utility constant gives:

$$\frac{dU(.)}{dp} = (1-p).u_a'(W) - u_a(W) + p.u_d'(W) + u_d(W) = 0 \qquad \text{[A14.3]}$$

so that

$$VOSL = \frac{dW}{dp}\bigg|_{EU=cons\tan t} = \frac{u_a(W) - u_d(W)}{(1-p).u_a'(W) + p.u_d'(W)} \qquad \text{[A14.4]}$$

The numerator shows the difference between utility if the individual survives or dies in the current period. The denominator is the expected marginal utility of wealth, conditional on survival and dying, each event being weighted by the relevant probabilities. The denominator is often called the "expected utility cost of funds" or the "expected utility cost of spending".

Baseline risk

Given the inequalities A14.2, VOSL > 0. VOSL also increases with baseline risk, p, the so-called "dead anyway" effect (Pratt and Zeckhauser, 1996). Hammitt (2000) points out that this effect cannot be large for small risk changes because survival probabilities for any year are much higher than mortality probabilities [(1 – p) is large, p is small]. As p increases, the numerator in A14.4 is unchanged because p does not affect it. But the denominator changes since the first expression declines and the second increases. Given the likely probabilities, the decline outweighs the increase and the denominator thus decreases. VOSL rises with baseline risk, but not by much.

Wealth

The effect of wealth changes on VOSL depends on financial risk aversion in the two states – survival and death. Risk neutrality and risk aversion are sufficient to ensure that VOSL rises with W. Since $u_a'(W) > u_d'(W)$ the numerator increases in wealth. Since $u_a''(W) < 0, u_d''(W) < 0$, the denominator declines with wealth. Hence VOSL rises with wealth.

Health status

The relationship between VOSL and health status on survival is strictly indeterminate, although many studies assume that VOSL will be higher for survival in good health than for survival in poor health, which seems intuitively correct. Hammitt (2000) points out that survival in bad health may limit the individual's ability to increase utility by spending money – the marginal utility of wealth may be lower for survival in bad health than in good health. The denominator in A14.4 is smaller if survival means bad health. But the numerator is also smaller, so the relationship between VOSL and health state is dependent on exact values and could be positive or negative.

Latency

Equation A14.4 says nothing about latency, i.e. exposure to risks now may result in death much later (e.g. arsenicosis, asbestosis, etc.). The relevant VOSL (call it $VOSL_{lat}$) is:

$$VOSL_{lat} = \frac{VOSL_T}{(1+s)^T}.P_T \qquad \text{[A14.5]}$$

where $VOSL_{lat}$ is the VOSL now for an exposure risk occurring now, T is the latency period after which the individual dies, s is the discount rate (technically, the individual's discount rate) and P_T is the probability that the individual will survive the latency period, *i.e.* the probability that he/she does not die from other causes in the interim period. Essentially, then, the relevant VOSL is the discounted value of the future VOSL at the time the risk effect occurs, adjusted for the probability of surviving during the latency period. If WTP varies with income and income increases with time, then, rather than discounting future WTP at the relevant discount rate, a *net* discount rate may be used. If *s* is the discount rate and WTP grows as n % per annum, the net discount rate will be (s-n) % per annum. A convenient case occurs where s = n since this reduces the problem to one of using undiscounted values.

Hammitt and Liu (2004) present a somewhat more sophisticated version of A14.5 for a latent effect where the risk change occurs as a "blip", *i.e.* a temporary risk reduction as opposed to a permanent reduction of risk. (For a permanent risk reduction, WTP needs to be summed for each of the future periods). Their equation is:

$$WTP_0 = \frac{WTP_T}{\left(1/(1+s)\right)^T . a_T . (1+g)^{T\eta}}$$

[A14.6]

where WTP_0 is willingness to pay for a risk reduction now, WTP_T is willingness to pay for a risk reduction in T years time, s is the personal discount rate, a is a factor linking age to WTP (a = 1 if age has no effect on willingness to pay, with a < 1 being the usual expectation), g is the growth rate of income and η is the income elasticity of willingness to pay for risk reduction. Equation A14.6 thus makes an explicit attempt to modify the VOSL equation for *a)* age and *b)* interim income growth during a latency period.

Age

Equation A14.4 does not tell us if WTP (and hence VOSL) varies with age. Age is usually thought to have two potentially offsetting effects: *a)* the older one gets, the fewer years are left so the benefit of any current reduction in risk declines – we would expect VOSL to decline with age; *b)* the opportunity cost of spending money on risk reduction declines as time goes by because savings accumulate, so WTP for risk reduction may actually rise with age. Technically, therefore, VOSL may vary with age in an indeterminate manner.

ISBN 92-64-01004-1
Cost-Benefit Analysis and the Environment
Recent Developments
© OECD 2006

Chapter 15

Equity and Cost-benefit Analysis

Conventional CBA for the most part continues to regard distributional or equity concerns as having little or no place in social decisions about project selection and design. Yet challenges to this perspective form a rich tradition within the CBA literature. Proposals, considered in this chapter, to make appraisals more sensitive to concerns about distributional justice or equity can be viewed as a hierarchy necessitating ever more explicit judgement, about the social desirability of possible distributional outcomes. These include: identifying and cataloguing how project-related costs and benefits are distributed; calculating implicit distributional weights: e.g. what weight would need to be assigned to the gains of a particular societal group for that project to be deemed socially valuable?; and lastly, re-calculating the project's net benefit based on assigning explicit distributional weights to the benefits received and costs incurred by different societal groups. A crucial question, addressed in this chapter, then is where cost-benefit practitioners should locate themselves upon this hierarchy?

15.1. Introduction

Cost-benefit analysis (CBA) is concerned (primarily) with efficiency in allocation of economic resources. The corresponding rules are: choose projects with benefits greater than costs or, alternatively, allocate available funds across those projects, which collectively secure the largest net benefits. Of course, in practice, efficiency is not sole criterion used to distinguish between the desirability or otherwise of proposals as a look at a number of real-life examples of public policies makes clear. One reason for this is that cost-benefit thinking does not take place in a moral vacuum. Project or policy selection and design can give rise to challenging issues with regards to the "rightness" of a given action or the social desirability of a particular distribution of benefits and costs. The focus of this chapter is on how distributional implications of projects and policies reasonably can be accommodated within cost-benefit appraisals. This, in turn, reflects an assertion, not necessarily shared by all, for appraisals to be more sensitive to concerns about distributional justice or equity within the current generation.

Distributional considerations can enter implicitly or explicitly into cost-benefit thinking by, for example, not counting the costs and benefits that arise beyond national boundaries or within certain groups. Indeed, the way in which a distributional issue might manifest itself is potentially diverse. For example, Boardman *et al.* (2001) suggest that conflicts can be between consumers, producers and taxpayers, project participants and non-participants, nationals and non-nationals as well as rich and poor. In the case of environmental policies, we might also add polluter and victim/beneficiary to this list. As an illustration of this latter point, Freeman (2003) argues that choice between willingness to accept and willingness to pay, in cost-benefit appraisals, is in many ways an ethical one: that is, based on a judgement about underlying property rights (see Chapter 11).

Various proposals exist about how to bring the distributional consequences of projects and policies within the ambit of cost-benefit appraisals. One recent suggestion, which we follow in this chapter, is to view these proposals as a hierarchy necessitating ever more explicit judgement, on the part of the cost-benefit analyst, about the social desirability of possible distributional outcomes. At the heart of any such judgement lies a standpoint or appeal to evidence about how society ought to distribute well-being, income, wealth or some more specific good such as environmental quality.

A related issue is what this implies about the trade-off between efficiency and equity; that is, how far should a conventional cost-benefit test be moderated in the light of equity and distributional considerations? In essence, placing equity or distributional within a cost-benefit framework implies that access to goods or avoidance of bads, facilitated by policy interventions, is not solely made on the basis of individual or household willingness to pay. Practical examples of these concerns permeate many areas of public policy. For example, in health policy, decision-makers might seek a balance between maximising the overall benefits of health-care interventions and directing interventions towards certain groups (*e.g.* low-income, vulnerable, low capabilities). Indeed, the consideration of the role of equity in framing health policies such as health-care delivery and finance decisions is relatively well-established (see, for comprehensive reviews, Williams and Cookson, 2000; Wagstaff and van Doorslaer, 2000). It is arguable that a consideration of equity in the context of the economic appraisal of environmental policies and projects with environmental impacts is less well established. There are a number of notable exceptions. In the debate concerning climate change, equity concerns, if anything, have dominated much of the broader discussion of this problem (although this has not been reflected in the actual behaviour of many governments around the world).

The remainder of this chapter is organised as follows. Section 15.2 outlines some a number of broad issues that arise in incorporating distributional or equity concerns within the cost-benefit framework. We then turn, in Section 15.3, to consider some (related) proposals to extend or sensitise cost-benefit appraisals to the distributional consequences of projects and policies. Section 15.4 considers broader principles of equity and assesses how these principles conflict with one another. Using the example of environmental policy, this section examines a proposal for balancing competing principles of equity such the polluter-pays-principle and ability to pay. Lastly, Section 15.5 offers conclusions and guidance for policy-makers.

15.2. Equity and efficiency

Projects and policies with environmental impacts inevitably have distributional consequences. Indeed, for a great many environmental policies this is the point of these interventions in that these work by favouring (relative to the *status quo*) victims of pollution at the expense of polluters. Typically, the economic justification for these interventions is couched in terms of their efficiency (in the sense of giving rise to higher overall social welfare). However, this application of the polluter pays principle (*e.g.* OECD, 1975) owes as much to the perceived desirable distributional consequences of assigning property rights to the victims of pollution.

By contrast, some policies or projects might deliver greater efficiency at the cost of distributional outcomes, which are not viewed as desirable. Road pricing or congestion charging – such as the London Congestion Charge (LCC) – provides a good example. Under the LCC from February 2003, those motorists wishing to enter the congestion charge zone around central London during designated peak hours on any weekday now pay a uniform charge. While this is not an optimal congestion charge in the sense of setting this charge equal to the marginal social cost of making a vehicle journey, its objectives are similarly to reduce congestion by making motorists take greater account of the social costs of their journeys. Interestingly, a cost-benefit appraisal of this scheme carried out on behalf of the Greater London Authority (GLA) – the body responsible for administering the LCC – indicated that its (*ex ante*) net benefits were likely to be positive. However, congestion charging, in general, has a number of distributional outcomes, which are of significance as well. One particular concern is that rationing road-use to the "highest bidders" – while according to the GLA's cost-benefit appraisal is a more efficient use of economic resources – means that those motorists who cannot afford the charge are "forced" to use public transport or simply not to make their journey at all. In the case of the former option, public transport systems might become overcrowded causing a disamenity to new and existing users.

Clearly, one response could be to invoke the Kaldor-Hicks criterion. As long as winners can potentially compensate the losers from a congestion charge then all is well. Perhaps it is thought that, in the round, net losers of such a project will be net winners for efficient projects implemented elsewhere. Therefore, it makes sense to select projects so as to maximise the size of society's economic pie. If there remained distributional concerns then policy-makers could separately worry about how this pie is divided using alternative redistributive policy instruments at their disposal. According to this view, concerns about efficiency legitimately can be separated from equity or distributional concerns. In practice, however, efficiency and equity might not be as straightforwardly separated as this standard approach implies. Moreover, distributional impacts of a project or a policy may have an important bearing on the public or political acceptability of that intervention. For example, in the case of the LCC, a variety of distributional concerns were anticipated in the way in which the congestion charge was designed. Certain groups are exempt or face a lower charge while the revenues collected are reinvested in London's bus services. Such provisions plausibly entail some sacrifice in efficiency as, for example, those with exemptions still treat road-use as being "free" at the point of access. However, presumably it is the case that London's decision-makers have reasoned (rightly or wrongly) that this sacrifice is worth it if allays at least some of the public's concerns about the distributional impacts of the LCC.

The question is how such distributional concerns can be considered routinely within a cost-benefit framework? One general way to of achieving this is by writing the net (social) benefits (NB) calculation as follows. Assume, for simplicity, that a project will affect only two individuals. Taking account of the distribution of gains and losses could be achieved by assigning a weight (a_i) to the net benefits received by each individual: *i.e.* $NB = a_1 NB_1 + a_2 NB_2$.

An important feature of conventional CBA is now apparent. It assumes that $a_1 = a_2 = 1$; that is, weights of unity are assigned to the net benefits of individuals regardless of who it is that receives a unit of benefit or suffers a unit of cost. This approach might be justified on a number of grounds. Perhaps, for example, it is the case that distribution of income or well-being is considered to be optimally distributed (in terms of its implications for social welfare). If we interpret these weights, a_i, as providing a numerical description about the preferences of society regarding distribution then the conventional approach amounts to a judgement that it is of no consequence how net benefits are distributed even if it is the case that individuals affected by the project had very different levels of socio-economic characteristics. By contrast, if distribution is not optimal – *e.g.* maybe there are political or administrative obstacles to introducing the requisite distributive measures – there is a rationale for varying the weights assigned to the net benefits of different individuals if these differences reasonably can be argued to reflect legitimate distributional and equity concerns. What this amounts to is a judgement that project selection or design might be another means of addressing society's distributional goals. Not surprisingly, much of the controversy about distributional weighting surrounds debates about the relative merits of using projects in this way as well as the problems entailed in surmising what society's distributional goals are.

Distributional concerns refer to the distribution of something; that is, some development outcome. Before turning to these issues of how these distributional concerns might be integrated within cost-benefit appraisals, it is worth considering what it is that is to be supposed to be the focus of this concern. That is, what is it that is to be distributed? Kriström (2005) notes at least two possibilities.

First, it might be that it is well-being that is to be distributed. This could, in turn, be interpreted as a concern about income distribution although the notion of income here needs to be broadly construed. For example, non-markets costs and benefits can be thought of as determining in part the income of individuals (see Chapter 16). However, in practice, much of distributional CBA has been concerned with a narrower (but more easily measurable) definition of income.

Second, evidence can be found to support the view that policy-makers and the public are also concerned about how particular goods and bads are distributed across different societal groups. The environmental justice movement in the United States has argued that unwanted or hazardous land-uses (such as waste disposal and transfer facilities) are unfairly or inequitably distributed: *i.e.* located predominately in areas, which are relatively highly populated by low-income groups or ethnic minorities. Notwithstanding the debate about the (policy or market) mechanisms that might lead to this outcome, the environmental justice perspective advocates allocating these environmental burdens in a rather different way. Similar themes can be found for other environmental bads such as air quality and goods such as the amenity provided by the distribution of green open spaces in urban areas.

15.3. Analysing the distributional impacts of projects within a cost-benefit framework

A simple illustration of how specific distributional concerns can be analysed within a cost-benefit framework is as follows. Again, assume there are just two individuals in society, this time denoted by R and P, affected by a project and that the net benefit to each individual (R and P) of this project is:

- Individual R: +GBP 200
- Individual P: –GBP 100

The total net benefit of the project is GBP 100; therefore, the project is worthwhile in the sense that it increases economic efficiency. However, what if individual P – the net loser – is poor relative to the net beneficiary of this project? In other words, the project worsens an already unequal distribution of income and wealth.

An array of proposals exists to analyse this type of distributional issue within the cost-benefit framework. Kriström (2005) has shown how these proposals can be thought of as a hierarchy of options. These include: 1) identifying and cataloguing how project-related costs and benefits are distributed; 2) calculating *implicit* distributional weights: *e.g.* if a project generates net aggregate losses but net gains are enjoyed by a group that society is particularly worried about, what weight would need to be assigned to these gains such that the project was deemed to have a positive social value?; and lastly, 3) re-calculating the project's net benefit based on assigning *explicit* distributional weights to the benefits received and costs incurred by different societal groups.

15.3.1. Identifying distributional impacts

CBA is frequently criticised as being pre-occupied with a project's or policy's "bottom-line" in the form of its net social benefits. Assuming, for the moment, that this criticism is justified, it is problematic for a number of reasons. For example, as noted earlier in this chapter, policy-makers often worry about precisely the details that such an aggregation abstracts from: namely, how net benefits are distributed. However, thinking beyond this cataloguing of distributional impacts to the uses of these data, this information might be valuable for a number of reasons. There may be pragmatic reasons for knowing which groups win and which groups lose from implementing the project. Perhaps it is the case the project's losers are in a position to affect the project's success or failure (in the sense of net benefits being realised).

This suggests that, at a minimum, one useful element of a CBA would be the provision of detailed information about distributional impacts. Put this way, there is no requirement that the cost-benefit analyst makes a judgement about the empirical evidence as regards how to weight the impacts enjoyed or suffered by different groups. It requires only that these be documented to the extent that the data and other resources permit. How these distributional consequences might translate into an assessment of the social value of the project can be left to the political process. Of course, it would naïve to assume that value judgements are wholly eliminated. For example, a decision must be made at some point, about which societal groups are to be described. However, as later sections will illustrate, there is less need for tricky judgements relative to other analytical options in the hierarchy.

There may be practical difficulties in identifying "winners" and "losers" and their incomes and/or some other aspect of their relative position in society in sufficient detail. Of course, without this basic building block, any more ambitious analysis of distributional concerns (described below) cannot be contemplated either. This problem is likely to be a matter of degree and it is just as likely that many cost-benefit appraisals do not generate these data simply because they are not compelled to do so rather than because of the unfeasibility of the task. It is interesting that much of modern benefit assessment in the form of stated preference methods such as the contingent valuation method (Chapter 8) already may contain a wealth of data about the distribution of non-market impacts. That is, these studies typically elicit information about respondent's demographic and socio-economic characteristics as well as detailed data about, for example, uses and experiences of an environmental good under consideration. Such data could provide valuable insights into how certain project impacts are distributed.

15.3.2. Implicit distributional weights

Should cost-benefit appraisals limit the analysis of distributional issues to carefully identifying and cataloguing how costs and benefits are distributed? Broadly speaking there are two further options. Both are premised on thinking about how distributional information might be used by policy-makers but in a way that is comparable with the standard net benefit rule. This entails revising the CBA decision rule on the basis of adjusted or distributionally weighted net benefits as indicated in Section 15.2. The distributional net benefit criterion is that a project should go ahead if:

$$\sum_i a_i NB_i \geq 0$$

where a_i varies across individuals, households or – more realistically – societal groups (i.e. depending on the level of aggregation that available data will allow). That is, go ahead with a project, if the sum of distributional weighted net benefits is at least as great as zero.

While, as we shall see, there is considerable debate about choosing the "correct" weights, a convenient way around this controversy is to ask instead what set of weights would be required to "tip the balance" between recommending that the project go-ahead (*i.e.* positive total NB) or not go-ahead (*i.e.* negative total NB) (Gramlich, 1990; Kanninen and Kriström, 1993)?

i.e. $0 = NB = NB_R + a_P NB_P \Rightarrow a_P{}^* = \dfrac{NB_R}{NB_P}$

Hence, this is an implicit distributional test, as it does not require that weights (a_i) be imputed directly. Rather it asks, for $a_R = 1$ and setting $NB = 0$, how large would the implicit weight $a_P{}^*$ need to be to affect the decision about the social worth of the project?

For the simple example above, the answer is 2: *i.e.* $a_P{}^* = \dfrac{NB_R}{NB_P} = \dfrac{200}{100}$.

Once we know this "tipping point", what can be done with this information? Perhaps most importantly, it could be asked whether assigning this weight (or these weights) is justified perhaps in the sense of whether or not it is commensurate with society's preferences or what is known about political acceptability. The answer could depend, in our simple example, on the relative income difference between the two individuals as well as the distance that each is from recognised thresholds such as poverty levels or average income. The catch is that this question arguably cannot be answered properly unless we have recourse to reliable and direct estimates of a_P. Yet, the point of this implicit weighting approach is to allow the cost-benefit analyst to avoid these potentially deep waters. Nevertheless, implicit weights at least can be compared with the range of estimates in the literature, which we discuss in Section 15.3.3 below.

Gramlich (1990) notes a further use of the data previously discussed. Project selection or design is only one of many redistributive mechanisms available to governments. Moreover, critics of distributional CBA such as Harberger have argued that it must be asked whether these alternative measures are generally a less socially wasteful means of addressing distributional concerns. For example, this would certainly be true if say some fiscal mechanism could say costlessly redistribute income. In such instances, it would always be desirable to shelve inefficient but equitable projects and address distributional disparities using this other redistribution mechanism. Needless to say, any redistributive scheme is inefficient to a greater or lesser extent.[1] However, this emphasis on "extent" is important. One issue then is to compare, as a means of addressing distributional concerns, project selection or design with (practical) alternatives such as direct ways of transferring incomes across individuals (perhaps via the tax system) or other public programmes, which explicitly focus on say raising low incomes.

Assuming that there is information about how inefficient various practical and alternative redistributive mechanisms are, then this sets an upper bound on how much inefficiency is permissible in choosing and designing projects on the basis on distributional criteria. Formally, this entails a comparison of the terms $a_P{}^*$ and $1/(1-c)$. The coefficient, c, is an indicator of how inefficient alternative redistributive mechanisms are (*i.e.* what proportion of total resources is lost in the "act" of redistribution) and its value will lie between 0 and 1. In the example above, the project should go ahead as long as it is the case that $c \leq 0.5$. In this way, distributional concerns are allowed to influence project choice subject to this being the most cost-effective means of addressing some distributional goal.

15.3.3. *Explicit distributional weights*

The last broad analytical option departs from simply asking what values distributional weights would *need to take*. A rather more prescriptive approach would be to impute explicit weights perhaps based on the findings of past studies. For example, one approach is based on a judgement about the importance of income to those who gain or lose from the project. The assumption of diminishing marginal utility of income implies that the utility value of a unit change in a poor individual's income is greater than the utility value of the same unit change in income of a rich person. Other things being equal, this implies that a dollar or euro of benefit received by the latter receives less weight than the same change for the former, reflecting this difference in its relative contribution to social welfare. One possible weight, following this rationale, is:

$$a_i = (\overline{Y} / Y_i)^e$$

where: $\overline{Y}$ is average or mean income per capita; Y_i is income of the ith individual (or group); and e is the elasticity of the marginal utility of income or society's valuation of an increment to that individual's income. (The derivation of this weight is illustrated in the annex to this chapter.) Clearly, whereas data on the two former parameters are (in principle) easily measurable it is information about e, which is crucial. Intuitively, this elasticity is said to reflect society's degree of inequality aversion. A logical starting point then for determining its likely magnitude is to ask the question as to how much inequality "society" is willing to tolerate?

In principle, e could range from: $0 \le e < \infty$ although, fortunately for analysts, the literature as discussed below suggests that the plausible range is considerably narrower than this. Note that conventional or "unweighted" CBA is equivalent to assuming $e = 0$ (as this would result in $a_i = 1$). At the other extreme, as the degree of inequality aversion becomes ever larger ($e \to \infty$), the cost-benefit test amounts to always "ruling-out" any project that adversely affects the very worse off. (Conversely, it will always "rule-in" a project that positively affects the very worse off.) And while the simplest assumption, in terms of ease of computation, is to set $e = 1$ (and thus compare each individual's income relative to the mean) ultimately it must be asked whether or not this seems to imply stronger societal preferences towards income equality than observed evidence suggests.

To reiterate, distributional weights reflect a judgement about the value to be placed on each dollar or euro received by or taken away from each individual or group. A variety of data might be sought in order to justify this judgement. Typically, it is argued that this judgement should be made on the basis of the revealed behaviour of (democratic and accountable) governments with regard to say redistributive policies. That is, by examining public policies where distributional issues are a predominant concern, something can be learned about the relative weights to be placed on the costs and benefits of different societal groups. A usual reference point is the income tax system where it is argued that the different marginal tax rates that people, with different incomes, face tells the analyst something useful about society's preferences towards the social value of that income. A prominent variant of this notion is based on equal *absolute* sacrifice and argues that tax system operates by imposing an equal burden in terms of utility losses on all income classes relative to some utility function (Young, 1994; although see, for example, Gramlich, 1990, for a discussion of the problems of using information about marginal tax rates in this way).

Table 15.1. **Distributional weights and CBA – illustrative example**

Degree of inequality aversion: e	Net benefits: Individual R	Net benefits: Individual P	Total net benefits
0	200	−100	100
0.5	163	−141	22
1	109	−283	−174
2	48	−1 131	−1 083

The implication of a range of values for e, for the simple illustrative data used earlier in this chapter, is indicated in Table 15.1. To this example, we add the assumption that the ratio of the income of our wealthier individual R to our poorer individual P is equal to 3: i.e. $Y_R = 3Y_P$. Note that, in general, the effect of assuming values of e, which are greater than 0, is to shrink the positive net benefits of individual R and to boost the negative net benefits of individual P. The magnitude of e determines how large this relative adjustment is going to be. Thus, for $e = 0.5$ the project still has a small but positive NB. However, for $e = 1$, the sum of distributional weighted NB is negative. It is also apparent from the table that larger values of e very quickly result in relatively extreme weights to be placed on the losses suffered by the individual with income below the mean.

Table 15.2. **Relative social value of gains and losses**

	Value of e			
	0	0.5	1.0	2.0
Loss to R as a fraction of gains to P	1.00	0.60	0.30	0.10

Source: Adapted from Pearce (2003b).

This is illustrated further in Table 15.2. This indicates the implied social value attached to a dollar received by P relative to a dollar taken away from R (or *vice versa*). For example, for $e = 1$, R's loss would be valued at only 30% of P's gain. For $e = 2$, R's loss is valued at only 10% of P's gains and so on. In other words, if we were to set $a_R = 1$, then for $e = 2$, this would imply that a_P should be 10 times this amount: i.e. $a_P = 10$.

Some empirical debate has centred specifically on the magnitude of e. Comprehensive reviews of this literature can be found in Pearce and Ulph (1999) and Cowell and Gardiner (1999). While the latter survey concludes that "a reasonable range seems to be 0.5 ... to 4" (p. 33), Pearce and Ulph (1999) argue for a much narrower range in the region of 0.8. On this basis, Pearce (2003b) argues that values of e in the range of 0.5 to 1.2 are defensible in the cost-benefit appraisal of climate change policy. Identifying such a range is of more than theoretical interest. It provides a useful benchmark with which, for example, to scrutinise environmental policy proposals that use distributional concerns as their rationale (see Box 15.1).

15.4. **Competing principles of equity**

Much of the discussion about weighting net benefits in CBA has been limited to the consideration of disparities in income and wealth. Nevertheless, as noted at the very beginning of this chapter, equity and distributional concerns are multi-dimensional concepts. Thus, it is entirely possible, and indeed likely, that policy-makers do not always choose one ethical perspective over another but rather it may be that different approaches

Box 15.1. **Distributional CBA and climate change**

A re-emergence of interest in distributional CBA has arisen in the literature on the economics of climate change damage. While the origins of this particular debate can be traced to the wrong-headed notion that economics has little useful to say about climate change policy, this has on a more positive note led to an interesting and new line of inquiry with regard to CBA and equity. Specifically, this has embodied concern about the treatment, in economic analysis, of the way in which the burdens of climate change damage are likely to be distributed between countries, which can be characterised as either rich or poor and vulnerable. As a result, an increasing number of influential studies of climate change damage have reflected this concern by adopting some form of equity or distribution weighting.

Pearce (2003b) outlines an example of the consequences of distributional weighting for the calculation of climate change damage. This is based on data drawn from the much-cited study of Fankhauser (1995). Initial (i.e. unweighted) estimates of damage levels – arising from a doubling of pre-industrial concentrations of carbon dioxide ($2 \times CO_2$) – and their distribution between rich and poor countries are adjusted using distributional weights. Total global damage (arising from $2 \times CO_2$) (D_{WORLD}) is the sum of the dollar value of damage that occurs within poorer countries (D_P) and the dollar value of damage that occurs within richer countries (D_R). These values are adjusted using equity weights, respectively: a_P and a_R. That is,

$D_{WORLD} = a_P D_P + a_R D_R$.

The weights a_P and a_R are calculated as $a_i = (\overline{Y} / Y_i)^e$, where $\overline{Y}$ is (the global) average per capita income; Y_i is a (rich or poor) country's average per capita income (itself adjusted for differences in purchasing power across countries); and e is the elasticity of the marginal utility of income. The expression above then becomes:

$$D_{WORLD} = \left[\left(\frac{\overline{Y}}{Y_P} \right)^e \times D_P \right] + \left[\left(\frac{\overline{Y}}{Y_R} \right)^e \times D_R \right]$$

The basic data, for re-estimating climate change damages in the light of distributional considerations, are as follows: D_P = USD 106 billion; D_R = USD 216 billion; Y_P = USD 1 110; Y_R = USD 10 000; and, $\overline{Y}$ = 3 333. Distributional weighted climate change damage can thus be estimated as:

$$D_{WORLD} = \left[\$106bn \times \left(\frac{\$3,333}{\$1,110} \right)^e \right] + \left[\$216bn \times \left(\frac{\$3,333}{\$10,000} \right)^e \right]$$

Table 15.3 indicates the effect, depending on the assumed value of e, of adjusting estimates of climate change damages to take account of per capita income disparities between rich and poor countries. Column 2 ($e = 0$) reproduces the damage estimates cited earlier. For $e = 0.5$ (column 3), this weighting provides a boost to poor countries' damage estimate and shrinks that of rich countries. Indeed, the dollar value of adjusted D_P is greater than adjusted D_R. Overall, however, global damage is less; relative to the case of unweighted damages ($e = 0$). For $e = 1$ (column 4), the boost to D_P is much more significant; that is, it increases far more rapidly than D_R shrinks. However, global damage is less than 30% higher than in the case of unweighted damages (row 5, columns 2 and 4). Finally, for $e = 2$ (column 5), the impact of weighting damages is dramatic and any assessment of the relative burden of climate change is, as a consequence, substantially altered.

Box 15.1. **Distributional CBA and climate change** (*cont.*)

Table 15.3. **Estiamtes of distributional weighted climate change damages**

USD billions

	Value of e			
	E = 0	E = 0.5	E = 1.0	E = 2.0
Poor countries	106	184	318	954
Rich countries	216	125	72	24
Total	322	309	390	978

Source: Adapted from Pearce (2003b).

These findings suggest at least three considerations:

First, it is important to ask: what is a justifiable range of values for the parameter *e*? The answer to this question is not necessarily straightforward as it plausibly entails assessing what is global society's aversion to inequality. However, unless it is the case that climate change damage presents distinct justice principles, it can be argued that a worsening of income distribution as a result of climate change can be analysed in much the same way as for any project. Pearce (2003b) suggests that a cautious but defensible reading of the literature is that *e* lies in the range of 0.5 and 1.2. In the context of Table 15.3, this means that the findings of columns 3 and 4 are those which should interest policy-makers.

Second, thinking in terms of the appropriate range of values for distributional weights is, in general, a useful way of scrutinising the stringency (or otherwise) of a country's proposals to limit its emissions of greenhouse gases. For example, Pearce (2003b) argues forcibly that the UK Government has used an unjustifiably high weight to the welfare burden of climate change damage in poor countries in its cost-benefit appraisals. That is, this weight is unreasonably high given the UK's revealed behaviour in *e.g.* foreign aid allocation. In essence, in order for the UK position (which is currently under review) to be analytically defensible, it must be argued that the situation of a poorer country losing a dollar of income because of climate change is somehow significantly worse than that same country losing a dollar of income in some different way. While it is not entirely implausible that this is the case, it is not sufficient simply to (implicitly or explicitly) assert it without basis.

Third, whether or not the findings of Table 15.3 (columns 3 and 4) would markedly alter the results of a global cost-benefit assessment of climate change policies is debatable. Global damage is not that much different from the unweighted case in either example. Of course, assessing the net worth of any programme that sought to limit say CO_2 emissions depends also on a number of other factors including, notably, cost estimates and these must be similarly weighted. Thus, it should also be noted that if distributional weighting is used then not only should benefits of a given climate change policy (*i.e.* foregone climate change damages) be adjusted but also the costs of mitigating greenhouse gases under this policy.

are balanced against one another depending on the policy context. For example, in the case of environmental policy, a dominant theme is that it is the polluter that should pay for environmental improvements. Thus, while it might be just as efficient to require that the victims of pollution (*i.e.* the beneficiaries) should foot the bill for environmental improvements, it is the notion that it is polluters – having created the problem – who should get their "just desserts" that strikes many as being intuitively the fairer approach.

Box 15.2. **Balancing competing principles of environmental equity**

A study by Atkinson *et al.* (2000) suggests that stated preference methods can be used to evaluate trade-offs between efficiency and equity and can also provide insights into the values attached to different concepts of equity. The scenario presented to respondents is an urban air quality programme, which is assumed to have benefits in excess of costs. The issue is how to distribute the costs of the programme across the city's residents. Residents are assumed that vary in their characteristics with a three-fold classification: whether they cause the pollution, the extent to which they benefit from the programme and their ability to pay.

A contingent ranking study (see Chapter 9) was conducted in Lisbon. In one experiment, respondents were first asked to rank different groups of individuals according to the respondent's view of who should pay first for the programme. The combinations are shown below in Figure 15.1, where blanks are interpreted as meaning does not benefit and is not responsible. Respondents were asked to say of which of these groups should pay first (ranked 1), which next (ranked 2) and so on.

A second experiment focused on ranking groups of individuals according to two out of the three equity principles. For example, in one version of this question, it was assumed that income was same across the six groups, so that respondents were asked to rank groups by benefits and responsibility alone. This time each attribute had three levels (low, medium and high) where the aim here was to account for "non-linearities" in the property rights issue (*e.g.* who should pay: the polluter or the victim?). Another version of this question assumed benefits were equal and groups were ranked according to income and responsibility alone. This permits an analysis of property rights and concern for the distribution of income. Roughly 250 people were sampled in each of the two experiments. The results suggested the following conclusions based on the econometric analysis of the rankings.

Figure 15.1. **Sample ranking card for Experiment 1**

| | Group | | | | | |
	A	B	C	D	E	F
Health state	Benefits	Benefits			Benefits	
Income level	Low	High	Low	High	Low	High
Responsibility	Polutes		Polutes			Polutes
RANK						

Experiment 1: Responsibility for pollution was regarded as the single most important attribute; that is, respondents appeared to embrace the polluter-pays-principle in their answers. However, this was only part of the story. The findings also suggested that there was a trade-off between responsibility and a combination of income and benefits. Those with high income and high benefits should pay more than somebody who has low income and low benefits. These findings are largely unaltered when the results are adjusted for selfish behaviour; that is, high-income respondents biasing their answers away from assigning responsibility (in effect) to themselves.

If individuals refuse to trade-off between the various attributes, their responses are said to be "lexical"; that is, they decide on the basis of one attribute alone regardless of the values taken by the other attributes. Lexicality is potentially important because it would strike at the heart of the cost-benefit assumption that people are willing to make trade-offs. Initial analysis suggested that some 20% of respondents appeared to rank lexically on the basis of responsibility alone being the determinant of who should pay. However, such rankings can be consistent with making trade-offs; that is, they may just imply underlying preferences that place a very high value on the attribute in question.

> **Box 15.2. Balancing competing principles of environmental equity** (*cont.*)
>
> *Experiment 2*: while the two approaches are not strictly comparable, the findings of experiment 2 appeared to largely bear out those of experiment 1. In other words responsibility matters most but people, in general, do trade-off attributes. The research suggests some important lines of inquiry. The net benefits of the hypothetical programme were taken to be positive and the focus was on who should pay for the costs. The findings of both experiments suggest that they could be extended to see if equity and efficiency (net benefits) themselves have trade-offs from the point of view of individual respondents.

Nevertheless, most environmental policies do not apply this principle uncompromisingly. For example, certain groups of polluters such as low-income or vulnerable households or small businesses might also receive concessions or exemptions from the burden of paying for environmental improvements. In the case of road pricing, the London Congestion Charge discussed previously provided one real-life example of this.

More generally, benefits or burdens are often allocated in everyday life according to pragmatic and acceptable rule of thumb or formula that reflects a balance between competing and diverse principles. This is the essence of Elster's (1992) concept of local justice. Similarly, Young (1994) reasons that practical responses to distributional or equity concerns emerge as rules of thumb in response to specific policy questions. Each of these responses implies a set of weights attached to the benefits received and costs incurred by certain groups. The point is that typically, however, these weights will not be assigned according to any observable formula or with reference to some general theories of distributive justice. However, it may be possible to observe how institutions distribute goods and bads in practice. An alternative means of deriving weights, which reflect the importance attached to say different notions of equity in the context of a particular environmental policy problem, is to use survey instruments administered to samples drawn randomly from the public. For example, stated preference methods, such as choice modelling, designed to elicit preferences for environmental goods provide a promising vehicle for evaluating these issues (see Chapter 9 as well as Box 15.2).[2]

15.5. Summary and guidance for decision-makers

Conventional CBA for the most part continues to regard distributional or equity concerns as having little or no place in social decisions about project selection and design. While this approach strikes some critics as an oddity, it would be a mistake to conclude that this downgrades the usefulness of CBA. Even if efficiency is only one piece of the puzzle in understanding the social worth of a project, it remains extremely important. Moreover, there are cogent reasons why cost-benefit analysts typically take this singular approach to the appraisal of the costs and benefits of projects and policies. That is, it is not merely unmindful neglect. For example, in the round, project gains and losses could even out across groups. Furthermore, policy-makers have an array of possibly superior re-distributive mechanisms at their disposal if they wish to take a more proactive stance with regard to reaching society's distributional objectives. Far better then, for economic resources not to be "wasted" but rather put to their best use in the strict sense of Kaldor-Hicks. However, as we have noted in this chapter, each of the reasons supporting this assertion in favour of conventional CBA is contestable. This suggests greater scope for scrutinising the distributional consequences of projects within the cost-benefit framework.

There are, of course, important issues about what it is that should be distributed. Intuitively, it could be some measure of well-being or income broadly construed; that is, reflecting as much as possible of the provision of market and non-market goods and bads that affects people's quality of life. However, other perspectives arrive at a narrower interpretation of what is to be distributed on the basis of practical issues (about what portion of well-being and income is readily observable) and concerns about particular aspects of distributional justice (in the case of distributing environmental risks).

Whatever the particular interpretation that is adopted, incorporating distributional concern implies initially identifying and then possibly weighting the costs and benefits of individuals and groups on the basis of differences in the characteristic of interest. Kristöm's hierarchy is a useful way to understand the demands that various proposals place on the cost-benefit analyst. First, there is the relatively straightforward but possibly arduous task of assembling and organising raw (i.e. unadjusted) data on the distribution of project costs and benefits. Second, these data could then be used to ask what weight or distributional adjustment would need to placed on the net benefits (net costs) of a societal group of interest for a given project proposal to pass (fail) a distributional cost-benefit test. Third, explicit weights reflecting judgement about society's preferences towards distributional concerns can be assigned and net benefits re-estimated on this basis.

A crucial question then is where should cost-benefit analysts locate themselves upon this hierarchy? Given that cost-benefit appraisals are sometimes criticised for ignoring distributional consequences altogether then the apparently simplest option of cataloguing how costs and benefits are distributed could offer valuable and additional insights. This suggests that, at a minimum, cost-benefit appraisals arguably should routinely provide these data. Whether more ambitious proposals should be adopted is a matter of deliberating about whether 1) the gains in terms of being able to scrutinise the (weighted) net benefits of projects in the light of societal concerns about both efficiency and equity outweighs; 2) the losses arising from the need for informed guesswork in interpreting the empirical evidence with regards to the treatment of the latter.

On the one hand, empirical evidence about the "correct" magnitudes of distributional weights can be usefully employed in distributional CBA as the application to the case of climate change discussed in this chapter illustrates. On the other hand, even apparently small changes in assumptions about the size of distributional weights – indicated by the range of values in available empirical studies – can have significant implications for recommendations about a project's social worth. This finding should not be a surprise for it primarily reflects the complexity involved in trying to disentangle society's distributional preferences. As a practical matter, the danger is whether the most ambitious proposals for distributional CBA generate more heat than light. While it would worthwhile for research to seek further understanding of these preferences – perhaps making greater use of stated preference methods as discussed elsewhere in this chapter – in the interim, estimating implicit weights might be the most useful step beyond the necessary task of cataloguing the distribution of project cost and benefits.

Notes

1. Explanations of why this is the case typically have used Arthur Okun's analogy of the leaky bucket used to equalise the water volumes in two receptacles. Assuming that the distribution of water between the two receptacles is unequal in the first instance, the transfer, via a leaky bucket, inevitably leads to an overall loss of water in pursuit of the goal of a more equal distribution. This is the essence of society's problem: how much efficiency should be traded-off for more equity? For example, in the case of taxation of incomes the leaky bucket represents incentives affecting the work-leisure choice. That is, ever higher marginal tax rates discourage high income earners from working more and thereby decreases, in some degree, the total amount of income that society has available to redistribute.

2. Examples of experimental and survey based approaches to examining health-related equity questions are reviewed in Williams and Cookson (2000).

ANNEX 15.A1

Deriving a Marginal Utility of Income Weighting Procedure

Let utility be related to income, *i.e.* $U = U(Y)$, such that the marginal utility of income function has a constant elasticity. The marginal utility of income function for individual i can then be written:

$$U_i^{'} = \frac{dU}{dY_i} = aY_i^{-e}$$

where $-e$ is now the elasticity of the function. For the average income $\overline{Y}$ we shall therefore have

$$U_{\overline{Y}}^{'} = a\overline{Y}^{-e}$$

and the relative weight for the ith individual would then be

$$\frac{U_{\overline{Y}}^{'}}{U_i^{'}} = \frac{a\overline{Y}^{-e}}{aY^{-e}} = \left(\frac{\overline{Y}}{Y_i}\right)^{-e}$$

ISBN 92-64-01004-1
Cost-Benefit Analysis and the Environment
Recent Developments
© OECD 2006

Chapter 16

Sustainability and Cost-benefit Analysis

The notions of sustainability and "sustainable development" have permeated significant parts of policy and public discourse about the environment. This chapter discusses the handful of recommendations do exist with regards to how CBA can be extended to take account of these concerns. One perspective starts from the assertion that certain natural assets are so important or critical (for future, and perhaps current, generations) so as to warrant protection at some target level. In terms of the conduct of CBA, this has resulted in the idea of a shadow or compensating project, meaning that projects that cause environmental damage are "covered off" by projects that result in environmental improvements. The overall consequence is that projects in the portfolio maintain the environmental status quo. More broadly, the sustainability debate has focussed attention on assets and asset management. This might emphasise the need for an "asset check". That is, what the stocks of assets are before the project intervention and what they are likely to be after the intervention?

16.1. Introduction

The call for countries to pursue policies aimed at achieving "sustainable development" or "sustainability" was established in the Brundtland Report in 1987, the Earth Summit in 1992 and, more recently, at the World Summit in 2002. Sustainable development has been now adopted as an over-arching goal of economic and social development by United Nations agencies and by many individual nations, local governments and even corporations and further has generated a huge literature. It is clear that formidable challenges confront policy-makers who have publicly stated their commitment to the goal of sustainable development; not least in determining what exactly it is that they have signed up to. Most fundamentally, however, most discussions about sustainability typically have centred upon establishing a wider understanding of our obligations to future generations and identifying the actions implied by observing these obligations. The subject of this chapter is how such concerns about *intergenerational* equity can be integrated into the appraisal of public projects.

Not surprisingly much of the early literature reflected debates about whether to "discount" or "not discount". That is, what is the appropriate way in which we should weigh costs and benefits that occur in the future relative to the present? A familiar argument was that social discount rates typically used by, for example, finance ministries and development agencies were "too high". Many worried that this created, in effect, an in-built bias against projects which entail substantial up-front costs but benefits coming on-stream only in the distant future, with climate change mitigation options perhaps being the pre-eminent example. While these debates are far from wholly resolved, there is arguably a consensus that at least some of the proposed cures for this dilemma – such as using a zero social discount rate – may actually make matters worse in other directions. Moreover, recent developments in the literature on social (and private) discounting – reviewed in Chapter 13 – have provided a more level playing field for appraising projects with impacts in the far-off future.

The objective of this chapter then is to review a variety of more recent proposals for how cost-benefit analysis (CBA) might be interpreted in the light of concerns about sustainability. It is worth noting at the outset that some have been altogether more critical of the applying the concept of sustainability to CBA. Little and Mirrlees (1994), whose pioneering theoretical work has been a guiding light in the modern application of cost-benefit thinking to the appraisal of projects, is one example. Their criticisms are two-fold. First, they argue that sustainability is "more of a buzzword … than a genuine concept" (p. 213). Second, they view sustainability as flimsy grounds for accepting or rejecting projects in that it would rule out, almost by definition, some productive activities such as mining.

With regards to the former charge, while there remains some debate about what precisely "sustainability" means (or what it means for development to be sustainable), in the past decade or so there has been remarkable and genuine progress in understanding the concept of sustainability both in theory and in practical terms (see, for recent and comprehensive reviews, Pezzey and Toman, 2002; Hamilton and Atkinson, 2006). Of course, a number of debates still exist. Nevertheless, most would argue that sustainability is a meaningful concept.

That claim, however, says nothing in particular about how this concept affects project appraisal and cost-benefit thinking more generally. Hence, the second charge brought by Little and Mirrlees, needs careful consideration. On the one hand, critics might argue that the best way in which policy-makers can contribute to sustainability is by selecting the best projects, where "best" is defined relative to a standard cost-benefit test. Furthermore, if we define sustainability concerns as synonymous with greater environmental protection (it is more complicated than this, as we shall see below) then, relative to the case where non-market or intangible environmental impacts are ignored, proper shadow pricing will reduce the number of environmentally damaging projects within a portfolio (relative to the case where non-market environmental impacts are ignored by analysts). Put another way, simply conducting a proper state-of-the-art CBA of projects could have a favourable impact on prospects for sustainable development.

On the other hand, these comments by no means capture the entirety of the sustainability debate, which crucially is concerned about the distribution of well-being (or net benefits) over time. Establishing methods that permit the routine shadow pricing of environmental impacts is just one piece of the puzzle in understanding intergenerational consequences of project selection. Other prominent aspects of the sustainability debate focus on whether projects, in the aggregate, are creating enough wealth for future generations as well as arguing for a more specific focus on whether enough *natural* wealth is being conserved. One concern is that too many "projects" involve the current generation enjoying benefits now (or in the near future) at the expense of those living in future generations. What this amounts to is a suggestion that project selection criteria should be more sensitive to the impacts of actions taken now on future generations. However, sustainability as we discuss in more detail in what follows is a concept that is relevant to the project *portfolio* rather each individual project. Taking this perspective avoids counter-intuitive claims (about project desirability) arising from an overly literal translation of the sustainability concept to each individual project.

16.2. Sustainability: background

It is approaching two decades since the early shaping of the sustainability problem in the Brundtland Report. In that time, substantial progress has been made in clarifying the many controversial issues that have emerged. The concept of sustainable development itself has been defined in a number of ways. The Brundtland Report defined it as "development that meets the needs of the present generation without compromising the ability of future generations to meet their own needs" (WCED, 1987, p. 43). Economists have tended to reinterpret this as a requirement to follow a development path where human welfare or well-being (per capita) does not decline over time (see, for example, Pezzey, 1989). Achieving sustainability, in turn, has been equated with propositions regarding how an economy should manage its wealth over time. Guiding principles in this respect include that of *weak sustainability* which emphasises changes to the real value of wealth in the aggregate and *strong sustainability* which (typically) also emphasises the conservation of *critical* natural capital, *i.e.* critically important resources for which there are essentially no substitutes. While this terminology arguably has been rather unhelpful in deflecting attention from complementarities between the two perspectives, as it been dominant in much of the sustainability discourse over the past 10 to 15 years, we continue to use it here. Hence, in what follows, we consider each of these conditions for sustainability and their implications for CBA in turn.

16.3. Weak sustainability and CBA

For *weak sustainability* (WS) any one form of asset or capital can be run down provided "proceeds" are reinvested in other forms of asset or capital. Put another way, it is the "overall" portfolio of wealth that is bequeathed to the future that matters (*e.g.* Solow, 1986). This, in turn, is based on a rule of thumb known as the Hartwick rule (or sometimes the Hartwick-Solow rule) (Hartwick, 1977; Solow, 1974). Following this rule requires that the change in the (real) value of total wealth should not be negative in the aggregate. A good illustration of the theory of WS is provided by the literature on green national accounts. This work arises from a concern that economic indicators, such as Gross National Product (GNP), do not reflect the depletion and degradation of the environment and so may lead to incorrect development decisions, in much the same way that cost-benefit analyses that do not include the values people place on the environment may yield poor investment decisions.

Before proceeding to consider the implications of WS for cost-benefit analysis, some basic results from this theoretical work are briefly discussed below. This literature builds on important contributions by Weitzman (1976), Hartwick (1990) and Mäler (1991). The focus in most contributions is on accounting for the value of changes in total wealth in national income. National income is typically defined along the (optimal) path of a simple economy with stocks of goods (including natural assets used in production) and bads (including environmental liabilities, *i.e.* degradation of environmental stocks such as clean air, that negatively affect utility or well-being). A general expression for a (net) national income aggregate or green Net National Product (*gNNP*) is:

$$gNNP = C + \sum p_i \dot{X}_i = C + S_G \qquad [16.1]$$

Equation [16.1] states that *gNNP* is equivalent to consumption (C) plus the sum of net changes in assets ($\dot{X}_i$) each valued at its shadow price (p_i). Alternatively, this can be written as consumption plus adjusted net or genuine saving (S_G): that is, $\sum_i p_i \dot{X}_i = S_G$ where the changes in assets might refer to *net* investments in produced, human and natural capital.

An interpretation of *gNNP* is that it measures extended Hicksian income: that is, the maximum amount of produced output that could be consumed at a point in time while leaving wealth (instantaneously) constant (Pemberton and Ulph, 2001). Given an interpretation of (weak) sustainability that the change in the (real) value of total wealth should not be negative in the aggregate, this definition of income suggests that our focus should be on the genuine saving or S_G component of the expression for *gNNP* above. The reason for this is that S_G tells us about the (net) change in total wealth: *i.e.* it can be shown that,

$$\dot{W} = 0 \text{ if } S_G = 0 \qquad [16.2]$$

That is, the change in total wealth ($\dot{W}$) is zero if genuine saving is zero (Dasgupta and Mäler, 2000). More specifically, the key finding in this literature is that a point measure of $S_{G_t} < 0$ means that a development path is unsustainable (Hamilton and Clemens, 1999).

Negative genuine saving implies that the level of well-being over some interval of time in the future must be less than current well-being – development is not sustained.[1]

Interestingly, the proposition that negative genuine saving is unsustainable holds for (characterisations of) non-optimal development paths (Dasgupta and Mäler, 2000) and other extensions such as exogenous technological change (Weitzman and Löfgren, 1997). In addition, Hamilton and Hartwick (2005) and Hamilton and Withagen (2004) show that if S_G is persistently greater than zero – arguably a sensible policy target in a risky world – then not only is wealth (the present value of well-being) increasing but development can, in certain circumstances, also be said to be sustained.[2] The key conclusion, then, is that (persistent) *negative* genuine savings is a sure sign of unsustainability, i.e. of declining aggregate wealth. This is consistent with more popular notions of "not eating into one's capital" or "not selling the family silver". Persistent *positive* genuine savings is fairly indicative of sustainability, although the conclusion in this respect is less certain than for negative genuine savings.

An interesting recent development in the literature is proposed by Hamilton (2002) in response to the question as to how (weak) sustainability should be measured when population is growing. That is, S_G measures only the change in total wealth whereas, in much of the developing world, the reality is that population is growing at relatively rapid rates. In such circumstances, the net change in total wealth per capita is a better measure of sustainability (than the genuine savings rate). This can be written as follows:

$$\frac{d}{dt}\left(\frac{W}{N}\right) = \frac{\dot{W}}{N} - \frac{gW}{N} \qquad [16.3]$$

where W is total wealth, N is total population and *g* is the population growth rate. Hence, the net change in total wealth per capita, $d/dt(W/N)$, is equal to change in total wealth (i.e. $\dot{W}$ or S_G) divided by total population (N) minus the product of total wealth per capita (W/N) and the population growth rate (*g*). Hamilton (2002) refers to this latter component of the (right-hand side of the) above expression as a "wealth-diluting" term, which represents the sharing of total wealth with the extra people implied by a country's growth in population. Clearly, for a population growth rate that is strongly positive then $d/dt(W/N)$ could provide a very different signal to policy-makers about sustainability prospects than the "traditional" genuine savings rate. Indeed, Box 16.1 below provides an illustration of this for six countries.

How does CBA relate to this particular explanation of the sustainable development? At least five issues seem relevant here:

First, public projects (almost) invariably have characteristics of investments; that is, expenditures incurred early on in the project's lifetime to finance provision of a stream of benefits in the future. For example, projects might increase the supply of physical infrastructure or augment the stock of human capital via additional spending on say education and primary health-care. Thus, to the extent that a project entails the (net) accumulation of produced assets or human assets then, other things being equal, it contributes to sustainability. In other words, discussions about sustainable development should not ignore these desirable wealth-increasing properties of many projects. Of course, to the extent that projects give rise to environmental liabilities or deplete resource stocks then this loss of natural assets decreases, other things being equal, sustainability. However, as previously discussed, the net effect is signalled by aggregate indicators such as genuine saving or the net change in per capita net wealth.

Box 16.1. **Changes in wealth per capita**

The main source of year-on-year cross-country information about genuine savings is *e.g.* World Bank (2003). The World Bank typically defines genuine savings, for a nation, as gross saving *plus* education expenditures *minus* consumption of fixed (produced) capital *minus* depletion of mineral, energy and forest (timber) resources *minus* carbon dioxide damage. While the net or genuine saving rate provides useful information about how much total wealth is, on balance, being accumulated, where population is growing (or declining), the net change in (real) wealth per capita is a better measure of sustainability. Recently, Hamilton (2002) has provided empirical estimates of the change in wealth per capita (including natural resources) across a range of countries.[*]

Table 16.1. **Change in wealth per capita, selected countries, 1999**

	S_G/N	Population growth	W/N	Percentage change in wealth per capita
	USD	%	USD	%
US	3 597	1.2	86 255	3.0
Germany	2 203	0.0	79 761	2.7
Malaysia	827	2.4	19 200	1.9
Indonesia	−46	1.6	4 148	−2/7
Pakistan	10	2.4	2 258	−2.0
Colombia	111	1.8	9 265	−0.6

Source: Hamilton (2002).

Table 16.1 reports some of Hamilton's findings. For example, in Germany, population growth is about zero and hence the change in wealth per capita is simply equal to $\dot{W}/N$ or S_G/N. In the US, despite a relatively high percentage rate of population growth in developed country terms (mostly explained by net migration to the US), the change in wealth per capita is positive. This is also the case in Malaysia despite a percentage rate of growth of population of around 2.4%. In Indonesia, however, the wealth per capita reducing impact of a negative value of S_G/N is exacerbated by growth in population. The two remaining cases of Pakistan and Colombia are interesting in that a positive S_G/N (although somewhat marginal in the case of Pakistan) is insufficient to offset the impact on wealth per capita of an increasing population. Thus, in Pakistan and Colombia the change in wealth per capita is negative, although both of these countries had avoided negative genuine saving. In such cases, Hamilton (2002) shows that it is relatively straightforward to then calculate the savings effort that would have been consistent with a constant (real) value of wealth per capita.

[*] See World Bank (1997) for estimates of cross-country total wealth (including natural wealth).

To return to the example of mining cited in the introduction to this chapter, by definition, an investment in a mine that enables the extraction of a valuable but finite deposit of some natural resource is financing an unsustainable activity. That is, mining can continue only up to point that the resource is exhausted (either physically or economically). Whether there are broader implications for sustainability is another matter. Much depends on whether or not the proceeds from mining the resource are invested in an alternative (productive) asset. If the proceeds of mining are ploughed back into new and productive projects then development can be sustained.[3] From a cost-benefit perspective, a related question is whether relevant shadow prices need to be adjusted for the fact that commercial natural resources used up today are not available for future use? In economic language, there is a "user cost" associated with the depletion of such resources. Assuming that impacts of resource scarcity are priced properly in markets, then they need no further adjustment. That is, the "user cost" will be reflected in the resource's market price.[4]

Second, while the literature on WS has been effective in emphasising the importance of raising savings rates as one element of how policy can realise concern for future generations, less attention has been given to the productivity of investments. Clearly, this latter issue falls squarely within the domain of CBA. Not only can projects, selected by cost-benefit appraisals, increase net wealth but also can further contribute to sustaining development by ensuring that savings are put to the most productive use.

Third, discussions about WS are inherently about whether an economy is saving enough for the future. In other words, there is a premise that say, a nation's savings effort might be insufficient to sustain levels of consumption or well-being over the development path. As Box 16.1 illustrates, emerging data also seem to bear out this prediction at least for certain countries. For such countries, projects – on balance – lead to wealth being liquidated. Put this way, there is an analogy with discussions about the social value of investment (*vis-à-vis* consumption) in some of the seminal contributions on shadow pricing (*e.g.* Little and Mirrlees, 1974; Squire and van der Tak, 1975). In countries where savings rates are "low", it was argued that a project that results in greater amounts of investment should get more credit (in a cost-benefit test) than a project that generates additional consumption. The rationale here was that fostering higher economic growth rates is a relative priority particularly in developing countries and raising saving and investment rates aids this goal, at least over the short- to medium-term. If so, then postponing consumption has an additional pay-off that is not reflected in the observed data. An analogous argument could be made in the context of sustainable development. However, in this case, the rationale is the proposition that *net* saving rates are too low to sustain development. If ensuring that consumption and well-being does not decline over time is a priority for public policy then this suggests that any project that raises the (net) savings rate, perhaps by investing in some asset or generating funds to be reinvested, might be assigned a premium to reflect this additional social value.

Fourth, although this approach to sustainable development is largely concerned with greening national accounts, the theoretical framework underpinning WS also gives rise to cost-benefit rules. An example is illustrated in Box 16.2. This describes a cost-benefit test of the desirability of switching land-use from standing forest to farmland. The link to sustainability, in this instance, is that land is an asset that has a distinct (social) value depending on the use to which it is put. In theory, for a country with abundant tropical forest resources it might be expected that initially there are net benefits to converting land but that in the longer term, (costless) deforestation will occur up to the point where the value of land (*i.e.* the marginal hectare) under these two competing uses is equal. In the real world, however, it would be expected that a variety of policy distortions and market imperfections can easily lead to *excess* deforestation, where "excess" can be interpreted as deforestation yielding a decline in the social value of the land asset. In other words, a cost-benefit test of the land-clearing decision would indicate that the costs of deforestation outweigh the benefits.

Box 16.2. **Sustainability and cost benefit analysis of tropical deforestation**

For many forest resources, such as tropical forests, the valuation of depletion raises an interesting challenge. The issue is essentially one of land use, with standing forests being one use among many for a particular land area. This suggests, as in Hartwick (1992, 1993), that the correct way to value deforestation is to measure the change in land value (which should represent the present value of the net returns under the chosen land use). A recent paper by Hamilton and Atkinson (2006) has provided an empirical application of this notion to deforestation in the Peruvian Amazon. While this paper focuses on the better measurement of income and wealth, in a green national accounting framework, it is also suited to evaluating whether the switch of land-use from forest to agriculture is actually wealth increasing (or "sustainable").

While Hamilton and Atkinson (2006) investigate how Peru might green its national accounts for current "excess" deforestation, arising from slash-and-burn farming, this is in essence also a cost-benefit exercise. Focusing on a broad range of costs and benefits of deforestation, the net costs of "excess" deforestation is defined as the sum of the (present) values of sustainable timber harvest and the value of the carbon sequestered by that natural growth, local and global willingness to pay (WTP) for conservation minus agricultural returns on deforested land. Using a range of market and non-market data, reflecting these changes, the authors' results are summarised in Table 16.2. These data assume that slash-and-burn farming is replaced by pasture, a social discount rate of 5% and a 20-year period for the calculation of present values. This indicates that excess deforestation is USD 1286/hectare (ha) in the year 1995. Regarding the components of excess deforestation, it is evident that the sum of (present values of) local and global WTP (where the latter is made up of non-use value) – i.e. USD 1015/ha -is only a little in excess of the (present) value of agricultural returns. In other words, the estimated value of excess deforestation in the table is sensitive to the estimate of the timber and carbon value of the (foregone) sustainable harvest in that it is these values that "tip" the balance such that the switch from forest to slash-and-burn agriculture can be characterised as, other things being equal, wealth-decreasing.

Regarding the bigger picture, the authors show that the effect of accounting for (net) changes in wealth that arise when forestland is cleared for slash-and-burn farming is to reduce the estimated genuine savings rate for Peru. Despite this, however, this adjusted saving rate remains strongly positive in the study year. Of course, the genuine saving calculation is an estimate of *total* saving effort, whereas the Peruvian population is growing at a rate of 1.7% per year. Performing the savings analysis in per capita terms requires, first, calculating genuine saving per capita, roughly USD 58 (for a population of 25.6 million). Then a "wealth-diluting" term, representing the sharing of total wealth with this extra 1.7% of the population in 1995, must be subtracted – this can be calculated to be about USD 131 in 1999 using the figures in Hamilton (2002). Atkinson *et al.* argue that this indicates that genuine saving per person in Peru is probably not robust, at USD 58, and that the change in wealth per capita is quite likely negative.

Table 16.2. **Value of excess derorestration, 1995**

	Components of excess deforestation (USD current)
+ Local willingness to pay for conservation	868
+ Global willingness to pay for conservation	147
+ Value of sustainable timber harvest	858
+ Value of carbon stored in sustainable timber harvest	310
? Agricultural returns	897
= Value of excess deforestation	1 286

Notes: Data refer to present values (PV); assumed social discount rate equals 5%; lifetime for PV calculations is 20 years.

> **Box 16.2. Sustainability and cost benefit analysis of tropical deforestation** *(cont.)*
>
> A number of points should be made in evaluating these findings. There is considerable uncertainty regarding the data needed to calculate these terms and, for example, the appropriate magnitude of discount rates. This gives rise to potentially wide ranges of values for much of the data (but not reflected in Table 16.2). With respect to policy implications, in this application, local forest clearance decisions reduce welfare in other countries (via loss of non-use value and a [net] contribution to climate change). In other words, the optimal mix of forest and agricultural land is different to that which currently prevails given that farmers, for some reason, cannot capture the value of conservation benefits. In reality, attempts to reduce excess deforestation will have to translate these values into transfers that farmers in Peru can appropriate. Such mechanisms, in essence, have been put into effect by the Global Environment Facility (GEF) and endorsed in international environmental agreements such as the Convention for Biodiversity.

Fifth, while project sustainability is often interpreted as depending on the achievement of the projected or forecast net benefit or rate of return,[5] the meaning of sustainable development prompts a concern about the relationship between the project intervention and its effects on the various asset bases. Projects may secure an acceptable rate of return but may not contribute as much as they might to the goal of sustainable development just as projects may also fail to secure the highest gains for the poorest people in the current generation.

The contribution of a project to sustainable development could be gauged by way of an "*asset check*", to examine what the stocks of assets are before the project intervention and what they are likely to be after the intervention. In other words, the project could be appraised in the context of the overall asset stock and the extent to which it is depreciating or appreciating independently of the project. In contrast to a standard benefit-cost appraisal, this would force the focus to be more specifically on capital assets. This approach also raises the issue of whether any of the asset stocks are "critical" (the strong sustainability approach).

An asset check procedure could separately address total assets, specific critical assets, technological effects on asset productivity, the background rate of population growth and asset resilience, for example. In each case an assessment of the "baseline" value of the asset stock would be required, *i.e.* the size of the asset stock at any point of time, allowing for any levels of asset depreciation taking place independently of the project. Next the effects of the project on these assets could be estimated.

16.4. Strong sustainability and CBA

Important as it might be, discussions about sustainable development in the context of project appraisal seldom focus primarily on the desirable wealth increasing properties of these projects. Rather the focus of these contributions more usually has been on what has been termed strong sustainability (SS, or strong sustainable development).[6]

Advocates of SS as a guiding principle argue that it is the physical protection of absolute levels of ecological goods that is a prerequisite for sustainability. If individual preferences cannot be counted on to fully reflect this importance, there is a paternal role for decision-makers in providing this protection. Reasons for this include the complexity of ecosystems and the view that the diminished capacity of the environment to provide functions, such as waste absorption and ecological system maintenance, cannot be replaced or substituted (Norton and Toman, 1997). Furthermore, it is argued that natural assets are characterised by important thresholds, that if exceeded lead to large-scale and irreversible ecological losses with possibly dramatically negative impacts on human well-being. There are several variants on this proposition. For example, very few supporters of SS (explicitly) argue that all natural assets must be separately conserved. More usually it is argued that there is a subset of *critical* natural assets, which are both crucial for human welfare and have no substitutes: therefore, it follows that such assets cannot be simply traded off for other forms of wealth and must be managed according to more case-specific criteria (Pearce *et al.* 1989).

Defining more precisely which natural assets are critical and which are not is clearly a fundamental element in ensuring that this approach is useful for policy-making and appraisals. Before we turn to this issue in more detail, we firstly marshal the broad implications of SS. Focusing on the essential idea that a given physical amount of a resource must be preserved intact in order that it may continue to provide critical services, a two-tier approach to sustainability is suggested. For example, Farmer and Randall (1998) outline the implications of the (long-established) concept of a "safe minimum standard" (SMS) whereby policy-makers follow standard cost-benefit rules unless there is a compelling reason not to; *e.g.* to conserve a critical natural asset. However, this SMS conservation rule can itself be overridden if its costs are "intolerable".

Pearce *et al.* (1996) provide an illustration of how this two-tier approach might operate in the case of a tropical rainforest. In this example, preserving some quantity of the forest is assumed to be critical for the long-term well-being of humanity. The effect of this preservation is to reduce the amount of forest that can be considered to be an economic resource (*i.e.* it reduces the quantity of harvest or clearance that can be carried out from the non-conserved stock). The key indicators for a country with tropical forest operating under this regime will be twofold: are stocks of this critical natural asset declining? and are genuine savings rates (*i.e.* savings net of the change in the non-conserved resource stock) negative? A positive answer to either of these questions would be an indication of unsustainability.

If analysts were able to monetise critical natural assets, then the policy implications of the SS perspective, in cost-benefit terms, become even plainer. One means of capturing the notion of the value of a critical amount of a resource or natural asset is by assuming that,

$$p_i \to \infty \text{ as } X_i \to \overline{X}_i^+$$

where, $\overline{X}_i^+$ is the critical amount of the natural asset – *i.e.*, as the resource declines to the critical amount, arbitrarily large losses in welfare are associated with depletion of a marginal unit (Hamilton and Atkinson, 2006). This could correspond to a physical process, such as rapid deterioration in forest quality and diversity once a critical threshold has been breached (Pearce *et al.* 1996). Approaching this physical threshold would show up as a correspondingly large loss in value of the critical natural asset. Hence, if preferences for critical resources are taken into account, then the optimal or most socially desirable policy is to be strongly sustainable (*i.e.* set limits on resource depletion so as to avoid the prospect of rapidly increasing losses in welfare). Yet, while this approach can handle strong sustainability in principle, in practice it requires good measures of willingness to pay for a critical resource and sufficient scientific and economic information (concerning the relative importance of the loss of the resource) for preferences to reflect the appropriate trade-offs that would underpin this willingness to pay estimate.

With regards to project appraisal, a number of studies, beginning with Barbier *et al.* (1990), have sought to examine the specific implications of concern about strong sustainability for CBA. While these are largely conceptual contributions, there is also growing practical interest in the application of, for example, resource compensation in assessing real world examples of damage to natural and environmental resources. The basic approach taken, in theory and in practice, is to recognise that strong sustainability is a concept that is most relevant to the management of a *portfolio* of projects. That is, for example, imposing a constraint on project selection that each individual project does not damage the environment is arguably too stringent (in the sense that very few projects would presumably yield net benefits yet not damage the environment at all).

More accommodating proposals for selecting projects subject to a (strong) sustainability constraint usually advocate that the *net effect* on the environment of projects in a portfolio should be, at least, zero. Leaving aside, for the moment, the issue of what it is precisely that projects should (on balance) seek to conserve, we examine in more detail the broad principles of the approaches, for example, in Barbier *et al.* (1990) and later in Pires (1998) for subjecting a cost-benefit test to a (strong) sustainability constraint.

Each project i is associated with environmental costs, E. How these costs are to be measured is largely ambiguous. While monetary valuation would seem to be one candidate method, if shadow prices could be correctly estimated then it is unclear why sustainability concerns simply could not be built into standard net benefit estimates. The apparent need for additional sustainability constraints implicitly suggests that certain environmental costs are not measurable in this way. This point aside, the basic issue is that some projects "on offer" will lead to depletion or degradation of natural or environmental resource stocks: i.e. $E_i > 0$. Other projects "on offer" will lead to resource stocks being restored or augmented: i.e. $E_i < 0$. Two general constrained decision-rules have been put forward as capturing concern for strong sustainability within a cost-benefit setting.

First, a stringently strong constraint, for cost-benefit tests, might be imposed that in choosing projects that maximise net benefits, the *aggregate* environmental costs, i.e. $\sum_{i=1}^{n} E_{it}$, of all projects chosen for inclusion in the portfolio should be zero in each time period, t (which, for example, might correspond to a year). That is,

$$\sum_{i=1}^{n} E_{it} \leq 0 \quad \forall t \qquad [16.4]$$

The matrix in Figure 16.1 describes project selection criteria in more detail. Either of four cases might arise for any given project i for different possible permutations of net benefits (NB) and environmental costs (E), both of which may be either positive or negative. Decision-making in case where $NB_i > 0$ and $E_i < 0$ is relatively straightforward; that is, the project should be unambiguously accepted. Similarly unproblematic are cases where $NB_i < 0$ and $E_i > 0$ as such projects should be unambiguously rejected. However, deciding about the remaining cases necessitates additional judgements about say whether environmental costs ($E_i > 0$) for the current project under consideration can be compensated by environmental gains provided by another project within the portfolio ($E_j < 0$). However, the portfolio constraint that should be observed is that environmental costs, across all projects in the portfolio, should be at least zero. If the same is required of total net benefits then what this means is that the portfolio at least breaks-even on the basis of non-environmental benefits and costs as well as maintaining the environmental *status quo*.

Figure 16.1. **Project selection and strong sustainability**

	$E_i < 0$	$E_i > 0$
$NB_i > 0$	Accept	?
$NB_i < 0$	?	Reject

Note: Adapted from Bateman *et al.* (2002).

Second, a more flexible strong constraint might be imposed that the net environmental effect of all projects in a portfolio should be zero over some longer time horizon, T (where $T > t$). That is,

$$\sum_{t=1}^{T}\sum_{i=1}^{n} E_{it} \leq 0 \qquad\qquad [16.5]$$

Put another way, the constraint here is that it is the present value of environmental costs that should be zero over this time horizon. Hence, this is less stringent (than previously) in that it permits a greater degree of temporal flexibility in meeting the specified sustainability constraint. Arguably, environmental costs in equation [16.5] should also be discounted – *e.g.* weighted by $[1/(1 + s)^t]$ where s is the social discount rate. This would simply reflect the fact that a project that restores environmental quality at some point in the future is less valuable than a project which restores environmental quality now.

Quite how long this planning horizon should be is an interesting question although most contributions have offered little practical guidance on this matter. On the one hand, environmentally improving projects are primarily intended as compensation for future generations, which might suggest no requirement for haste in implementing these compensating projects. On the other hand, if the current generation receives substantial amenity from at least some of these resources, then this might suggest a greater degree of urgency.

Observing the sustainability constraint in the expression immediately above requires that any environmental loss is compensated by an environmental gain of equal (present) value. What this amounts to is a requirement that the value of a natural asset is eventually kept intact, a basic tenet of (strong) sustainability. However, in the interval between damage and compensation occurring there is some loss of well-being as the natural asset, during that time, does not provide the same level of environmental services. Of course, asking how far all this matters in practical terms is a valid question. Nevertheless, it is far from a purely theoretical issue. Sustainability is fundamentally about ensuring (at least) a constancy of a development path. Whether permitting actions, which result in a development path where there is a drop in well-being at some early stage followed by an offsetting jump in well-being at some later point, is consistent with this emphasis is likely to hinge on issues about how steep the initial drop is and how long before the corresponding gain is realised. As ever, the issue is the correct balance. That is, defining T to be too short-term brings us back to the stringently strong constraint defined above. Interestingly, some of these issues are illustrated in the context of climate change policy as Box 16.3 shows.

> ### Box 16.3. **Climate change and shadow projects**
>
> While few, if any, would argue that the Kyoto Protocol will contribute to strong sustainable development, some of its provisions, which mandate legally binding reductions in greenhouse gas emissions (GHGs) across relatively high-income countries and economies in transition, illustrate the ideas introduced by those who have examined strong sustainability in the context of project appraisal. For example, countries have to achieve GHG targets, *on average*, over a 5-year period (2008-12). That is, it allows any country to say undershoot its target in any one year as long as this is made-up by a corresponding overshoot in some other period. Of course, permitting this flexibility is simply the exercise of commonsense in assisting countries meet a costly objective. However, it also illustrates how the broad idea of shadow projects might be conceived in practice. Moreover, the Kyoto Protocol also allows parties to "bank" (*i.e.* receive credit in the future for) any GHG reductions resulting from over-compliance within the first control period or "trades" under the Clean Development Mechanism (CDM). Interestingly, however, it does not allow countries to "borrow" future emission reductions. The case of the CDM is also interesting in that it implies compensating for emissions of carbon dioxide arising from one "project" (*e.g.* coal-fired electricity generation), in one country, by the financing of a project that sequesters (more than off-setting) reductions in atmospheric carbon dioxide in another country (*e.g.* "clean" energy or planting trees).

Both of the methods for integrating SS criteria into a cost-benefit test broadly correspond to what has become known as the shadow and compensating projects approach. For example, projects that cause environmental damage are "covered off" by projects that result in environmental improvements. Quite what this means in practice is another matter. The timing of compensations is just one issue. Another is that natural assets are heterogeneous and so questions arise as to whether this term – "net effect" – refers to a specific natural asset (*e.g.* wetlands) or natural assets in general. In principle, requiring that projects in a portfolio leave the overall (present) value of natural assets intact, raises the prospect of allowing a project which damage wetlands as long as these are accompanied by a compensating project which seeks to improve say urban air quality.

Typically, however, most of the discussion about shadow projects has centred on replacing "like-with-like": *e.g.* a wetland for a wetland. A number of analytical dilemmas still arise. Depending, for example, where original and compensating resources are located, the winners and losers in each case could be either wholly or very different. Other issues include the measurement of what is lost and what is replaced. Some degree of quantification must be implied in this process. Otherwise, how can it be credibly claimed that compensation has taken place? Such issues, and others, are discussed in Box 16.4 which also outlines a somewhat different rationale for shadow projects – the "Public Trust Doctrine" – to that embodied in the "critical capital" terminology.

16.5. Summary and guidance for decision-makers

The notion of "sustainable development" has permeated significant parts of policy and public discourse about the environment. While there remains debate about it means for development to be sustainable, there is now a coherent body of academic work that has sought to understand what a sustainable development path might look like, how this path

Box 16.4. **The public trust doctrine and shadow projects**

Chapman and Hanemann (2004), in the US public policy context, provide a distinct variant on the justification for shadow projects, which they term the "Public Trust Doctrine". This approach does not appeal *directly* to contested ethical or scientific imperatives (as typically, accounts about strong sustainability do). Rather it draws on the authority of legislative or constitutional requirements that (certain specified) natural and environmental resources are held in trust for the public (now and in the future). Put another way, this view holds that there is a legal basis for stating that particular resources be replaced "like-for-like". Interestingly, actions entailing resource compensation – implied by this Doctrine – is potentially to become a lively issue in the European context as it is part of the proposed EU Directive on Liability.

In the US, this Doctrine apparently has a relatively long lineage dating back, at least, to the late 19th century. At the national or federal level, it assigns broad power to the government to protect certain resources and, more recently, has been extended to the public interest in the natural environment. Additionally, at the state level it has formed the basis for natural resource damage assessment. One high profile and recent impetus to this Doctrine was the creation of the Superfund to finance the remedial cleanup of existing hazardous waste sites. This established a liability to pay damages for injury, destruction or loss of natural resources in addition to the costs of cleanup, remediation and other response costs.

More generally, the Public Trust Doctrine motivates shadow projects in requiring that restoration the natural asset in question acts as compensation for natural resource damage. Put another way, if the resource is, in effect, held in trust for future generations then liquidating that asset – even with financial (or some other) recompense – will not suffice. Rather the asset itself must be restored and so it is the cost of restoration that forms the basis for this claim especially "… when replacement resources are of similar type, quality and comparable value" (NOAA Guidelines cited in Chapman and Hanemann, 2004). Resource compensation might take two forms. First, "value-to-value" – a given resource is replaced elsewhere by the similar resource of equivalent value. Second, "service-to-service" – a given resource is replaced elsewhere by the similar resource, which provides equivalent (non-monetised) services. An example of the former, outlined by Chapman and Hanemann is Lavaca Bay, a Marine Superfund site in south Texas. This is a site which has suffered injury to its ecological resources (salt marsh and fish and migratory birds). Restoration involved developing the area of acreage of habitat restoration required and damages owing were based on cost of implementing the "appropriate" restoration actions.

A number of issues arise from the application of the restoration cost approach to real world examples. Wetland restoration provides a prominent illustration. "Wetland banking" in the US allows a party to substantially alter a wetland if they purchase credit earned by another party for protection or enhancement of another wetland. These credits are then traded through a "wetland bank". The overall requirement is that there is no net loss in wetlands. In other words, this is a form of resource compensation or institution for facilitating the "purchase" of shadow projects. While this seems an inventive means of conserving wetlands, in the aggregate, it is not surprisingly associated a number of problems. First, data requirements can be large and burdensome (although this is hardly a conclusion unique to this type of work). Second, the created ecosystem can fail in the sense of not providing an adequate substitute habitat or some other ecological function. Third, inevitably there is the problem of whether "like" being replaced with "like". For example, a cross-habitat assumption of equal per unit value (*e.g.* a hectare) may be invalid as it is entirely possible that the "created" ecosystem is likely to be less valuable than a degraded natural ecosystem. Proposals to deal with this latter problem include that of "two-for-one": *i.e.* replacing one lost wetland with two new ones.

can be achieved and how progress towards it might be measured. While it is hardly surprising that these efforts have not generated a consensus, there has been considerable progress in understanding where agreement and disagreement is and why this arises.

Much of this work considers the pursuit of sustainable development to be an aggregate or macroeconomic goal. By-and-large cost-benefit analysts have not sought actively to engage with this broader debate except insofar as it relates to factors affecting a project's forecast net benefit or rate of return. However, it should be noted that recent developments discussed elsewhere in this volume – most notably on valuing environmental impacts and discounting costs and benefits – are relevant to this issue. In this chapter, we have discussed a number of additional speculations about how cost-benefit appraisals can be extended to take account of recent concerns about sustainable development.

According to one perspective there is an obvious role for appraising projects in the light of these concerns. This notion of strong sustainability starts from the assertion that certain natural assets are so important or critical (for future, and perhaps current, generations) so as to warrant protection at current or above some other target level. If individual preferences cannot be counted on to fully reflect this importance, there is a paternal role for decision-makers in providing this protection. With regards to the relevance of this approach to cost-benefit appraisals, a handful of contributions have suggested that sustainability is applicable to the management of a *portfolio* of projects. This has resulted in the idea of a shadow or compensating project. For example, this could be interpreted as meaning that projects that cause environmental damage are "covered off" by projects that result in environmental improvements. The overall consequence is that projects in the portfolio, on balance, maintain the environmental status quo. Practical applications of this approach include wetland loss and compensating restoration in the US.

There remain a number of outstanding questions about the broader applicability of this approach. Specifically, the demarcation between those assets which can be thought of as critical and those which are not is, in practice, far from clear. Indeed, any practitioner familiar with this on-going debate may be forgiven for developing a sinking feeling at the prospect of having to translate these discussions in practical lessons for appraising projects, for there are arguably few clear signs that any dramatic progress has been made in this regard. This is despite the fact that the "critical capital" terminology (and sweeping claims about its policy implications) is now commonplace in the literature.

Some have sought to characterise "criticality" according to ecological criteria while others have drawn on political or constitutional precedents (*e.g.* the Public Trust Doctrine). In the case of the former, for example, proponents have been tempted into defining critical assets very broadly perhaps to include most types of natural assets. Yet, the evidence on which this broad sweep relies is dependent on weighting decision-making heavily in favour of precaution. This raises important issues. On the one hand, there is a benefit to avoiding untoward and irreversible damage to (possibly) critical resources. On the other hand, there are likely to be significant costs to applying the shadow projects approach as widely as this perspective would imply. Interestingly, while specific real world examples can be found that approximate the notion of a shadow project there is arguably little evidence of wider enthusiasm for this particular approach.

There are further ways of viewing the problem of sustainable development. Whether these alternatives – usually characterised under the heading "weak sustainability" – are complementary or rivals has been a subject of debate. This debate would largely dissolve if it could be determined which assets were critical. As this latter issue is itself a considerable source of uncertainty, as we have discussed, the debate continues. However, the so-called "weak" approach to sustainable development is useful for a number of reasons. While it has primarily be viewed as a guide to constructing green national accounts (*i.e.* better measures of income, saving and wealth), the focus on assets and asset management has a counterpart in thinking about project appraisal. For example, this might emphasise the need for an "asset check". That is, what the stocks of assets are before the project intervention and what they are likely to be after the intervention? It might also add another reason for the tradition in cost-benefit analysis of giving greater weight to projects which generate economic resources for saving and investment in economies where it is reckoned that too little net wealth (per capita) is being passed on to future generations.

Notes

1. However, it is important to note that a point measure of positive SG, *i.e.* $S_{G_i} > 0$, does not necessarily mean that a development path is sustainable (Asheim, 1994; Pezzey and Withagen, 1998). In other words, S_G is strictly speaking a one-sided indicator of sustainability.

2. Specifically, this requires that the growth rate in genuine saving does not exceed the interest rate.

3. For many countries, in practice, it appears that the prudent path of saving the proceeds of resource depletion has been difficult to achieve. Indeed, a number of contributions have sought to identify explanatory factors that account for the inability of resource-rich economies to transform this natural good fortune into saving (see, for example, Atkinson and Hamilton, 2003).

4. Johansson (1993) notes that where extraction (or harvest) is not optimal – in the sense of the gain from using up a unit now exactly matches the loss from not having that unit in the future – that there is an additional imputation to reflect the mismatch between current gains and future losses.

5. For example, the World Bank's Operations Evaluation Department refers to the resilience to risk of net benefits flows over time, where these risks are broadly construed to include financial risk, institutional risks and so on (see, for example, Belli *et al.*, 1998).

6. Some contributions refer to "environmental sustainability" or "environmentally sustainable development". However, the definition of these terms accords with the definition of strong sustainability and strong sustainable development used in this chapter.

ISBN 92-64-01004-1
Cost-Benefit Analysis and the Environment
Recent Developments
© OECD 2006

Chapter 17

Benefits Transfer

Transfer studies are the bedrock of practical policy analysis in that only infrequently are practitioners afforded the luxury of conducting original studies. This is no less true in the case of borrowing or transferring WTP values to policy questions involving environmental or related impacts which are the subject of this chapter. Although there are no generally accepted practical transfer protocols, a number of elements of what might constitute best practice have been discussed widely. These include scrutinising the accuracy and quality of the original studies and taking adequate account of a possible variety of differences between the study site (where a WTP estimate exists) and policy site(s) (where this estimate needs to be transferred to). The holy grail of benefits transfer is the consolidation of data on non-market values in emerging transfer databases. While a welcome development, there is a corresponding need for a better understanding of when transfers work and when they do not as well as developing methods that might lead to transfer accuracy being improved.

17.1. Introduction

Advances in methods to value non-market goods have been a striking feature of modern cost-benefit analysis. Increasingly such benefit assessment techniques are being used to inform policies and project choice across a number of countries. However, there is some recognition that the key to the routine policy use of non-market values is a greater reliance on benefits transfer: that is, taking a unit value of a non-market good estimated in an original or primary study and using this estimate (perhaps after some adjustment) to value benefits that arise when a new policy is implemented. It should be noted that transfers can relate to benefits or costs (*i.e.* foregone benefits) depending on the change in provision from the *status quo* proposed by the project. However, we retain the prevailing terminology of "benefits transfer" throughout this chapter.

Benefits transfer is the subject of a rapidly growing literature. The reason is obvious. If benefits transfer were a valid procedure, then the need for costly and time-consuming original (or "primary") studies of non-market values would be vastly reduced. For example, for policies, programmes and projects with multiple non-market impacts, conducting original studies may not be possible. If so, benefits transfer might be the answer. Benefits transfer, for example, could be used to provide an interim assessment of whether (or not) a more in-depth analysis is worthwhile. For many, however, the ultimate prize of benefits transfer is a comprehensive database of non-market values, which can be taken "off the shelf" and applied to new policies and projects as needed. Attainment of this goal is still some way off even given the ever-growing number of good quality (original) non-valuation studies that are emerging. Interestingly, as we discuss later in this chapter, the building blocks of this process are in place in the context of environmental values.

Unfortunately, there is a more fundamental obstacle to the uptake of benefits transfer than the abundance (or otherwise) of studies. This is that the validity of benefits transfer remains, in many respects, open to scrutiny. An interim conclusion (interim, because so much research is emerging on this issue) is that benefits transfer can give rise to inaccuracy of varying degrees of magnitude. This conclusion needs to be qualified to some extent. Benefits transfer seems to work in some contexts better than in others, for reasons that are sometimes not very clear. However, conclusions about validity (or otherwise) need to be placed in their appropriate context. Put another way, a degree of inaccuracy is almost inevitable and some benefits transfer analysts have asked whether criteria used to judge transfer validity are too demanding relative to the accuracy needed to help evidence-based policy making. As a practical matter, it may be that some degree of imprecision "does not matter" and that more pragmatic (but clear) rules of thumb are needed about the hurdle of accuracy that any transfer must attain.

The remainder of this chapter is organised as follows. Section 17.2 provides a definition of benefits transfer and then goes on to outline the steps that a benefits transfer approach typically might take and looks at ways in which unit values (to be transfer) might be adjusted to "fit better" the characteristics (of the good and the affected population) that accompany a new policy. Section 17.3 describes efforts to develop comprehensive databases of values for use in future transfers. A more critical assessment of the validity of benefits transfer is then offered in Section 17.4. Section 17.5 offers concluding remarks on issues such as best practice in the light of the preceding discussion.

17.2. Benefits transfer: basic concepts and methods

17.2.1. Defining benefits transfer

Benefits transfer (BT) concepts have been advanced in a number of articles over the past 15 years or so. Early developments include the pioneering contributions in the 1992 issue of Water Resources Research (Vol. 28, No. 3), which was dedicated specifically to BT. A definition of BT offered in that volume was: "… the transfer of existing estimates of non-market values to a new study which is different from the study for which the values were originally estimated" (Boyle and Bergstrom, 1992). Since then the number and quality of BT studies have increased significantly. Another milestone was Desvousges, Johnson and Banzhaf (1998) one of the first major published studies of the validity of BT. That volume distinguished two basic definitions of BT.

The first definition is a broader concept based on the use of existing information designed for one specific context (original context) to address policy questions in another context (transfer context). These types of transfer studies are not limited to cost-benefit analysis (CBA) and related applications. They occur whenever analysts draw on past studies to predict effects of policies in another context. Put this way, benefits transfer – in some shape or form – is far more pervasive to policy analysis than many perhaps would fully realise.

The second definition is a narrower concept based on the use of values of a good estimated in one site (the "study site") as a proxy for values of the (same) good in another site (the "policy site"). This is the type of BT most commonly used in CBA and thus it is this more specific definition that is the basis of this chapter. However, the application of this type of benefits transfer covers a remarkably wide range of goods. For example, the provision of a non-market good at a policy site might refer to a river at a particular geographical location (where study sites relate to rivers at different locations). However, relevant impacts at a site might also entail some change in a human health state. A policy-site also might be a wholly different country to that where the study was originally conducted. That is, perhaps values are being transferred from countries, which are data-rich (i.e. the minority) to countries where is a paucity of such information (i.e. the majority).

17.2.2. Transfer methods

An important point is that benefits transfer is not necessarily a passive or straightforward choice for analysts. Once benefits transfer has been selected as the assessment method (itself a choice requiring some reflection), then judgment and insight is required for all of the basic steps entailed in undertaking a BT exercise. For example, information needs to be obtained on baseline environmental quality and changes as well as relevant socio-economic data. In addition, original studies for transfer need to be identified. Published and unpublished (e.g. so-called "grey") literature might be sought in this regard. It may be, however, that a database of past studies exists in which case consulting this source would seem an appropriate starting point. Later on in this chapter, we describe efforts to construct databases of environmental valuation studies (see

Section 17.2.3). In general rule a transfer can be no more reliable than the original estimates upon which it is based. Given a lack of good quality original studies for many types of non-market values and the fact that even good studies typically have not been designed specifically for transfer applications care must be taken here. Clearly, the analyst needs to have some criteria for judging the quality of studies if no "official" (or other) guidance exists.

Perhaps the most crucial stage is where existing estimates or models are selected and estimated effects are obtained for the policy site (*e.g.* per household benefits). This is the point at which the actual transfer occurs and implies choosing a particular transfer approach (see below). In addition, the population at the relevant policy site must be determined. Aggregation is achieved by multiplying per individual or household values by the relevant population. While it is worth noting that this choice may entail controversy – especially when deciding how the large the population is that holds non-use values for a given environmental resource (see Box 17.1) – in what immediately follows we focus upon summarising the findings of past studies with reference to a unit value (or perhaps range of unit values) as well as whether this value (or these values) need to be adjusted. Adjustments might be contemplated most commonly to reflect differences at the original study site(s) and the new policy site. There are at least three different types of adjustment of increasing sophistication for the analyst to choose from. These options are reviewed in what follows.

Unadjusted (or naïve) WTP transfer

The procedure here is to "borrow" an estimate of WTP in context S (the study site) and apply it to context P (the policy site). The estimate is usually left unadjusted.

$$WTP_S = WTP_P$$

A variety of unit values may be transferred, the most typical being mean or median measures. Mean values are readily compatible with CBA studies as they allow simple transformation to aggregate benefit estimates: *e.g.* multiply mean (average) WTP by the relevant affected population to calculate aggregate benefits.

The virtue of this approach is clearly its simplicity and the ease with which it can be applied once suitable original studies have been identified. Of course, the flipside of this relative straightforwardness is that it fails to capture important differences between the characteristics of an original study site (or sites) and a new policy site. If these differences are significant determinants of WTP, then this transfer approach – which is sometimes more prescriptively known as a naïve transfer – will fail to reflect likely divergences in WTP at the study and policy sites.

Determinants of WTP that might differ between study and policy sites include (Bateman *et al.*, 2000):

- The socio-economic and demographic characteristics of the relevant populations. This might include income, educational attainment and age.
- The physical characteristics of the study and policy sites. This might include the environmental services that the good provides such as, in the case of a river, opportunities for recreation in general and angling in particular.
- The proposed change in provision between the sites of the good to be valued. For example, the value of water quality improvements from studies involving small

improvements may not apply to a policy involving a large change in quantity or quality (*e.g.* WTP and quantity may not have a straightforward linear relationship).

● Differences in the "market" conditions applying to the sites. For example variation in the availability of substitutes in the case of recreational resources such as rivers. Two otherwise identical rivers might be characterised by different levels of alternative recreational opportunities. Other things being equal, mean WTP to prevent a lowering of water quality at a river where there are few substitutes should be greater than WTP for avoiding the same quality loss at a river where there is an abundance of substitutes. The reason for this is that the former is a more scarce recreational resource than the latter.

● Temporal changes. There may be changes in valuations over time, perhaps because of increasing incomes and/or decreasing availability of clean rivers.

As a general rule, there is little evidence that the conditions for accepting unadjusted value transfer hold in practice. Effectively, those conditions amount to saying that the various conditions listed above all do not hold, *i.e.* "sites" are effectively "identical" in all these characteristics (or that characteristics are not significant determinants of WTP, a conclusion which sits at odds with economic theory).

WTP transfer with adjustment

A widely used formula for adjusted transfer is:

$$WTP_P = WTP_S (Y_P/Y_S)^e,$$

where Y is income per capita, WTP is willingness to pay, and e is the income elasticity of WTP. This latter term is an estimate of how the WTP for the (non-market) good in question varies with changes in income. According to this expression, if e is assumed to be equal to one then the ratio of WTP at sites S and P is equivalent to the ratio of per capita incomes at the two sites (*i.e.* $WTP_P/WTP_S = Y_P/Y_S$). In this example, values are simply adjusted upwards for projects affecting people with higher than average incomes and downwards for projects that affect people with lower than average incomes. As an example, Krupnick *et al.* (1996) transfer WTP for various health states (mortality and morbidity) from the USA to Eastern Europe using the ratio of wages in the two areas (and various assumptions about the income elasticity of WTP). This produces a WTP in Eastern Europe that is some proportion less than WTP for the USA.

In the above commonly used adjustment, the only feature that is changed between the two sites is income. The rationale for this is perhaps because it is thought that this is the most important factor resulting in changes in WTP. Of course, to the extent that say income is not the sole determinant of WTP then even this improvement may well fall short of approximating actual WTP at the study site. However, it is also possible to make a similar adjustment for, say, changes in age structure between the two sites, changes in population density, and so on. Making multiple changes of these kind amounts to transferring benefit functions and it is to this last transfer approach that we now turn.

WTP function transfer

A more sophisticated approach is to transfer the benefit or value function from S and apply it to P. Thus, if it is known that WTP at the study site is a function of range of physical features of the site and its use as well as the socio-economic (and demographic) characteristics of the population at the site then this information itself can be used as part of the transfer. For example, $WTP_S = f(A, B, C, Y)$ where A, B, C are additional and significant factors affecting WTP (in addition to Y) at site S, then WTP_P can be estimated using the coefficients from this equation in combination with the values of A, B, C, Y at site P: *i.e.*

$WTP_S = f(A, B, C, Y)$

$WTP_S = a_0 + a_1A + a_2B + a_3C + a_4Y$,

where the terms a_i refer to the coefficients which quantify the change in WTP as a result of a (marginal) change in that variable. For example, assume that WTP (simply) depends on the income, age and educational attainment of the population at the study site and that the analysts undertaking that study estimated the following relationship between WTP and these (explanatory) variables.

$WTP_S = 3 + 0.5Y_S - 0.3\ AGE_S + 2.2\ EDUC_S$

That is, WTP_S increases with income and educational attainment but decreases with age as described. In this transfer approach, the entire benefit function would be transferred as follows:

$\Rightarrow WTP_P = 3 + 0.5Y_P - 0.3\ AGE_P + 2.2\ EDUC_P$

As an example of the implications of this approach, if the population at the policy site is generally much older than that at the study site then WTP_P – other things being equal – will be lower than WTP_S.

A still more ambitious approach is that of meta-analysis (*e.g.* Bateman *et al.*, 2000). This is a statistical analysis of summary results of a (typically) large group of studies. At its simplest, a meta-analysis might take an average of existing estimates of WTP, provided the dispersion about the average is not found to be substantial, and use that average in policy site studies. Alternatively, average values might be weighted by the dispersion about the mean, the wider the dispersion the lower the weight that an estimate would receive.

The results from past studies can also be analysed in such a way that persistent variations in WTP can be explained. This should enable better transfer of values since the analyst can learn about what WTP systematically depends on. In the meta-analysis case, whole functions are transferred rather than average values, but the functions do not come from a single study, but from collections of studies. As an illustration, assume that the following function is estimated using past valuation studies of wetland provision in a particular country:

WTP = a_1 + a_2 TYPE OF SITE + a_3 SIZE OF CHANGE + a_4 VISITOR NUMBERS +
a_5 NON-USERS + a_6 INCOME + a_7 ELICITATION FORMAT + a_8 YEAR

This illustrative meta-analysis seeks to explain WTP with reference not only to the features of the wetland study sites (type, size of change in provision in the wetland, numbers of visitors and non-users) and socio-economic characteristics (income) but also process variables relating to the methods used in original studies (elicitation format in stated preference studies and so on) and the year in which the study was undertaken. Application of meta-analysis to the field of non-market valuation has expanded rapidly in recent years. Studies have taken place in respect of urban pollution, recreation, the ecological functions of wetlands, values of statistical life, noise and congestion.

Many commentators have concluded that, at least in theory, the more sophisticated the approach is the better, in terms of accuracy of the transfer. The rationale for this conclusion presumably being that there is little to commend BT if it is inaccurate and misleading. However, many have understandably also combined this aspiration for accuracy with some pragmatism about dismissing simplistic approaches altogether. Thus, there seems to be a suspicion that is also little to commend BT if it cannot be routinely applied, as for many this is its fundamental rationale. This latter point means that the appeal of BT is likely to be diminished if it is always and everywhere the preserve of the highly trained specialist. This conflict will only be resolved once analysts have learned more about when and where simple approaches are justified and when they are not.

17.3. Benefits transfer guidelines and databases

Without a readily accessible stock of benefit studies any BT exercise may be hampered by the daunting task of collecting past studies. It has long been claimed that it is necessary to establish national and international databases of valuation studies which are accessible for the researcher who intends to conduct benefit transfer. Established international collaboration between Environment Canada, the US EPA and the UK Ministry with environmental responsibilities (DEFRA) has resulted in the development of a substantial library of benefit estimates: the EVRI system (*www.evri.ca*). This database was designed with the specific goal of easing benefit transfer analyses. EVRI is a searchable (and web-based) database of empirical studies on the economic value of environmental benefits and human health effects. Currently, EVRI has more than 1 600 study entries, which are accessible to subscribers. Each entry contains a summary of the original study (*e.g.* by topic, area/population, method, results) and thus permits identification of suitable studies for BT. Clearly, this provides a useful function in reducing the search costs of finding transferable studies, which might be considerable for researchers in many countries.

Benefits transfer has been propounded in a number of the guideline documents in the context of specific environmental policy "sectors". One example is the RPA methodology (1998) for application in the water industry in England and Wales. It is intended as a preliminary methodology, a "stop gap" until further research is undertaken, and within these terms of reference it has been used to generate crude value indicators. The applications of this methodology include the appraisal of proposals for river and groundwater abstractions, reservoir construction and use and so on. Adjusted transfer values are categorised into "low", "medium" and "high" and are expressed in readily aggregated units of measure such as UK pounds (GBP) per kilometre of river affected per annum or GBP per kilometre per household per annum. Impact categories include the welfare gains or losses of anglers, day-trippers and non-users (in a 60 km radius). Table 17.1 provides an illustration of the unit values arising from this methodology.

Table 17.1. **An illustration of the RPA methodology**

Location	Access	Facilities	Bound	Value (GBP/km/yr)
Urban	Accessible along whole reach of river	Good facilities and considered a "honeypot" site	Upper	GBP 8 000
	Access to only part of river reach	Some to limited facilities	Central	GBP 4 000
	Limited access	Few to no facilities	Lower	GBP 1 000
Mixed	Accessible along whole reach of river	Good facilities and considered a "honeypot" site	Upper	GBP 8 000
	Access to only part of river reach	Some to limited facilities	Central	GBP 4 000
	Limited access	Few to no facilities	Lower	GBP 1 000
Rural	Accessible along whole or part of river	Good facilities: acts as a local park	Central	GBP 4 000
	Some to limited access	Few	Lower	GBP 1 000

Benefits transfer databases and manuals, in general, are a welcome development in the literature, as those analysts who have spent time searching for values no doubt would testify. There are caveats of course. While the EVRI database seems to constitute a major step in increasing the uptake of benefits transfer, there is still the need for expert judgement and analysis in selecting and adjusting values. In principle, the database provides information on the likely quality of the studies, although how this evaluation might work in practice is less clear at this point in time. That the analyst's job is made much easier and more defensible as the findings of previous valuation studies are systematically distilled and organised, this is generally a welcome addition to the BT "tool-kit".

As regards the RPA methodology, while its relative ease of calculation means that the approach can be widely practised, many analysts might blanche at the potential over-simplicity of this approach. Perhaps the most worrying aspect is that this work has run ahead of any serious and sustained effort to validate whether and when benefits transfer works in this context in England and Wales. But much depends on how the data are being used as well as whether resulting summary values are based on an abundance of good quality evidence or not. To the extent that values such as those in Table 17.1 simply are being "pulled off-the-shelf" and applied unadjusted then the questions that arise are what degree of accuracy is being sacrificed (by ignoring important determinants of WTP) and whether this inaccuracy is tolerable given the policy uses to which the analysis is being put to. The latter question in particular, while interesting, is not straightforward to answer. There is some cause for optimism yet there are also cautionary tales. Hence, we return to this issue in Section 17.4 below. The general lesson is that benefits transfer database approaches are to welcomed but it would be worthwhile allying these efforts to the establishment of widely agreed and authoritative protocols as to what is best practice with regards to using catalogued values. Moreover, as Box 17.1 indicates there is a risk that, without such provision, decisions based on this type of approach and subjected to official scrutiny will be found wanting.

17.4. The validity of benefits transfer

Why might benefits transfer not always be a valid procedure? One example arises from concerns about the merits (or otherwise) of transferring values in the literature on health and safety valuation. As an illustration of this debate, a recent study by the UK Home Office (HO) sought to estimate the aggregate yearly burden (*i.e.* cost) of criminal offending in England and Wales (Brand and Price, 2000). One important component of these burdens arises from violent crime. Specifically, victims suffer an array of tangible (*e.g.* financial) and intangible (*e.g.* psychological and physical distress) losses when they are subjected to a crime involving violence. Given that intangible losses are essentially non-market costs – and given that studies that have sought to value these impacts in England and Wales (at that time) were absent, the HO study values each (statistical) crime victim's injury by borrowing values from non-crime – *i.e.* road transport – contexts for equivalent injury categories (*e.g.* black-eyes, broken limbs etc.).

The issue surrounding this example of benefits transfer is that there are good reasons to think that people's WTP to reduce crime risks could be very different than their WTP to reduce road transport risks. Such insights are relatively well known from the risk perception literature. There is growing and parallel recognition that degree to which a particular health and safety risk is perceived as voluntary, well understood and easy to control could be a significant determinant of WTP (Bateman *et al.*, 2000). Of course, in the

Box 17.1. **Benefits transfer and the policy process: The case of the River Kennet**

Cost-benefit analysis is practised with varying degrees of sophistication. If it is poorly executed, critics will use poor practice as a basis for criticising the technique *per se*. The risks of poor practice are highest in benefits transfer since the temptation to use existing studies to provide estimates for "new" sites is strong : it saves the costs of an original study and is highly suited to approaches based on guidelines and manuals of practice. An interesting illustration of such problems arose with the public inquiry into Thames Water Company's proposal to extract borehole water from near the River Kennet in England. The proposal was opposed by the Environment Agency (for England and Wales) on the grounds that the abstractions would affect the flow of the Kennet. The Agency chose to use benefit assessment as its main case against Thames Water, adopting economic valuations recorded in an existing "benefits manual". No original study was carried out with respect to the Kennet. In this case there was only one such study and it related to the River Darent in Kent (*e.g.* Garrod and Willis, 1996). The Darent study was itself of interest because non-use values, i.e. willingness to pay for flow improvement by individuals who did not visit the Darent at all, amounted to just under 90% of the total benefits. The public expenditure part of the Darent low flow alleviation was not fully authorised by government, even though they had received the Darent benefit assessment study which showed benefits greatly exceeding costs. Garrod and Willis (1996) speculate that failure to secure the full authorisation arose from scepticism about the non-use value estimates in the Darent study. Despite this experience, the Environment Agency borrowed the Darent study estimates for both use and non-use values and applied them to the Kennet. The risks in such an exercise are considerable, and the problem was compounded by multiplying the individual non-use values per person by an arbitrary population defined as the population served by the Thames Water company. The end result was that Thames Water's appeal against the Agency's original restriction on abstraction was upheld by a public inquiry. The Inquiry Inspector reduced the non-use value component of the Kennet benefits by 98% to just GBP 0.3 million compared to GBP 13.2 million as estimated by the Agency. The adjustment reflected the reduction of the "affected" non-use population from the 7.5 million people in the Thames Water area to just 100 000.

For some, the Kennet decision was a serious blow to CBA. But an alternative view is that the Agency was pursuing a risky misuse of CBA by borrowing figures from a manual which in turn had to rely on just one, albeit well-executed, study of a single river. Benefits transfer is controversial in its own right and few practitioners adopt it without serious reservations. Misusing benefits transfer is not a criticism of CBA in itself. The proper course of action in the Kennet case should have been an original benefit assessment. But the controversy has focused attention of an important issue of how to define the relevant population for non-use values, a subject that is still debated in the literature.

case of the HO study, benefits transfer was all that was available if economic appraisal was not to be wholly silent on an important component of the costs of violent crime. Yet, this is only an interim measure at best. Put another way, benefits transfer in this case is not an alternative to original crime-based valuations.

In the example above, the problem for benefits transfer was that while the goods being measured in the original study and new policy study superficially appear to be similar (*e.g.* broken limbs in each instance), it may be the case that the goods are actually dissimilar.

This could be the case if people care about the cause of the incident. While a plausible assertion, it is worth noting that not all studies have found that the cause of some impact is a significant determinant of WTP. (See Chapter 14 for an assessment of the direct evidence on this issue to date.) Ready *et al.* (2004a), for example, do not find that specifying the cause of an ill-health episode influences respondents' stated WTP to avoid five illness episodes of varying severity across a number of European countries. (See Box 17.2 for a fuller description of this contingent valuation study.)

Generally speaking, however, there has been growing concern that existing studies – in both the health and the environmental valuation fields – have been used as the basis for transfers to goods which are actually divergent in terms of the equivalence of their likely WTP values. This apparent dissimilarity can be a complicated matter. As discussed previously, it may be that study sites and policy sites have different features such as socioeconomic and demographic characteristics of the respective populations. Such differences can be taken account of, perhaps by benefit function transfer. Less straightforward to control for are instances where the cause of, for example, an environmental problem, how it would be avoided or how money (to cover the costs of a proposal) would be collected are the source of differences in WTP. However, even in these instances, meta-analysis may be able to sort out the implications of these differences for WTP. The greatest challenge is where differences in WTP are based on wholly unobserved differences in preferences. Box 17.2 provides a pan-European example where this was one plausible reason for the findings of the study.

This example investigates a question of some practical importance. That is, can values be transferred across countries? There are few estimates of non-market values outside of the USA and certain countries in Europe for many categories of environmental and other non-market goods. How then are we to take account of these goods in the appraisal of projects in developing countries where the data are currently scarce? Original studies are one option. But this is expensive and there is a clear potential for cost savings if benefit/value estimates (or functions) can be developed that can be transferred from data-rich countries to countries, which are data-poor primarily because they lack the economic resources needed to fill this informational gap. Interestingly, transfers between countries are routinely undertaken by, for example, The World Bank (Silva and Pagiola, 2003).

A small number of studies have looked at this question of the validity of transfers from developed to developing countries. Barton and Mourato (2003) describes the findings of two comparable CV surveys which elicited WTP to avoid ill-health symptoms associated with exposure to polluted coastal water in Portugal and Costa Rica. Unfortunately, the findings of this single transfer study are far from encouraging. Statistically significant differences were found for three ill-health states investigated with transfer errors in the range of 87-130%. Alberini *et al.* (1997) find that in an original study of WTP to avoid morbidity episodes in Taiwan, transferring WTP values from the US results in, on balance, a reasonable approximation of their findings at the study site (*i.e.* Taiwan). However, the authors find that adjusting the WTP value to be transferred did not appear to have any marked effect on accuracy relative to the unadjusted case. We return to this latter finding later in this chapter.

The example in Box 17.2 is one (large-scale example) of a growing number of studies that have sought to test the validity of the benefits transfer. Another illustration is described in Box 17.3. This examines the important question of the temporal reliability of

Box 17.2. **Valuing health in the European Union – Are values consistent across countries?**

Richard Ready *et al.* (2004b) examine whether when benefit transfer is attempted between two countries unique problems can arise, even where the goods being valued are identical. First, there are likely to be differences between the countries in the measurable characteristics of the populations. However, such differences can be taken account of when transferring values. Second, and more worryingly, there may be differences in preferences not related to measurable differences in demographics, associated with for example differences in cultures or shared experiences. By their very (unobservable) nature, these differences cannot be straightforwardly taken account of.

The Ready *et al.* study seeks to estimate and compare the benefits of a specific improvement in health as measured in simultaneous contingent valuation surveys conducted in five different European countries: England, Norway, Portugal, the Netherlands and Spain. Five identical illness episodes of varying severity formed the basis of this cross-country comparison: *i*) itchy eyes (lasting one day); *ii*) coughing (one day); *iiii*) home bed-rest (three days); *iv*) accident and emergency room visit and home bed-rest (five days); and, *v*) hospital admission (three days) and home bed-rest (five days). Respondents were told to assume that they would, with certainty, experience the episode some time within the near future but could, with certainty, avoid it by paying some amount of money.

Before values can be compared across countries, they must first be translated into a common currency. Translation of values from pesetas (Spain), escudos (Portugal), kroner (Norway) and guilder (Netherlands) into UK pounds (the common currency used in this study) is somewhat more complicated than simple use of financial exchange rates. The correct exchange rate to use when converting WTP values is the exchange rate that holds purchasing power constant, rather than the exchange rate seen in financial markets. However, for three of the countries involved in this study the surveys were conducted in large cities (Oslo, Amsterdam, and Lisbon) rather than the country as a whole, where price levels tend to be higher than the respective national averages. Using national average PPP values would overvalue WTP in those countries and so where possible this should be taken into account as well.

Comparing results across countries, the most relevant reference point is expected WTP for a "standard" individual: that is, a respondent in each country of identical age, gender, income and so on. Clear patterns emerge, with Spain and Portugal having the highest WTP, England having the lowest WTP, and Norway and the Netherlands having intermediate WTP. This pattern holds for all of the ill-health episodes valued. If differences in WTP could be mostly explained by observable differences in characteristics of the populations in the five study countries then WTP to reduce each symptom – for a standard individual – should be more or less the same. However, given the fact that clear differences persist it would appear that there are divergences in preferences as well.

WTP values. In a sense, what this is asking is how old can a valuation study be – upon which WTP values are based – before it is no longer "accurate". What all such validation tests are doing is to carry out an original study at the policy site as well. The proposed value to be transferred can then be compared with the value that was obtained from the primary study. A successful indication of the overall merits of the transfer is clearly indicated by whether or not the transferred value and the primary estimate are similar judged on the basis of some (statistical or other) criterion or criteria. Bateman *et al.* (2000) argue that if

---

Box 17.3. **Temporal reliability of transfer estimates**

An important check of the reliability of WTP estimates, from stated preference studies, is temporal stability of these values. As discussed in Chapter 8, "test-retest" studies – which seek to estimate WTP at a study site after some time has elapsed since an initial and comparable study – have indicated that WTP values are relatively stable over time. This is encouraging for a number of reasons. However, from the perspective of benefits transfer, it suggests that the findings from older studies can continue to be used to evaluate contemporary policy or project proposals.

Most of these studies have evaluated stability over a two-year interval. A study by Brouwer and Bateman (2005) examines WTP over a five-year interval. Contingent valuation surveys were carried out in 1991 and 1996 holding constant the area in which the survey was administered – the Norfolk Boards – and the environmental good that was valued as well as its provision – flood protection ensuring wetland conservation and recreational amenity. Temporal reliability of values was investigated by applying a variety of tests of statistical equality of unit WTP values and WTP functions obtained at each of these two different points in time (i.e. 1991 and 1996).

The authors find that, even after taking account of inflation and changes in purchasing power that occur between the dates of the two studies, the balance of evidence suggests there are significant differences between WTP values obtained in 1991 and 1996, with mean WTP increasing significantly in real terms over the period. In addition, the determinants of WTP are somewhat different between the two periods as well. However, the authors note that their conclusions about the temporal reliability of these estimates are also rather sensitive to the type of statistical test used to detect differences. As such a conclusion of this study – echoed elsewhere in the benefits transfer literature – is for more research on the consistency of these tests used to scrutinise the validity of transfer exercises.

sufficient comparisons can be made and found to be "similar" then this is eventually a justification for assuming that transferred values can be used without the need to validate them with primary studies.

Benefits transfer tests are typically used to measure how large any error will tend to be. To do this, each site in a BT test is, in turn, treated as the "target" or policy site of a transfer, that is, each is treated as the site for which a benefits estimate is needed. The transferred estimate is then compared to the own-study estimate for the target site, and the transfer error can be calculated as follows:

$$\text{Transfer error} = \frac{(\text{transferred estimate} - \text{own-study estimate})}{\text{own-study estimate}} \times 100$$

As an illustration of the implications of a benefits transfer test for assessing the accuracy of this practice, we discuss in more detail the findings of the Ready et al. (2004b) health valuation study described in Box 17.2. Table 17.2 shows the average absolute transfer error for each of the three transfer methods described earlier in this chapter, when the goal is to predict average WTP in a particular country. This test consisted of valuing five ill-health states (of varying symptom severity and duration) in four European countries (Portugal, England, the Netherlands and Norway).* The transfer error here refers to the

---

* This transfer error calculation excludes Spain.

percentage difference between a transferred estimate of WTP and the estimate obtained in the country itself. In other words, the average transfer error in the table refers to roughly how much inaccuracy is entailed, on average, when a value from any one of these ill-health states is transferred from a group of three countries to a fourth country. Interestingly, the results indicate that when the goal is to predict average WTP in a country, the three different transfer methods performed equally well (or poorly). That is, the level of sophistication of the transfer method does not alter conclusions as to the likely size of the transfer error. On average, a transfer from a group of three countries to a fourth country resulted in an over- or under-estimate of about 38%.

Table 17.2. **Performance of transfer methods – an example**

%

	Average Transfer Error
Value (naïve) transfer	38
Value transfer with income adjustment	37
Value/benefit function transfer	39

Source: Ready et al. (2004b).

Broader reviews of benefit transfer tests by Brouwer (2000) and Rosenberger and Loomis (2003) have summarised the findings of a number of studies that have looked at recreational resources, water quality improvements and landscape amenities. Distilling a message from simple value transfers is not straightforward. Some of these studies indicate that transfer error ranges are small while other studies indicate that these ranges are extremely large.

As described in Table 17.2, value function transfer tests appear to perform little better in terms of reducing transfer errors (although there are exceptions). Brouwer (2000) speculates that one problem is likely to be the generally low explanatory power of WTP functions. That is, much of the variability of stated WTP values is not explained by, for example, the additional information that is gathered about respondents' socio-economic/ demographic characteristics. Other variables of possible importance could be included if these data are collected at both the study site and the policy site. These could include uses/ experiences of a recreational resource. However, some variables might not be easily observable or quantifiable. Rosenberger and Loomis (2003) note that such interpretations of benefits transfer tests have given an additional impetus to efforts to measure policy and study site characteristics.

One interesting development is the use of Geographical Information Systems (GIS). For example, Lovett et al. (1997) outline the potential benefits of this approach in the context of recreational value transfers. GIS offers one means of obtaining considerable improvements in recreational demand modelling via greater accuracy in calculating travel times and description of available substitutes to a particular recreational resource. To the extent that data availability permits, GIS offers a way of routinely and comprehensively tackling such geographical issues through detailed mapping and so on.

Finally, at least one study finds that values obtained from pooled data (i.e. more than one study site) and transferred to a target site leads to a smaller error range than transfers based on a single study site value only. This finding (if a generality) might be interpreted as suggesting that a benefits transfer based on one original study only is likely to be less valid than those based on broader evidence (see also Box 17.1).

Notwithstanding this understandable and vital concern for improving the accuracy of benefit transfers, it is also worth asking how much transfer error policy-makers (or analysts) are willing to expose themselves to in order to inform better policy advice. One interpretation is that whether these (and other) margins of error should be considered "large" or "too large" might depend on the use of the results. For some project and policy applications it is probably acceptable for errors of the magnitude suggested in Table 17.2. Indeed, Ready *et al.* (2004b) argue that, as a practical matter, relative to other sources of uncertainty in a policy analysis, the scale of error that they find is probably acceptable. Any uncertainty of the final results can be dealt with through sensitivity analysis.

Figure 17.1. **Continuum of decision settings and the required accuracy of a benefits transfer**

Low				High
Gains in knowledge	Screening/Scoping	Policy decisions	Compensatory damages	

Source: Brookshire (1992).

There is a legitimate discussion to be had regarding how much accuracy is required. An early but valuable contribution to the benefits transfer literature by Brookshire (1992) provides more detail as to what this might imply. Figure 17.1 indicates that if the objective of a benefits transfer study is to gain more knowledge about some benefit at a policy site or provide an initial assessment of the value of policy options (*i.e.* scoping/screening) then it may be that a relatively low level of accuracy is acceptable. Once the analyst moves towards undertaking a transfer study to inform an actual policy decision or resource damage compensation litigation then a greater degree of accuracy is arguably desirable. In such cases, presumably, either compelling evidence for the validity of benefits transfer needs to exist or an original valuation may be warranted.

17.5. Summary and guidance for decision-makers

Transfer studies are the bedrock of practical policy analysis in that only infrequently are policy analysts afforded the luxury of designing and implementing original studies. In general then, analysts must fall back on the information that can be gleaned from past studies. This is likely to be no less true in the case of borrowing or transferring WTP values to policy questions involving environmental or related impacts. Almost inevitably, benefits transfer introduces subjectivity and greater uncertainty into appraisals in that analysts must make a number of additional assumptions and judgements to those contained in original studies. Of course, the same could be said of almost any modelling exercise. The key question is whether the added subjectivity and uncertainty surrounding the transfer is acceptable and whether the transfer is still, on balance, informative.

Surprisingly given its potentially central role in environmental decision-making, there are no generally accepted practical transfer protocols to guide analysts. It is likely, however, that these will emerge in the near future given the progress made in establishing, for example, US and UK guidelines for stated preference studies.

However, a number of elements of what might constitute best practice in benefits transfer might include the following. First, the studies included in the analysis must themselves be sound. Initial but crucial steps of any transfer are very much a matter of carefully scrutinising the accuracy and quality of the original studies. Second, in conducting a benefits transfer, the study and policy sites must be similar in terms of population and population characteristics. If not then differences in population, and their implications for WTP values, need to be taken into account. Just as importantly, the change in the provision of the good being valued at the two sites also should be similar. This particular consideration raises many issues including that of whether the context in which a good is being provided is an important determinant of WTP. Of course, this consideration is not without its problems. As we have discussed previously, there is speculation that one reason why a number of prominent transfer tests have indicated a lack of accuracy lies in the difficultly of adequately taking account of all relevant differences between study sites and policy site.

The holy grail of benefits transfer is the consolidation of data on non-market values in emerging transfer databases (such as EVRI). Yet, while databases are to be welcomed and encouraged, these developments still need to be treated with some caution. This is because an interim conclusion of much of the benefits transfer literature is that the validity and accuracy of benefits transfer can be questioned. Thus, there is a widely acknowledged need for more research to secure a better understanding of when transfers work and when they do not as well as developing methods that might lead to transfer accuracy being improved. However, it is clear that this agenda unavoidably would entail conducting considerable new research. Yet, if adequate knowledge about validity is desired, then this is the investment cost that is needed to realise this objective.

In the meantime, it is arguable that it would be too cautious, not to say naïve, to propose that practitioners hoping to transfer say WTP values should await this new evidence. However, a competent application of transfer methods demands informed judgement and expertise and sometimes, according to more demanding critics, as advanced technical skills as those required for original research. At the very least, it suggests that practitioners should be explicit in their analysis about important caveats regarding a proposed transfer exercise as well as take account of the sensitivity of their recommendations to changes in assumptions about economic values based on these transfers.

ISBN 92-64-01004-1
Cost-Benefit Analysis and the Environment
Recent Developments
© OECD 2006

Chapter 18

Cost-benefit Analysis and Other Decision-making Procedures

CBA is often contrasted with other decision-making aids such as cost-effectiveness analysis (CEA) and multi-criteria analysis (MCA). But the assumption that these aids are substitutable is not valid and great care is needed in defining the question to be asked and in determining which technique is most relevant to helping with the decision. This chapter provides an overview of various techniques. In addition to CEA and MCA it looks at risk assessment, environmental impact assessment, strategic environmental assessment, risk-benefit, risk-risk, and health-health analysis. Each of these approaches reveals insights into features of good decision-making, but CBA tends to have a more comprehensive approach.

18.1. A gallery of procedures

This volume is concerned with recent developments in cost-benefit analysis (CBA). In Chapter 19 we look at some of the reasons that some decision-makers are distrustful of CBA. This distrust is one reason (and it is important to understand it may not be the dominant reason) that some people look for alternatives to CBA. Other reasons for looking for alternatives include:

- A desire to have decision-aiding procedures that are not so demanding in informational terms.

- A desire to have procedures that can be widely understood and which are not reliant on expert.

- A desire to have "rapid" procedures given that political decisions cannot always wait for the results of a CBA.

Over the years, various techniques of appraisal have emerged in the environmental field. We list these as:

- Environmental Impact Assessment (EIA) or Environmental Assessment (EA).
- Strategic Environmental Assessment (SEA).
- Life Cycle Analysis (LCA).
- Risk Assessment (RA).
- Comparative Risk assessment (CRA).
- Risk-Benefit Analysis (RBA).
- Risk-Risk Analysis (RRA).
- Health-Health Analysis (HHA)
- Cost-Effectiveness Analysis (CEA).
- Multi-Criteria Analysis (MCA).

In the remainder of this chapter we look very briefly at each of these procedures. Space forbids a detailed assessment which can be found, for example, in EFTEC (1998). The idea is simply to "locate" CBA in this range of procedures. It is important to understand that the procedures vary significantly in their comprehensiveness and that it cannot be assumed that each is a substitute for the other.

18.2. Environmental Impact Assessment (EIA)

EIA is a systematic procedure for collecting information about the environmental impacts of a project or policy, and for measuring those impacts. It will immediately be obvious that EIA is not a comprehensive evaluation procedure. It ignores non-environmental impacts and it ignores costs. Less obviously, it may not account in a detailed way for the ways in which impacts vary with time. Nonetheless, EIA is an essential part of any evaluative procedure. If we use the benchmark of CBA, then EIA is an essential input to

CBA. CBA covers the other impacts of projects and policies, and it goes one stage further than EIA by attempting to put money values on the environmental impacts. Most EIAs do make an effort, however, to assess the significance of environmental impacts. Some may go further and give the impacts a score (the extent of the impact) and a weight (its importance). Weights might be derived from public surveys but more usually are determined by the analyst in question. Unlike CBA, EIA has no formal decision rule attached to it (*e.g.* benefits must exceed costs), but analysts would typically argue that its purpose is to look at alternative means of minimising the environmental impacts without altering the benefits of the project or policy.

In general, then:

- EIA is an essential input to any decision-making procedure.

- Impacts may be scored and weighted, or they become inputs into a CBA.

- EIA would generally look for ways to minimise environmental impacts without changing (significantly anyway) the benefits or costs of the project or policy.

18.3. Strategic Environmental Assessment (SEA)

SEA is similar to EIA but tends to operate at a "higher" level of decision-making. Instead or single projects or policies, SEA would consider entire programmes of investments or policies. The goal is to look for the synergies between individual policies and projects and to evaluate alternatives in a more comprehensive manner. An SEA is more likely than an EIA to consider issues like: is the policy or project needed at all; and, if it is, what are the alternative options available? In this sense, SEA is seen to be more pro-active than EIA which tends to be reactive. Proactive here means that more opportunity exists for programmes to be better designed (from an environmental perspective) rather than accepting that a specific option is chosen and the task is to minimise environmental impacts from that option. Again, while it encompasses more issues of concern, SEA remains non-comprehensive as a decision-guiding procedure. Issues of time, cost and non-environmental costs and benefits do not figure prominently. Relative to the benchmark of CBA, SEA goes some way to considering the kinds of issues that would be relevant in a CBA – *e.g.* the "with/without" principle and consideration of alternatives.

18.4. Life Cycle Analysis (LCA)

LCA is similar to EIA in that it identifies the environmental impacts of a policy or project and tries to measure them. It may or may not measure the impacts in the same units, any more than EIA tries to do this. Typically, when attempts are made to adopt the same units they do not include money, although some LCAs have done this. The chief difference between EIA and LCA is that LCA looks not just at the impacts directly arising from a project or policy, but at the whole "life cycle" of impacts. For example, suppose the policy problem is one of choosing between the "best" forms of packaging for a product, say fruit juice. The alternatives might be cartons, bottles and cans. LCA would look at the environmental impacts of each option but going right back to the materials needed for manufacturing of the container (*e.g.* timber and plastics, glass, metals) and the ways in which they will be disposed of once consumers have consumed the juice. Included in the analysis would be the environmental impacts of primary resource extraction and the impacts from landfill, incineration etc. LCAs proceed by establishing an inventory of impacts and then the impacts are subjected to an assessment to establish the extent of impact and the weight to be attached to it. Relative to the benchmark of CBA, LCA is essentially the physical counterpart to the kind of environmental impact analysis that is required by a CBA. In itself LCA offers no obvious decision rule for policies or projects. Though widely advocated as a comprehensive decision-guidance, LCA does not (usually) consider non-environmental costs and benefits. Hence it is not a comprehensive decision-guide. However, if the choice context is one where one of several options has to be chosen (we must have cans or bottles or cartons, but not none of these), then, provided other things are equal, LCA operates like a cost-effectiveness criterion (see below).

18.5. Risk Assessment (RA)

Risk assessment involves assessing either the health or environmental risks (or both) attached to a product, process, policy or project. Risk assessments may be expressed in various ways:

- As the probability of some defined health or ecosystem effect occurring, *e.g.* a 1 in 100 000 chance of mortality from continued exposure to some chemical.

- As a number of incidences across a defined population, *e.g.* 10 000 premature deaths per annum out of some population.

- As a defined incidence per unit of exposure, *e.g.* X% increase in premature mortality per unit air pollution.

- As a "no effect" level of exposure, *e.g.* below one microgram per cubic metre there may be no health effect.

Risk assessments may not translate into decision rules very easily. One way they may do this is if the actual or estimated risk level is compared to an "acceptable" level which in turn may be the result of some expert judgement or the result of a public survey. A common threshold is to look at unavoidable "everyday" risks and to judge whether people "live with" such a risk. This may make it acceptable. Other procedures tend to be more common and may define the acceptable level as a no-risk level, or even a non-risk level with a sizeable margin or error. Procedures establishing "no effect" levels, *e.g.* of chemicals, define the origin of what the economist would call a "damage function" but cannot inform decision-making unless the goal is in fact to secure that level of risk. Put another way, "no effect" points contain no information about the "damage function".

18.6. Comparative Risk Assessment (CRA)

CRA involves analysing risks but for several alternative projects or policies. The issue is then which option should be chosen and the answer offered by CRA is that the option with the lowest risk should be chosen. Efforts are made to "normalise" the analysis so that like is compared to like. For example, one might want to choose between nuclear energy and coal-fired electricity. One approach would be to normalise the risks of one kilowatt hour of electricity and compute, say, deaths per kWh. The option with the lowest "death rate" would then be chosen. However, in this case, the normalisation process does not extend to cost, so that CRA may want to add a further dimension, the money cost of generating one kWh. Once this is done, the focus tends to shift to cost-effectiveness analysis – see below. A further problem concerns the nature of risk. "One fatality" appears to be a homogenous unit, but if people are not indifferent to the manner of death or whether it is voluntarily or involuntarily borne, then, in effect, the normalisation has failed. Once again, one can see that CRA is not a comprehensive decision-guide since the way it treats costs (if at all) may not be all-embracing. Nor would CRA deal with benefits.

18.7. Risk-Benefit Analysis (RBA)

RBA tends to take two forms, each of which is reducible to another form of decision rule. In other words, RBA is not a separate procedure. The first meaning relates to benefits, costs and risks, where risks are treated as costs and valued in money terms. In that case the formula for accepting a project or policy would be:

[Benefits – Costs – Risks] > 0

This is no different to a CBA rule.

In the second case the RBA rule reduces to CRA. Benefits might be standardised, *e.g.* to "passenger kilometres" and the risk element might be fatalities. "Fatalities per passenger kilometre" might then be the thing that should be minimised. As with CRA, cost may or may not enter the picture. If it does, then RBA tends to result in CBA or cost-effectiveness analysis.

18.8. Risk-Risk Analysis (RRA)

RRA tends to focus on health risks and asks what would happen to health risks if some policy was adopted and what would happen if it was not adopted. The "with/without" focus is familiar in CBA. The novelty tends to be the fact that not undertaking a policy may itself impose costs in terms of lives or morbidity. For example, a policy of banning or lowering consumption of saccharin might have a justification in reducing health risks from its consumption. But the with-policy option may result in consumers switching to sugar in place of the banned saccharin, thus increasing morbidity by that route. The advantage of RRA is that it forces decision-makers to look at the behavioural responses to regulations. Once again, however, all other components in a CBA equation are ignored, so the procedure is not comprehensive.

18.9. Health-Health Analysis (HHA)

HHA is similar to RRA but instead of comparing the risks with and without the behavioural reaction to a policy, it compares the change in risks from a policy with the risks associated with the *expenditure* on the policy. As such, it offers a subtle focus on policy that is easily overlooked. Since policies costs money, the money has to come from somewhere and, ultimately, the source is the taxpayer. But if taxpayers pay part of their taxes for life-saving policies, their incomes are reduced. Some of that reduced income would have been spent on life-saving or health-enhancing activities. Hence the taxation actually increases life risks. HHA compares the anticipated saving in lives from a policy with the lives lost because of the cost of the policy. In principle, policies costing more lives than they save are not desirable. HHA proceeds by estimating the costs of a life-saving policy and the number of lives saved. It then allocates the policy costs to households. Life risks are related to household incomes through regression analysis, so that it is possible to estimate lives lost due to income reductions. Once again, the procedure is not comprehensive: policies could fail an HHA test but pass a CBA test, and *vice versa*.

18.10. Cost-Effectiveness Analysis (CEA)

The easiest way to think about CEA is to assume that there is a single indicator of effectiveness, E, and this is to be compared to a cost of C. Suppose there is now just a single project or policy to be appraised. CEA would require that E be compared to C. The usual procedure is to produce a cost-effectiveness ratio (CER):

$$CER = \frac{E}{C} \qquad\qquad [18.1]$$

Notice that E is in some environmental unit and C is in money units. The fact that they are in different units has an important implication which is, unfortunately, widely disregarded in the literature. A moment's inspection of [18.1] shows that the ratio is perfectly meaningful – *e.g.* it might be read as US Dollars per hectare of land conserved. But the ratio says nothing at all as to whether the conservation policy in question is worth undertaking. In other words, CEA cannot help with the issue of whether or not to undertake any conservation. It should be immediately obvious that this question cannot be answered unless E and C are in the same units.

CEA can only offer guidance on which of several alternative policies (or projects) to select, given that one has to select one. By extension, CEA can *rank* any set of policies, all of which could be undertaken, but given that at least some of them must be undertaken. To see the limitation of CEA, equation [18.1] should be sufficient to show that an entire list of policies, ranked by their cost-effectiveness, could be adopted without any assurance that any one of them is actually worth doing. The notion of "worth doing" only has meaning if one can compare costs and benefits in a manner that enables one to say costs are greater (smaller) than benefits. In turn, that requires that costs and benefits have a common *numeraire* which, in principle, could be anything. In CBA the numeraire is money.

If we suppose that there are i = 1...n potential policies, with corresponding costs C_i and effectiveness E_i then CEA requires that we rank the policies according to

$$CER_i = \frac{E_i}{C_i} \qquad\qquad [18.2]$$

This ranking can be used to select as many projects as fit the available budget $\bar{C}$, *i.e.*:

$$Rank \quad by \quad CER_i \quad s.t \quad \sum_i C_i = \bar{C} \qquad\qquad [18.3]$$

A further issue with CEA is the process of selecting the effectiveness measure. In CBA the principle is that benefits are measured by individuals' preferences as revealed by their willingness to pay for them. The underlying value judgement in CBA is "consumer" or "citizen sovereignty". This amounts to saying that individuals are the best judges of their own well-being. Technically, the same value judgement could be used in CEA, *i.e.* the measure of effectiveness could be based on some attitude survey of a random sample of individuals. In practice, CEA tends to proceed with indicators of effectiveness chosen by experts. Rationales for using expert choices are *a)* that experts are better informed than individuals, especially on issues such as habitat conservation, landscape, etc., and *b)* that securing indicators from experts is quicker and cheaper than eliciting individuals' attitudes.

18.11. Multi-Criteria Analysis (MCA)

MCA is similar in many respects to CEA but involves multiple indicators of effectiveness. Technically, CEA also works with multiple indicators but increasingly resembles simple models of MCA since different effectiveness indicators, measured in different units, have to be normalised by converting them to scores and then aggregated via a weighting procedure. Like CEA, policy or scheme cost in an MCA is always (or should always be) one of the indicators chosen. The steps in an MCA are as follows:

● The goals or objectives of the policy or investment are stated.

● These objectives are not pre-ordained, nor are they singular (as they are in CBA which adopts increases in economic efficiency as the primary objective) and are selected by "decision-makers".

● Generally, decision-makers will be civil servants whose choices can be argued to reflect political concerns.

● MCA then tends to work with experts' preferences. Public preferences may or may not be involved.

● "Criteria" or, sometimes, "attributes" which help achieve the objectives are then selected. Sometimes, objectives and criteria tend to be fused, making the distinction difficult to observe. However, criteria will generally be those features of a good that achieve the objective.

● Such criteria may or may not be measured in monetary terms, but MCA differs from CBA in that not all criteria will be monetised.

● Each option (alternative means of securing the objective) is then given a score and a weight. Pursuing the above example, a policy might score 6 out of 10 for one effect, 2 out of 10 for another effect, and 7 out of 10 for yet another. In turn, experts may regard the first effect as being twice as important as the second but only half as important as the third. The weights would then be 2, 1 and 4 respectively.

● In the simplest of MCAs, the final outcome is a weighted average of the scores, with the option providing the highest weighted score being the one that is "best". More sophisticated techniques might be used for more complex decisions.

● To overcome issues relating to the need for criteria to be independent of each other (*i.e.* experts' preferences based on one criterion should be independent of their preferences for that option based on another criterion), more sophisticated techniques might be used, notably "multi-attribute utility theory" (MAUT). MAUT tends to be over-sophisticated for most practical decision-making.

The formula for the final score for a project or policy using the most simple form of MCA is:

$$S_i = \sum_j m_j . S_j \qquad [18.4]$$

where i is the ith option, j is the jth criterion, m is the weight, and S is the score.

MCA offers a broader interpretation of CEA since it openly countenances the existence of multiple objectives. Issues relating to MCA and which are the subject of debate are as follows:

● As with CEA, when effectiveness is compared to cost in ratio form MCA cannot say anything about whether or not it is worth adopting any project or policy at all (but see Annex 18.A1). Its domain is restricted to choices between alternatives in a portfolio of options some of which must be undertaken. Both MCA and CEA are therefore "efficient" in the sense of seeking to secure maximum effectiveness for a given unit of cost, but may be "inefficient" in the sense of economic efficiency. Annex 18.A1 illustrates the problem further and shows that MCA produces the same result as a CBA only when a) the scores on the attributes are the same, b) the weights in the MCA correspond to shadow prices in the CBA, and c), which follows from b), the weight on cost is unity.

- MCA generally proceeds by adopting scores and weights chosen by experts. To this extent MCA is not as "accountable" as CBA where the money units reflect individuals' preferences rather than expert preferences. Put another way, the raw material of CBA is a set of individuals' votes, albeit votes weighted by income, whereas experts are unelected and may not be accountable to individual voters.

- MCA tends to be more "transparent" than CBA since objectives and criteria are usually clearly stated, rather than assumed. Because of its adoption of multiple objectives, however, MCA tends to be less transparent than CEA with a single objective.

- It is unclear how far MCA deals with issues of time discounting and changing relative valuations.

- Distributional implications are usually chosen as one of the objectives in an MCA and hence distributional impacts should be clearly accommodated in an MCA.

18.12. Summary and guidance for decision-makers

A significant array of decision-guiding procedures are available. This chapter shows that they vary in the degree of comprehensiveness where this is defined as the extent to which all costs and benefits are incorporated. In general, only MCA is as comprehensive as CBA and may be more comprehensive once goals beyond efficiency and distributional incidence are considered. All the remaining procedures either deliberately narrow the focus on benefits, e.g. to health or environment, or ignore cost. Procedures also vary in the way they treat time. EIA and LCA are essential inputs into a CBA, although the way these impacts are dealt with in "physical terms" may not be the same in a CBA. Risk assessments, of which HHA and RRA are also variants, tend to be focused on human health only. The essential message is that the procedures are not substitutes for each other.

ANNEX 18.A1

Multi-criteria Analysis and the "Do Nothing" Option

For the "do nothing" option to be included correctly in an evaluation it is necessary for costs and benefits to be measured in the same units. When MCA adopts the form of cost-effectiveness, with the multiple criteria of effectiveness being compared *in ratio form* to cost, then MCA cannot evaluate the "do nothing" option. This is because the units of effectiveness are weighted scores whilst the measure of cost is money. Numerator and denominator are not in the same units. The "escape" from this problem is for costs to be given a score (usually the absolute level of money cost) and a weight. If we think of the weighted scores as "utils" (or any other unit of account) then MCA can handle the "do nothing" option. If the ratio of benefits to costs is less than unity, the "do something" option is rejected. Similarly, if utils of benefits minus utils of costs is negative, the do something option would also be rejected.

In this way, MCA can be modified to handle the do nothing option. However, it can easily be shown that MCA will give the same result as CBA under very limited conditions.

Table 18.A1.1 shows the procedure adopted in a simple MCA. Let the score for E1 be 10, E2 = 5 and E3 = 30. The scores are multiplied by chosen weights, assumed to be W1 = 4, W2 = 6, W3 = 10. Cost is weighted at unity. The sum of the weighted scores shows that "do something" is a "correct" choice. If the weights W1 ... W3 are prices, then Table 18.A1.1 would appear as a CBA, *i.e.* MCA and CBA would produce formally identical results.

Table 18.A1.1. **Weighted input data for an MCA: cost weighted at unity**

	Do something: raw scores	Do something: weighted scores
Cost	-50	-50
E1	+10	+40
E2	+5	+30
E3	+30	+300
Sum of (weighted) scores	-5	+320

Table 18.A1.1 shows that the selection of weights is important. An "unweighted" approach (which means raw scores are weighted at unity) would reject the policy but the weighted approach would accept it. As long as the weights in Table 18.A1.1 correspond to the prices in a CBA, however, then CBA and MCA would generate the same result.

Finally, if we assume shadow prices and MCA weights are the same, but that the weight applied to cost in the MCA is, say, 8, then weighted cost would appear as –400 in Table 18.A1.1 and weighted MCA would reject the do something option.

We can summarise the conditions for CBA and MCA to generate the same result:

a) Attribute scores must be the same.

b) MCA weights must correspond to shadow prices and, in particular.

c) Costs must be weighted at unity.

ISBN 92-64-01004-1
Cost-Benefit Analysis and the Environment
Recent Developments
© OECD 2006

Chapter 19

The Political Economy of Cost-benefit Analysis

CBA works with a well-defined "objective function" – the thing to be maximised. But this is unlikely to coincide with what political bodies actually do. This chapter reviews the goals that political entities might actually maximise (the "political welfare function") and shows why the resulting decisions are likely to diverge from those using CBA. The reasons for this divergence are then explored. It remains important to present CBA results in their un-politicised form so that any gaps between actual and efficient decisions can be identified.

19.1. The issue

The methodology of cost-benefit analysis (CBA) has been developed over a long period of time. It has also been subjected to many criticisms, as has its theoretical basis – welfare economics. Nonetheless, most (though certainly not all) economists continue to recommend the use of CBA as a "decision-informing" procedure. They would argue that, even if decisions are not finally made on the basis of CBA, decisions should be informed by CBA such that it is at least an input into decision-making, Many governments adopt that view as well, and there are numerous publications offering guidelines and manuals for the implementation of CBA – see Section 1.4. One immediate virtue of CBA is that its procedures have been very carefully thought through. That does not make it necessarily superior to other procedures for decision-making, but it does suggest that any recommended alternative should be subjected to similar critical analysis.

But if CBA commands widespread consensus from most economists, why are policy and investment decisions often made in manners inconsistent with CBA? This is a question of *political economy*. Economists' theoretical prescriptions are rarely met in practice. The main reason for this disparity between theory and practice is fairly obvious: governments cannot simply design policy measures without taking account of political realities. First, what economists may regard as an "optimal" instrument design tends to serve one overriding goal – *economic efficiency*. Political reality demands that other goals, which are not necessarily consistent with each other, also play a part in practical design and implementation. Second, governments are not all-knowing, all powerful guardians of social well-being in the manner usually assumed in textbooks. Rather, they have to contend with pressure groups and lobbies which, in turn, represent sets of conflicting interests. Put another way, the "social welfare function" that underlies CBA is not the same as the social welfare function that politicians adopt. As a result, actual policy and "optimal" policy rarely coincide. This "gap" is very much the subject of a political economy approach to policy analysis. One political economy issue is therefore to explain why actual policy design diverges from the alleged optimal design of those policies according to CBA.

The remainder of this chapter surveys recent suggestions as to why there is a divergence between optimal and actual policy design.

19.2. Political welfare functions

Chapters 1 and 2 explained that CBA works with a very precise notion of *economic efficiency*. A policy is efficient if it makes at least some people better off and no-one worse off, or, far more realistically, if it generates gains in well-being for some people in excess of the losses suffered by other people. These notions correspond to Pareto improvements and potential Pareto improvements. In turn, well-being (welfare, utility) is defined by people's preferences: well-being is increased by a policy if gainers prefer the policy more than losers "disprefer" it. Finally, preferences are measured by willingness to pay (accept) and this facilitates aggregation across the relevant population: the numeraire is money. The underlying social welfare function consists of the aggregate of individuals' changes in well-being and would typically take a form such as the following:

$$\Delta SW = \sum_{i,t} \Delta W_{i,t} \qquad [19.1]$$

where Δ signifies "change in", W is well-being and ΔW can be positive for some individuals and negative for others, i is the ith individual and t is time (discounting is ignored, for convenience). For a policy to pass a CBA test ΔW > 0.

Political economy suggests that actual decisions are not made on the basis of this social welfare function. While it is possible to suggest many different formulations, a function such as the following captures the essence of what might happen in practice (Grossman and Helpman, 1994; Aidt, 1998).

$$\Delta PW = \alpha \sum_{i,t} \Delta W_{i,t} + (1-\alpha) \sum_{n,t} \Delta W_{n,t} \qquad [19.2]$$

In this case there are two broad groups in society: individuals i, as in the CBA function, and "interested parties" or "pressure groups", n. To emphasise the difference, political welfare, "PW" is substituted for "SW". The weights α and $(1 - \alpha)$ reflect the strength of political regard for social well-being and the well-being of interest groups. In the limit, if $\alpha = 1$ the PW function is equivalent to the SW function. If $\alpha = 0$ then government is totally "captured" by interest groups, as in early models of political economy (Becker, 1983).[1] Note that interest groups can be pro- or anti-environmental so that political decisions may over- or under-regulate for environmental quality. The conditions for successful organisation of lobbies are not of direct relevance here – Olson (1965) remains the *locus classicus* in this respect.

While simplistic in many respects, the contrast between the two welfare functions immediately explains why CBA may be rejected at the political level: it simply fails to capture the various pressures on governments in making decisions. In turn, governments are sensitive to those pressures for their own reasons which may be a simple as staying in power or a concern to "buy" support in order to realise some social or economic programme. The essential point is that the textbook recommendation is formulated in a context that is wholly different from the political context. Of course, explaining differences does not justify them and the role of CBA remains one of explaining how a decision should look if the economist's social welfare function approach is adopted. Ultimately, there are no meta-rules for selecting social welfare functions beyond arguing for their "reasonableness" or the extent to which they might command consensus.

19.3. Efficiency as a social goal

Suppose now that politicians were everywhere persuaded of the need to adopt a social welfare function that was sensitive to the wishes of voters independently of any interest group or pressure group. Then the social welfare function could look like the textbook example above or it could be different because of the rejection of the notion of economic efficiency underlying the economist's welfare function. There are many ways in which a social welfare function sensitive to individuals' wishes could be devised. One example, widely countenanced in the literature involves accepting the general notion of a welfare function above, but rejecting the idea that willingness to pay (WTP) is a socially relevant measure of gain or loss. WTP is self-evidently affected by income or wealth. In general, the higher is income the higher is WTP. The economic efficiency social welfare function does not therefore accord "equal votes" to individuals. Rather it weights individual votes by income, and to many that seems unfair. As noted in Chapter 2, allowing for this unfairness is consistent with changing the social welfare function so that it takes the form:

$$\Delta wSW = \sum_{i,t} \lambda_{i,t} \Delta W_{i,t}$$

[19.3]

The notation is as before, but the lower case "w" reminds us that we are looking at a distributionally weighted social welfare, and the λs are now the weights to be attached to different groups in society. Typically, political regimes with a strong concern for low income groups and vulnerable groups (*e.g.* the aged) would attach high λs to those groups, and lower weights to other groups. These distributional concerns show up in various government guidelines (*e.g.* see the UK Treasury's "Green Book" guidance (UK HM Treasury 2002), or US EPA's guidance on environmental justice (US EPA 1998)).

Adoption of a distributionally weighted welfare function would effectively mean that the notion of economic efficiency underlying the orthodox CBA formula is being rejected, or at least modified. Actual decisions based on this welfare function will not therefore necessarily pass a CBA test. On the other hand, as Chapter 2 noted, the general guideline documents on CBA issued in the 1970s by OECD, UNIDO and the World Bank all contained this distributionally weighted welfare function. The issue is not so much rejecting CBA as choosing a different form of it. Nonetheless, if the issue is one of observing policies that fail a CBA test, one reason for that failure may well be the dominance given to distributional considerations.

19.4. Welfare and self-interest

On the face of it, the notion of economic efficiency underlying CBA rests on individuals' maximising their own self-interest. This appears to follow from the way in which individuals' "utility functions" are described in economics textbooks. Usually, they are presented in the form of U = U(X) where X is some vector of goods and services consumed by the individual. This portrayal of how individuals decide on issues can be contrasted with a public interest "ideal" whereby decisions are made in terms of what is best for society as a whole. Those who believe that political decisions are not about meeting individuals' self interests but are about maximising the "good" of society are therefore likely to reject an economic calculus based on self-interest. This is the view, for example, of Sagoff (1988, 2004). On this view, the proper procedure is to ensure that the context of decision-making is one where citizens' preferences are expressed. That context would appear to be the political arena, not the outcome of a context where, say, CBA experts collect questionnaires from respondents who are asked for their stated preferences.

The basis of this view is not always clear, however. On the one hand, it could be an argument about how decisions are actually made, and on the other about how decisions should be made. In the former case, which is the one relevant to the political economy argument, those who argue that CBA does not determine political decisions are saying that CBA rests on self interest but political decisions do not. But it is far from clear that preferences revealed in the political process are any less self-interested and more public-spirited than those revealed by the same people in the marketplace or in hypothetical questionnaires. The political social welfare function above would be a case in point.

If the argument is that CBA decisions *are* based on self-interest but political decisions *should not* be based on self-interest, then the debate is an ethical one. That issue is relevant to the political economy issue of why CBA is not adopted because what may be happening is that the underlying value judgment in CBA – that individuals' preference should count – is being rejected in the political arena. However, there is nothing in the notion of a utility function or in CBA that declares actual preferences and choices to be made solely on the basis of self-interest. Indeed, the notion of "total economic value" (Chapter 6) quite explicitly acknowledges bequest values and existence values which are other-related expressions of value. Revealed economic values may reflect the individual speaking on his/her behalf, on behalf of their family, on behalf of society in general, or on behalf of future generations. It has been argued that hypothetical questionnaire approaches to willingness to pay – contingent valuation – elicit not self-interested preferences but "warm glow" or "moral satisfaction" (Kahneman and Knetsch, 1992). Even if true, this is not an argument for calling such values "non-economic" – see Harrison (1992). It is not essential for preferences to be motivated by pure self interest for them to qualify for economic relevance, a point that has been made fairly often in the economics literature from Arrow (1951), through Becker (1993), to Hanemann (1996).

19.5. Money as the numeraire

Just as the *perception* that CBA is based on self-interest alone may explain some of the hostility towards CBA, and hence a reluctance to be guided by it, so the role of money as numeraire in CBA causes further perceptual problems. The underlying theory of CBA is clear in that money is simply the numeraire, the means where preferences are expressed and choices made. But expressing maximands in terms of money clearly can cause misperceptions that money *per se* is the objective that is being maximized, rather than well-being. For all kinds of cultural, religious and historical reasons, money is identified with greed and avarice. Basing decision guidance on a calculus expressed in terms of money thus risks a false word association and the resulting picture thinking.

19.6. Interest groups again

The political welfare function introduced above makes explicit recognition of the fact that, desirably or not, interest groups influence political decisions. In turn, interest groups may be multi-objective or single objective in their aims. An environmental pressure group, for example, may have a single objective in pursuing the goal of environmental quality but can be multi-objective in embracing many different types of environmental goal. An interest group with these goals will tend to have the belief that environmental assets are somehow "different" and should not be subject to trade-offs. Academic studies which claim that individuals do not trade-off environment and other goods – so called "lexical preferences" – give some comfort to this view. Hostility to CBA arises because it is thought that the use of a money metric "debases" the environment, making it appear as if it is as saleable as a supermarket good. The obvious economic response is that environmental conservation is not costless and any cost is a foregone benefit since the resources that make up cost could have been used elsewhere. In turn, forgone benefits embrace potential rights or obligations: perhaps the right to a livelihood, the right to work, the right to health care etc. (Beckerman and Pasek, 1997). Opportunity cost therefore "embodies" rights and obligations, so that the correct ethical context is one of trade-offs between rights and obligations.

Nonetheless, if the issue is one of explaining why actual and economically optimal policy prescriptions diverge, the rejection of or refusal to consider trade-offs can be very important. Since trade-offs are, as indicated above, logically unavoidable, the issue becomes one of trying to explain how pressure groups and politicians can ignore them. The political economy literature suggests the following explanations.

First, from the standpoint of the pressure group, the goal is the lexical objective. In terms of its own welfare function, the pressure group is placing a very low, even zero, weight on any other set of objectives. But it can only place a low weight on the costs of its actions, *e.g.* the cost of a stricter environmental policy, if it does not bear those costs directly. Since environmental policy has a very strong public good nature, policy costs are shared very broadly in society and do not fall disproportionately on the pressure group. As such, the pressure group has no incentive to take account of costs in an economically rational manner. It acts as a free rider. On the other hand, politicians as public trustees presumably should consider cost. Their incentive to ignore it can arise from several sources. Whilst fairly obviously a political fiction, politicians may prefer to believe that cost is unimportant if it facilitates a politically comfortable stance. Facing up to trade-offs means confronting pressure groups in one form or another. Adopting what appear (falsely) to be "win win" strategies in which no one appears to be made worse off is far more convenient. Hence politicians may not always face up to the problems of making hard choices. One other source of influence leading to a neglect of cost can be the law itself. Notably in environmental policy areas, "no cost" doctrines have emerged which argue that the state as trustee of the people has a legal obligation to secure specific environmental goals regardless of cost. This "public trust" philosophy has been notable in some US liability cases relating to hazardous waste sites and oil pollution (see Chapter 16). While an economist would argue that such legal notions are themselves invalid because of the neglect of cost, the doctrines lend support to the notion that politicians need not always take account of cost.

Overall, it is quite possible that politicians and pressure groups will rationalise a refusal to consider trade-offs of the kind that CBA was explicitly designed to confront. As such, a rejection of trade-offs, rational or not, implies a rejection of CBA.[2]

19.7. Flexibility in politics

CBA is, quite explicitly, a normative procedure. It is designed to prescribe what is good or bad in policy-making. But politics can be thought of as the art of compromise, of balancing the various public and specialised interests embodied in the political welfare function. If, in the extreme, all decisions were to be made on the basis of CBA, decision-makers would have no flexibility to respond to the various influences that are at work demanding one form of policy rather than another. In short, CBA, or, for that matter, *any* prescriptive calculus, compromises the flexibility that decision-makers need in order to "act politically". Unsurprisingly, they will therefore give low weight to decision-making processes that embrace a high profile for CBA.

19.8. Is CBA participatory?

Where the political system is sensitive to the public interest there is likely to be emphasis on consultation and participation. If, on the other hand, CBA appears to be non-participatory, there could be serious objections to giving it high profile in decision-making. As it happens, while participation is often seen as an end in itself, it is also a necessary ingredient for economic efficiency. The reason for this is that lack of participation can easily engender opposition to a project or policy, making it difficult to implement and costly to reverse. Participation may also produce better policy and project design since those most affected are closer to the issue than analysts and decision-makers. In the economic development literature, it is well established that development projects are more likely to succeed if communities and gender groups are involved in the process. Appraisal techniques are often criticised because they may omit this participatory feature of decision-making. Stated preference approaches (see Chapters 8 and 9), however, have an important role to play in securing participation, a role that emanates directly from the fact that techniques elicit all kinds of information about attitudes, motivations, preferences and willingness to pay. In short, CBA should be wholly consistent with public participation since CBA rests on the basis of recording and valuing public preferences.

But the meaning of the term "participation" is not always clear and one reason why CBA may be rejected for actual decision-making is that what is meant by participation differs from the meaning in terms of recording individuals' preferences. At least three versions of the term appear: a) participation as consultation, i.e. taking account of the preferences of affected parties; b) participation as influence, i.e. ensuring that affected parties influence the direction and form of the project or policy; and c) participation as benefit-sharing, i.e. ensuring that affected parties receive a share of the resulting benefits. Frequently what is meant by participation is not the recording of public preferences, but the need to consult with pressure groups who would otherwise stand in the way of policy. It is senses b) and c) above that matter in political decision-making rather than sense a). Yet a) is what underlies CBA whereas b) and c) are not accorded status in CBA. In consequence, CBA may appear to be non-participatory and can be rejected or downgraded as a result.

19.9. Uncertainty

CBA may be afforded low status in decision-making because it appears to be very uncertain. Where benefits can be measured in money terms, valuations may often appear to have unacceptably high ranges of confidence. In some cases benefits may not be measurably in money terms.

The standard defence of CBA would emphasise arguments along the following lines. Social science data are not like "physical" data. While both are subject to uncertainty, social science data are far more probabilistic since they reflect the behaviour of millions of individuals. Thus uncertainty is endemic to social science. In terms of choosing between decision-making guidance, however, uncertainty per se is not the issue. What matters is whether any one form of guidance is more uncertain than the others. This "baseline" issue is usually ignored in debates over uncertainty – it is far from clear that CBA scores any worse on grounds of uncertainty than any other decision-guiding techniques. Even if CBA is more uncertain than other techniques, it does not follow that some alternative technique is better. The greater uncertainty of CBA is simply being exchanged for a somewhat illusory certainty, illusory because it is achieved by ignoring other factors that should bear on how to make decisions. Consider CBA "versus" risk assessment. CBA may appear to be more uncertain than risk assessment because the money values appear to add to the variables that are uncertain. Risk assessment avoids monetary assessment and hence reduces the level of uncertainty. But it does so by sacrificing a basic requirement of decision-rules, namely conveying whether something is good or bad, desirable or undesirable. In effect, risk assessment conveys no idea of whether any decision is "correct" because it offers no absolute standard against which good or bad is measured.

A second source of uncertainty of relevance to CBA is that pertaining to stated preference methodologies. These approaches, which are increasingly used in cost-benefit studies, are thought by some to *add* to the uncertainty in CBA. The reason for this is that the questionnaires are hypothetical and hence the answers are hypothetical. The hypothetical nature of the questionnaire is not itself a criticism. After all, the reason hypothetical questions are being asked is invariably because there are no "real" markets for the analyst to refer to. If the real markets existed, there would be no need to ask hypothetical questions. Nonetheless, the answers could be biased (upwards or downwards, but more usually it is thought the bias is upwards). The issue becomes one of finding out how likely it is that the hypothetical answers diverge from the respondents' "true" WTP. To this end, stated preference techniques adopt many tests of validity – see Chapters 8 and 9. But bias is likely to remain. This may not matter too much if there is some idea of the direction of bias and its probable scale. Research suggests that there is an upwards bias in WTP responses, but it is not easy to say what the scale of this bias is. In some cases, questionnaires are very good predictors of what people will actually choose – as with election opinion polls.

While arguments of the kind advanced above may be valid, the feeling that questionnaire answers are not reliable indicators of true preferences remains. As far as the political economy question is concerned, what matters is how the uncertainty in CBA is *perceived*, not whether it can be justified or not. Similarly, the baseline issue is difficult to convey: uncertain as CBA is, the alternatives may be even more uncertain.

19.10. Economic literacy

A further obstacle to the acceptance and use of CBA is the fact that, like all economic techniques, it requires an input of time and effort in order to understand the underlying rationale and some of the technical details. However well trained decision-makers are, there will always be a residual element that does not invest time in trying to understand CBA. This may reflect unwillingness, prior training in other disciplines, perceptions about problems with CBA, or, simply limited time. One distinguished economic advisor in the UK remarked, for example, on the distinction between:

> "the theorists who seek to trap the inner secrets of the economy in their models and the practitioners who live in a world of action where time is precious, understanding is limited, nothing is certain and non-economic considerations are always important and often decisive" (Cairncross, 1985).

CBA, with its elaborate theoretical underpinnings and reasonably well-defined but extensive rules for valid implementation, may therefore be too complex for the busy civil servant. The situation will be worse if there are policies of appointing non-economists to positions at the higher end of the decision-making hierarchy, or if economic advice is regarded as an "appendage" to higher-level decision-making. There are two views of such situations: a) that they reflect a poor understanding of the relevance of CBA, and economic techniques in general, or b) that the decision-making structure itself reflects the distrust that is felt about economic evaluation techniques.

Henderson (1985) notes a very different problem of getting economics into decision-making processes. While economists are very much aware of the rigorous discipline needed to understand even basic economics, non-economists, and especially scientists and lawyers, frequently are not. Both disciplines are used to the notion of acquiring other disciplinary knowledge on a fairly casual basis, with notable exceptions. The result is what Henderson calls "Do it Yourself Economics", a body of beliefs that appears to resemble economic knowledge but is invariably at odds with economic science. Henderson remarks:

"All over the world, ideas and beliefs which owe nothing to recognized economics textbooks still retain their power to influence people and events" (Henderson, 1985, p. 11).

With respect to CBA there are two outcomes. Either CBA is ignored because the "do it yourself" economist "knows better", or some watered down form of CBA is adopted. The latter shows up particularly in the adoption of decision-making procedures that are either incomplete or just as problematic as CBA (if not more so). Examples include life cycle analysis, cost-effectiveness and multi-criteria analysis – see Chapter 18. All have a role to play but none of them can answer all the questions that CBA can answer. But, even if this viewpoint is accepted, "do it yourself" economics opens the way to embracing such techniques which are less difficult to understand. For the advocate of CBA the challenge is to understand why DIY economics occurs.

19.11. Summary and guidance for decision-makers

Political economy, or "political economics", seeks to explain why the economics of the textbook is rarely embodied in actual decision-making. As discussed above, the reasons lie in the role played by "political" welfare functions rather than the social welfare functions of economics, distrust about or disbelief in monetisation, the capture of political processes by those not trained in economics, beliefs that economics is actually "common sense" and easily understood, and, of course, genuine mistrust of CBA and its theoretical foundations based on the debates that continue within the CBA community and outside it. But explaining the gap between actual and theoretical design is not to justify the gap. Theoretical economists need a far better understanding of the pressures that affect actual decisions, but those who make actual decisions perhaps also need a far better understanding of economics.

Notes

1. The political economy literature largely began by assuming that interest groups captured most regulatory processes. Later, the existence of "public interest" motives on the part of politicians was readmitted, thus producing a "PW" notion of the kind presented here. See, for example, Kalt and Zupan (1984).

2. One might add that while the notion of a trade-off, or opportunity cost, is the most fundamental principle of economics, some agents in political debates act as if they are not aware of it. The arguments in the text above concern situations in which the agent is aware but has an incentive to ignore it.

ISBN 92-64-01004-1
Cost-Benefit Analysis and the Environment
Recent Developments
© OECD 2006

References

Adamowicz, W., J. Louviere and J. Swait (1998), *Introduction to Attribute-Based Stated Choice Methods*, Final Report to NOAA, US.

Adamowicz, W.L., V. Bhardwaj and B. Macnab (1993), "Experiments on the Difference Between Willingness to Pay and Willingness to Accept", *Land Economics*, Vol. 69, No. 4, pp. 416-427.

AEA Technology (1999), *Cost-Benefit Analysis for the Protocol to Abate Acidification, Eutrophication and Ground Level Ozone in Europe,* Publication No. 133, The Hague, Ministry of Housing, Spatial Planning and the Environment.

AEA Technology (1998a), *Cost-Benefit Analysis of Proposals under the UNECE Multi-Pollutant Multi-Effect Protocol,* Report to UK Department of Environment, Transport and Regions, London and to UNECE Task Force on Economic Aspects of Abatement Strategies, Geneva.

AEA Technology (1998b), *Economic Evaluation of the Control of Acidification and Ground Level Ozone,* Report to DGXI of the European Commission, Brussels, European Commission.

AEA Technology (1998c), *Economic Evaluation of Air Quality Targets for CO and Benzene,* Report to DGXI of the European Commission, Brussels, European Commission.

AEA Technology (1998d), *Cost-Benefit Analysis for the Protocol to Abate Acidification, Eutrophication and Ground Level Ozone in Europe*, Ministry of Housing, Spatial Planning and the Environment, The Hague, Netherlands, Publication No. 133.

Agee M.D. and T. Crocker (2005), "Transferring Measures of Adult Health Benefits to Children: Some Issues and Results", in *Economic Valuation of Environmental Health Risks to Children*, OECD, Paris, forthcoming.

Agee M.D. and T. Crocker (2001), "Smoking Parents' Valuations of own and Children's Health", Paper presented at the Association of Environmental and Resource Economists conference, Bar Harbor, Maine, 13-15 June, 2001.

Aidt, T. (1998), "Political Internalisation of Economic Externalities and Environmental Policy", *Journal of Public Economics*, Vol. 69, pp. 1-16.

Aimola, A. (1998), "Individual WTPs for Reductions in Cancer Death Risks", in R. Bishop and D. Romano (eds.), *Environmental Resource Valuation: Applications of the Contingent Valuation Method in Italy,* Dordrecht, Kluwer, pp. 196-212.

Alberini, A., M. Cropper, A. Krupnick and N.B. Simon (2004), "Does the Value of Statistical Life Vary with Age and Health Status? Evidence from the US and Canada", *Journal of Environmental Economics and Management,* Vol. 48, pp. 769-792.

Alberini, A., M. Cropper, T.-T. Fu, A. Krupnick, J.-T. Liu, D. Shaw and W. Harrington (1997), "Valuing Health Effects of Air Pollution in Developing Countries: The Case of Taiwan", *Journal of Environmental Economics and Management*, Vol. 34, No. 2, pp. 107-126.

Albers, H., A. Fisher and W. Hanemann (1996), "Valuation and Management of Tropical Forests: Implications of Uncertainty and Irreversibility", *Environmental and Resource Economics,* No. 8, pp. 39-61.

Arabsheibani, R. and A. Marin (2000), "Stability of the Estimates of the Compensation for Danger", *Journal of Risk and Uncertainty*, Vol. 20, No. 3, pp. 247-269.

Arrow, K. (1951) (2nd edition 1963), *Social Choice and Individual Values*, New York, Wiley.

Arrow, K., G. Daily, P. Dasgupta, S. Levin, K.-G. Maler, E. Maskin, D. Starrett, T. Sterner and T. Tietenberg (2000), "Managing Ecosystem Resources", *Environmental Science and Technology,* Vol. 34, pp. 1401-1406.

Arrow, K. and A. Fisher (1974), "Environmental Preservation, Uncertainty and Irreversibility", *Quarterly Journal of Economics,* Vol. 88, pp. 312-319.

Arrow, K., R. Solow, P. Portney, E. Leamer, R. Radner and H. Schuman (1993), *Report of the NOAA Panel on Contingent Valuation*, Federal Register, Vol. 58, No. 10, pp. 4016-4064.

Arthur, W. (1981), "The Economics of Risks to Life", *American Economic Review*, Vol. 71, pp. 54-64.

Asheim, G.B. (1994), "Net National Product as an Indicator of Sustainability", *Scandinavian Journal of Economics*, Vol. 96, pp. 257-265.

Atkinson, G., B. Day, S. Mourato and C. Palmer (2004a), "'Amenity' or 'Eyesore'? Negative Willingness to Pay for Options to Replace Electricity Transmission Towers", *Applied Economic Letters*, Vol. 14, No. 5, pp. 203-208.

Atkinson, G., W.R. Dubourg, K. Hamilton, M. Munasinghe, D.W. Pearce and C.E.F. Young (1997), *Measuring Sustainable Development: Macroeconomics and Environment*, Cheltenham, Edward Elgar.

Atkinson, G. and K. Hamilton (2003), "Savings, Growth and the Resource Curse Hypothesis", *World Development*, Vol. 31, No. 11, pp. 1793-1807.

Atkinson, G., F. Machado and S. Mourato (2000), "Balancing Competing Principles of Environmental Equity", *Environment and Planning A*, Vol. 32, No. 10, pp. 1791-1806.

Barbier, E., A. Markandya and D.W. Pearce (1990), "Environmental Sustainability and Cost-Benefit Analysis", *Environment and Planning A*, Vol. 22, pp. 1259-1266.

Barton, D.N. and S. Mourato (2003), "Transferring the Benefits of Avoided Health Effects from Water Pollution between Portugal and Costa Rica", *Environmental and Development Economics*, Vol. 8, pp. 351-371.

Bateman, I., R.T. Carson, B. Day, M. Hanemann, N. Hanley, T. Hett, M. Jones-Lee, G. Loomes, S. Mourato, E. Ozdemiroglu, D.W. Pearce, R. Sugden and J. Swanson (2002), *Economic Valuation with Stated Preference Techniques: A Manual*, Cheltenham, Edward Elgar.

Bateman, I., A.P. Jones, N. Nishikawa and R. Brouwer (2000), *Benefits Transfer in Theory and Practice: A Review and Some New Studies*, Norwich, Centre for Social and Economic Research on the Global Environment (CSERGE) and School of Environmental Sciences, University of East Anglia.

Bateman I., B. Rhodes, C. Starmer and R. Sugden (1997), "A Test of the Theory of Reference-Dependent Preferences", *The Quarterly Journal of Economics*, Vol. 112, No. 2, pp. 479-505.

Beattie, J., J. Covey, P. Dolan, L. Hopkins, M. Jones-Lee, G. Loomes, N. Pidgeon, A. Robinson and A. Spencer (1998), "On the Contingent Valuation of Safety and the Safety of Contingent Valuation: Part 1 – *Caveat Investigator*", *Journal of Risk and Uncertainty*, Vol. 17, pp. 5-25.

Becker, G. (1993), "Nobel Lecture: the Economic Way of Looking at Behaviour, *Journal of Political Economy*, Vol. 101, No. 3, pp. 385-409.

Becker, G. (1983), "A Theory of Competition among Pressure Groups for Political Influence", *Quarterly Journal of Economics*, Vol. 98, pp. 371-400.

Beckerman, W. and J. Pasek (1997), "Plural Values and Environmental Valuation", *Environmental Values*, Vol. 6, pp. 65-86.

Beggs, S., S. Cardell and J. Hausman (1981), "Assessing the Potential Demand for Electric Cars", *Journal of Econometrics*, Vol. 16, pp. 1-19.

Belli, P., J. Anderson, H. Barnum, J. Dixon and J.-P. Tan (1998), *Handbook on Economic Analysis of Investment Operations*, Washington DC, The World Bank.

Ben-Akiva, M., T. Morikawa and F. Shiroishi (1991), "Analysis of the Reliability of Preference Ranking Data", *Journal of Business Research*, Vol. 23, pp. 253-268.

Bergson, A. (1938), "A Formulation of Certain Aspects of Welfare Economics", *Quarterly Journal of Economics*, Vol. 52, No. 2, pp. 310-334.

Biller, D. (ed.) (2001), *Valuation of Biodiversity Benefits: Selected Studies*, OECD, Paris.

Bishop, R. (1978), "Endangered Species and Uncertainty: The Economics of a Safe Minimum Standard", *American Journal of Agricultural Economics*, Vol. 60, pp. 10-18.

Boadway, R. (1974), "The Welfare Foundations of Cost-Benefit Analysis, *Economic Journal*, Vol. 84, pp. 926-939.

Boardman, A., D. Greenberg, A. Vining and D. Weimer (2001), *Cost–Benefit Analysis: Concepts and Practice*, 2nd edition, Upper Saddle River, New Jersey, Prentice Hall.

Bockstael, N., A.M. Freeman, R. Kopp, P. Portney and V.K. Smith (2000), "On Valuing Nature", *Environmental Science and Technology*, Vol. 34, No. 8, pp. 1384-1389.

Bohara, A.K., J. Kerkvliet and R.P. Berrens (2001), "Addressing Negative Willingness to Pay in Dichotomous Choice Contingent Valuation", *Environmental and Resource Economics*, Vol. 20, pp. 173-195.

Boyle, K.J. (2003), "Introduction to Revealed Preference Methods", in P.A. Champ, K.J. Boyle and T.C. Brown (eds.), *A Primer on Nonmarket Valuation*, Dordrecht, Kluwer, pp. 259-268.

Boyle, K.J. and J.C. Bergstrom (1992), "Benefits Transfer Studies: Myths, Pragmatism and Idealism", *Water Resources Research*, Vol. 28, No. 3, pp. 657-663.

Brand, S. and P. Price (2000), "The Economic and Social Costs of Crime", Research Study 217, London, Home Office.

Brent, R. (1996), *Applied Cost-Benefit Analysis*, Cheltenham, Edward Elgar.

Bresnahan, B.W., M. Dickie and S. Gerking (1997), "Averting Behaviour and Urban Air Pollution", *Land Economics*, Vol. 73, No. 3, pp. 340-357.

Brookshire, D.S. (1992), "Issues Regarding Benefits Transfer", paper presented at the Association of Environmental and Resource Economists Workshop, Utah, June 1992.

Broome, J. (1992), *Counting the Cost of Global Warming*, Cambridge, White Horse Press.

Brouwer, R. (2000), "Environmental Value Transfer: State of the Art and Future Prospects", *Ecological Economics*, Vol. 32, pp. 137-152.

Brouwer, R. and I. Bateman (2005), "The Temporal Stability of Contingent WTP Values", *Water Resources Research* (in press).

Brouwer, R., I. Langford, I. Bateman and R.K. Turner (1999), "A Meta-analysis of Wetland Contingent Valuation Studies", *Regional Environmental Change*, Vol. 1, No. 1, pp. 47-57.

Brown, T.C., I. Ajzen and D. Hrubes (2003), "Further Tests of Entreaties to Avoid Hypothetical Bias in Referendum Contingent Valuation", *Journal of Environmental Economics and Management*, Vol. 46, No. 2, pp. 353-361.

Bulte, E., M. Joenje and H. Jansen (2000), "Is There Too Much or Too Little Forest in the Atlantic Zone of Costa Rica?", *Canadian Journal of Forest Research*, Vol. 30, pp. 495-506.

Bulte, E., D. van Soest, C. van Kooten and R. Schipper (2002), "Forest Conservation in Costa Rica when Nonuse Benefits are Uncertain and Rising", *American Journal of Agricultural Economics*, Vol. 84, No. 1, pp. 150-160.

Cairncross, A. (1985), "Economics in Theory and Practice", *American Economic Review*, Vol. 75, No. 2, pp. 1-14.

Cairns J. (2005), "Discounting of Children's Health: Conceptual and Practical Difficulties", in *Economic Valuation of Environmental Health Risks to Children*, OECD, Paris, forthcoming.

Carson, R. (1998), "Contingent Valuation Surveys and Tests of Insensitivity to Scope" in R. Kopp, W. Pommerhene and N. Schwartz (eds.), *Determining the Value of Non-Marketed Goods: Economic, Psychological and Policy Relevant Aspects of Contingent Valuation Methods*, Chapter 6, Boston, Kluwer.

Carson, R.T., N. Carson, A. Alberini, N. Flores and J. Wright (1995), *A Bibliography of Contingent Valuation Studies and Papers*, La Jolla, California, Natural Resource Damage Assessment Inc.

Carson, R., N.E. Flores, K. Martin and J. Wright (1996), "Contingent Valuation and Revealed Preference Methodologies: Comparing the Estimates for Quasi-Public Goods", *Land Economics*, Vol. 72, pp. 80-99.

Carson, R.T., N.E. Flores and N.F. Meade (2001), "Contingent Valuation: Controversies and Evidence", *Journal of Environmental and Resource Economics*, Vol. 19, pp. 173-210.

Carson, R.T., T. Groves and M.J. Machina (1999), "Incentive and Informational Properties of Preference Questions", Plenary Address, Ninth Annual Conference of the European Association of Environmental and Resource Economists (EAERE), Oslo, Norway, June.

Carson, R., W.M. Hanemann, R. Kopp, J. Krosnick, R. Mitchell, S. Presser, P. Ruud and V.K. Smith with M. Conaway and K. Martin (1997), "Temporal Reliability of Estimates from Contingent Valuation", *Land Economics*, Vol. 73, pp. 151-163.

Carson, R.T. and R.C. Mitchell (1995), "Sequencing and Nesting in Contingent Valuation Surveys", *Journal of Environmental Economics and Management*, Vol. 28, No. 2, pp. 155-173.

Carson R.T., R.C. Mitchell, M. Hanemann, R.J. Kopp, S. Presser and P.A. Ruud (2003), "Contingent Valuation and Lost Passive Use: Damages from the Exxon Valdez Oil Spill", *Environmental and Resource Economics*, Vol. 25, No. 3, pp. 257-286.

Carthy, T., S. Chilton, J. Covey, L. Hopkins, M. Jones-Lee, G. Loomes, N. Pidgeon and A. Spencer (1999), "On the Contingent Valuation of Safety and the Safety of Contingent Valuation: Part 2 – The CV/SG Chained Approach", *Journal of Risk and Uncertainty*, Vol. 17, pp. 187-213.

CEC (Commission of the European Communities) DGXII, (1995), *ExternE: Externalities of Energy*, Vols. 1-6, Brussels, Commission of the European Communities.

CEC DGXII (1998), *ExternE: Externalities of Energy*, Vols. 7-10, Brussels, Commission of the European Communities.

Champ, P.A., K.J. Boyle and T.C. Brown (eds.) (2003), *A Primer on Nonmarket Valuation*, Dordrecht, Kluwer.

Champ, P.A., N.E. Flores, T. Brown and J. Chivers (2002), "Contingent Valuation and Incentives", *Land Economics,* Vol. 78, No. 4, pp. 591-604.

Chapman, D. and W.M. Hanemann (2004), "Use of Economic Valuation to Establish Compensation under the E.C Environmental Liability Directive", paper presented at "Envecon 2004", Applied Environmental Economics Conference, Royal Society, London, March 26.

Chapman, R.G. and R. Staelin (1982), "Exploiting Rank Ordered Choice Set Data within the Stochastic Utility Model", *Journal of Marketing Research,* Vol. 19, pp. 288-301.

Chichilnisky, G. (1996), "An Axiomatic Approach to Sustainable Development", *Social Choice and Welfare*, Vol. 13, pp. 231–257.

Chilton, S., J. Covey, L. Hopkins, M. Jones-Lee, G. Loomes, N. Pidgeon and A. Spencer (2002), "Public Perceptions of Risk and Preference-based Values of Safety", *Journal of Risk and Uncertainty*, Vol. 25, No. 3, pp. 211-232.

Chilton, S., J. Covey, M. Jones-Lee, G. Loomes and H. Metcalf (2004), *Valuation of Health Benefits Associated with Reductions in Air Pollution: Final Report,* London, Department for Environment, Food and Rural Affairs.

Ciriacy-Wantrup, C.V. (1968), *Resource Conservation: Economics and Policies*, 3rd edition, Berkeley, University of California.

Clinch, P.J. and A. Murphy (2001), "Modelling Winners and Losers in Contingent Valuation of Public Goods: Appropriate Welfare Measures and Econometric Analysis", *Economic Journal*, Vol. 111, pp. 420-443.

Conrad, K. (1999), "Computable General Equilibrium Models for Environmental Economics and Policy Analysis", in van den Bergh, J.C.J.M. (ed.), *Handbook of Environmental and Resource Economics*, Cheltenham, Edward Elgar, pp. 1060-1088.

Corso, P.S., J.K. Hammitt and J.D. Graham (2001), "Valuing Mortality-risk Reduction: Using Visual Aids to Improve the Validity of Contingent Valuation", *Journal of Risk and Uncertainty*, Vol. 23, pp. 165-84.

Costa, D. and M. Kahn (2002), "Changes in the Value of Life 1940-1980", Working Paper 9396, National Bureau of Economic Research.

Costanza, R., R. d'Arge, R. de Groot, S. Farber, M. Grasso, B. Hannon, K. Limburg, S. Naeem, R. O'Neill, J. Paruelo, R. Raskin, P. Sutton and M. van den Belt (1997), "The Value of the World's Ecosystem Services and Natural Capital", *Nature*, Vol. 387, pp. 253-260.

Costello, C. and M. Ward (2003), "Search, Bioprospecting, and Biodiversity Conservation: Comment", Santa Barbara, Donald Bren School of Environmental Science and Management, University of California at Santa Barbara, *mimeo*.

Cowell, F. and K. Gardiner (1999), *Welfare Weights. Report to the Office of Fair Trading*, London, Office of Fair Trading.

Craft, A. and D. Simpson (2001), "The Social Value of Biodiversity in New Pharmaceutical Product Research", *Environmental and Resource Economics*, Vol. 18, No. 1, pp. 1-17.

Cummings, R.G. and L.O. Taylor (1999), "Unbiased Value Estimates for Environmental Goods: a Cheap Talk Design for the Contingent Valuation Method", *American Economic Review*, Vol. 89, No. 3, pp. 649-665.

Cummings, R.G., D.S. Brookshire and W.D. Schulze (eds.) (1986), *Valuing Environmental Goods: An Assessment of the Contingent Valuation Method,* Rowman and Allanhed, Totowa, New Jersey.

Daily, G. (ed.) (1997), *Natures Services: Societal Dependence on Natural Ecosystems*, Washington DC, Island Press.

Dasgupta, A.K. and D.W. Pearce (1972), *Cost-Benefit Analysis: Theory and Practice*, London, Macmillan.

Dasgupta, P. (1982), *The Control of Resources*, Oxford, Blackwell.

Dasgupta, P. and K.-G. Mäler (2000), "Net National Product, Wealth and Social Well-being", *Environment and Development Economics*, Vol. 5, pp. 69-93.

Dasgupta, P., S. Marglin and A. Sen (1972), *Guidelines for Project Evaluation*, Vienna, UNIDO (The "UNIDO Manual").

Day, B. (2002), "Valuing Visits to Game Parks in South Africa", in D.W. Pearce, C. Pearce and C. Palmer (eds.), *Valuing the Environment in Developing Countries: Case Studies*, Cheltenham, Edward Elgar, pp. 236-273.

Day, B. (2001), *The Valuation of Non-Market Goods 2*, Imperial College London, *mimeo*.

de Blaeij, A., R.J.G. Florax and P. Rietveld (2003), "The Value of Statistical Life in Road Safety: a Meta-analysis", *Accident Analysis and Prevention*, Vol. 35, pp. 973-986.

de Graaf, J.V. (1957), *Theoretical Welfare Economics*, Cambridge, Cambridge University Press.

Desvousges, W., F.R. Johnson and H.S. Banzaf (1998), *Environmental Policy Analysis with Limited Information: Principles and Applications of the Transfer Method*, Cheltenham, Edward Elgar.

Desvousges, W. *et al.* (1993), "Measuring Natural Resource Damages with Contingent Valuation: Tests of Validity and Reliability", in J. Hausman (ed.), *Contingent Valuation: A Critical Assessment*, Amsterdam, North-Holland, pp. 91-164.

Diamond, P. (1996), "Discussion of the Conceptual Underpinnings of the Contingent Valuation Method by A.C. Fisher", in D. Bjornstad and J. Kahn (eds.), *The Contingent Valuation of Environmental Resources: Methodological Issues and Research Needs*, Cheltenham, Edward Elgar, pp. 61-71.

Dickie, M. and F. Brent (2002), "Family Behavior and the Economic Value of Parent and Child Health", paper presented at the 2002 World Congress of Environmental and Resource Economists, Monterey, California, June 24-27.

Dickie M. and S. Gerking (2005), "Valuing Children's Health: Parental Perspective", in *Economic Valuation of Environmental Health Risks to Children*, OECD, Paris, forthcoming.

Dickie, M. and S. Gerking (2002), "Willingness to Pay for Reduced Morbidity", Department of Economics Working Paper 02-07, University of Central Florida.

Dickie, M. and S. Gerking (2001), "Parents' Valuation of Latent Health Risks to their Children", Working Paper presented at the US Environmental Protection Agency Workshop "Valuing a Statistical Life: Assessing the State of the Art for Policy Applications", 6-7 November, Silver Spring, Maryland.

Dickie, M. and V.L. Ulery (2001), "Valuing Health in the Household: Are Kids Worth More Than Parents?" Paper presented at the Association of Environmental and Resource Economists 2001 Workshop: "Assessing and Managing Environmental and Public Health Risks", 13-15 June.

Dillingham, A.E., T. Miller and D.T. Levy (1996), "A More General and Unified Measure for Valuing Labour Market Risk", *Applied Economics*, Vol. 28, pp. 537-542.

Dillon, W.R., T.J. Madden and N.H. Firtle (1994), *Marketing Research in a Marketing Environment*, 3rd Edition, Boston, Irwin.

Dinwiddy, C. and F. Teal (1996), *Principles of Cost-Benefit Analysis for Developing Countries*, Cambridge, Cambridge University Press.

Dixit, A. and R. Pindyck (1995), "The Options Approach to Capital Investment", *Harvard Business Review*, May-June, pp. 105-155.

Dixit, A. and R. Pindyck (1994), *Investment Under Uncertainty*, Princeton, Princeton University Press.

Dubourg, W.R., M.W. Jones-Lee and G. Loomes (1997), "Imprecise Preferences and Survey Design in Contingent Valuation", *Economica*, Vol. 64, pp. 681-702.

Dupuit, A.J. (1853), "On Utility and its Measure – On Public Utility", *Journal des Économistes*, Vol. 36, pp. 1-27.

Dupuit, A.J. (1844), "On the Measurement of the Utility of Public Works", (Trans. R. Barback), *International Economic Papers*, Vol. 2, 1952.

Eckstein, O. (1958), *Water Resource Development: the Economics of Project Evaluation*, Cambridge, Mass., Harvard University Press.

ECMT (European Conference of Ministers of Transport) (1998), *Strategic Environmental Assessment in the Transport Sector*, OECD, Paris.

Eeckhoudt, L. and J. Hammitt (2001), "Background Risks and the Value of Statistical Life", *Journal of Risk and Uncertainty*, Vol. 23, No. 3, pp. 261-279.

EFTEC (2003), *The Thames Tideway: Stated Preference Survey*, Report to Thames Water plc, London, EFTEC.

EFTEC (Economics for the Environment Consultancy Ltd) (1998), *Review of Technical Guidance on Environmental Appraisal*, London, Department of Environment, Transport and the Regions.

Elster, J. (1992), *Local Justice: How Institutions Allocate Scarce Goods and Necessary Burdens*, Cambridge, Cambridge University Press.

Fankhauser, S. (1995), *Valuing Climate Change: The Economics of the Greenhouse*, London, Earthscan.

Farmer, M.C. and A. Randall (1998), "The Rationality of a Safe Minimum Standard", *Land Economics*, Vol. 74, No. 3, 287-302.

Fischhoff, B., P. Slovic, S. Lichtenstein, S. Read and B. Combs (1978), "How Safe is Safe Enough? A Psychometric Study of Attitudes towards Technological Risks and Benefits", *Policy Sciences*, Vol. 8, pp. 127-152, reprinted in P. Slovic (ed.), *The Perception of Risk*, London, Earthscan, 2001.

Fisher, A. (2000), "Investment under Uncertainty and Option Value in Environmental Economics", *Resource and Energy Economics*, Vol. 22, pp. 197-204.

Flores, N. and R. Carson (1997), "The Relationship between Income Elasticities of Demand and Willingness to Pay", *Journal of Environmental Economics and Management*, Vol. 33, pp. 287-295.

Florio, M. (2004), *Guide to Cost-Benefit Analysis of Investment Projects*, Brussels, European Commission, DG Regional Policy.

Foster, V. and S. Mourato (2002), "Testing for Consistency in Contingent Ranking Experiments", *Journal of Environmental Economics and Management*, Vol. 44, pp. 309-328.

Foster, V. and S. Mourato (2003), "Elicitation Format and Sensitivity to Scope: Do Contingent Valuation and Choice Experiments Give the Same Results?", *Environmental and Resource Economics,*Vol. 24, pp. 141-160.

Foster, V., I. Bateman and D. Harley (1997), "A Non-experimental Comparison of Real and Hypothetical Willingness to Pay", *Journal of Agricultural Economics*, Vol. 48, No. 2, pp. 123-138.

Frederick, S., G. Loewenstein and T. O'Donoghue (2002), "Time Discounting and Time Preference: a Critical Review", *Journal of Economic Literature*, Vol. XL, pp. 351–401.

Freeman, A.M. III (2003), *The Measurement of Environmental and Resource Values*, 2nd edition, Resources for the Future, Washington, DC.

Garrod, G. and K.G. Willis (1996), "Estimating the Benefits of Environmental Enhancement: A Case Study of the River Darent", *Journal of Environmental Planning and Management*, Vol. 39, pp. 189-203.

Garrod, G. and K.G. Willis (1999), *Economic Valuation of the Environment: Methods and Case Studies*, Cheltenham, Edward Elgar.

Georgiou, S., I.H. Langford, I.J. Bateman and R.K. Turner (1998), "Determinants of Individuals' Willingness to Pay for Perceived Reductions in Environmental Health Risks: A Case Study of Bathing Water Quality", *Environment and Planning A*, Vol. 30, pp. 577-594.

Gerdtham, U.-G. and M. Johannesson (2002), "Do Life-saving Regulations Save Lives?", *Journal of Risk and Uncertainty*, Vol. 24, No. 3, pp. 231-249.

Gittinger, J.P. (1984), *Economic Analysis of Agricultural Projects*, Baltimore, Johns Hopkins University Press.

Gollier, C. (2002), "Discounting an Uncertain Future", *Journal of Public Economics*, Vol. 85, pp. 149-166.

Government of Canada (1995), *Benefit-Cost Analysis Guide for Regulatory Programs*, Ottawa, Canadian Treasury Board Secretariat.

Gowdy, J. (2004), "The Revolution in Welfare Economics and its Implications for Environmental Valuation and Policy", *Land Economics*, Vol. 80, No. 2, pp. 239-257.

Gramlich, E M. (1990), *A Guide to Benefit–Cost Analysis*, 2nd Edition, Prospect Heights, Illinois, Waveland Press.

Green, P. and V. Srinivasan (1978), "Conjoint Analysis in Consumer Research: Issues and Outlook", *Journal of Consumer Research*, Vol. 5, pp. 103-123.

Greene, W.H. (1997), *Econometric Analysis*, 3rd Edition, New York, US, Macmillan.

Grossman, G. and E. Helpman (1994), "Protection for Sale", *American Economic Review*, Vol. 84, pp. 833-850.

Hahn, R. (2000), *Reviving Regulatory Reform: A Global Perspective*, Washington DC, AEI-Brookings Joint Center for Regulatory Studies.

Hamilton, K. (2002), *Sustaining Per Capita Welfare with Growing Population: Theory and Measurement*, Washington, DC, World Bank Environment Department.

Hamilton, K. and G. Atkinson (2006), *Wealth, Welfare and Sustainability: Advances in Measuring Sustainable Development*, Cheltenham, Edward Elgar, forthcoming.

Hamilton, K. and M. Clemens (1999), "Genuine Savings Rates in Developing Countries", *World Bank Economic Review*, Vol. 13, No. 2, pp. 333-356.

Hamilton, K. and J.M. Hartwick (2005), "Investing Exhaustible Resource Rents and the Path of Consumption", *Canadian Journal of Economics*, Vol. 38, No. 2, pp. 615-621.

Hamilton, K. and C. Withagen (2004), "Savings, Welfare and Rules for Sustainability", Washington DC, the World Bank, *mimeo*.

Hammitt, J. (2002), "Commentary on What Determines the Value of Life? A Meta-analysis", *Journal of Policy Analysis and Management*, Vol. 21, No. 2, pp. 271-273.

Hammitt, J. (2000), "Valuing Mortality Risk: Theory and Practice", *Environmental Science and Technology*, Vol. 34, pp. 1396-1400.

Hammitt, J. and J. Graham (1999), "Willingness to Pay for Health Protection: Inadequate Sensitivity to Probability?", *Journal of Risk and Uncertainty*, Vol. 18, pp. 33-62.

Hammitt, J. and J.-T. Liu (2004), "Effects of Disease Type and Latency on the Value of Mortality Risk", *Journal of Risk and Uncertainty*, Vol. 28, No. 1, pp. 73-95.

Hanemann, W.M. (1999), "The Economic Theory of WTP and WTA", in I. Bateman and K. Willis (eds.), *Valuing Environmental Preferences: Theory and Practice of theContingent Valuation Method in the US, EU and Developing Countries*, Oxford, Oxford University Press, pp. 42-96.

Hanemann, W.M. (1996), "Theory *versus* Data in the Contingent Valuation Debate", in D. Bjornstad and J. Kahn (eds.), *The Contingent Valuation of Environmental Resources: Methodological Issues and Research Needs*, Cheltenham, Edward Elgar, pp. 38-60.

Hanemann, W.M. (1991), "Willingness to Pay and Willingness to Accept: How Much Can they Differ?", *American Economic Review*, Vol. 81, pp. 635-647.

Hanemann, W.M. (1984), "Welfare Evaluations in Contingent Valuation Experiments with Discrete Responses", *American Journal of Agricultural Economics*, Vol. 66, pp. 332-341.

Hanemann, W.M. and B. Kanninen (1999), "The Statistical Analysis of Discrete-Response CV Data", in I.J. Bateman and K.G. Willis (eds.), *Valuing Environmental Preferences: Theory and Practice of the Contingent Valuation Method in the US, EU, and Developing Countries*, Oxford, Oxford University Press, pp. 302-441.

Hanley, N. and B. Kriström (2003), "What's It Worth? Exploring Value Uncertainty Using Interval Questions in Contingent Valuation", Department of Economics, University of Glasgow, *mimeo*.

Hanley, N. and C.L. Spash (1993), *Cost Benefit Analysis and the Environment*, Edward Elgar, Cheltenham.

Hanushek, E.A. (1992), "The Trade-off Between Child Quantity and Quality", *Journal of Political Economy*, Vol. 100, No. 1, pp. 84-117.

Harrison, G.W. (1992), "Valuing Public Goods with the Contingent Valuation Method: A Critique of Kahneman and Knetsch", *Journal of Environmental Economics and Management*, Vol. 22, pp. 57-70.

Hartwick, J.M. (1993), "Forestry Economics, Deforestation and National Accounting", in E. Lutz (ed.), *Toward Improved Accounting for the Environment*, World Bank, Washington DC, pp. 289-314.

Hartwick, J.M. (1992), "Deforestation and National Accounting", *Environmental and Resource Economics*, Vol. 2, pp. 513-521.

Hartwick, J.M. (1990), "Natural Resources, National Accounting and Economic Depreciation", *Journal of Public Economics*, Vol. 43, pp. 291-304.

Hartwick, J.M. (1977), "Intergenerational Equity and the Investing of Rents from Exhaustible Resources", *American Economic Review*, Vol. 67, pp. 972-974.

Hausman, J. (ed.) (1993), *Contingent Valuation: A Critical Assessment*, North Holland, Amsterdam.

Hausman, J. and D. McFadden (1984), "Specification Tests for the Multi-nomial Logit Model", *Econometrica*, Vol. 52, pp. 1219-1240.

Hausman, J. and P. Ruud (1987), "Specifying and Testing Econometric Models for Rank-ordered Data", *Journal of Econometrics*, Vol. 34, pp. 83-104.

Hausman, J. and D. Wise (1978), "A Conditional Probit Model for Qualitative Choice: Discrete Decisions Recognising Interdependence and Heterogeneous Preferences", *Econometrica*, Vol. 46, pp. 403-426.

Hazilla, M. and R. Kopp (1990), "The Social Cost of Environmental Regulations: A General Equilibrium Analysis", *Journal of Political Economy*, Vol. 98, pp. 853-873.

Heal, G. (1998), *Valuing the Future: Economic Theory and Sustainability*, New York, Columbia University Press.

Heinzerling, L. and F. Ackerman (2004), *Priceless: On Knowing the Price of Everything and the Value of Nothing*, New York, The New York Press.

Henderson, N. and I. Bateman (1995), "Empirical and Public Choice Evidence for Hyperbolic Social Discount Rates and the Implications for Intergenerational Discounting", *Environmental and Resource Economics*, Vol. 5, pp. 413-423.

Henderson, P.D. (1985), *Innocence and Design: the Influence of Economic Ideas on Policy – The 1985 BBC Reith Lectures*, Oxford, Blackwell.

Henry, C. (1974), "Investment Decision under Uncertainty: The Irreversibility Effect", *American Economic Review*, Vol. 64, No. 6, pp. 1006-12.

Hensher, D. (1994), "Stated Preference Analysis of Travel Choices: The State of Practice", *Transportation*, Vol. 21, pp. 107-133.

Hepburn, C. (2003), *Resource Collapse and Hyperbolic Discounting*, Oxford University Department of Economics, Discussion Paper.

Hicks, J.R. (1943), "The Four Consumer's Surpluses", *Review of Economic Studies*, Vol. 1, pp. 31-41.

Hicks, J.R. (1939), "Foundations of Welfare Economics", *Economic Journal*, Vol. 49, pp. 696-712.

Hoehn, J.P. and A. Randall (1989), "Too Many Proposals Pass the Benefit Cost Test", *American Economics Review*, Vol. 79, pp. 544-551.

Hoffmann S., A. Krupnick and V. Adamowicz (2005), "Economic Uncertainties in Valuing Reductions in Children's Environmental Health Risks", in *Economic Valuation of Environmental Health Risks to Children*, OECD, Paris, forthcoming.

Holland, M. and W. Krewitt (1996), *Benefits of an Acidification Strategy for the European Union*, Brussels, European Commission.

Horowitz, J. and K. McConnell (2002), "A Review of WTA/WTP Studies", *Journal of Environmental Economics and Management*, Vol. 44, pp. 426-447.

IVM, NILU and IIASA (1997), *Economic Evaluation of Air Quality for Sulphur Dioxide, Nitrogen Dioxide, Fine and Suspended Particulate Matter and Lead*, Report to DGXI, Brussels, European Commission.

Jenkins, R.R., N. Owens and L.B. Wiggins (2001), "Valuing Reduced Risks to Children: The Case of Bicycle Safety Helmets", *Contemporary Economic Policy*, Vol. 19, No. 4, pp. 397-408.

Johannesson, M. and P.-O. Johansson (1997), "Quality of Life and the WTP for an Increased Life Expectancy at an Advanced Age", *Journal of Public Economics*, Vol. 65, pp. 219-228.

Johannesson, M. and P.-O. Johansson (1996), "To Be or Not Be, That Is the Question: An Empirical Study on the WTP for an Increased Life Expectancy at an Advanced Age", *Journal of Risk and Uncertainty*, Vol. 13, pp. 163-174.

Johannesson, M. and P.-O. Johansson (1995), "Is the Value of a Life Year Gained Independent of Age?", Stockholm School of Economics, *mimeo*.

Johannesson, M., P.-O. Johansson and K. Löfgren (1997), "On the Value of Changes in Life Expectancy: Blips *versus* Parametric Changes", *Journal of Risk and Uncertainty*, Vol. 15, pp. 221-239.

Johansson, P.-O. (2002), "On the Definition and Age-Dependency of the Value of a Statistical Life", *Journal of Risk and Uncertainty*, Vol. 25, No. 3, pp. 251–263.

Johansson, P.-O. (1993), *Cost-Benefit Analysis of Environmental Change*, Cambridge, Cambridge University Press.

Jones-Lee, M.W., M. Hammerton and P.R. Phillips (1985), "The Value of Safety: Results from a National Sample Survey", *Economic Journal*, Vol. 95, pp. 49-72.

Just, R., D. Hueth and A. Schmitz (1982), *Applied Welfare Economics and Public Policy*, New York, Prentice Hall.

Just, R., D. Hueth and A. Schmitz (2004), *The Welfare Economics of Public Policy: a Practical Guide to Project and Policy Evaluation*, Cheltenham, Edward Elgar.

Kahneman, D. and A. Tversky (eds.) (2000), "Choice, Values and Frames", Cambridge Universtity Press, Cambridge.

Kahneman, D. and A. Tversky (1979), "Prospect Theory: An Analysis of Decision under Risk", *Econometrica*, Vol. 47, No. 2, pp. 263-291.

Kahneman, D. and J. Knetsch (1992), "Valuing Public Goods: The Purchase of Moral Satisfaction", *Journal of Environmental Economics and Management.*, Vol. 22, pp. 57-70.

Kaldor, N. (1939), "Welfare Propositions of Economics and Interpersonal Comparisons of Utility", *Economic Journal*, Vol. 49, pp. 549-552.

Kalt, J. and M. Zupan (1984), "Capture and Ideology in the Economic Theory of Politics", *American Economic Review*, Vol. 74, No. 3, pp. 279-300.

Kanninen, B.J. and B. Kriström (1993), "Welfare Benefit Estimation and Income Distribution", Beijer Discussion Paper Series No. 20, Stockholm, Beijer Institute of Ecological Economics.

Knetsch, J. (1989), "The Endowment Effect and Evidence of Non-reversible Indifference Curves", *American Economic Review*, Vol. LXXIX, pp. 1277-1284.

Knetsch, J. and J. Sinden (1984), "Willingness to Pay and Compensation Demanded: Experimental Evidence of an Unexpected Disparity in Measures of Value", *Quarterly Journal of Economics*, Vol. XCIX, pp. 507-21.

Kolstad, C.D. (1999), *Environmental Economics*, Oxford, Oxford University Press.

Koopmans, T.C. (1965), "On the Concept of Optimal Economic Growth", *Pontificae Academiae Scientiarum Scripta Varia*, Vol. 28, pp. 225-300.

Kopp, R.J., A.J. Krupnick and M. Toman (1997), *Cost-Benefit Analysis and Regulatory Reform: An Assessment of the Science and the Art*, RFF Discussion Paper 97-19, Resources for the Future, Washington, DC.

Kopp, R. and V.K. Smith (1993), "Introduction", in R. Kopp, R and V.K. Smith (eds.), *Valuing Natural Assets: the Economics of Natural Resource Damage Assessment*, Resources for the Future, Washington, DC, pp. 1-5.

Krewitt, W., M. Holland, A. Trukenmüller, T. Heck and R. Friedrich (1999), "Comparing Costs and Environmental Benefits of Strategies to Control Acidification and Ozone in Europe", *Environmental Economics and Policy Studies*, Vol. 2, pp. 249-266.

Krinsky, I. and A. Robb (1986), "Approximating the Statistical Properties of Elasticities", *Review of Economics and Statistics*, Vol. 68, pp. 715-719.

Kriström, B. (2005), "Framework for Assessing the Distribution of Financial Effects of Environmental Policies", in Y. Serret and N. Johnstone (eds.), *The Distributional Effects of Environmental Policy*, Cheltenham, Edward Elgar and OECD, Paris, forthcoming.

Krugman, P. (1996), "Making Sense of the Competitiveness Debate", *Oxford Review of Economic Policy*, Vol. 12, No. 3.

Krupnick, A.J., A. Alberini, M. Cropper, N. Simon, K. Itaoka and M. Akai (1999), "Mortality Risk Valuation for Environmental Policy", Discussion Paper 99-47, Resources for the Future, Washington, DC.

Krupnick, A., A. Alberini, M. Cropper, N. Simon, B. O'Brien, R. Goeree and M. Heintzelman (2002), "Age, Health and the Willingness to Pay for Mortality Risk Reductions: A Contingent Valuation Survey of Ontario Residents", *Journal of Risk and Uncertainty*, Vol. 24, No. 2, pp. 161-186.

Krupnick, A.J., W. Harrington and B. Ostro (1990), "Ambient Ozone and Acute Health Effects: Evidence from Daily Data", *Journal of Environmental Economics and Management*, Vol. 18, No. 1, pp. 1-18.

Krupnick, A., K. Harrison, E. Nickell and M.A. Toman (1996), "Value of Health Benefits from Ambient Air Quality Improvements in Central and Eastern Europe: An Exercise in Benefits Transfer", *Environmental and Resource Economics,* Vol. 7, pp. 307-332.

Krutilla, J. and A. Fisher (2nd edition, 1985), *The Economics of Natural Environments,* Baltimore, Johns Hopkins University Press.

Krutilla, J. and O. Eckstein (1958), *Multipurpose River Development,* Baltimore, Johns Hopkins University Press.

Lancaster, K. (1966), "A New Approach to Consumer Theory", *Journal of Political Economy,* Vol. 84, pp. 132-157.

Leggett, C.G. and N.E. Bockstael (2000), "Evidence of the Effects of Water Quality on Residential Land Prices", *Journal of Environmental Economics and Management,* Vol. 39, No. 2, pp. 121-144.

Li, C.Z. and K.G. Lofgren (2000), "Renewable Resources and Economic Sustainability: A Dynamic Analysis with Heterogeneous Time Preferences", *Journal of Environmental Economics and Management,* Vol. 40, pp. 236-250.

Lind, R.C. (1982), "Introduction", in R.C. Lind, K. Arrow, G. Corey, P. Dasgupta, A. Sen, T. Stauffer, J. Stiglitz, J. Stockfisch and R. Wilson (eds.), *Discounting for Time and Risk in Energy Policy,* Baltimore, Johns Hopkins University Press, pp. 1-20.

Lind, R.C., K. Arrow, G. Corey, P. Dasgupta, A. Sen, T. Stauffer, J. Stiglitz, J. Stockfisch and R. Wilson (eds.) (1982), *Discounting for Time and Risk in Energy Policy,* Baltimore, Johns Hopkins University Press.

Lipsey, R. and K. Lancaster (1956-1957), "The General Theory of Second Best", *Review of Economic Studies,* Vol. 24, pp. 11-32.

Little, I. (1950) (2nd edition 1957, reissued 2002), *A Critique of Welfare Economics,* Oxford, Oxford University Press.

Little, I. and J. Mirrlees (1994), "The Costs and Benefits of Analysis: Project Appraisal and Planning Twenty Years on", in R. Layard and S. Glaister (eds.), *Cost-Benefit Analysis,* Cambridge, Cambridge University Press, pp. 199-234.

Little, I. and J. Mirrlees (1974), *Project Appraisal and Planning for Developing Countries,* Oxford, Oxford University Press (The "OECD Manual").

Liu, J.T., J.K. Hammitt, J.D. Wang and J.L. Liu (2000), "Mothers' Willingness to Pay for her Own and her Child's Health: A Contingent Valuation Study in Taiwan", *Health Economics,* Vol. 9, pp. 319-326.

Londero, E. (1996), *Benefits and Beneficiaries,* Washington DC, Inter-American Development Bank.

Londero, E.H. (2003), *Shadow Prices for Project Appraisal: Theory and Practice,* Cheltenham, Edward Elgar.

Loomes, G. and M. Jones-Lee (2004), *Valuation of Health Benefits Associated with Reductions in Air Pollution. Draft Final Report to DEFRA,* London, Department of the Environment, Food and Rural Affairs.

Loomis, J.B., T. Lucero and G. Peterson (1996), "Improving Validity Experiments of Contingent Valuation Methods: Results of Efforts to Reduce the Disparity of Hypothetical and Actual Willingness to Pay", *Land Economics,* Vol. 72, No. 4, pp. 450-61.

Louviere, J. and D. Hensher (1982), "On the Design and Analysis of Simulated Choice or Allocation Experiments in Travel Choice Modelling", *Transportation Research Record,* Vol. 890, pp. 11-17.

Louviere, J., D. Hensher and J. Swait (2000), *Stated Choice Methods: Analysis and Application,* Cambridge, Cambridge University Press.

Louviere, J. and G. Woodworth (1983), "Design and Analysis of Simulated Consumer Choice or Allocation Experiments: An Approach Based on Aggregate Data", *Journal of Marketing Research,* Vol. 20, pp. 350-367.

Lovett, A.A., J.S. Brainard and I.J. Bateman (1997), "Improving Benefit Transfer Demand Functions: A GIS Approach", *Journal of Environmental Management,* Vol. 51, pp. 373-389.

Luce, R.D. (1959), *Individual Choice Behavior: A Theoretical Analysis,* New York, John Wiley and Sons.

Lutter, R. (2001), "Improving Regulatory Analysis at the Environmental Protection Agency", Testimony before the House Committee on Small Business, Subcommittee on Regulatory Reform and Oversight, Washington DC, US Senate.

Maass, A. (1962), *Design of Water Resource Systems,* New York, Macmillan.

Maddison, D. (2000), *Valuing the Morbidity Effects of Air Pollution,* Centre for Social and Economic Research on the Global Environment (CSERGE), University College London, London, *mimeo.*

Maddison, D. and S. Mourato (2002), "Valuing Difference Road Options for Stonehenge", in S. Navrud and R. Ready (eds.), *Valuing Cultural Heritage*, Edward Elgar, Cheltenham, pp. 87-104.

Maguire, K.B., N. Owens and N.B. Simon (2002), "Willingness to Pay to Reduce a Child's Pesticide Exposure: Evidence from the Baby Food Market", National Center for Environmental Economics Working Paper, No. 02-03, Washington DC, US EPA.

Mäler, K.-G. (1991), "National Accounts and Environmental Resources", *Environmental and Resource Economics*, Vol. 1, pp. 1-15.

Mäler, K.-G. (1974), *Environmental Economics: a Theoretical Inquiry*, Baltimore, Johns Hopkins University Press.

Mäler, K.-G. (1971), "A Method of Estimating Social Benefits from Pollution Control", *Swedish Journal of Economics*, Vol. 73, pp. 121-133.

Markandya, A., A. Hunt, R. Ortiz and A. Alberini (2004), "EC NewExt Research Project: Mortality Risk Valuation – Final Report – UK", Brussels, European Commission.

Markandya, A. and D. Rübbelke (2003), "Ancillary Benefits of Climate Policy", FEEM Working Paper, 105.03, Fondazione Eni Enrico Mattei (FEEM), Milan.

Marshall, A. (1890), *Principles of Economics*, London, Macmillan.

McConnell, K., I. Strand and S. Valdes (1997), "Testing Temporal Reliability and Carry-over Effect: The Role of Correlated Responses in Test-Retest Reliability Studies", *Environmental and Resource Economics*, Vol. 12, pp. 357-374.

McFadden, D. (1981), "Econometric Models of Probabilistic Choice", in C. Manski and D. McFadden (eds.), *Structural Analysis of Discrete Data with Econometric Applications*, MIT Press, Cambridge.

McFadden, D. (1973), "Conditional Logit Analysis of Qualitative Choice Behaviour", in P. Zarembka (ed.), *Frontiers in Econometrics*, Academic Press, New York.

McKean R. (1958), *Efficiency in Government through Systems Analysis*, New York; Wiley.

Merkhofer, M. (1987), *Decision Science and Social Risk Management: a Comparative Evaluation of Cost-benefit Analysis, Decision Analysis and Other Formal Decision-aiding Approaches*, Boston, D. Reidel.

Mishan, E.J. (1988), *Cost-Benefit Analysis*, 4th edition, London, Unwin Hyman.

Mitchell, R. and R. Carson (1989), *Using Surveys to Value Public Goods: The Contingent Valuation Method*, Johns Hopkins University Press for Resources for the Future, Washington DC.

Morrall, J. (2003), "Saving Lives: Reviewing the Record", *Journal of Risk and Uncertainty*, Vol. 27, No. 3, pp. 221-237.

Morrall, J. (1986), "A Review of the Record", *Regulation*, Vol. 10, pp. 25-34.

Morrison, G. (1997), "Resolving Differences in Willingness to Pay and Willingness to Accept: Comment", *American Economic Review*, Vol. 87, No. 1, pp. 236-240, March.

Morrison, G. (1996), "Willingness to Pay and Willingness to Accept: Some Evidence of an Endowment Effect", Discussion Paper 9646, Department of Economics, Southampton University.

Morrison, M., J. Bennett, R. Blamey and J. Louviere (1998), "Choice Modelling and Tests of Benefit Transfer – Choice Modelling Research Report 8", Canberra, University College, University of New South Wales.

Morrison, M., R. Blamey, J. Bennett and J. Louviere (1999), "A Review of Conjoint Techniques for Estimating Environmental Values", University of New South Wales, Canberra.

Mount, T., W. Weng, W. Schulze and L. Chestnut (2001), "Automobile Safety and the Value of Statistical Life in the Family: Valuing Reduced Risks for Children, Adults and the Elderly", paper presented at the 2001 Association of Environmental and Resource Economists Workshop, Bar Harbor, Maine, June 13-15, 2001.

Mrozek, J.R. and L.O. Taylor (2002), "What Determines the Value of Life? A Meta-Analysis", *Journal of Policy Analysis and Management*, Vol. 21, No. 2, pp. 253-270.

Munro, A. and N. Hanley (1999), "Information, Uncertainty and Contingent Valuation", in I.J. Bateman and K.G. Willis (eds.), *Contingent Valuation of Environmental Preferences: Assessing Theory and Practice in the USA, Europe, and Developing Countries*, Oxford, Oxford University Press, pp. 258-279.

Murdoch, J. and M. Thayer (1990), "The Benefits of Reducing the Incidence of Nonmelanoma Skin Cancers: a Defensive Expenditures Approach", *Journal of Environmental Economics and Management*, Vol. 18, pp. 107-119.

Norton, B.G. and M.A. Toman (1997), "Sustainability: Economic and Ecological Perspectives", *Land Economics*, Vol. 73, No. 4, pp. 663-568.

OECD (2005), *Economic Valuation of Environmental Health Risks to Children*, OECD, Paris, forthcoming.

OECD (2004), "Regulatory Impact Analysis (RIA) Inventory", internal document, OECD, Paris.

OECD (1997), *Regulatory Impact Analysis: Best Practice in OECD Countries*, OECD, Paris.

OECD (1983), *Product Safety: Risk Management and Cost-benefit Analysis*, OECD, Paris.

OECD (1981), *The Costs and Benefits of Sulphur Oxide Control*, OECD, Paris.

OECD (1975), *The Polluter Pays Principle: Definition, Analysis and Implementation*, OECD, Paris.

Olson, M. (1965), *The Logic of Collective Action*, Cambridge MA, Harvard University Press.

Olson, M. and M. Bailey (1981), "Positive Time Preference", *Journal of Political Economy*, Vol. 89, No. 1, pp. 1-25.

Olsthoorn, X., M. Amann, A. Bartonova, J. Clench-Ass, J. Cofala, K. Dorland, C. Guerreiro, J. Henriksen, H. Jansen and S. Larssen (1999), "Cost-benefit Analysis of European Air Quality Targets for Sulphur Dioxide, Nitrogen Dioxide and Fine and Suspended Particulate Matter in Cities", *Environmental and Resource Economics*, Vol. 14, pp. 333-351.

Palmquist, R.B. (1992), "Valuing Localized Externalities", *Journal of Urban Economics*, Vol. 31, pp. 59-68.

Parsons, G.R. and M.J. Kealy (1992), "Randomly Drawn Opportunity Sets in a Random Utility Model of Lake Recreation", *Land Economics*, Vol. 68, No. 1, pp. 93-106.

Pearce, D.W. (2005), "Conceptual Framework for Analysing the Distributive Impacts of Environmental Policies", in Y. Serret and N. Johnstone (eds.), *The Distributional Effects of Environmental Policy*, Cheltenham, Edward Elgar and OECD, Paris, forthcoming.

Pearce, D.W. (2004a), *The Costs and Benefits of Crime Prevention and Control Revisited: A Fresh Look at the Conceptual Foundations*, London, Home Office.

Pearce, D.W. (2004b), "Does European Union Environmental Policy Pass a Cost-Benefit Test?", *World Economics*, Vol. 5, No. 3, pp. 15-138.

Pearce, D.W. (2004c), "Environmental Market Creation: Saviour or Oversell?", *Portuguese Economic Journal*, Vol. 3, No. 2, pp. 115-144.

Pearce, D.W. (2003a), *The Role of "Property Rights" in Determining Economic Values for Environmental Costs and Benefits*, Report to the UK Environment Agency, Bristol, Environment Agency.

Pearce, D.W. (2003b), "The Social Costs of Carbon and Its Policy Implications", *Oxford Review of Economic Policy*, Vol. 19, No. 3, pp. 362-384.

Pearce, D.W. (2001), "Controversies in Economic Valuation", in P. McMahon and D. Moran (eds.), *Economic Valuation of Water Resources: Policy and Practice*, London, Terence Dalton, pp. 49-63.

Pearce, D.W. (2000), "Policy Frameworks for the Ancillary Benefits of Climate Change Policies", in OECD, *Ancillary Benefits and Costs of Greenhouse Gas Mitigation*, OECD, Paris, pp. 517-560.

Pearce, D.W. (1998a), "Environmental Appraisal and Environmental Policy in the European Union", *Environment and Resource Economics*, Vol. 11, pp. 1-13.

Pearce, D.W. (1998b), "Auditing the Earth", *Environment*, Vol. 40, No. 2, March, pp. 23-28.

Pearce, D.W. (1986), *Cost-Benefit Analysis* (2nd edition), London, Macmillan.

Pearce, D.W., B. Groom, C. Hepburn and P. Koundouri (2003), "Valuing the Future: Recent Advances in Social Discounting", *World Economics*, Vol. 4, No. 2, pp. 121-141.

Pearce, D.W., K. Hamilton and G. Atkinson (1996), "Measuring Sustainable Development: Progress on Indicators", *Environment and Development Economics*, Vol. 1, No. 1, pp. 85-101.

Pearce, D.W. and A. Markandya (1989), *Environmental Policy Benefits: Monetary Valuation*, OECD, Paris.

Pearce, D.W., A. Markandya and E.B. Barbier (1989), *Blueprint for a Green Economy*, London, Earthscan.

Pearce, D.W., D. Moran and D. Biller (2002), *Handbook of Biodiversity Valuation: a Guide for Policy Makers*, OECD, Paris.

Pearce, D.W. and C. Nash (1981), *The Social Appraisal of Projects: a Text in Cost-Benefit Analysis*, Basingstoke, Macmillan.

Pearce, D.W. and C. Pearce (2001), *The Value of Forest Ecosystems*, Montreal, Convention on Biological Diversity.

Pearce, D.W., J. Powell and A. Craighill (1998), "Integrating Life Cycle Analysis and Economic Valuation: Waste Management", in F. Berkhout, R. Heintz and P. Vellinga (eds.), *Substances And Materials Flows Through Economy and Environment*, Dordrecht, Kluwer, pp. 127-146.

Pearce, D.W. and D. Ulph (1999), "A Social Discount Rate for the United Kingdom", in D.W. Pearce (ed.), *Economics and Environment: Essays on Ecological Economics and Sustainable Development*, Cheltenham, Edward Elgar, pp. 268-85.

Pearce, D.W., D. Whittington and S. Georgiou (1994), *Project and Policy Appraisal: Integrating Economics and Environment*, OECD, Paris.

Pemberton, M. and D. Ulph (2001), "Measuring National Income and Measuring Sustainability", *Scandinavian Journal of Economics*, Vol. 103, No. 1, pp. 25-40.

Persson, U., A. Norinder, K. Hjalte and K. Gralén (2001), "The Value of a Statistical Life in Transport: Findings from a New Contingent Valuation Study in Sweden", *Journal of Risk and Uncertainty*, Vol. 23, No. 2, pp. 121-134.

Pezzey, J. (1989), *Economic Analysis of Sustainable Growth and Sustainable Development*, Environment Department Working Paper No. 15, Washington DC, World Bank.

Pezzey, J. and M. Toman (2002), "Progress and Problems in the Economics of Sustainability", in T. Tietenberg and H. Folmer (eds.), *International Yearbook of Environmental and Resource Economics 2002/3*, Cheltenham, Edward Elgar, pp. 165-232.

Pezzey, J. and C.A. Withagen (1998), "The Rise, Fall and Sustainability of Capital-Resource Economies", *Scandinavian Journal of Economics,* Vol. 100, No. 2, pp. 513-527.

Pigou, A. (1920), *The Economics of Welfare*, London, Macmillan.

Pires, C. (1998), "Sustainability and Cost-Benefit Analysis", *Environment and Planning A,* Vol. 30, No. 12, pp. 2181-2194.

Pitt, M. and M. Rosenzweig (1990), "Estimating the Intrahousehold Incidence of Illness: Child Health and Gender-Inequality in the Allocation of Time", *International Economic Review*, Vol. 31, pp. 969-989.

Poe, G., M. Welsh and P. Champ (1997), "Measuring the Difference in Mean Willingness to Pay When Dichotomous Choice Valuation Responses Are Not Independent", *Land Economics*, Vol. 73, No. 2, pp. 255-267.

Pope, C., M. Thun, M. Namboodri, D. Dockery, J. Evans, F. Speizer and C. Health (1995), "Particulate Air Pollution as a Predictor of Mortality in a Prospective Study of US Adults", *American Journal of Respiratory Critical Care Medicine*, Vol. 151, pp. 669-674.

Porter, R. (1982), "The New Approach to Wilderness Conservation through Benefit-Cost Analysis", *Journal of Environmental Economics and Management*, Vol. 9, pp. 59-80.

Portney, P. and J. Weyant (eds.) (1999), *Discounting and Intergenerational Equity*, Resources for the Future, Washington, DC.

Postle, M. (2002), *Technical Guidance Document on the Use of Socio-Economic Analysis in Chemical Risk Management Decision-making*, OECD, Paris.

Rabl, A. (2003), "Interpretation of Air Pollution Mortality: Number of Deaths or Years of Life Lost?", *Journal of Air and Waste Management Association*, January 2003, Vol. 53, No. 1, pp. 43-50.

Ramsey, F.P. (1928), "A Mathematical Theory of Saving", *Economic Journal,* Vol. 38, pp. 543–559.

Randall, A. and J.R. Stoll (1980), "Consumer's Surplus in Commodity Space", *American Economic Review,* Vol. 70, No. 3, pp. 449-455.

Rausser, G. and A. Small (2000), "Valuing Research Leads: Bioprospecting and the Conservation of Genetic Resources", *Journal of Political Economy*, Vol. 108, No. 1, pp. 173-206.

Rawls, J. (1971), *A Theory of Justice*, Oxford, Oxford University Press.

Ray, A. (1984), *Cost-Benefit Analysis: Issues and Methodologies*, Baltimore, Johns Hopkins University Press.

Ready, R., S. Navrud, B. Day, W.R. Dubourg, F. Machado, S. Mourato, F. Spanninks and M. Rodriquez (2004a), "Benefit Transfer in Europe: How Reliable are Transfers between Countries?", *Environmental and Resource Economics,* Vol. 29, pp. 67-82.

Ready, R., S. Navrud, B. Day, W.R. Dubourg, F. Machado, S. Mourato, F. Spanninks and M. Rodriquez (2004b), "Contingent Valuation of Ill-Health Caused by Pollution: Testing for Context and Ordering Effects", *Portuguese Economic Journal 3,* (in press).

Reed Johnson, F., E. Fries and H. Banzaf (1996), "Valuing Morbidity: An Integration of the Willingness-to-Pay and Health-Status Literature", TER Technical Working Paper 9601, Durham, North Carolina, Triangle Economic Research.

Robbins, L. (1938), "Interpersonal Comparisons of Utility: a Comment", *Economic Journal,* Vol. 48, pp. 635-641.

Roe, B., K. Boyle and M. Teisl (1996), "Using Conjoint Analysis to Derive Estimates of Compensating Variation", *Journal of Environmental Economics and Management,* Vol. 31, pp. 145-159.

Rosenberger, R.S. and J.B. Loomis (2003), "Benefits Transfer", in P.A. Champ, K.J. Boyle and T.C. Brown (eds.), *A Primer on Nonmarket Valuation,* Dordrecht, Kluwer Academic Publishers, pp. 445-482.

Rowe, R., C. Lang, L. Chestnut, D. Latimer, D. Rae and S. Bernow (1995), *The New York Electricity Externality Study,* New York, Oceana Publications.

Russell, C.S. (2001), *Applying Economics to the Environment,* Oxford, Oxford University Press.

Sagoff, M. (2004), *Price, Principle and the Environment,* Cambridge, Cambridge University Press.

Sagoff, M. (1988), *The Economy of the Earth,* Cambridge, Cambridge University Press.

Samuelson, P. (1942), "Constancy of the Marginal Utility of Income", in O. Lange (ed.), *Studies in Mathematical Economics and Econometrics – In Memory of Henry Schultz,* Chicago, Chicago University Press.

Sandy, R. and R.F. Elliott (1996), "Unions and Risk: Their Impact on the Level of Compensation for Fatal Risk", *Economica,* Vol. 63, No. 250, pp. 291-309.

Scapecchi, P. (2005), "Valuation Differences Between Adults and Children", in *Economic Valuation of Environmental Health Risks to Children,* OECD, Paris, forthcoming.

Schmid, A. (1989), *Benefit-Cost Analysis: a Political Economy Approach,* Colorado, Westview Press.

Scitovsky, T. (1941), "A Note on Welfare Propositions in Economics", *Review of Economic Studies,* Vol. 9, pp. 77-88.

Serret, Y. and N. Johnstone (eds.) (2005), *The Distributional Effects of Environmental Policy,* Cheltenham, Edward Elgar and OECD, Paris, forthcoming.

Shepard, D. and R. Zeckhauser (1982), "Life Cycle Consumption and Willingness to Pay for Increased Survival", in M. Jones-Lee (ed.), *Valuation of Life and Safety,* Amsterdam, North Holland.

Shogren, J. (1999), *Benefits and Costs of Kyoto,* Laramie, Department of Economics, University of Wyoming, *mimeo.*

Shogren, J.F., S.Y. Shin, D.J. Hayes and Kliebenstein, J.B. (1994), "Resolving Differences in Willingness to Pay and Willingness to Accept", *American Economic Review,* Vol. 84, No. 1, pp. 255-70.

Sidgwick, H. (1883), *Principles of Political Economy,* London, Macmillan.

Siebert, W.S. and X. Wei (1994), "Compensating Wage Differentials for Workplace Accidents: Evidence for Union and Nonunion Workers in the UK", *Journal of Risk and Uncertainty,* Vol. 9, No. 1, pp. 61-76.

Silva, P. and S. Pagiola (2003), "A Review of the Valuation of Environmental Costs and Benefits in World Bank Projects", Environmental Economics Series Paper No. 94, Environment Department, Washington DC, The World Bank.

Simpson, D. and A. Craft (1996), *The Social Value of Biodiversity in New Pharmaceutical Product Research,* Resources for the Future, Discussion Paper 96-33, Washington DC.

Simpson, D., R. Sedjo and J. Reid (1996), "Valuing Biodiversity for Use in Pharmaceutical Research", *Journal of Political Economy,* Vol. 104, No. 1, pp. 163-185.

Slovic, P. (1987), "Perception of risk", *Science,* Vol. 236, No. 4799, pp. 280-285.

Smith, V.K. (1992), "Arbitrary Values, Good Causes, and Premature Verdicts", *Journal of Environmental Economics and Management,* Vol. 22, pp. 71–89.

Smith, V.K. and W. Desvousges (1986), *Measuring Water Quality Benefits*, Boston, Kluwer-Nijhoff.

Smith, V.K. and L. Osborne (1996), "Do Contingent Valuation Estimates Pass a Scope Test? A Meta Analysis", *Journal of Environmental Economics and Management*, Vol. 31, pp. 287-301.

Solow, R.M. (1986), "On the Intergenerational Allocation of Natural Resources, *Scandinavian Journal of Economics*, Vol. 88, No. 1, pp. 141-149.

Solow, R.M. (1974), "Intergenerational Equity and Exhaustible Resources", *Review of Economic Studies*, Vol. 41, pp. 29-45.

Squire, L. and H.G. van den Tak (1975), *Economic Analysis of Projects*, Johns Hopkins Press, Baltimore.

Steer Davies Gleave (SDG) (1999), *Bus Station Passenger Preferences*, report for London Transport Buses.

Steer Davies Gleave (SDG) (2000), *London Underground Customer Priorities Research*, report for London Underground.

Strotz, R. (1956), "Myopia and Inconsistency in Dynamic Utility Maximisation", *Review of Economic Studies*, Vol. 23, pp. 165-180.

Sugden, R. and A. Williams (1978), *The Principles of Practical Cost-Benefit Analysis*, Oxford, Oxford University Press.

Sutton, P. and R. Costanza (2002), "Global Estimates of Market and Non-Market Values Derived from Nighttime Satellite Imagery, Land Cover, and Ecosystem Service Valuation", *Ecological Economics*, Vol. 41, pp. 509-527.

Swierzbinski, J. (2002), "A Simplified Arrow-Fisher Model of Option Value with Irreversible Investment", Department of Economics, University College London, *mimeo*.

Tamburlini, G. (2005), "Overview of the Risk Differences Between Adults and Children", in *Economic Valuation of Environmental Health Risks to Children*, OECD, Paris, forthcoming.

ten Kate, K. and S. Laird (1999), *The Commercial Use of Biodiversity: Access to Genetic Resources and Benefit–Sharing*, London, Earthscan.

Tengs, T. (1995), "500 Life-saving Interventions and their Cost-Effectiveness ", *Risk Analysis*, Vol. 15, pp. 369-390.

Thaler, R. (1984), "Towards a Positive Theory of Consumer Choice", *Journal of Economic Behaviour and Organisation*, Vol. 1, pp. 29-60.

Thomas, H.A. (1963), "The Animal Farm: a Mathematical Model for the Discussion of Social Standards for Control of the Environment", *Quarterly Journal of Economics*, Vol. 77, pp. 143-148.

Tilman, D. and S. Polasky (n.d.), *Ecosystem Goods and Services and their Limits: The Role of Biological Diversity and Management Practices*, St Paul, University of Minnesota.

Toman, M. (1998), "Why Not to Calculate the Global Value of the World's Ecosystems and Natural Capital", *Ecological Economics*, Vol. 25, pp. 57-60.

Tourangeau, R., L.J. Rips and K. Rasinski (2000), *The Psychology of Survey Response*, Cambridge, Cambridge University Press.

Train, K.E. (1998), "Recreation Demand Models with Taste Differences Across People", *Land Economics*, Vol. 74, No. 2, pp. 230-239.

Turner, R.K., J. Pavavola, P. Cooper, S. Farber, V. Jessamy and S. Georgiou (2003), "Valuing Nature: Lessons Learned and Future Research Directions", *Ecological Economics*, Vol. 46, pp. 493-510.

Tversky, A. (1972), "Elimination by Aspects; A Theory of Choice", *Psychological Review*, Vol. 79, pp. 281-299.

Tversky, A. and D. Kahneman (1991), "Loss Aversion in Riskless Choice: A Reference-dependent Model", *Quarterly Journal of Economics*, Vol. 106, No. 4, pp. 1039-1061.

UK Cabinet Office (2003), *Better Policy Making: a Guide to Regulatory Impact Assessment*, London, Cabinet Office.

UK HM Treasury (2002), *The Green Book: Appraisal and Evaluation in Central Government* (Draft), London, HM Treasury.

Ulph, A. and D. Ulph (1997), "Global Warming, Irreversibility and Learning", *Economic Journal*, Vol. 197, pp. 646-650.

UNIDO (1980), *Manual for Evaluation of Industrial Projects*, Vienna, United Nations Industrial Development Organisation (The "UNIDO Manual").

US Environmental Protection Agency (2000), *Guidelines for Preparing Economic Analyses*, Washington DC, US EPA.

US Environmental Protection Agency (1999), *The Benefits and Costs of the Clean Air Act 1990 to 2010*, Report EPA-410-R-99-001, Springfield, VA, National Technical Information Service.

US Environmental Protection Agency (1998), *Final Guidance for Incorporating Environmental Justice Concerns in EPA's NEPA Compliance Analysis*, Washington DC, Government Printing Office.

US Environmental Protection Agency (1997), *The Benefits and Costs of the Clean Air Act 1970–1990*, Washington DC, US EPA.

Vassanadumrongdee, S., S. Matsuoka and H. Shirakawa (2004), "Meta-analysis of Contingent Valuation Studies on Air Pollution Related Morbidity Risks", *Environmental Economics and Policy Studies*, Vol. 6, No. 1, pp. 11-48.

Viscusi, W.K. (2004), "The Value of Life: Estimates with Risks by Occupation and Industry", *Economic Inquiry*, Vol. 42, No. 1, pp. 29-48.

Viscusi, W.K. (1995), "The Automobile Risk Metric for Valuing Health Risks", in N. Schwab, Christe and N. Soguel (eds.), *Contingent Valuation, Transport Safety and the Value of Life*, Dordrecht, Kluwer, pp. 171-93.

Viscusi, W.K. and J. Aldy (2003), "The Value of Statistical Life: a Critical Review of Market Estimates Throughout the World", *Journal of Risk and Uncertainty*, Vol. 27, No. 1, pp. 5-76.

Viscusi, W.K., W.A. Magat and J. Huber (1991), "Pricing Environmental Health Risks: Survey Assessments of Risk-Risk and Risk-Dollar Trade-Offs for Chronic Bronchitis", *Journal of Environmental Economics and Management*, Vol. 21, No. 1, pp. 32-51.

Viscusi, W.K., W.A. Magat and J. Huber (1987), "An Investigation of the Rationality of Consumer Valuations of Multiple Health Risks", *RAND Journal of Economics*, Vol. 18, No. 4, pp. 465-479.

Vitousek, P., H. Mooney, J. Lubchenco and J. Melillo (1997), "Human Domination of Earth's Ecosystems", *Science*, Vol. 277, pp. 494-499.

Wagstaff, A. and E. van Doorslaer (2000), "Equity in Health Care Finance and Delivery", in A.J. Culyer and J.P. Newhouse (eds.), *Handbook of Health Economics – Volume 1*, Amsterdam, Elsevier, pp. 1803-1862.

Walshe, G. and P. Daffern (1990), *Managing Cost-Benefit Analysis*, London, Macmillan.

Ward, W., B. Deren and E. D'Silva (1991), *The Economics of Project Analysis: a Practitioner's Guide*, Washington DC, World Bank.

WCED – World Commission on Environment and Development (1987), *Our Common Future*, The Report of the World Commission on Environment and Development, Oxford, Oxford University Press.

Weitzman, M.L. (2001), "Gamma Discounting", *American Economic Review*, Vol. 91, pp. 260-271.

Weitzman, M.L. (1999), "Just Keep on Discounting, but...", in P. Portney and J. Weyant (eds.), *Discounting and Intergenerational Equity*, Washington DC, Resources for the Future, pp. 23-30.

Weitzman, M.L. (1998), "Why the Far Distant Future Should Be Discounted at its Lowest Possible Rate", *Journal of Environmental Economics and Management*, Vol. 36, pp. 201–208.

Weitzman, M.L. (1976), "On the Welfare Significance of National Product in a Dynamic Economy", *Quarterly Journal of Economics*, Vol. 90, pp. 156-162.

Weitzman, M.L. and K.-G. Löfgren (1997), "On the Welfare Significance of Green Accounting as Taught by Parable", *Journal of Environmental Economics and Management*, Vol. 32, pp. 139-153.

Wesseler, J. (2000), "Temporal Uncertainty and Irreversibility: a Theoretical Framework for the Decision to Approve the Release of Transgenic Crops", in W. Lesser (ed.), *Transitions in Agbiotech: Economics of Strategy and Policy*", Connecticut, Food Marketing Policy Centre, pp. 375-385.

Whitehurst, P. (1999), *Risk-risk Analysis of Life-saving Expenditures in the UK*, Dissertation for M.Sc in Environmental Economics, London, University College London.

Williams, A. and R. Cookson (2000), "Equity in Health", in A.J. Culyer and J.P. Newhouse (eds.), *Handbook of Health Economics – Volume 1*, Amsterdam, Elsevier, pp. 1863-1910.

Willig, R. (1976), "Consumers' Surplus without Apology", *American Economic Review*, Vol. 66, No. 4, pp. 589-597.

Winpenny, J. (1995), *Economic Appraisal of Environmental Projects and Policies: a Practical Guide for Decision-Makers*, OECD, Paris.

Woodward, R. and Y. Wui (2001), "The Economic Value of Wetland Services: a Meta-Analysis", *Ecological Economics*, Vol. 37, No. 257, pp. 257-270.

World Bank (2003), *World Development Indicators 2003*, CD-ROM, Washington DC, World Bank.

World Bank (1997), *Expanding the Measure of Wealth*, Washington DC, The World Bank.

Young, H.P. (1994), *Equity: In Theory and Practice*, Princeton University Press, Princeton.

Zhao, J. and C. Kling (2001), "A New Explanation for the WTP/WTA Disparity", *Economics Letters*, Vol. 73, pp. 293-300.

Indexes

I

K

L

M

N

O

T

U

V

W

OECD PUBLICATIONS, 2, rue André-Pascal, 75775 PARIS CEDEX 16
PRINTED IN FRANCE
(97 2006 01 1 P) ISBN 92-64-01004-1 – No. 54459 2006